The Fragility of Manhood

The Fragility of Manhood

HAWTHORNE, FREUD, AND THE POLITICS OF GENDER

David Greven

THE OHIO STATE UNIVERSITY PRESS · COLUMBUS

Copyright © 2012 by The Ohio State University.
All rights reserved.

Library of Congress Cataloging-in-Publication Data
Greven, David.
  The fragility of manhood : Hawthorne, Freud, and the politics of gender / David Greven.
     p. cm.
  Includes bibliographical references and index.
  ISBN 978-0-8142-1200-4 (cloth : alk. paper)—ISBN 978-0-8142-9301-0 (cd)
  1. Hawthorne, Nathaniel, 1804–1864—Criticism and interpretation. 2. Psychological fiction, American—History and criticism. 3. Psychology in literature. 4. Narcissism in literature. 5. Masculinity in literature. I. Title.
  PS1892.P74G74 2012
  813'.3—dc23
                              2012021599

Cover design by Judith Arisman
Text design by Juliet Williams
Type set in Adobe Garamond Pro

∞ The paper used in this publication meets the minimum requirements of the American National Standard for Information Sciences—Permanence of Paper for Printed Library Materials. ANSI Z39.48-1992.

9 8 7 6 5 4 3 2 1

CONTENTS

Acknowledgments   vii

INTRODUCTION
    The Paradox of Desire   1

CHAPTER 1
    Paradise Lost:
    Hawthorne's Traumatic Narcissism   24

CHAPTER 2
    As His Mother Loved Him:
    "The Gentle Boy" and Freud's Theory of Male Homosexuality   40

CHAPTER 3
    Revising the Oedipal Hawthorne:
    Criticism and the Forms of Narcissism   69

CHAPTER 4
    Struck by the Mask:
    Narcissism, Shame, Masculinity, and the Dread of the Visual   91

CHAPTER 5
    In a Pig's Eye:
    Masculinity, Mastery, and the Returned Gaze of *The Blithedale Romance* 114

CHAPTER 6
    The Gaze in the Garden:
    Femininity, Fetishism, and Tradition in "Rappaccini's Daughter"   141

CHAPTER 7
    Visual Identity:
        Hawthorne, Melville, and Classical Male Beauty   180

CHAPTER 8
    A Certain Dark Beauty:
        Narcissism, Form, and Race in Hawthorne's Late Work   210

EPILOGUE
    The Haunted Verge:
        Aesthetics, Desire, History   243

Notes   255
Bibliography   292
Index   306

ACKNOWLEDGMENTS

It took more than one Hawthorne conference to turn me into the author of this book. Numerous scholars have nurtured and emboldened my work on Hawthorne. While many deserve acknowledgment here, I especially want to thank, for early and generous encouragement, Robert K. Martin, Millicent Bell, Nina Baym, Brenda Wineapple, Fred Newberry, Alison Easton, Sam Coale, Magnus Ullén, Richard Millington, Lee Person, Wyn Kelley, Monika Elbert, David Diamond, Roberta Weldon, and Jana Argersinger. I have been fortunate to meet and to learn from so many Hawthorne scholars from around the world, and I happily salute the emergence of a global Hawthorne scholarly community. Jane J. Benardete's seminar on Hawthorne and James at Hunter College was a crucial one for my intellectual development. As ever, I thank my friend and mentor Timo Gilmore, my dissertation advisor at Brandeis, for his unceasing guidance. My debt to Timo is inexpressible, as are the depths of my admiration. I also thank John Burt and Wai Chee Dimock for their support and friendship. Tim Dean's generosity and guidance at a crucial stage in my intellectual development and early immersion in psychoanalytic thinking were deeply helpful. His work exemplifies the best qualities of psychoanalytic theory. Both for their galvanizing example and for their support, I also thank David Leverenz and the late Robin Wood.

I gratefully acknowledge two scholarly journals for allowing me to republish, in revised, chapter form, previously published articles. An earlier version of chapter 2 was published as "Rereading Narcissism: Freud's Theory of Male Homosexuality and Hawthorne's 'The Gentle Boy'" in *Mod-*

ern Psychoanalysis 34, no. 2 (2009). This article was the winner of a Phyllis W. Meadow Award for Excellence in Psychoanalytic Writing, 2007 (Honorable Mention). An earlier version of chapter 5 was published as "In a Pig's Eye: Masculinity, Mastery, and the Returned Gaze in *The Blithedale Romance*," *Studies in American Fiction,* 34, no. 2 (2006): 131–59. Some of the language in chapter 4 regarding Ora Gannett Sedgwick is lifted from my review of Richard Millington's 2011 Norton Critical Edition of *The Blithedale Romance* published in *The Nathaniel Hawthorne Review*, vol. 37, no. 2 (Fall 2011): 148–53.

I also humbly and gratefully thank the two anonymous readers of the manuscript for The Ohio State University Press, who provided me with critical feedback that was as penetratingly insightful as it was emboldening. These readers have truly helped me to write a better book, and I offer them my thanks. I also profusely thank my wonderful editor at OSU Press, Sandy Crooms, for her unfailingly warm, thoughtful, and scrupulous support of the project, and the accomplished staff at the press.

And, as ever, I thank Alex Beecroft for being so much more than my friend of friends forever.

INTRODUCTION

The Paradox of Desire

A YOUNG MAN stares into a pool and sees his own reflection. At first, his reflection appears to be another person, endowed with great beauty. Enflamed with desire, the young man reaches out to the image in the pool, which dissolves at his touch. Gradually, he comes to understand that this image is just that, an image, and moreover a reflection of himself. Recognition brings with it neither relief nor release; this self-encounter leads to frustration, sorrow, and, ultimately, death.

The myth of Narcissus has played a central role in understandings of the self, its predicaments and potential dangers, throughout the Western tradition. Despite the avid interest in classical myth exemplified by his two collections of Greek myths rewritten for children, Nathaniel Hawthorne never mentions Narcissus in print.[1] Yet the figure of Narcissus and the thematic concerns of his myth suffuse Hawthorne's writings. Belying the textual absence of his naming, the myth of Narcissus informs several Hawthorne works, sometimes fairly obviously, as in the tellingly titled "Monsieur du Miroir" (1837), but more often, and more subtly, in the stories that prominently feature a young man. What Hawthorne's youthful male characters share with Narcissus is a male identity intricately, if not entirely, bound to the power and the demands of the eye. This relationship to vision is deeply conflictual, acts of seeing and responses to being seen fraught with anxiety, aggressivity, and even terror. The young man's conflict over his own image is one of the most consistently developed themes in Hawthorne's oeuvre. Young Goodman Brown, Minister Hooper, Robin Molineux, Giovanni

Guasconti, Arthur Dimmesdale, Holgrave, Coverdale, Donatello: all of these immediately recognizable male characters are, as I will show, depicted in ways that emphasize their relationship to vision, a relationship always rendered in highly ambivalent terms. Moreover, Hawthorne's male characters are particularly provocative extensions of the symbolic meanings of the figure of Narcissus because, in addition to their conflict with their own image, they are at once physically beautiful and morally dubious.

A brief tour of the beautiful young men that recur in Hawthorne's pages conveys his wide-ranging interests in this figure: following the trope of "handsome," we find descriptions such as Coverdale's of Westervelt in *The Blithedale Romance*: "He was still young, seemingly a little under thirty, of a tall and well-developed figure, and as handsome a man as ever I beheld" (3: 92); of Fanshawe, the protagonist of Hawthorne's first novel, whose identity as a scholar is apparently augmented by his personal attractiveness: "The stranger could scarcely have attained his twentieth year, and was possessed of a face and form, such as Nature bestows on none but her favorites" (3: 346); of Donatello in *The Marble Faun* as being so "full of animal life as he was, so joyous in his deportment, so handsome, so physically well developed, he made no impression of incompleteness, of maimed or stinted nature" (4: 14); of the English soldier in Hawthorne's late, unfinished masterpiece *Septimius Felton* as "A young officer, a petulant boy, extremely handsome, and of gay and buoyant deportment" (13: 21). What is especially noteworthy is the license this ostentatious male attractiveness gives women to wield the sexually appraising gaze. In the early story "David Swan," a pretty young woman sees the titular young man, sleeping, like Narcissus's double, Endymion, beneath her eyes: blushingly,

> she stole a glance at the youthful stranger, for whom she had been battling with a dragon in the air [a bee].
> "He is handsome!" thought she, and blushed redder yet. (9: 187)

Many of Hawthorne's men are "striking," such as the guilt-wracked Dimmesdale, "a person of very striking aspect, with a white, lofty, and impending brow, large, brown, melancholy eyes"; that Dimmesdale's mouth, "unless when he forcibly compressed it, was apt to be tremulous, expressing both nervous sensibility and a vast power of self-restraint," tellingly reveals the emotional tensions that simmer beneath a striking aspect, and the authorial disposition toward these attributes (1: 66). Beneath Dimmesdale's beauty, tormenting feelings of self-doubt and self-disdain seethe; his hypocrisy renders his outward beauty especially problematic, for it defies the Victorian assumption that outer beauty reveals inner goodness. Most often in Hawthorne, the beauty of men masks an inner depravity, to the extent that this beauty seems the hallmark of this depravity rather than a contrast to it. Or male beauty causes great discomfort. Coverdale's apprehension of Westervelt's attractiveness seems only to deepen Coverdale's distaste toward the mesmerist: "The style of his beauty, however, though a masculine style, did not at all commend itself to my taste. . . . he had no fineness of nature; there was in his eyes (although they might have artifice enough of another sort) the naked exposure of something that ought not to be left prominent" (3: 86). Though his face and form reveal him to be a favorite of Nature, Fanshawe is besieged by "a blight, of which his thin, pale cheek and the brightness of his eye were alike proofs, [and that] seemed to have come over him ere his maturity" (3: 346).

Hawthorne appears to have needed to put a beautiful man on the page. The question to which we will repeatedly return is why he took such a consistently skeptical view of this attractive figure. Beatrice Rappaccini, the victim of her scientist-father's genetic experiments on her body, poses a question to the handsome and callow man who has voyeuristically spied on her as she tends to the poison plants whose DNA she shares. Her question to this young man, Giovanni Guasconti—"O, was there not, from the first, more poison in thy nature than in mine?" (10: 91)— can be restated this way: Having had a father who interfused my blood with that of his poisonous plants, I have a literal reason for the poison in my system. What accounts for the poison coursing through yours? His most consistent themes indicate that Hawthorne asks this question along with Beatrice.

Yet Hawthorne also views beautiful young men with empathy: he shares with them an empathetic fearfulness at the power of the gaze—not an avaricious desire to wield it but rather a desire to avoid falling *under* it. The theme of painful, violent, and violating looking informs Hawthorne's work. The dubious desire to look and possess by looking in works such as "Wakefield," "Rappaccini's Daughter," and *The Blithedale Romance* and the encounter with a troubling and even terrifying mirror image in stories such as "Feathertop" and longer works such as *The Scarlet Letter* together provide an apposite model for what Sándor Ferenczi diagnosed as "spectrophobia," "the dread of catching sight of one's own face in a mirror."[2] Hawthorne's work plumbs spectrophobia for all of its ethical, aesthetic, and emotional depth, consistently thematizing traumatic seeing and being seen. It is little wonder that by his last complete novel, *The Marble Faun,* Hawthorne depicts a look that kills, Miriam's blinding glare that impels Donatello to kill the Model.

HAWTHORNE, FREUD, AND LACAN

Freudian theory is the theoretical foundation of this study. Through Freud and his extraordinarily and enduringly provocative insights into the difficulties of gender and sexual identity, I make the case that Hawthorne's representation of male subjectivity defies and even at times transcends the normative demands of hegemonic masculinity. As a methodology, however, Freudian theory must undergo stringent revision, given that many of Freud's positions and conclusions are often in deep need of updating. Jacques Lacan's reformulation of Freud's theory of narcissism is especially helpful to one of our central themes, the relationship between gender and vision. Lacan's theory of the mirror stage is very familiar by now, but it retains a revelatory power for Hawthorne's work.[3]

Lacan theorized that there are three "orders" of existence (the Imaginary, the Symbolic, and the Real).[4] The mirror stage is the key component of the Imaginary order, in which the ego is formed through a narcissistic fascination with one's own image. Before the mirror stage, the very young child is a body in pieces (*le corps morcelé*). One sense, the visual, is more advanced than any other. When the child stares at his image in the mirror, he mistakes the *image* of wholeness in the mirror for an actual, authentic wholeness. This profound misrecognition (*méconnaissance*) is the basis from which a self is formed. Our mesmerizing and seductive counterpart in the mirror, what Lacan calls the "small other," seizes us (*captation*), holding us its captive always.

Lacan, intertextually competing with Freud, transforms the Narcissus myth into the narrative of subjectivity. He associates narcissism with the aggressivity, rivalry, strife, and even suicidal despair that all stem from this primary encounter with one's own image. In that it is formed through identification with an image, the ego's foundations are fragile and tenuous. That the ego emerges from the mirror stage and the Imaginary order is a crucial aspect of Lacanian theory, which opposes ego-psychology and its constitutive belief in the reconstruction of the "healthy" ego. In completely destabilizing the concept of the ego, Lacan renders any psychoanalytic effort to restore it inherently suspect.

Also of importance, the mirror stage incorporates the social and the gaze. The child, apprehending its own seemingly complete and mesmerizing image, turns around to look at its mother looking at the child as it looks at and "recognizes" itself. The formation of our own subjectivity depends on the mother's approving, knowing nod of recognition. An awareness of and dependence on visual affirmation of one's own existence—existence *as* a visual subject—is a fundamental aspect of the formation of subjectivity. As

I will be arguing, Hawthorne's work elaborates endlessly on these dynamics, especially the implications of visuality's centrality both for the subject and for all social relations, (relations between the mother and child, as I will show in chapter 2, being the template for these).

For Lacan, narcissism is pathological because it is a subjectivity based on a mirage. Yet, as Lacan lays out his theories, all subjectivity and libidinal attachments would appear to derive from the same evanescent sources. The Lacanian theorist Joan Copjec discusses Lacan's understanding of narcissism within a larger discussion of Lacan's theory. For Copjec, Lacan's theory of the gaze differs both from Foucault's theory of the panoptical gaze and from film theory's uses of Lacan. For Foucault, power is invested in monitoring the subject, hence its deployment of a panoptical gaze and hence the feeling subjects unceasingly have that they are being watched, whether or not they are, indeed, being watched. For film theory, the gaze defines the spectator, which is presented as a stable heterosexual male subject. In Copjec's view, Lacan's theory of the gaze is distinct from these other theories because, for Lacan, the gaze does not define, and certainly does not monitor, the subject, but is, rather, quite indifferent to it. I will return to film theory's treatment of Lacan in chapter 1. For now, I want to draw on Copjec's reading of Lacan, in which she offers a particularly insightful summary of the Lacanian revision of Freud's theories of narcissism, which will be considered at greater length in chapters 1 and 2. As Copjec puts it,

> Narcissism, too, takes on a different meaning in Lacan, one more in accord with Freud's own. Since something always appears to be missing from any representation, narcissism cannot consist in finding satisfaction in one's own visual image. It must, rather, consist in the belief that one's own being exceeds the imperfections of the image. Narcissism, then, seeks the self beyond the self-image, with which the subject constantly finds fault and in which it constantly fails to recognize itself. What one loves in one's image is something more than the image ("in you more than you"). Thus is narcissism the source of the malevolence with which the subject regards its image, the aggressivity it unleashes on all its own representations. And thus does the subject come into being as a transgression of, rather than in conformity to, the law. It is not the law, but the fault in the law—the desire that the law cannot ultimately conceal—that is assumed by the subject as its own. The subject, in taking up the burden of the law's guilt, goes beyond the law.[5]

In Copjec's reading of Lacan, narcissism emerges as a kind of malevolent defensiveness against a simultaneously held and urgent set of disappointments *and* desires. One of the sources of the aggression within narcissism is a dissatisfaction with one's visual image and the insistent corollary belief that one is *more* than this image, more resplendently beautiful and complete.

Hawthorne offers an analogous treatment of these themes. He is a Freudian-Lacanian theorist of the visual and its relationship to gender who sees gender as unintelligible without the visual, and both gender and the visual as fundamentally imbricated. The visual is also what constricts, wounds, and unceasingly antagonizes the gendered subject in his work. At the same time, Hawthorne, so obsessively an explorer of the guilty subject's agonized relationship to the law, presages Foucault's understanding of the panoptical gaze, as exemplified by Rappaccini's invasive, controlling, and totalizing surveillance of the young lovers in one of Hawthorne's greatest tales. Hawthorne, however, does not view, as Foucault does, the law as positive and nonrepressive, as *inciting* desire, but as the force that represses desire, and with dire consequences. Hawthorne's psychoanalytic sensibility, therefore, emerges from his acute sense of profound discrepancies between a subject's desires and the law's dictates.

One of the means of registering these discrepancies is narcissism, which memorializes a subject's state of oneness, however illusory and evanescent, before the inevitable process of socialization. It is within what Lacan describes as the Symbolic order, the domain of the father's language and law, that this socialization occurs. Which is to say, we acquire and achieve subjectivity through a rebirth into language and the inscriptions of the law and the name of the father. Narcissism, imbued with plangent urgency and fueled by malevolent anger, memorializes the Imaginary and the mirror stage.

Narcissism can be understood as the subject's experience of being unceasingly haunted by its own mesmerizing image before the onset of subjectivity. Narcissism memorializes what "belonged" to the subject before it became a Symbolic entity: its ties to nature and the Real, and the heady state of oneness and connection that Freud theorized as the "oceanic feeling," a profound feeling of unity in which the infant's and the mother's bodies were indistinguishable. (The infant has no idea, for example, that the breast is the *mother's* breast, a bodily zone separate from his own body.) A violent disruption of mother–child bonds links Freudian oedipal theory and Lacan's theory of the passage from the Imaginary to the Symbolic order, both of which are narratives of identification with the "Father." Narcissism memorializes not just the subject's indescribable feeling of a prior oneness—for the subject is irreducibly a split subject after its formation through language—but also the connection to the mother, which must be forsaken for Symbolic socialization. Narcissism retains a power to resist and stall this socialization, even as it is incorporated into a "properly oedipalized," male-dominated social order.

Little wonder, then, that the properly functioning subject—properly functioning because it believes itself to *be* a subject—is always already a haunted, wandering subject, forever estranged from itself. What I call Hawthorne's "traumatic narcissism" relates to this haunted disposition: a sense of being fundamentally bereft while imagining a prior state of fulfillment and connection to which the subject can never return but that haunts and on some fundamental level continues to shape the present. Narcissism marks the points of disparity between one's fantasies and experiential realities; it is precisely its ability to link and even to embody these gulfs that makes narcissism a useful, indeed provocatively vivid, index of anxieties, hostilities, and wishes.

Narcissism has profound implications for sexual as well as gendered identity. In his difficult, exasperating, and undeniably compelling *No Future: Queer Theory and the Death Drive,* Lee Edelman argues against the societal valuation of the Child, which he views as the linchpin of a heterosexist emphasis on reproductive futurity that queer sexuality not only nobly resists but must, self-consciously embodying the death drive, actively oppose. Edelman cites some of this same penetratingly insightful passage from his fellow Lacanian Copjec.[6] I do not share Edelman's philosophical positions, especially about queer sexuality's proper value (as the apparently resistant embodiment of the death drive), and I therefore do not follow him in his subsequent conclusion that what Lacan and Copjec are theorizing is narcissism's chief significance as a "life-denying economy."[7] But, as I will show in the first two chapters especially, the fates of narcissism and homosexuality have been intimately, if not inextricably, intertwined in psychoanalytic theory and also in popular receptions of it. Certainly, within this gay male imaginary, homosexuality is seen as life-denying, a quality linked to the perceived nullity of narcissism. As I will be attempting to show in my Janus-faced book—which has one eye on traditional close readings of a canonical author, the other on revising literary studies, psychoanalytic theory, and the related topic of Freud studies through queer theory—narcissism is a potentially resistant mode of affectional attachment and response. What Hawthorne, Freud, and Lacan evoke so movingly is the anguish within narcissism, its contested nature and the struggles it suggests over identity and self-knowledge, qualities that in their irreducibility to any one stagnant view pointedly deny life-denial.

NARCISSISM AND ITS DISCONTENTS

Apart from an excellent 1983 essay by Shernaz Mollinger and an expansive and thoughtful dissertation by MaryHelen Cleverley Harmon, the importance of narcissistic themes in Hawthorne has been largely overlooked. In an important essay, Joseph Adamson does discuss the subject, but places narcissism within the larger context of shame in Hawthorne's work, arguing that narcissism functions as a defense against shame. Christopher Castiglia also discusses the central role of shame in the "queer sociality" of Hawthorne's work, especially in *The House of the Seven Gables* (1851), and makes quite bracingly novel uses of shame as a force that can trigger and undergird progressive new social arrangements.[8] Shame is, as I will have frequent occasion to discuss, undoubtedly one of the chief affects in Hawthorne. But, following Andrew Morrison's theory of shame as the "underside" of narcissism, I argue that in Hawthorne's work shame proceeds from a larger framework of narcissism. In order to understand the full importance of Hawthorne's uses of the Narcissus myth, it will be helpful to this analysis to chart some of the trends in the myth's reception, which has been historically prohibitive and phobic.

In her feminist study *The American Narcissus,* Joyce W. Warren takes canonical American literature before the Civil War to the severest task, arguing that, in its focus on male individualism, it is narcissistic in the most pathological sense of the word. Emerson and Cooper come under particularly critical scrutiny. Interestingly enough, however, Hawthorne is spared the most stringent of Warren's analyses, emerging as an exception to the general narcissistic male rule. He escapes Warren's judgment precisely because, unlike his contemporaries, and "despite personal and cultural inhibitions," Hawthorne "was acutely aware of the personhood of the female other and was able to create female characters who stand out in American literature as women of substance and individuality."[9] Though writing in 1984, Warren articulates a view with a sturdy provenance, the term "narcissistic" still able to cast its pejorative light on any subject. While I agree with Warren about the salutary qualities of Hawthorne's still controversial representation of women, I argue that Hawthorne's depictions of male sexuality are also a crucial aspect of the ways in which his work resists normative structures of gendered and sexual identities. Hawthorne's modulations of the myth of Narcissus throughout his work allowed him to develop a resistant attitude toward patriarchal constructions of masculinity, which in turn was an important dimension of his overall critique of gendered power in the United

States, a project that culminates in his extraordinary late, unfinished *Septimius Felton/Norton* manuscripts.

In order to make a case for the political value of the Narcissus theme in Hawthorne, it is necessary to establish the legitimacy of narcissism as an erotic and social economy. In most contexts, narcissism connotes a self-regard unseemly in its excessiveness, an egotism run amok; transatlantic Romanticism seems especially rife with such monstrous egotism. For Lillian R. Furst, the crux of the Romantic hero's tragedy is that "his egotism is such as to pervert all his feelings inwards on to himself till everything and everyone is evaluated only in relationship to that precious self, the focus of his entire energy," the result being that "no genuine, let alone altruistic love is possible."[10] Furst's view of the "blatant egotism" of the Romantic writer emblematizes the general view of Romantic male authorship.[11] The "egotism" of which some critics accuse Hawthorne stems from this larger accusation of solipsism in transatlantic Romanticism.[12] In addition to being framed as the bastion of white male privilege (Mulvey, Warren), narcissism has also been a pathological medical condition in several areas of psychoanalytic thought, including Freud's, a problematic history which this study reexamines.

Perhaps a good place to start in our challenge to broad understandings of narcissism as pathological egotism is with the Romantics, whose work deeply influenced Hawthorne and other American writers of the nineteenth century. Percy Bysshe Shelley's description of the titular phenomenon of his essay *On Love* goes directly to the heart of narcissistic self-representation:

> Thou demandest what is Love. It is that powerful attraction towards all we conceive, or fear, or hope beyond ourselves. . . . If we reason, we would be understood; if we imagine, we would that the airy children of our brain were born anew within another's; if we feel, we would that another's nerves should vibrate to our own, that the beams of their eyes should kindle at once and mix and melt into our own; that lips of motionless ice should not reply to lips quivering and burning with the heart's best blood. This is Love.[13]

For Shelley, desire for another person is desire for self-likeness. While a longstanding tradition in the West has taken a similar view, it has done so in terms of the misogynistic construction of "woman" as the reflection of man, who sees in woman's eyes the mirror image of his own beauty, physical and intellectual at once. Shelley, who was very much like the young Hawthorne a cynosure of the eye, was perhaps personally guilty of taking this view of women in life. But in any event, in this essay his evocation of a desire for someone whose "nerves should vibrate to our own" resonantly evokes the intimacy of narcissism, or, more properly, the desire for intimacy of a particularly intense kind within narcissism. Moreover, it exposes the narcissistic core of desire, which, as Freud put it, has neither aim nor object, but, on the other hand, proceeds from the basis of a desire to replicate and rediscover the self. There is, too, an inherent vulnerability in narcissistic desire, a need for some kind of affirmation of one's own worth on emotional and physical levels that is given through complementary resemblance. Male subjectivity is always figured as border-patrolled, as locked-down. Writers such as Shelley and Hawthorne suggest the porousness and fluidity of the male subject as well as the fragility of its constitution, the intense effort needed to maintain its surface logic of coherence and stability.

If psychoanalysis, as I will show, has no less consistently than the Western tradition put forth the view of narcissism as pathological, it can also be used provocatively to explore the centrality rather than the retrogressive role narcissism plays in desire.[14] As psychoanalyst Wilhelm Stekel wrote:

> Virtually every auto-erotic act is a manifestation of narcissism. For the pleasure is derived from one's own body. Moreover, close psychologic scrutiny of human love relations discloses that every human being seeks his self, or his self-reflecting image, in others, and that every love, in a certain sense, is love of self. We but love ourselves in others and hate ourselves through our hatred of others.[15]

Stekel provides a psychoanalytic version of Shelley's desire for reassuring likeness. By adding the factor of autoeroticism, Stekel also reminds us of the sexual dimensions of self-fascination. I will discuss the distinctions between autoeroticism and narcissism in the first chapter, but let me establish here that, in Hawthorne's own time, autoeroticism was a very troubling concept to many people. Broadly understood, it was, if anything, a more publicly denounced form of sexual expressiveness than homoeroticism. Autoeroticism was embodied negatively in the figure of the *onanist*, or masturbator. (From a psychoanalytic perspective, just as autoeroticism and narcissism are distinct from one another, autoeroticism cannot simply be reduced to onanistic practice; each has its own psychic characteristics.[16]) The voluminous antebellum literature on the dangers of onanism, linked with same-sex sexual practices by such high-profile health reformers as John Todd, Sylvester Graham, and Mary Gove Nichols, classified autoerotic desire as no less pernicious than same-sex desire, a bane to the emotional, spiritual, and physical integrity of the normative body.[17] As Stephen Nissenbaum observed in his penetrating study of the Jacksonian era's reformers, *Sex, Diet, and Debility*, Hawthorne's work has much in common with themes in Graham's tracts, especially.[18]

Yet Hawthorne's work also challenges the reformers' uniformly phobic disdain for the autoerotic. He floods the concept of solitary pleasure with the free-floating urgency of phantasy. A prime example of his sensibility is the almost nakedly autobiographical story "The Haunted Mind" (1835), about the nighttime reveries of a young man on the verge of sleep (9: 304–9). As a phalanx of phantasms invade his drowsy mind, Hawthorne's young man fitfully responds to each oneiric visitation, ranging from the intimidating, stern, masculine figure of "Fatality," a demon that "touches" the "sore place" of the young man's heart and embodies "Shame," to a female presence whose "tenderer bosom" and softer breathing would be, the narrator "whispers," such a pleasant addition to these "night solitudes." By the last paragraph, the drowsy young man seems to achieve some form of climax: "the knell of a temporary death." This work implies that the self is an ample and suitable site of erotic contemplation. Adding to this idea is Hawthorne's rare use of the second person in the narrator's description of these nighttime reveries. Addressing both his sleepy and contemplative protagonist and, implicitly, the reader as "You," Hawthorne's narrator maintains an emotional distance from both that is also redolent of spectatorial fascination. Mirror images, or more properly a chain of mirror images, narrator, protagonist, and reader reflect and double one another, simultaneously inciting desire, delaying climactic release, and then collectively experiencing this little death and its dreamlike, floating bodilessness.

Hawthorne's work generally both supports and troubles the idea of solitary pleasure—supports by suggesting its possibility repeatedly, troubles by rendering the idea ominous. Giovanni Guasconti's onanistic reveries in "Rappaccini's Daughter" seem fueled as much by his own self-fixation as they do by the disturbing beauty of the story's titular figure, but these reveries are harbingers of his own doom. Coverdale in *The Blithedale Romance* onanistically forereckons "the abundance of my vintage" high up in his inviolate bower, but he uses this vantage point to facilitate his obsessive voyeurism, as if to repudiate knowledge of his own onanistic desires. There is in Hawthorne a constant struggle between conflicted modes—empathy and scorn, desire and revulsion, respectful distance and invasive intrusion, and so on. Narcissism emerges as the chief site of these affectional and social struggles, their conductor and psychic source.

JACKSONIAN AMERICA AND HAWTHORNE'S VIEW OF MASCULINITY

Before proceeding to a further clarification of my psychoanalytic method here, I want to establish my understanding of what makes Hawthorne, on balance, a radical writer—however many conservative tendencies inform his work at times—of the antebellum period. Critical treatments of Hawthorne, especially those written by prominent critics such as Sacvan Bercovitch, Jonathan Arac, and John Carlos Rowe, from the early 1990s to the present have framed him as a racist and a misogynistic writer, or, at best, a writer who failed to make his politics sufficiently active, decisive, visible, or resistant.[19] Or, Hawthorne has been framed as a writer who couched his own quite adamant conservative politics in a coy rhetorical pose of political indifference. In my view, these critiques have at times misrepresented Hawthorne's politics and art; more troublingly, they have stemmed from a larger critique of Hawthorne's suspect "inaction" or passivity. While matters remain unsettled in terms of making sense of Hawthorne's admittedly conflicted and often frustrating politics, Larry Reynolds in *Devils and Rebels* has done a salutary job of providing new cultural contexts for them. The themes of inaction and passivity, whatever they may have meant for Hawthorne as a member of his northern abolitionist community, emerge as central to his fiction. It is precisely in the strange passivity of Hawthorne's men that the radicalism of his treatment of masculinity lies. Hawthorne evinces a career-long willingness to acknowledge the unspeakable and culturally silenced vulnerability in American manhood; moreover, he insists on viewing hegemonic masculinity from a skeptical perspective that emerges as a critique. Unsilencing the strictures of what T. Walter Herbert identifies as *code masculinity*, which demands a stoic reserve that kills off the range of human feeling in males, and offering a valuable, anguished, sometimes even angry critique of it, Hawthorne managed to resist the normative gendered standards of his era while also illuminating their pressures and effects.[20] This book attempts to show just how illuminating Hawthorne's work remains.

Building on the work of historians such as David G. Pugh, Michael Kimmel, E. Anthony Rotundo, and Andrew Burstein, I argued in my 2005 study *Men Beyond Desire: Manhood, Sex, and Violation in American Literature* that Jacksonian America produced a recognizably modern version of American manhood that privileged male competitiveness and physical strength and targeted nonnormative masculine behaviors—effeminacy, especially—as threats to the gendered stability of the nation.[21] The diverse discursive forces at work in antebellum America, sometimes with wildly competing interests and agendas—ideologies of self-made manhood and Jacksonian man-on-the-make market competiveness; religious reformers and temperance advocates; medical, health, and sexual reformers—united in the focus of their reconstructive programs: the young white male and his often errant, volatile body as well as spirit. Male sexuality—controlling, regulating, harnessing, and properly directing it—emerged as the chief battleground of these ideological battles. The particular form of male sexuality that emerged in antebellum literature—the figure that I call *the inviolate male*—was a reaction not only to the intensity of programs that sought to control male sexuality but also to the sheer incommensurability of their competing demands.

Hawthorne's work teems with emotionally, physically, and sexually inviolate male figures who reject both female and male companionship, who are in flight from marriage *and* other men. The formation of homosocial bonds, or what I call compulsory fraternity, was (and, I would argue, remains) no less a normative demand for the subject than marriage. At the same time, if broadly speaking the gendered protocols of Jacksonian America demanded phallic aggression and relentless ambition from its competitive, enterprising male subjects (and, from its female subjects, conformity to a new model of female passionlessness and domesticity embodied by the emergent Cult of True Womanhood), Hawthorne's work abounds with men, particularly young men, who eschew these market-driven models and attitudes. Hawthorne's male characters retreat when they might be expected to drive ahead, hide when others unceasingly seek. The passivity of Hawthorne's males, reflected in key patterns of his own life, especially in his politics, may reflect an unwillingness to pursue proper (and prescribed) political values. But their secretive, sensual slinking to the sidelines also refuses the gendered dictates of Hawthorne's own era, which, on so many levels, demanded maximal visibility from its male subjects.

Hawthorne, born in 1804, came of age in an America being shaped by the masculinist and anti-European cult of Andrew Jackson. Though elected in 1828 and re-elected four years later, Jackson had, in many ways, a three-term presidency. Although John Quincy Adams, in what Richard Hofstadter, in his classic study *Anti-Intellectualism in American Life,* describes as "a freakish four-way election," defeated Jackson the first time he ran for office in 1824, "Jackson was by far the more popular candidate."[22] The Battle of New Orleans in 1815 was a decisive moment for both Jackson and the nation's self-definition. The famous battle—in which Jackson was celebrated for having defeated the British, as if single-handedly—established him as a military hero throughout the nation and solidified the American distrust of and distaste for its own substantive European heritage. As an embodiment of European values and valences, John Quincy Adams only managed to maintain a tenuous, unsteady hold on his own presidency. As Hofstadter describes,

> Adams's administration was the test case for the unsuitability of the intellectual temperament for political leadership in early nineteenth-century America. . . . Adams became the symbol of the old order and the chief victim of the reaction against the learned man. . . . As Adams embodied the old style, Andrew Jackson embodied the new. . . . In headlong rebellion against the European past, Americans thought of "decadent" Europe as more barbarous than "natural" America; they feared their own advancing civilization was "artificial" and might estrange them from Nature . . . [In Jackson] was a man of action, "educated in Nature's schools," who was "artificial in nothing" . . . Against a primitivist hero [like Jackson] . . . who brought wisdom straight out of the forest, Adams . . . seemed artificial . . . . [When Jackson challenged Adams again in 1828], Adams was outdone in every section of the country but New England.[23]

As Hofstadter put it, the terms of the election that resulted in Andrew Jackson's 1828 presidency could be viewed as a battle between, in the words of a popular couplet of the time, "John Quincy Adams who can write / And Andrew Jackson who can fight" (159).[24]

Rather than put up a fight, Hawthorne's men forfeit their roles as social and sexual contenders and instead focus intensely on the self. This focus on the self was, in Hawthorne's treatment, a parody of the cult of self-made manhood that ran the gamut from Jacksonian market-values to the loftier principles of Emerson-Thoreauvian Transcendentalism, with its focus on self-reliance and self-culture. Self-focus in Hawthorne promises subversively pleasurable possibilities while threatening to immure the subject in the narrow confines of solipsism. Passivity emerges as a strategy for allowing for these potential pleasures while staving off an impending obsolescence.

A great deal more work needs to be done on the schism between Hawthorne's publicly avowed love not only for Jackson but for the very aggressive purposefulness he embodied, not just generally but in Hawthorne's own view, and the thoroughgoing critique of masculinist power in Hawthorne's work. Hawthorne offers scabrous critiques of men such as Judge Pyncheon in *The House of the Seven Gables* and Westervelt, Hollingsworth, Old Moodie, and even the narrator, Coverdale, in *The Blithedale Romance,* men who principally wield their power against those whose disadvantages leave them ill-equipped for a fight (the fragile elderly brother and sister Clifford and Hepzibah in *Gables;* wan and withdrawn Priscilla as the Veiled Lady in *Blithedale;* that novel's general populace subjected to Coverdale's rapaciously voyeuristic gaze).[25] While there are certainly masculinist attitudes in Hawthorne's life and work, Hawthorne consistently strives to undermine the stability from which hegemonic masculinity proceeds to wield its various forms of power. As I will attempt to show in this book, Hawthorne was a resistant critic of the increasing masculinism of his culture in ways that have not always been apparent to his critics.

THE PURPOSE OF PSYCHOANALYTIC CRITICISM

To return to the question of method: in speaking of psychoanalytic theory and of myth in relation to Hawthorne, I am both recalling earlier, no longer favored approaches to literary art and making a new, updated case for these approaches. While providing valuable insights distinctively its own, the historical approach to literature currently favored by Americanists cannot tell the full story of literature's effects on readers nor of readers' investments in literature. Though I believe that literary criticism must be sensitive to matters of history, I also believe that psychoanalytic theory is acutely adept at treating the affectional aspects of literary experience. One of my goals in this book is to make a case for the relevance, usefulness, and complementarity of psychoanalytic theory to historical studies of literature. I return to the question of the relationship between Americanist literary studies and psychoanalysis in chapter 3.

While I will have several occasions to establish, anew, why I feel that psychoanalytic theory is a useful means of studying Hawthorne's work, I want to take a moment both to situate myself within a psychoanalytic literary studies framework and to explain why my approach also stands apart from this framework as well as from historical approaches to nineteenth-century literature. In his 1968 *The Dynamics of Literary Response*, once a well-known work, Norman N. Holland summarizes the elements of psychoanalytic literary criticism in chapters on fantasy, "form as defense," displacement, character, affect, and related topics. Some of his comments in the 1975 edition seem to me enduringly apt:

> [As] readers, you and I bring certain characteristic expectations to a literary work and defend against or adapt the text to suit them. As I accept the text through my characteristic defenses, I project my preferred fantasies into it and transform those fantasies, using the text as absorbed, into a meaning

and coherence that matters to me. You do the same for you. The literary experience is the transformation described in *Dynamics*, but it takes place within each of us differently, because we each transform the resources the work offers us so as to express our different identity themes.[26]

Writing before identity politics, Holland presciently includes the idea of "identity themes." While I am not writing from a standard identity-politics position, which focuses on positive images and an affirming group identity, my personal identity certainly shapes my politics and therefore my work. Writing as a multiracial gay man about a white and presumably heterosexual author, and writing very much from a presentist position while also striving to be historically scrupulous, I am quite self-consciously creating my own versions of Hawthorne and his work here which, while they may bear resemblances to the authentic manifestations of these, are very much shaped by my own sensibility. Certainly, I will concur with Holland that I am projecting my preferred fantasies into Hawthorne's work and transforming those fantasies, using the text as absorbed, into a meaning and coherence that matters to me. (For Holland, "the reader introjects a process of psychological transformation [from unconscious fantasy toward conscious significance] that is embodied in the literary work.") In so doing, I genuinely hope to speak to something that is authentically and independently alive and vital in Hawthorne's work. But it is no more "explained" by psychoanalytic theory than it is by a scrupulous historical study—no more, that is, *explained away* by either. Because of Hawthorne's genius as a thinker as well as prose stylist, his work not only withstands but also exceeds critical analysis. Yet critical analysis also has a life—a consecration, if you will—of its own, and its own meanings and reasons for existence. What I hope happens throughout this study is that my own identity themes and Hawthorne's work as well as Freud's can converge in ways that produce new meanings and readings of value.

As Stanley J. Coen writes in his fine study *Between Author and Reader*, psychoanalytic criticism is ill-advised to attempt to reconstruct the biographical author, as it did in the past (and as, it should be noted, many contemporary and decidedly nonpsychoanalytic approaches continue to do). "Beginning with a careful literary analysis, we must then demonstrate that a psychoanalytic perspective does indeed add something further to clarifying and enhancing multiple meanings and perspectives for enriching our reading experience of the text. Often the value in psychoanalytic literary criticism is not the psychoanalytic perspective or language but simply that it is good criticism."[27] I agree with Coen, and certainly hope to have produced good criticism. But at the same time, psychoanalytic theory is not indistinguishable from other critical approaches. My commitment to it, which involves extensive revision of it from within, has a great deal to do with my political stances but also my own sensibility.

Psychoanalytic theory, to my mind, takes the best aspects of New Criticism—which, as has been amply shown, had many inherent flaws and ideological blindnesses—to a new level of theoretical sophistication, specifically in the belief in the importance and efficacy of close reading that both approaches share. But beyond this, psychoanalytic theory is particularly responsive, or at least can be made to be, to the emotional and other kinds of experiential aspects of gender and sexuality and also, though this area needs much more development within the discipline, racial identity. When informed by feminism, queer theory, and race theory, psychoanalysis can be a profoundly empathetic and suggestive means of developing enhanced, broad, and intimate understandings of identity and its implications.

For Hawthorne, writing in a literary era that placed severe restrictions on content, especially in matters of sexuality, and that, from the presidency of Andrew Jackson forward, set severe limits on gendered behavior for both men and women, literature was a means of expressing often taboo subjects in life as well as art. In my view, Hawthorne problematizes and even undermines normative gender and sexual roles (which is not to suggest that he does so with entire consistency or that a real conservatism in this and other regards is not also present in Hawthorne, only that it is not preponderant). But because Hawthorne does so, as he did just about everything, enigmatically, psychoanalytic theory, with its avowed interest in the unconscious and with *parapraxis,* slips of the tongue and other unintended revelations of unconscious thoughts and dynamics, becomes particularly useful for decoding his messages.

Hawthorne's work remains deliberately, constitutionally enigmatic in ways that simultaneously resist and beckon interpretation. Psychoanalytic theory should be more than a figural attempt to pry open locked boxes with beguiling patterns on their surfaces. Instead, its own difficulties and its own biases as well as capacity for insight dynamically interact and intersect with the textual object to which the theoretical methodology is applied. My effort is not to *apply* psychoanalytic theory to Hawthorne's work, but rather to compare both as modes of inquiry while letting each discover the other. What motivates me to study Hawthorne at length—beyond my belief that he is the greatest American writer of the nineteenth century—is that, in my view, Hawthorne is a radical theorist of gender, sexuality, and American masculinity. However many inherent and varied critical and literary dangers lurk within such a treatment of an author, the allure of engagement and insight surpasses the fears they produce. In the end, any critical project is a work in progress to be, if not completed, at least extended and enlarged by the reader.

As Meredith Anne Skura writes in *The Literary Use of the Psychoanalytic Process,*

> Using the psychoanalytic process as a model for literary texts does not imply that all conventions, all literal meanings, or all ordinary functions in a text are there only to be questioned. But it does provide a reminder that the questions are always there and that the uncertainty they produce is part of what the text conveys, even if this uncertainty is slight and finally resolved. Texts are more unstable than we might think; they are less fixed than simpler models that merely look for "hidden material" might indicate.[28]

Psychoanalytic theory is a complex model for the study of literature—complex both because it produces problems of its own that must be dealt with and because of the density and range of its invaluable insights. To use a Skura term, what psychoanalytic theory illuminates for us is "discrepancy": the tension between what a work ostensibly strives to achieve and what it *does* achieve, the indications it gives that, on the way to its idiosyncratic achievement, the work has encountered numerous forks in the road, that numerous fissures have developed.

There are tantalizing discrepancies in Hawthorne's work, ways in which he undermines the surface agendas of his narratives. Yet, at the same time, Hawthorne takes the very idea of narrative as an opportunity to subvert, to stage malevolent and upsetting fun and games. Moreover, as I have been suggesting, a genuine anguish courses through his witty menace. Psychoanalytic theory holds as a central premise that all is not what it seems, that all has not been made clear, in other words, that the unconscious has a powerful place in our lives that we struggle to understand. As I attempt to make use of it in this book, psychoanalytic theory can help us more fully and empathetically to understand the sources of Hawthorne's anguish—in life, to a certain extent, but more importantly and expansively within the realms of his art. While my specific subject is the startling discrepancy between the nineteenth-century American model of hegemonic or code masculinity and Hawthorne's representation of it, this focus leads to a broader set of reflections on the nature, or perhaps we should say the cultures, of gendered identity.

CHAPTER SUMMARIES

The book takes the following trajectory. In chapter 1, I discuss, in relation to Hawthorne's work, both the Narcissus myth and the psychoanalytic treatment of narcissism as an early stage in human development that provokes a sense of "paradise lost" in the nostalgic adult subject. This nostalgia relates to the concept I develop of "traumatic narcissism." I use this concept to interpret emotional patterns that recur in Hawthorne's fiction—its deep senses of loss, anger, betrayal, cruelty, and sorrow. The discussion turns to the valences among narcissism and male homosexuality in Freud's thought, the Ovidian version of the Narcissus myth, and Hawthorne's particular uses of it. I then establish the terms whereby one of the most important areas of inquiry in the study—visuality and the sense of vision, related to shame and sadistic forms of looking such as voyeurism—will be discussed. Looking at Jacques Lacan's and Laura Mulvey's revisions of Freudian visual theory (the mirror stage and the gaze, and the male gaze, respectively), I discuss how their work helps us to understand the potential uses that can be made of Freud as well as certain pervasive themes in Hawthorne, in particular the confrontation with his own image on the part of the figure of the young man.

In chapter 2, I take these propositions further. I re-examine Freud's often disputed if not altogether debunked theory of male homosexual psychosexual development, in which narcissism plays a central role, arguing that this theory, while not without some considerable difficulties, retains a value as an analysis of mother-identified male identity and the implications such an identity has for social relations. I reread Freud's essay "On Narcissism: An Introduction" as an understanding of human subjectivity that provides a provocative alternative to the theory of the Oedipal complex. From the basis of this reading, I argue that Hawthorne explores same-sex love in his story "The Gentle Boy," which I read as a complementary narrative to Freud's theory of the male homosexual child's psychosexual development, particularly in the centrality of the mother–son bond in both the tale and Freud's theory. In this chapter, I begin to address the relationship between shame and narcissism in Hawthorne's fiction as well as the relationship both thematics have to the equally substantial one in Hawthorne of vision and the gaze.

Chapter 3 discusses Frederick Crews's Freudian interpretation of Hawthorne in his 1966 book *The Sins of the Fathers* and Crews's later anti-Freudianism. From the 1980s to the present, Crews has emerged as one of Freud's chief critics. In this chapter, I discuss Crews's revisionist project, arguing that Crews's early Freudian critique of Hawthorne was itself a misrepresentation of both Freud and Hawthorne. Challenging the emphasis that Crews placed on the Oedipus complex in Hawthorne's work, I explore the narcissistic themes at play within it, through close readings of the tales "Roger Malvin's Burial" and "My Kinsman, Major Molineux." In the reading of "Burial," I develop the concept I call "murderous narcissism" as an alternative to the oedipal schema Crews sees at work in the story. In addition, I discuss the homoerotic significance of the classical allusions in the tale. With "Molineux," I develop, from my readings of Freud, Lacan, and Mulvey, the concept of the "narcissistic gaze" in Hawthorne. The goal of this chapter is not to replace one powerful critical term with another—narcissism for the Oedipus complex—but, instead, to establish that a consideration of Hawthorne's narcissistic themes allows us to shed new light on his interests in male sexuality, vision, and the gaze.

Chapter 4 refines the theoretical and thematic terms of the study as a whole. Here, I develop, through engagements with psychoanalytic and film theory, the ideas that Hawthorne's narcissistic themes are informed by a career-long preoccupation with vision, especially in sadistic forms such as voyeurism, and with shame. I argue that, while an important theme in and of itself, shame proceeds *from* narcissism in Hawthorne's work. Shame plays a key role in the "narcissistic crisis" that Hawthorne repeatedly stages. This chapter argues that Hawthorne's critique of normative masculinity proceeds from his awareness of the potentialities of shame in narcissism and the relation both have to vision and masculinity. The particular, consistent ways in which Hawthorne conveys the affect of shame in his male characters are explored, as are the related experiences of gender alienation and heterosexual ambivalence. In this chapter, I introduce the concept of "self-overseeing." Hawthorne foregrounds a heightened sense of panic within the male self's encounter with the visual evidence of its existence. The moments in which male characters glimpse themselves, as if for the first time, are fraught with anxiety and even terror. Extending the themes of the Narcissus myth, with its ban on self-knowledge, these instances of self-overseeing reveal some core truth of the self, but this revelation fills the subject with dread and self-revulsion.

Chapter 5 builds on the previous chapter in its examination of the ethics of looking and the gaze. Through a close reading of *The Blithedale Romance* that draws on film theory as well as Freud and Lacan, I explore Hawthorne's construction of a voyeuristic male subjectivity, unpacking psychoanalytic interpretations of voyeurism as a form of sadism, and the ways in which it is informed by both homoerotic desire and homophobic defenses. I treat voyeurism as an alternative form of narcissism while also considering the ways in which the novel thematizes the "pornographic gaze." Miles Coverdale's ravenous desire to look at the other characters is read not as male mastery expressed through vision but, rather, as indicative of the essential fragility, as well as potential for cruelty and prejudice, in his persona. His own confrontation with images of normative, nonnormative, and even nonhuman masculinity provides some of the most dramatic moments in the novel. I examine these moments in terms of Hawthorne's deconstruction of both the male gaze and the conventional male subject's relationship to masculinity as a gendered standard. One of the main themes of the chapter is the propensity that the objects of Coverdale's gaze have for *returning* the gaze and subjecting him to its own paralyzing effects. The chapter concludes with a comparison of the returned gaze in Hawthorne and Hitchcock.

In chapter 6, I switch gender lenses and focus instead on Hawthorne's representation of femininity, arguing that, on balance, Hawthorne's work is feminist in its identification with female figures and critical hostility toward masculinist power. This chapter compares Hawthorne's tale "Rappaccini's Daughter" to Freud's essay "Medusa's Head." I discuss the myth figures of Medusa and Narcissus as complementary metaphors for the difficulties in gendered subjectivity. Male narcissism emerges here as a defense against female sexuality and homoerotic desire. I also insert the tale within the contexts of literary tradition and intertextuality that are, I feel, crucial to any understanding of Hawthorne. Among other intertexts, the Bible, Christianity, particularly the myth of the fortunate fall, and Ovid's *Metamorphoses* are discussed as source materials revised through Hawthorne's particular interests in questions of gender, sexuality, and their psychological dimensions. Freud's theory of male fetishism is discussed at length and used as a critical lens through which to analyze the deep structures of misogyny that Hawthorne, in my view, critiques in this work.

In chapter 7, I turn to a comparative discussion of Hawthorne and Melville that focuses on each writer's reception of classical works of art, and classical male beauty in particular. Beginning with each writer's impressions in his journals of the classical figure of Antinous, a legendary homoerotic icon, I explore the implications of Melville's greater comfort with registering and recording homoerotic appreciation than that which Hawthorne exhibited. Considering his reconstructed late 1850s essay "Statues in Rome" and his *Billy Budd,* left in manuscript form and unpublished in his lifetime, I consider the ways in which Melville thematizes what I call *visual identity* and its relationship to male sexuality. Hawthorne's equally vivid and intensive thematization of the concept occurs through means that are less explicit than Melville's, but equally relevant to Hawthorne's work. Between them, Melville and Hawthorne should be viewed as crucial contributors to what I term transatlantic homoerotic visual culture. Considering each writer's familiarity with the eighteenth-century German art historian Winckelmann's theories of art, I argue that Melville and Hawthorne both take Winckelmann's complex nonsensual homoeroticism to suggestive and provocative levels of engagement. Turning to Hawthorne's 1860 novel *The Marble Faun,* I consider the significance of the titular figure to the narcissistic and homoerotic crisis Hawthorne thematizes in his work, and the ways in which the faun represents a kind of closure to this crisis.

In chapter 8, I turn my attention to matters of race, and the ways in which homoerotic narcissism intersects with race and gender. I argue for the aesthetic and political value of Hawthorne's unfinished *Septimius Felton* and *Septimius Norton* manuscripts. First, I propose that Hawthorne's late period deserves much more critical scrutiny and acknowledgment than it has been traditionally accorded. The "unfinished" nature of both of these texts may, I argue, be a strategic aspect of their political aims, or at least reflective of them on some level. Second, I discuss Hawthorne's exploration of racial identity and the ways in which his narcissistic themes and interests in the gaze inform this exploration of race. I discuss the implications of Hawthorne's "black" sensibility, as Melville put it, for his depiction of the multiracial Septimius Felton. Given the controversies that currently attend Hawthorne's representation of race in the slavery era, my analysis makes the case that Hawthorne, in his late phase, much more thoughtfully engaged with matters of race and racism than he had in previous phases of his career. This argument seeks not to exculpate Hawthorne for his racism, but to provide a better context for it and also to enlarge the discussion of it. One way I do this here is to insert Hawthorne's work within the growing field of "whiteness" studies. In psychoanalytic terms, I discuss the concepts of "ego ideal" and "ideal ego" in order to theorize the nature of Septimius's desire, both for the Revolutionary War English soldier he kills and the mysterious woman (actually the soldier's sister) with whom he develops a relationship.

In the epilogue, I discuss some fresh aspects of Hawthorne's work that further illuminate its narcissistic thematic: his aesthetics and his representation of history as crisis for the individual subject. Revisiting Hawthorne's elaboration of his aesthetic theory in "The Custom-House," what I call his *textual narcissism,* I explore the ways in which Hawthorne represents art as a mirror in which the unconscious and matters of social reality have equal weight and can be brought into mutual dialogue. I insert Hawthorne's aesthetics within philosophical treatments of narcissism's relationship to language, considering the ways in which, first, the predicaments of the mythic Narcissus have been interpreted as indicative of the difficulties inherent in writing and art generally, and, second, Hawthorne's work illuminates and interacts with these philosophical questions. I then turn to Hawthorne's idiosyncratic representation of history and its relationship to the individual subject in *The Marble Faun*. This discussion allows me to revisit the controversial issue of Hawthorne's supposed ahistoricism. While critics such as Sacvan Bercovitch, Lauren Berlant, Eric Cheyfitz, and John Carlos Rowe have critiqued Hawthorne for his political conservatism and hypocritical poses of political naiveté, I argue here that Hawthorne offers a radical account of history as contingent upon individual experience and the question of desire. Hawthorne's emphasis on the narcissistic dimensions of historical experience makes his interpretation of the historical no less challenging but also considerably more interesting than contemporary critical treatments have maintained.

CHAPTER 1

Paradise Lost

HAWTHORNE'S TRAUMATIC NARCISSISM

THE CHIEF CLAIM of this book is that Nathaniel Hawthorne's work consistently evokes the core themes of the Narcissus myth: a beautiful young man whose beauty incites desire from both females and other males and whose cruel rejection of those in whom he has inflamed desire inflames a desire for vengeance in them; the staging of an encounter between a beautiful man and his reflection; the unattainability of this image of beauty, always tantalizingly out of reach; the often suppressed issue of same-sex desire that inheres within this myth that is essentially about a beautiful young man desiring another; and the intertwining of desire with death, as emblematized by the moment in which Narcissus stares at his image even in the River Styx on his way to the underworld in Ovid's telling. The myth of Narcissus is also the myth of Echo, a powerful interpretation of women's role in patriarchy. Echo is of great relevance to Hawthorne, whose work abounds with Echo figures struggling to make their voices heard even as they are denied a voice. In that all of these themes also preoccupy Freud, whose influence over my treatment of Hawthorne is considerable, the Narcissus myth looms above every aspect of the present study, from primary texts to a critical methodology itself under reconsideration.

The approach I take combines Freudian literary criticism with psychoanalytic queer theory. My view is that a comparative analysis of primary author and critical method yields a richer understanding of both. In comparing Hawthorne and Freud, reading them each through the other, I aim to develop a better understanding of the psychological and cultural components of social constructions of normative male subjectivity and of literature's role in both shaping and potentially undermining this subjectivity.

Both the Narcissus myth and the philosophical discussions it has engendered allow us to contemplate the essentially *paradoxical* nature of desire. The barriers to self-knowledge are many and formidable; we are strangers to ourselves. How much greater is the impasse between us and another. Is it really possible for us to connect to another person? For that matter, what, exactly, do we want to connect *with* in another person? Is it really possible for someone else to forge a connection with *us*? The Narcissus myth and its tradition provide a resonant treatment of such questions and opportunities for them to be raised anew. In Hawthorne's evocation of the myth and Freud's reimagining of it as a human being's initial experience of the world, one he or she desperately attempts to regain, and in Lacan's theory of the mirror stage, the child's identification with and captivation by its own image, the Narcissus myth finds a potent new symbolic force. Hawthorne's work demonstrates that narcissism can create discordant effects, register a wide range of erotic responses, and challenge hierarchies of gendered and sexual identity. Proceeding from the basis of the self allowed Hawthorne to write affectingly of the multifaceted complexity of human experience.

Given the deep controversies that attend all uses of Freudian theory, the first order of business for a study that calls for a return to Freud—albeit a most idiosyncratic one!—is to define the terms of my revision. I will be turning to Freud more directly in chapter 2; in this chapter, I provide a series of contexts for my specific uses of Freud's concepts of narcissism, and especially for its centrality in his theory of male homosexuality. While many other Freudian concepts will be used in this study, the theory of male homosexual narcissism, which I argue can be used more generally as the model of mother-identified male psychology, is central to my analysis of Hawthorne's work, its potential radicalism, and his treatment of male subjectivity. At the same time, by revisiting some of Freud's most controversial and least critically supported arguments, I will attempt to demonstrate that they often retain a usefulness for questions of gender and sexuality. Before commencing psychoanalytic ventures into Hawthorne's work, it will be helpful to revisit the Narcissus myth and its associations between same-sex desire and gendered anxieties.

A crucial thematic linking all of these concerns in the myth is the sense of vision. From Ovid to Hawthorne to Freud, vision is associated inextricably with masculinity and male sexual desire, whereas voice, or more properly voicelessness, as Echo's role in the Narcissus myth achingly suggests, becomes symbolic of femininity and the female subject position in patriarchy. Freud's theories of vision, particularly its relationship to shame and sadistic forms of looking such as voyeurism, will be central to later chapters. In this chapter, I will turn to the two most important revisions of Freudian visual theory, Jacques Lacan's theory of the mirror stage and the gaze and Laura Mulvey's theory of the male gaze in the Hollywood cinema, both of which foreground narcissism and are crucial to the understanding of visual desire in Hawthorne's depiction of masculinity. I outlined the Lacanian theory of the mirror stage in the introduction; here, my discussion of Lacan's theory of the gaze allows me to establish my understanding of Hawthorne's work as a scopic field in which the male subject is only one figure in a much broader visual expanse, which is to say, finds his own abilities to look and to wield power by looking entirely dwarfed by the larger scopic regime. Thinking about Hawthorne's work in terms of the gaze makes it possible to think about its relevance to theories of film spectatorship such as Mulvey's, and, more broadly, to think about literature's relationship to visual art forms such as film. I discuss theoretical concepts such as narcissism, masochism, the mirror stage, the double, the male gaze, voyeurism, and fetishism in relation to Hawthorne's work, not in order to "apply" psychoanalytic and film theory concepts to Hawthorne, but because I believe that, between Hawthorne and theory, a lively and affecting dialogue occurs about the constitutive psychological elements of gendered identity. In that Hawthorne troubles the meanings of these elements, his work is worth examining for its insights into the arbitrariness of their social standardization as gender-role norms.

OVID'S NARCISSUS

It will be helpful to this analysis to recall some of the particulars of the Ovidian version of the myth of Narcissus, which has been the most influential version of the myth by far in the Western tradition. Ovid makes it clear that Narcissus needs a comeuppance. Desired by both females and males, the beautiful Narcissus cruelly rejects his suitors of each sex, mocking "Hill-nymphs and water-nymphs and many a man" (*The Metamorphoses,* 3: 401). He is cursed by being forced to suffer the same fate to which he subjected all of his admirers, to love a beautiful boy who cannot return his love. The major interest in the myth isn't Narcissus's vanity and its rightful comeuppance, though, but rather his recognition of the pain his indifference to desire has caused his admirers. This recognition occurs only as the result of the curse. Maddened by the unending elusiveness of the boy he desires, Narcissus finally realizes that

> Oh, I am he! Oh, now I know for sure
> The image is my own; it's for myself
> I burn with love; I fan the flames I feel.
> What now? Woo or be wooed? Why woo at all?
> My love's myself—my riches beggar me.
> Would I might leave my body! I could wish
> (Strange lover's wish!) my love were not so near! (3: 463–69)

Narcissus, the boy who mocked others' desire, now burns with the same desire, forced to experience the same maddening longing he instigated in others. From Ovid forward, the myth has functioned as a cautionary tale on several levels, principally against pride and vanity; but it has also served as a template for normative desire, for desire *itself* as normative: Narcissus must learn how to desire. Paradoxically, in learning how to desire, Narcissus also learns how *not* to desire, and experiences the pain he caused others of having a desire that cannot be fulfilled.

Another important myth-figure is embedded within Ovid's version of the Narcissus myth: Echo. Obsessed with Narcissus, Echo is constantly "following him," as Robert Graves limns Ovid's version of the myth, "through the pathless forest, longing to address him, but unable to speak first," forever iterating her plea "Lie with me!" Narcissus's harsh treatment of Echo as he adamantly dismisses her advances—"I will die before you ever lie with me!"—evince his cruelty.[1] Yet Echo is cursed as a result of *female* rage against male power. A laughing, charming nymph, Echo distracted Juno while her spouse Zeus was off philandering with another nymph. Upon discovering Echo's duplicity, Juno punishes her by denying her the ability to speak, rendering Echo capable only of repeating what someone else has said to her. One of the most poignant figures from classical myth, Echo can be used, in feminist terms, to represent women's problematic role within patriarchy. If the position of Woman in the West, as Hélène Cixous argues, is one of decapitation—the denial of mind and voice—the myth of Echo encapsulates this position.[2] If Narcissus, the beautiful man who falls in love with his own reflection, stands in for the conventional male protagonist, then Echo, the nymph denied her own voice, able only to echo the words spoken by others, provides the template for the traditional image of Woman, who can ostensibly only support, reflect—in a word, echo—narcissistic male leads.

"As Narcissus rejects Echo and the boys who want him," Steven Bruhm describes, "he rejects not only the dictate to desire another (a socially prescribed and approved other), but also the drive to stabilize a range of binarisms upon which gender in Western culture is founded." Bruhm lists some of the binarisms associated with the "problem of Narcissus" thusly: solipsism versus communality; surface versus depth; regression versus growth; madness versus sanity; self-obsession versus democracy; and sterility versus signification.[3] Like Cooper's Natty Bumppo, Stowe's Uncle Tom, and Melville's Billy Budd, Hawthorne's male characters are often sexually inviolate, figures who reject both heterosexuality and compulsory homosociality in the form of the enforced fraternity of separate gendered, public/private spheres in Victorian America. (The figure of the sexually inviolate male is the central topic of my book *Men Beyond Desire*, in which I consider the development of the figure in works by Irving, Cooper, Poe, Melville, Stowe, Augusta Jane Evans, and, especially, Hawthorne.) In that Hawthorne's sexually inviolate male characters reject both woman *and* man, they enact the Narcissus myth, as well as its terrible cautionary function: as Young Goodman Brown's fate emblematizes, these young, rejecting men are themselves profoundly rejected by narrative itself, left to live and die alone.

PARADISE LOST

Before turning to Freud, I want to try to paint a psychoanalytic picture generally of how Freud's theories of narcissism have contributed to our understanding of the subject's relationship to his or her own subjectivity. Whereas Freud made an adamant and frequent case for the centrality of the Oedipus complex, which we will discuss in greater detail in the next chapter, others have amplified the importance of his theories of narcissism. Béla Grunberger, one of the finest psychoanalytic thinkers in the Freudian tradition, argues that narcissism plays a central role in the psychic life. Grunberger's contribution is especially important because it implicitly challenges oedipal orthodoxy not only in Freud but also in psychoanalysis generally. The only normative oedipal outcome being properly achieved heterosexuality, any other kind of sexual orientation, such as homosexuality, will be seen as pathological and perverse. But this perspective overlooks and de-emphasizes not only the violence inherent within the *properly* resolved Oedipus complex but also the many deviations from it, the so-called negative Oedipus complexes that also account for a great deal of Freudian thought. Moreover, the focus on oedipal paradigms—emblematized, most significantly for this study, by Frederick Crews's interpretation of Hawthorne's work as principally a working out of the Oedipus complex—obscures the vital role that narcissism plays in the life of the body as well as the mind, when taken, as

Grunberger does, as an independent psychic agency. In chapter 2, I will demonstrate that narcissism provides a helpful alternative to the oedipal biases of Freudian theory.

"Narcissism should," writes Grunberger, "be recognized as an autonomous factor within the framework of Freudian topography and be promoted to the rank of psychic agency along with the id, the ego, and the superego." He argues that we should confer "on narcissism the rank of agency or motive force."[4] We long to return to an original, preverbal state of bliss, of "unrestricted autonomy and grandeur (the narcissist being one with the world, not delimited by the ego, which does not yet exist)," a state of well-being before trauma. We repress the "primal trauma" that shatters this once-experienced state of narcissistic bliss. "The repression remains superficial, however," he continues, in regards to the individual, "and the memory of 'paradise lost' will never cease to haunt him throughout life, especially as the individual's narcissism will always look on those 'substitute' pleasures with the scorn of the aristocrat for the rabble."[5]

In chapter 3, I will engage with Frederick Crews's work directly, but for now, let me note that it is difficult not to think here of his insightful description of "a certain impenetrable ceremoniousness that hints at aristocratic disdain for the coarse Jacksonian world" in Hawthorne's sardonic prose.[6] One thinks as well of the bitterness with which Hawthorne skewers those elderly Custom-House inspectors who dared to oust him from a job he hated. On some level, Hawthorne eulogizes a loss of something that he probably never possessed in life but may have had in *phantasy* (in psychoanalytic terminology, unconscious wishes). As Jean Laplanche and Jean-Bertrand Pontalis observe in their definitive *The Language of Psycho-Analysis,* "phantasy (or fantasy)," is an "imaginary scene in which the subject is a protagonist, representing the fulfillment of a wish (in the last analysis, an unconscious wish) in a manner that is distorted to a greater or lesser extent by defensive processes."[7] I would argue that the strange fascination with his Puritan forefathers that Hawthorne exhibits along with a revulsion toward them and their cruelly intolerant practices stems from his own narcissistic phantasy of having once possessed unlimited autonomy and control. Hawthorne's elegiac oeuvre, suffused with an intertextual awareness of Milton's poem about the Fall of Man (discussed at greater length in chapter 6), is haunted by a sense of paradise lost and unattainable. The vestiges of paradise that remain, such as the physical beauty of his Adamic characters, is a beauty tainted by postlapsarian blight, the shared trauma of human experience. Mark Edmunson helpfully reminds us that *Paradise Lost* was prominent among Freud's favorite literary works.[8] Both Hawthorne and Freud memorialize the moment in childhood in which narcissism ceded to the oedipal social order, an order forever haunted by this lost narcissism.

If it is true of Hawthorne personally that, in his narcissistic self-representations, he may be said, in Freud's language, to project before him as his ideal "the substitute for the lost narcissism of his childhood in which he was his own ideal," Hawthorne does not present this ego ideal or ideal ego in wholly idealized terms. (I discuss these concepts, and the distinctions between them, more fully in the last chapter.) The ideal image of man in Hawthorne is also often a violated, blighted image of man. Awash in the revealed depravity of all the people he has reverenced throughout his life, Young Goodman Brown discovers himself to be the most horrifying sight in the Satanic nighttime forest; described as notably physically attractive, the young scholar Fanshawe nevertheless bears the mark of an incipient blight; Giovanni Guasconti, described as a Grecian beauty, discovers that Beatrice Rappaccini's poison-plant blood now courses through *his* veins; beautiful young Donatello transforms into a haggard man over the course of *The Marble Faun;* and so forth.

Narcissism in Hawthorne carries with it an intense potential for dread; whatever form of self-investment manifests itself in his fiction is inextricably linked to pain, fear, and a predilection to aggressivity. Following Grunberger, we can understand that narcissism is above all else an agency that seeks a return to some mythic time—a paradise lost—*before* trauma. The fundamental trauma that shapes us, effects our individuation, and begins the process of our proper socialization is the separation from our mother's body, an event that shatters the ideal state of oneness in which we knew no distinction between her body and our own. However pessimistic Hawthorne's vision of the world, his pessimism flows out of a peculiarly ardent yearning for lost perfection, the idealized state of oneness in which child and mother's body were, if only for a moment, indissolubly linked, a transition I discussed in a Lacanian vein in the introduction as the individuating subject's passage into the Symbolic order. These themes are given their most acute treatment in "The Gentle Boy," which, as I will argue, is a tale central to Hawthorne's body of work. Within Hawthorne's depiction of narcissism as linked to horrifying feelings of loss is some persistent, urgent belief in a recapturable state of perfection, a belief always conjoined to an equally powerful refusal of or resistance to the belief, not a surprising stance in an author so committed to his own skepticism. For these reasons, I argue that Hawthorne's work foregrounds what I call a *traumatic narcissism,* a simultaneous nostalgia for a lost period of perfection and a bitter recognition of the impossibility of returning to this vanished, mythic state. If the Freudian concept of repetition-compulsion has emerged as a key means of understanding the patterns of American masculinity from the early republic to the present, Hawthorne's thematic of traumatic narcissism is a key aspect of what is politically resistant in his treatment of masculinity.[9] The desire to return—or to repeat—is met with a stringent, self-critical self-awareness. Hawthorne promotes neither narcissistic nor compulsive longings to return or to repeat; indeed, he critiques the motivations for either. At the same time, he treats these motivations with a certain degree of empathy.

The young men who populate Hawthorne's fictions reflect both nostalgia and a revulsion against it: nostalgia in that their state of physical perfection and ability to incite desire through the eye suggests an idealized representation of the self as youthful, desirable, and full of promise; revulsion in that their physical appeal jarringly contrasts with the inevitability of their ruin, on numerous levels. The loss and rage in Hawthorne parallel the psychoanalytic concept of grandiose narcissism, suffused with the pathological narcissist's anger at the world's failure to corroborate his own sense of his importance. Loss and rage also powerfully mock the promise of his comely male figures, making their pleasing outward show, paradoxically, the evidence of their doom and his despair. As I will further develop, male attractiveness appears to have provoked deep anxieties in Hawthorne, anxieties related to the cultural and social contexts of his own time, and to his personal experience of being a male in it. We will have several occasions throughout this study to revisit both these anxieties and their possible causes.

NARCISSISM AND THE PROBLEM OF HOMOSEXUALITY

Writers such as Ovid, Milton, Hawthorne, and Freud raise a question that will haunt the present study: To what extent is the narcissistic also the homoerotic? The episode in Book IV of Milton's *Paradise Lost* in which the newly made Eve recounts her nativity is exemplary in this regard. Eve falls in love with her own reflection and must be led back into properly heterosexual love by God and Adam. At least insofar as traditional readings allow, her narcissism evinces her immaturity, the vanity that will make her susceptible to Satanic seduction; but one could also argue that her disrupted, abandoned narcissism was the original sexual desire forcibly denied her. Though there is indubitably considerable homoerotic potentiality within narcissism, the extent to which narcissistic desire can be deemed homoerotic remains a productively difficult question. And as the predicament of Eve's desire more than suggests, female sexual desire, while linked in Milton to homoerotic narcissism, poses its own set of equally urgent difficulties for patriarchy. Precisely these questions will be the focus of chapter 6.

While the question of same-sex desire in Hawthorne's work looms large, the multivalent sexual registers of narcissism should not be ignored. I suggest that his narcissistic themes allowed Hawthorne to conduct a range of erotic energies; in making this suggestion, I aim to describe the capaciousness of narcissism as a textual experiment and an erotic sensibility. Given that my work represents a return to Freud from a queer theory perspective, it is important to acknowledge that the underpinnings of our current anti-narcissistic thought, enmeshed with homophobia, can be found in Freudian theory, albeit a Freudian theory, in my view, that has been distorted and misapplied.

In the life of the infant, narcissism is the stage between autoeroticism and object-love; Freud distinguished this "primary narcissism" from "secondary narcissism," one of the many enigmatic and controversial aspects of his theory. I will explore Freud's important 1914 essay "On Narcissism" in depth in the next chapter; for now, it will be helpful to consider some glosses of Freud's thought. Explicating Freud's 1914 essay, R. Horacio Etchegoyen importantly explains *the difference between autoeroticism and narcissism:*

> Childhood sexuality is not unitary and is not directed toward an object: it is at first anarchic, its various components each seeking its own pleasure and finding satisfaction in the subject's own body. Freud calls this stage "autoeroticism"; it precedes "alloeroticism," in which the object appears. There is a stage between these two, in which the unified sexual instincts take as their object the individual's own ego, which has been constituted at the same time. In this intermediate stage, called "narcissism," the subject behaves as if he were in love with himself; his egoistic instincts cannot yet be separated from his libidinal wishes.

"It is worth emphasizing," writes Etchegoyen, "that this condition is for Freud not only a stage in development but also a stable structure in the human being, who remains narcissistic even after finding an object."[10] As Janine Chasseguet-Smirgel notes, "Freud sees narcissism as not only one, or even several, stages of development, but as a permanent cathexis. It transforms the ego; as a result, objects can be cathected to different degrees, without the ego ever being able to give up entirely its libido in favour of its objects."[11]

Primary narcissism is the "original libidinal cathexis of the self"; in contrast, secondary narcissism, as Jeremy Holmes glosses Freud, is a regressive state in which the libido "(here conceptualized as a kind of psychic fluid)" of narcissists is "withdrawn from the external world and reinvested in themselves and their own bodies." As Holmes describes it, "Freud believed that people suffering from paranoia and schizophrenia, and to some extent hypochondriacal illnesses, regressed, often in the face of loss," to this secondary narcissistic state, described by Ronald Britton as "libidinal narcissism."[12] In other words, secondary narcissism is a regressive resurgence of the libidinal investment in one's own ego and body last experienced in infancy. Homosexuality has long been associated with this "regressive narcissism."[13]

One of the chief legacies of Freud is the view of narcissism and homosexuality as inextricably linked, the Siamese twins of psychoanalysis. Some scholars have sought to debunk entirely the relationship between homosexuality and narcissism, while others have reread the Freudian texts for precisely the value of the pairing.[14] I am in this latter camp (in more ways than one!). It is important to remember that Freud himself universalizes narcissism within his discussion of the two types of infant sexual object-choice, which he distinguishes as the "anaclitic" and the narcissistic. Freud argues that narcissism bears a much greater significance than its prevalence among "perverts and homosexuals especially" would suggest, an observation that "provides us with our strongest motive for regarding the hypothesis of narcissism as a necessary one." Though associated with the pathologization of homosexuality as narcissistic, Freud reveals narcissism, ostensibly the special penchant of perverts and homosexuals, as a universal sexual disposition: a primary narcissism exists in *everyone* (SE 14: 87–89).[15] Certainly, as I discuss in chapter 2, Freud's view of homosexual narcissism does indeed pose several great difficulties for queer theory, but I believe that it retains greater value than presently attributed to it.

A narcissistic sexual disposition is problematic for masculinity: on the one hand, narcissism is associated with homosexuality; on the other hand, it is associated with femininity. In Freud's view, notes Etchegoyen, "only men are capable of attaining complete—that is, anaclitic—object love; women conform to the narcissistic type, loving themselves and needing to be loved before loving."[16] In chapter 6, I complicate the view of an essentially narcissistic female sexuality. Historically, psychoanalysis has viewed male sexuality as anaclitic, fully object-based; this is one of the psychoanalytic orthodoxies that I contest even as I employ the insights of psychoanalysis to think through Hawthorne, narcissism, and gender. Moreover, I will throughout this book challenge American psychiatry's deployment of Freud to pathologize homosexuality as regressive narcissism, the specific subject of the next chapter.

HAWTHORNE AND LACAN
THE MIRROR STAGE AND THE GAZE

Hawthorne's work, in its increasing preoccupation with vision and visual culture, prefigures the cinema. The relationship between language and vision, in either representation or psychoanalytic theory, is a complex, indeed quite a vexed one. Freud's French reinterpreter Jacques Lacan's is best-known for his influential theories of language and its crucial relationship to the formation of a subject. Leaving behind the pre-oedipal world of the mother, the subject *becomes* a subject by entering the father's Symbolic order of language and law. If Lacan privileges the linguistic, his equally influential treatment of vision—exemplified in the mirror stage (which we outlined in the introduction) and the gaze—is well worth noting. Lacan's theories of subjectivity foreground not only language but also vision, perception, image, and illusion as fundamental to the subject's formation and lived experience.

In chapter 4, I will discuss Freud's theories of vision; for now, let me establish that Lacan's refinement of Freudian paradigms of vision into the theory of the gaze is crucial to our discussion. Lacan's theory of the gaze emerges from his disagreement with Sartre. Lacan disputed Sartre's conflation of the gaze and the act of looking. For Lacan, "the look" and "the gaze" are not the same thing. In Lacan's theory, the gaze actually becomes the object of the act of looking. When the subject looks at an object, this object is already looking back at the subject. Yet the subject can never see the object looking back at it; the object looks back at the subject from a vantage point that the subject can never see. For Lacan, there is a paradoxical blindness at the heart of vision.

As Lacan explains in *The Four Fundamental Concepts of Psychoanalysis*, "From the outset, we see, in the dialectic of the eye and the gaze, that there is no coincidence, but, on the contrary, a lure. When, in love, I solicit a look, what is profoundly unsatisfying and always missing is that—*You never look at me from the place from which I see you.*" "Conversely," Lacan adds, "*what I look at is never what I wish to see.*"[17] What is poignant in Lacan's discussion is that we are never *able* to see, certainly never able to see what we wish to see, never able really to see another, and never truly able to be seen *by* another. The emptiness and the disconnectivity of the gaze speak to narcissistic desire, a desire as unrealizable as it is maddening. In league with the Narcissus myth, psychoanalysis figures the relationships between the self and itself and between the self and the object of desire as equally and fundamentally impaired, the result of a profound, unbridgeable impasse. At the heart of the gaze is the plangency of narcissistic desire.

To explain the way that Lacan differentiates the eye or the "look" from the gaze, Kaja Silverman makes the analogy that the eye and the gaze are, in psychoanalytic theory, as distinct as penis and phallus. Whereas the penis is the male biological sexual organ, the phallus is the abstracted form of symbolic male power. (Indicative of our cultural misogyny, there is no correspondent abstract terminology for female sexuality. I would offer *yonic* as the female equivalent of phallic in terms of such symbolism.) Similarly, while the eye is the biological organ of sight, the gaze is the abstracted form of vision, far broader than any one individual's act of looking. As Silverman continues, "Although the gaze might be said to be 'the presence of others as such,' it is by no means coterminous with any individual viewer, or group of viewers. It issues 'from all sides,' whereas the eye '[sees] only from one point.'"[18]

As Lacan himself would have it, in an illustrative discussion of Sartre's *Being and Nothingness*, "The gaze in question is certainly the presence of others as such. But does this mean that originally it is in the relation of subject to subject, in the function of the existence of others looking at me, that we apprehend what the gaze really is? Is it not clear," Lacan presses, "that the gaze intervenes here only in as much as it is not the annihilating subject, correlative of the world of objectivity, who feels himself surprised, but *the subject sustaining himself in a function of desire?*"[19] If the gaze's chief usefulness is to the subject who wants to sustain his desire, the questions for our reading of Hawthorne works prominently include: What *is* the subject's desire?

Hawthorne devises theories of vision that prefigure Freudian and Lacanian paradigms, evoking the tensions that undergird them. His work makes the fearful encounter with one's own image and the subject's entrapment within the logic of the visual chief concerns, affectingly rendered. Hawthorne may be said to make the fateful encounter with the specular self his great subject. But more broadly, the powerlessness of Hawthorne's avid male lookers corresponds to the Lacanian understanding of the subject of the gaze as only one aspect of its larger scopic regime, engulfed within the overarching structures of vision in which subjects vie for illusory and impossible power. As I will show in chapter 5, *The Blithedale Romance* exemplifies the Lacanian aspects of Hawthorne's fictional staging of the gaze.

HAWTHORNE AND MULVEY

Narcissism in Hawthorne functions as an approach to masculinity that radically decenters and reorganizes it; in Hawthorne, men do not occupy clear-cut roles of dominance and mastery, which typically endow them with the power of the gaze, but instead come under visual scrutiny themselves as often as they subject others to it. In her famous 1975 essay "Visual Pleasure and Narrative Cinema," Laura Mulvey argued that the woman in classical Hollywood cinema connotes "to-be-looked-at-ness." In their effort to see their own reflections, men use women as mirrors for male resplendence, rendering women visual helpmeets. Yet in Hawthorne, males also connote this quality. Moreover, it is their own image they seek to find, a quest with homoerotic implications as well misogynistic ones.

Mulvey influentially but also controversially argued that the classical Hollywood cinema, a key manifestation of attitudes of the dominant culture, is organized around the male gaze, presumably the white, heterosexual male gaze, which objectifies women, the to-be-looked-at sex, by turning them into visual spectacles. Devoid of any autonomous power, the women in film exist to mediate the protagonist's own fears of castration. Todd McGowan has recently taken Mulvey to task for being insufficiently Lacanian in her theorization of the gaze, returning us to Lacan's original paradigms. Yet we can say that Mulvey, drawing on Lacan, formulates her own theory of the gaze in relation to Lacan as well as Freud; her version of the gaze is more local, immediate, and direct, the force of one person's eyes on another. The man's eyes are powerful because the entire field of vision is structured around traditional masculinity and its demands, which include an incessant staving off of castration fears. As Mulvey theorizes it, the protagonist has recourse to two strategies for fending off these fears: voyeurism (investigating the woman, solving her mystery) and fetishism (focusing on certain parts of her body, such as the face or the breasts). I rehearse Mulvey's views here, not to imply that I fully agree with them, either in terms of the classical Hollywood cinema or of Hawthorne's work, but to establish that they continue to be relevant to any understanding of the role of vision within theoretical concepts of gendered identity, generally. I do not accept Mulvey's view of the static and fixed nature of the male gaze in terms of identification and power; whereas Mulvey sees the spectator and the classical Hollywood protagonist sharing masculinist power, I see the process as much more unstable and much more fluid. There is nothing stable or coherent in the gendered gaze; moreover, the gaze itself is heterogeneous, multiple. Mulvey establishes a view of the Hollywood protagonist as well as the spectator as both male and stably heterosexual, which is clearly false on both counts. It should be added that Mulvey has simultaneously qualified her views over time and maintained her basic thesis. At the same time, I have yet to encounter any treatment of queer dimensions within the classical Hollywood cinema or in terms of the gaze in her work. This being said, though, my view of the gaze is closer to Mulvey's than it is to Lacan's. Like her, I see the gaze as a field of vision in which looking has a real-life impact on those being looked at, and on the looker, whereas for Lacan the major emphasis is on the blindness at the heart of vision, the *impossibility* of seeing, and the gaze as a vast structure that is quite indifferent to the individual subject.

For Mulvey, narcissism is thoroughly the domain of male privilege: the shared gaze of the spectator, who is gendered male, and the male screen protagonist return both to a pre-oedipal state of narcissistic omnipotence. I respect her feminist perspective though I do not agree with her here. If we take Mulvey's claims broadly as a problematic but nevertheless highly suggestive theory about the traditional, normative patterns of gendered vision in our culture, what is remarkable about Hawthorne's work is the extent to which he refuses and overturns assumptions about gender and the gaze. (Though I am aware that in making this comparison my argument threatens to descend into anachronism, I treat Mulveyan theory as an articulation of long-standing patterns of gender and vision in the Western tradition; Mulvey herself frames her discussion in this manner.)

Repeatedly, Hawthorne's male characters provoke and incite the gaze, becoming themselves entrapped within it; repeatedly, his male characters inspire the speculative sexual contemplation usually associated in narrative forms with desirable female figures. This is not to suggest that Hawthorne stints on depicting female beauty; far from it. Rather, as does Herman Melville, Hawthorne strives to give masculinity an equal claim to beauty. Very often, though, Hawthorne's interest in the beauty of his male characters bafflingly exceeds the parameters of the work. In ways that are indubitably linked to this last point, Hawthorne figures shame and trauma as central components of narcissism, and narcissism as fundamentally related to the relationship between gender and vision. These consistent associations make his work relevant for queer theory as well as psychoanalysis, and both relevant for an interpretation of his work.

In chapters 4, 5, and 6, I will consider voyeurism as another dimension of Hawthorne's narcissistic thematic. In the next chapter, I discuss Freud's controversial theory of male homosexual narcissism—which many will with justification feel has already been quite thoroughly debunked, but which still retains, in my view, an eerie relevance—in relation to Hawthorne's short story "The Gentle Boy." This chapter will begin to develop the relationship between shame affect and narcissism in Hawthorne's work. Before bringing this chapter to a close, I want to forecast a finding that I elaborate upon in chapter 7, which focuses on Hawthorne's (and Melville's) reception of classical male beauty.

VISUAL IDENTITY

Throughout his work, Hawthorne foregrounds a particular understanding of self, sexuality, and the body. His work thematizes what I call *visual identity*, the conceptualization of the self as a perceivable visual image, something extruded upon the surface of the world as a reflection of a private, interior self the existence of which can be affirmed only through this visualization. Which is to say, selves are only known or knowable through their outward manifestation in physical form. Visual identity is certainly not exclusive to males; indeed, the entire postclassical Western tradition has emphasized the visual aspects of beauty as a female domain. But what is of interest in Hawthorne is that the visual aspects of beauty are no less tangibly embodied in males than in females. Given the often idealizing tendencies of nineteenth-century American Romanticism, this might not be such a singular trait in an author's work. One readily recalls descriptions of male beauty in Cooper ("comely" young Jasper in *The Pathfinder*), Poe (the eerie, ruined beauty of Roderick Usher), Stowe (the louche handsomeness of Augustine St. Clare, and the sturdy one of Tom), and especially Melville (Marnoo, his island Apollo in *Typee*; his charming Carlo, always displaying his "organ," and vulnerable dandy Harry Bolton in *Redburn*; and his immortal Billy Budd). But what is resistant—and highly disturbing—in Hawthorne is how stringently he incorporates the male's beauty not only into the networks of the desiring gaze, making men equal-opportunity objects before it, but also into his fiction's moral schemes, in which beauty emerges as a troubling and troubled outgrowth of a view of the world as a visual regime. Melville, without question, may be said to be doing something quite similar, especially in *Billy Budd*. But the difference between both authors is that in Hawthorne, depictions of male and female beauty are equally weighted, whereas in Melville, beauty is disproportionately male. It would follow, then, that Melville is the "queerer" author, but such is not the case. Male beauty in Hawthorne emerges as a surprising disturbance within an exquisitely outlined and developed heterosexual economy of gender, difference, and desire, a self-undermining, inherent queerness within normative heterosexuality. To the extent that this is also true of Melville's writing, his relative lack of interest in femininity (and I do mean relative, since it would be quite inaccurate to say that women are not present, sometimes crucially present, in Melville's work) creates discrete, discordant effects. In short, Hawthorne and Melville are alike in their incorporation of queer themes, but each figures queerness in his own way.

The beauty of Hawthorne's men heightens their susceptibility to moral corruption. Or, as in the case of his gentle boy, it signifies his predicament in a culture that emphasizes normative masculinity, which Hawthorne everywhere shows to be indistinguishable from an overarching cultural and social structure of brutality. Hawthorne's work makes us consider anew the dynamics and the difficulties of a lived subjectivity that is inextricable from one's outward manifestation of this subjectivity, which is to say, one's visual identity.

CHAPTER 2

As His Mother Loved Him
"THE GENTLE BOY" AND FREUD'S THEORY OF MALE HOMOSEXUALITY

TO COMMENCE our exploration of the intersection of Freudian theories of narcissistic male sexuality and Nathaniel Hawthorne's fiction, I begin with a discussion of the most difficult aspect of Freud's theory of narcissism, its centrality in Freud's understanding of male homosexuality.[1] My reading of Hawthorne's work touches frequently on issues of same-sex desire, but I should make clear at the outset that the chief goal in my reading of Hawthorne is not to establish him as a prototype of the homosexual author, if it is to be accepted that modern homosexual identity is a phenomenon that can be dated from the latter nineteenth century into the twentieth. (I remain skeptical of this Foucauldian view of sexual history.)[2] Rather, I am interested in the ways in which Hawthorne's narcissism provides a conduit for the free play of sexuality, allowing for concepts such as same-sex desire, cross-gender identification, and gender liminality to intersect with traditional modes of sexual representation. Like many other antebellum American authors, Hawthorne, in classically Freudian terms, appears to have had a bisexual disposition in terms of responding to the beauty of both sexes. But Hawthorne doesn't simply respond to the varieties of beauty; indeed, beauty becomes a highly fraught, sustained discourse in his work with deep relevance for his career-long interests in gendered and sexual identity and, as his career develops, race.

Thinking through Freud's theory of narcissism from the perspective of male homosexuality allows us to accomplish several things at once. We can immediately address the controversial nature of the methodology this study uses, making a case for the methodology but also amply demonstrating that it will itself be subjected to reevaluation. Finding a persistent value, as I do, in one of Freud's most debunked theories, I make the case that Freudian theories of male homosexual narcissism retain a *general* relevance for male sexuality. In that Freud's theory focuses on the relationship between mother and son, it provides insights into Hawthorne, who throughout his work explores the nature of parent–child bonds, especially those between mother and child. As discussed in the previous chapter, a longing for lost origins, figured in the mother–child bond, suffuses Hawthorne's work. Hawthorne, in my view, challenges rather than perpetuates the oedipal logic of normative masculinity, the basis of which is a rejection of the mother. While there are certainly oedipal aspects to Hawthorne's work, and while Hawthorne himself idealized such man's-man figures as President Andrew Jackson, on balance it is maternal identification that informs his fiction.

In that Hawthorne foregrounds and illuminates the problematic nature of gendered identity itself, his work sheds reciprocal light on Freud's views of childhood psychosexual development, especially his insistence on the centrality of the Oedipus complex. If Freud provides a counternarrative to his own oedipal orthodoxy in his theory of narcissism, Hawthorne refuses any linear, clear-cut understanding of how normative gendered and sexual identity gets formed, thus refusing assimilation into oedipal orthodoxy. This view of Hawthorne runs counter to Frederick Crews's influential thesis of the oedipal paradigms of Hawthorne's work (discussed in the next chapter). By exploring narcissism in Hawthorne, I believe that we gain a deeper and more complex appreciation of Hawthorne's interest in several issues: gender, sexuality, race, but also trauma, shame, vision, power, and politics.

In their scrupulous study *Sexual Orientation and Psychodynamic Psychotherapy*, Richard C. Friedman and Jennifer I. Downey challenge the uses of Freud's theory of the Oedipus complex for the pathologization of homosexuality. Going through the Oedipus complex successfully in one's childhood means emerging as properly heterosexual. Traditionally, deviations from the normative resolution of the Oedipus complex, such as homosexuality, have been diagnosed as pathological forms of the complex and therefore of properly heterosexual adult sexuality. Friedman and Downey, making note of "profound change[s] in psychoanalytic theory in recent years in the areas of sexual orientation," argue that, contrary to classical psychoanalytic thought, "superego development, gender identity, sexual orientation, personality structure, the etiology of the neuroses (and the psychoses)—all seem to be subject to influences other than oedipal conflict resolution or failure thereof."[3] Salutary though their revisionist work proves to be for new, antihomophobic psychoanalytic methods of interpreting the dynamics of gay identity in a rapidly changing world, that the authors dispense with narcissism—a crucial aspect of Freud's thinking on homosexuality and, indeed, within his thought generally—altogether in their reassessment of classical psychoanalytic theory and survey of new approaches seems to me a disturbing and worrisome error.[4]

The opprobrium that narcissism has historically elicited—from its endurance as a cautionary tale throughout Western literature to its familiar usage as a pejorative assessment of an overly prideful character—intersects with the psychoanalytic diagnosis of narcissism as pathological. Freud's thinking on narcissism, particularly as it pertains to homosexuality, has contributed to this model. Yet it can also challenge the prevailing derogations of narcissism.[5]

The figure of the homosexual narcissist, who could also be described as the narcissistic homosexual, recurs throughout Freud's work. Great controversy over the Freudian view of homosexuality endures within queer theory: while many have contemned Freud's theory of homosexual narcissism as pathologizing and inherently homophobic (Warner, 1990; Fuss, 1995), others have found enough complexity in Freud's thinking on the subject to use his work not for the purposes of further pathologizing homosexual narcissism but, instead, to enlarge our view of desire and use psychoanalysis to challenge homophobic thinking (Dean, 2000; Dean and Lane, 2001; Bersani, 2001). My argument proceeds from this latter line of thought.

The historical psychoanalytic pathologization of narcissistic identity has hit homosexuals with particular force. Given that psychoanalysis has contributed to the pathologization of homosexuality generally (though not consistently), the pathologization of narcissistic personality also entails psychoanalytic homophobia. As I attempt to demonstrate here, homophobia can also be challenged *through* psychoanalytic means. My effort to recuperate narcissism, then, necessarily involves a challenge to this homophobia that emerges from within a psychoanalytic project. Finding the value in Freud's view of homosexuality as narcissistic is a jumping-off place for this effort.

Freud's theory of homosexual narcissism is only one piece of his larger thinking on narcissism. The narcissist and the homosexual, while distinct types, are sometimes indistinguishable from each other in Freudian thought, similarly "perverse" forms of identity. Moreover, they have consistently, as types, been broadly used as embodiments of the same negative character traits: obsessive if not pernicious self-involvement, an inability to love, arrested development, a hatred of the opposite sex, a deep and abiding penchant for surface rather than depth, and so on. Narcissism, it should be noted, is just as integral to Freud's view of heterosexuality as it is to homosexuality. Though it has not, to my knowledge, been read in this manner before, Freud's theory of homosexual male narcissism provides a *generally resonant* interpretation of the mother–son bond that exceeds the boundaries of a specific sexual orientation. To make an obvious point pointedly, heterosexual men have mothers, too.

The Hawthorne work that I discuss in this chapter, "The Gentle Boy," bears a striking resemblance in its thematic concerns to Freud's treatment of the homosexual child. Freud illuminates the aspects of Hawthorne's work that come closest to making a political statement about the ways in which males are socialized generally in Western patriarchy. Both provide insights into the experiential and social experience of maternally identified and narcissistically inclined male desire. Before turning to Freud's 1914 essay "On Narcissism: An Introduction" (SE 14: 67–105), it is important to address some of the reasons why Freud remains for many a homophobic thinker. In my view Freud is, on balance, a thinker who *challenges* sexual orthodoxies rather than establishes them. This holds true, as I will show, for his controversial theorization of homosexuality.

HOMOSEXUAL NARCISSISM
AN INTRODUCTION

In his aversive Foucauldian reading of Freud, Michael Warner argues that the concept of narcissism has been "primitively" used in psychoanalytic theory to calumniate queer sexuality as regressive and self-fixated.[6] I should make it clear that I do not concur with most of Warner's social-constructionist positions; when exclusively maintained, with little consideration for the psychic life, these positions are far too orthodox to be fully useful to an understanding of either sexuality or the phobias that various forms of sexuality incur. The most useful point of Warner's argument is his challenge to the prevailing view, in some circles, that homosexual desire is exclusively narcissistic, and that the homosexual subject chiefly desires himself or herself reflected in someone else. "Why is gender assumed to be our only access to alterity?" questions Warner. "Can it actually be imagined that people in homosexual relations have no other way of distinguishing between self and not-self? That no other marker of difference, such as race, could intervene; or that the pragmatics of dialogue would not render alterity meaningful, even in the minimal imaginary intersubjectivity of cruising?"[7] Warner specifically locates Freudian thought within heterosexual ideology, the "central imperative" of which is that "the homosexual be supposed to be out of dialogue on the subject of his being." Imagining the narcissistic homosexual's "unbreakable fixation on himself" serves two purposes: first, it allows "a self-confirming pathology by declaring homosexuals' speech, their interrelations, to be an illusion"; second, "*and more fundamentally it allows the constitution of heterosexuality as such.*"[8]

Warner wants us to understand that psychoanalysis, as an arm of power, facilitates the "utopian erotics of modern subjectivity" that works to obscure what institutionalized heterosexuality has in common with homosexuality, a dependence on "a self-reflexive erotics of the actual ego measured against its ideals," a dependence made visible in homosexuality but decisively obscured in heterosexuality. "Heterosexuality deploys an understanding of gender as alterity in order to mobilize, but also to obscure" what are its own "narcissistic sources," hence the crucial function of a "discourse about homosexuality as a displacement" of these disavowed sources.[9]

I am in agreement with Warner about the primitiveness of a view of homosexuality that reduces it to desire for sameness and as a stunted inability to recognize and erotically respond to "difference." Yet Warner's argument, which is not without value, hinges on a reductive reading of Freud that irons out the inconsistencies in his thought. It is these inconsistencies that make Freud an unpredictable and suggestive thinker. Freud returned to the subject of homosexuality several times, sometimes seeing it as one of the perversions, sometimes as the "most important of the perversions" (cold comfort, to be sure), but his attitude was not one of "complacent" hostility, as Warner describes it. How "inappropriate to use the word perversion as a term of reproach," he writes in his 1905 *Three Essays on the Theory of Sexuality* (SE 7: 160). Freud clarified that perversions become pathological when they assume "the characteristics of exclusiveness and fixation" (7: 161). In counterdistinction to Warner's presentation, Freud found, as a site of inquiry, homosexuality to be as interesting as it is disturbing, and his treatment of it cannot be simply dismissed as phobic. Moreover, Freud found exclusive heterosexuality no less perplexing a problem than homosexuality. For his era, and despite his lapses, particularly concerning lesbianism, Freud was a fairly progressive thinker on homosexuality.

The most surprising omission in Warner's critique of Freud's views on homosexuality is the centrality of the mother–son relationship to Freud's theory of homosexual development. In a footnote added in 1910 to his 1905 *Three Essays on the Theory of Sexuality,* Freud conjectures that homosexual identity emerges from an identification with the mother.

> In all the cases that we have examined we have established the fact that the

future inverts, in the earliest years of their childhood, pass through a phase of very intense but short-lived fixation to a woman (usually their mother), and that, after leaving this behind, they identify themselves with a woman and take *themselves* as their sexual object. That is to say, they proceed from a narcissistic basis, and look for a young man who resembles themselves and whom *they* may love as their mother loved *them*. Moreover, we have frequently found that alleged inverts have been by no means insusceptible to the charms of women, but have continually transposed the excitation aroused by women on to a male object. They have thus repeated all through their lives the mechanism by which their inversion rose. Their compulsive longing for men has turned out to be determined by their ceaseless flight from women. (SE 7: 145n1)[10]

Certain aspects of Freud's argument indisputably lend themselves to homophobic views and were perniciously exploited as a basis for homophobic practices at certain points in the history of American psychiatry. I argue, however, that Freud's theory of the mother–son relationship in terms of homosexuality should not necessarily be treated as itself pernicious; at the very least it should be re-examined.

The sheer range of cultural myths about the male homosexual encapsulated in this passage from *Three Essays* does, admittedly, stagger the mind: male homosexuals and their mother-fixation; male homosexuality as narcissistic self-love; male homosexual desire as desire for sameness, for the replica of the self (they "look for a young man who resembles *themselves*"); homosexual desire as an expression of panic over female sexuality; homosexual desire as a substitute for normative heterosexual desire; homosexual desire as a kind of repetition-compulsion through which some form of sexual trauma can be relived, re-experienced, but never "resolved" ("repeated all through their lives," "their compulsive longing"); male homosexuality as an attempt to escape women ("ceaseless flight"). Only a footnote, this passage wields a prescriptive power that managed to install a particular set of images about male homosexuality in the popular imagination. To be sure, there are difficulties with Freud's theories of homosexuality.

If one of the great phenomena of American culture is its profound receptivity to the new science of psychoanalysis, surely the Freudian view of homosexuality was one of the most widely assimilated of psychoanalytic concepts in the United States. Used to pathologize homosexuals and then to effect their elusive cure, Freud's theories were reduced to cartoonish essences of themselves, made to serve the ideological needs of a nation eager to normalize all of its citizens in every conceivable way, perhaps especially in sexual terms. Yet Freud's extraordinarily complex and often bizarrely contradictory ideas resisted such homogenization, much more its broad, normalizing application. In his complex approach to homosexuality, Freud was light-years ahead of figures such as Charles Socarides, one of the most prominent and virulently homophobic voices in American psychiatry.[11]

Warner leaves something else out of his discussion of Freud's view of homosexuality as a perversion: the centrality of perversity to Freud's thinking. As Jonathan Dollimore points out in his superb treatment of Freud in *Sexual Dissidence,* "Freud described homosexuality as the most important perversion of all," "as well as the most repellent in the popular mind," while also being "so pervasive to human psychology" that Freud made it "central to psychoanalytic theory."[12] As Dollimore writes, if the value of psychoanalysis lies in its exposure of the essential instability of identity, "then this is never more so than in Freud's account of perversion. At every stage perversion is what problematizes the psychosexual identities upon which our culture depends."[13] As Freud's own words in his famous *Three Essays on the Theory of Sexuality* attest, "a disposition to perversions is an original and universal disposition of the human sexual instinct" (SE 7: 231).

In Freud's most famous formulation, the Oedipus complex eradicates the infant and young child's access to polymorphous pleasure. In the process, we become properly socialized, learning how to desire normatively. For Freud, the oedipal conflict works differently in boys and girls. In boys, erotic attraction to the mother arouses aggressive, violent feelings in the form of sexual rivalry with the father whom he wishes to supplant. It is by learning to identify with, rather than to compete against, the father that the boy resolves his oedipal conflicts and becomes properly socialized. It is the boy's fear that his father, whom he imagines to be as competitively enraged against him, will castrate him that ends the boy's oedipal conflict. In contrast, for girls it is the recognition that they have been castrated that *commences* their Oedipus conflict. Freud frequently claimed to find the female Oedipus complex an essentially perplexing and mysterious process while nevertheless repeatedly submitting it to theoretical reformulations. Clearly, Freud is as frustrating a theorist of female psychosexual development as he is an illuminating one of the male's. As I will demonstrate in chapters 6 and 7, Freud's theories of femininity, however, are not altogether without value and interest.[14]

Part of socialization is the prohibition of both homosexuality and incest. By learning to identify rather than to compete with the same-sex parent and by learning to desire someone outside of the family and of the opposite sex, we find our way out of both homosexuality and incest and into normative desire and social identity. This is the area of Freud's thinking that has proven especially interesting to queer theory. Judith Butler wrote in her 1990 *Gender Trouble* of the "melancholia of gender identification" within Freud's model of normative childhood psychosexual development, the Oedipus complex. Butler drew out the implicit Freudian point that "it would appear that the taboo against homosexuality must *precede* the heterosexual incest taboo; the taboo against homosexuality in effect creates the heterosexual 'dispositions' by which the Oedipal conflict becomes possible."[15] Because homosexuality must be, along with incestuous relations, repudiated, same-sex relationships are always already haunted and left bereft by an internalized awareness of the prohibition against homosexual desires. That these desires were foundational to the formation of a sexual subjectivity makes the prohibitions against them especially wounding. An extraordinary range of queer theory treatments of these themes have followed Butler's line of argument.[16]

Socialization buries our polymorphous perversity under repressive decorum. What constitutes repression are an odd assortment of "social dams" such as the curious triumvirate of shame, disgust, and pity. The social and cultural neuroses that ensue are the "negative" of the perversions, the ills produced by their repression. Our oedipalization drives the pulsating waves and experiences of polymorphous pleasure underground, leaving a good deal of our libidinal energies repressed. But a burial is not an eradication, as Poe's writing makes so abundantly clear again and again: our perverse desires continue to destabilize the dams of repression.

As Freud consistently argued, civilization was a triumph for the human species and a tragedy for the individual. The lost histories of our childhood responses to the world—the unimaginable range of polymorphous pleasures, the sheer openness to feelings and sensations of all kinds—remain buried in our unconscious, largely hidden from us, accessible only in those unsettling moments of *parapraxis,* those slips of the tongue and other fissures through which our own truths slip out from beneath our repressive self-control. The Oedipus complex successfully transforms us into properly socialized beings, but this is not in and of itself a necessarily laudable process, only the one our culture demands. Freud's own ambivalence about the Oedipus complex hovers over his discussion of homosexuality. He unsettles his own account of childhood homosexual development through his frequent discussions of the *negative Oedipus complex,* an "inversion" of the "normal" version rather than an exceptional case of pathology. Indeed, there is in Freud a strange and unsettling continuum of childhood sexual "disturbances" that undermine the oedipal model. The negative Oedipus complex of heterosexual male masochism is particularly interesting as a complement to Freud's theory of male homosexuality.[17]

FREUD'S THEORY OF NARCISSISM AND ITS USES

The erotic predicament that lies at the heart of the Ovidian and Freudian versions of the Narcissus myth is the paradox of desire—the ultimate inaccessibility of another person. Our longing for the other person, our desire to connect to and at times to possess them despite the obvious and less apparent barriers that separate one person from another, is no less ardent despite their inaccessibility. The Narcissus myth is a heightened, particularly and peculiarly affecting version of the essential pathos of desire, the gulf between self and other. Moreover, thinkers such as Freud help us to see that what we long for is our self *in* the other, suggesting, as does Ovid, that desire may actually proceed not from a primary longing for the other but from an original desire for self.

As Leo Bersani puts it, all desire, at heart, has a narcissistic basis.

> We love . . . inaccurate versions of ourselves. . . . we relate to difference by recognizing and longing for sameness. All love is, in a sense, homoerotic. Even in the love between a man and a woman, each partner rejoices in finding himself, or herself, in the other. This is not the envy of narcissistic enclosure that Freud thought he detected in male heterosexual desire; it is rather an expression of the security humans can feel when they embrace difference as the supplemental benefit of a universal replication and solidarity of being. Each subject reoccurs differently everywhere.[18]

Recognizing our narcissistic disposition can lead to a utopian erotics of seeking sameness in difference and difference in sameness, an alterity not determined by such narrow concepts as gender (however decisive a role these concepts play in our lives).

The most valuable aspects of Jacques Lacan's work are his theory of the subject's development from identification with an illusory and misrecognized image of wholeness (*the mirror stage*) and his decoupling of desire from biological or physical needs.[19] Because desire is a term I use frequently here, some clarification of my understanding of it is in order. As the Lacanian queer theorist Tim Dean describes, "Distinguishing desire from biological or physical needs, Lacan conceived desire as the excess resulting from the articulation of need in symbolic form. Thus where bodies may be said to have needs such as biological sustenance and physical protection, subjects have desires—principally, overcoming the loss constitutive of subjectivity as such—hence the requirement to 'find the subject as lost object.' It is because desire remains distinct from need that sexuality is cultural rather than biological."²⁰ If desire is the differential between need and demand, desire always exists outside of corporeal wants and wishes. As Freud made sure we understood, desire has neither aim nor object. I mean always to evoke desire's possibilities in my use of the concept, which I leave deliberately open-ended; often, I mean to suggest sexual desire, but only as one of several forms desire can take.

Given the special emphasis that Freud will place on the homosexual narcissist, and that he begins his discussion with the specific problem of schizophrenia, it is intriguing that Freud frames the entire question of narcissism as a question of a fundamental human need and experience: love. In the "last resort we must," Freud writes, "begin to love in order not to fall ill, and we are bound to fall ill if, in consequence of frustration, we cannot love" (SE 14: 85). Freud uses narcissism primarily as an opportunity for the discussion of love and a rubric through which to explore it. Here, Freud's controversial penchant for universalization has its affecting dimension. Though narcissism has been both a pathologized and a minoritized identity, Freud actually makes it central to his understanding of human relationships.

Freud universalizes narcissism within his discussion of the two types of infant sexual object-choice, which he distinguishes as the "anaclitic" and the narcissistic. The first, the *anaclitic*, "or attachment," type of object-choice focuses on "the persons who are concerned with a child's feeding, care, and protection . . . that is to say, in the first instance the mother or her substitute." The second, the narcissistic, can be found "especially clearly in people whose libidinal development has suffered some disturbance, such as perverts and homosexuals, that in their later choice of their love object they have taken as a model not their mother but their own selves. They are plainly seeking *themselves* as a love object, and are exhibiting a type of object-choice which must be termed 'narcissistic.'" But the next line, which concludes this paragraph, anticipates Freud's argument that narcissism bears a much greater significance than its prevalence among "perverts and homosexuals especially" would suggest: "In this observation we have the strongest of the reasons which have led us to adopt the hypothesis of narcissism" (SE 14: 87–88). Freud not only establishes the validity of narcissism as another kind of sexual object-choice, he also takes great pains to emphasize that narcissism, far from a minority disposition, is as available a sexual object-choice as the only seemingly more normative anaclitic type:

> We have, however, not concluded that human beings are divided into two sharply distinguished groups, according as their object-choice conforms to the anaclitic or to the narcissistic type; we assume rather that both kinds of

object-choice are open to each individual, though he may show a preference for one or the other. We say that a human being has originally two sexual objects—himself and the woman who nurses him—and in doing so we are postulating a primary narcissism in everyone, which may in some cases manifest itself in a dominating fashion in his object-choice. (SE 14: 88)

This universal, primary narcissism is complexly significant (and enduringly controversial for psychoanalytic theory). First, it makes it clear that an individual will have not only another person upon whom to fix his erotic hopes but also himself (to use Freud's preferred gender for the moment). Although someone may "show a preference for one or the other," both kinds of object-choice—that involving someone else, that focusing on the self—are available to the desiring subject. I would go further than Freud and say that one can make *both* desiring choices; one can desire oneself as well as someone else. But Freud goes far enough; his language here about the choices open to every individual between anaclitic and narcissistic objects is remarkably neutral, even though in the previous paragraph he associates narcissism with those reliable transgressors, "perverts and homosexuals." By the time Freud describes, at a later stage in the essay, that the "aim and the satisfaction in a narcissistic object-choice is to be loved," one has a hard time distinguishing "normal" from narcissism—it is the rare person for whom being loved can be of no concern (SE 14: 98). Indeed, Freud reveals narcissism, the special penchant of perverts and homosexuals, as a universal sexual disposition: it is one of the two sexual object-choices available to everyone; moreover, we have all experienced the state of primary narcissism.

Freud then proceeds to distinguish anaclitic from narcissistic object-choice in terms that suggest the old, enduring problem of Freud's sexism: males are generally anaclitic in their object relations, females narcissistic. Sexism would appear to be at work here in that the more normative, the anaclitic, model of erotic attraction is generally the domain of males, whereas women and their sexuality are relegated to the sidelines of perversion. Yet because Freud's depiction of narcissism lies suspended between modes of universality and sexual specialism—just as his view of homosexuality lies between an offhand admiration and a steadfast understanding of it as deviant—the normal heterosexuality of males and the narcissistic perversity of women, while ostensibly the sexual order of things as Freud establishes it, will come to seem less secure and more odd. And, as if presciently aware of our contemporary objections to his limited and limiting views of women, Freud provides one of his most thoughtful demurrals when he qualifies what he has just said about the narcissistic sexuality of women.

Perhaps it is not out of place here to give an assurance that this description of the feminine form of erotic life is not due to any tendentious desire on my part to depreciate women. Apart from the fact that tendentiousness is quite alien to me, I know that these different lines of development correspond to the differentiation of functions in a highly complicated biological whole: further, I am ready to admit that there are quite a number of women who love according to the masculine type and who also develop the sexual overvaluation proper to that type. (SE 14: 89)

Had Freud consistently maintained the levelheaded and thoughtful tone of the above passage in his treatment of female sexuality, he would not remain burdened, as he will always be, by charges of misogyny. Here we have, as well, a reminder that what had seemed the normative mode of sexuality, the anaclitic sexuality of men, relies on "overvaluation," a kind of idealizing blindness that makes male desire something less than clear-eyed. Going back to the way that Freud theorized anaclitic male desire, the tendency to overvaluation that characterizes it stems from *"the child's original narcissism and thus corresponds to a transference of that narcissism to the sexual object"* (SE 14: 88, emphasis mine). In other words, at the heart of anaclitic object-choice, the normative choice that is in *opposition* to narcissism, that special penchant of homosexuals and other perverts . . . lies narcissism, which engenders the more normative choice. In other words, narcissism is the authentic core of *any* sexual object-choice.

I return to the issue of gendered object-choice below. But for now, what I want to establish is the centrality of narcissism to Freud's thinking about how we desire and how we love. Initially described as a heretofore unsuspected component of our erotic life, then as the characteristic of perverse sexualities, narcissism gathers momentum and achieves universality, finally emerging as one of the fundamental principles of desire.

Narcissism even impels the parental love for children. The "affectionate love" parents have for their children revives and reproduces their own, "long since abandoned narcissism" (SE 14: 90–91). Overwhelmed by their potent feelings for their offspring, parents indulge in newly reactivated narcissistic fantasies that they had long suppressed in accordance with "cultural acquisitions," and attempt to extend to their children the narcissistic "privileges" they had themselves long forfeited (SE 14: 91). If one of the major critiques of Freud's theory of the Oedipus complex is that, in his focus on the oedipal child, he pays insufficient attention to the desires and aggressions of the parents, here, Freud redresses this oversight in his theory of narcissism. One might say that he does so with a vengeance, rather frighteningly theorizing parental love for children—commonly perceived as the height of selfless love—as a passionate expression of narcissistic desire: "Parental love, which is so moving and at bottom so childish, is nothing but the parents' narcissism born again, which, transformed into object love, unmistakably reveals its former nature" (SE 14: 91). If parental love for children is one of narcissism's masks, it is certainly not the only one. Freud's depiction of narcissism here makes it hard to find a love that is not either a disguised form of narcissism or some kind of attempt to make up for its loss. "He who loves has, so to speak," Freud states, "forfeited a part of his narcissism, which can only be replaced by his being loved"—or, as Freud suggests in his depiction of the fond parent, in loving another (SE 14: 98).

The theme of parental narcissism proves crucial to an understanding of the broad relevance of narcissism to Freud's thinking and also to the depathologization of homosexual narcissism. It will be helpful to turn to Freud's thinking on heterosexual development and oedipalization—certainly the normative model of human sexual development for Freud—in order to frame our thinking on homosexual narcissism.

Jean Laplanche's theory of the "enigmatic signifier" illuminates the questions that attend to the mother–child relationship.[21] "Laplanche's concept of the enigmatic signifier," as Leo Bersani elucidates it, "refers to an original and unavoidable seduction of the child by the mother, a seduction inherent in the very nurturing of the child. The seduction is not intentional; simply by her care, the parent implants in the child 'unconscious and sexual significations' with which the adult world is infiltrated, and that are received in the form of an enigmatic signifier—that is, a message by which the child is seduced but that he or she cannot read, an enigmatic message that is perhaps inevitably interpreted as a secret. The result of this original seduction would be a tendency to structure all relations on the basis of an eroticizing mystification."[22] To take this point further, all sexuality flows from the essentially seductive mother–child relation, in that we always desire enigmatically and that we always desire the enigmatic.

As Steven Angelides further defines Laplanche's concept,

> The enigmatic signifier (of adult desire) is first inscribed in the infant's bodily, or, erotogenic zones. In a second phase, because the child cannot fully or successfully integrate the excessive libidinal excitation, or, unintelligible erotic messages from the parent, this enigmatic signifier undergoes a primal repression. The repressed, residual elements thereafter ensure a permanent conflictual relationship with the ego, producing a subjective core of

irreducible otherness. The child is thus split unto him or herself, and sexuality is ever after inflected by an enigmatic otherness. This universal theory of primal seduction and the enigmatic signifier is therefore the foundational structure for the constitution of the primordial unconscious, and thus sexuality, in the child.[23]

As Freud makes remarkably clear, the boundaries separating anaclitic from narcissistic desire are fluid; and as Laplanche suggests, desire begins in the relationship the child has with the mother. Given that the male homosexual's tie to and identification with the mother has been perhaps the most fundamental component of the view of homosexuality as pathological and the theory of male homosexuality itself, it seems well worth considering that desire understood in its *broadest* terms in Freudian thinking stems from the mother–child relationship.

Tim Dean writes of Freud on the Narcissus theme in his 1910 essay on Leonardo da Vinci as Freud at his "most inventive," and of this work as part of "a bizarre narrative of Freud's own construction—as if Freud felt compelled to rival Ovid's imaginative genius by creating a story of impossibly elaborate metamorphosis: the transformation of a boy into his mother."[24] "We might say," writes Dean," that psychoanalysis reveals the otherness within sameness, and so explodes the myth that sameness only involves self-sameness." To take just one example, the boy Leonardo, "by installing his mother in and as his own mind, has become other to himself."[25] This is the radical potential in Freud's treatment that critics such as Michael Warner have overlooked. (I will touch on Freud's study of Leonardo in chapter 7.)

Freud called narcissism a wound. If this wound is the customary psychoanalytic lack, lack marks our separation from the powerful being who gave us life alongside our desires—our mother, whose body we narcissistically mistook for our own. Following Otto Rank, who "argued that the universally traumatic experience of birth is the true origin of all anxiety, not castration," Marcia Ian describes the phallus as the phobic screen for something else: the umbilical cord, which literalizes and symbolizes the trauma of birth and our separation from the mother. Rank did not do away with the central Freudian notion of castration; rather, he theorized that it was birth trauma that alone explained it.[26] On some level, all sexuality stems from an essentially traumatic relationship with our mothers and our mothers' bodies. Lacan argued that desire emerges from the differential between need and demand, the moment when our need for the nourishment that comes from the mother's breast transmutes into a demand for the breast not related to the instinctual need for hunger. But we could also argue that desire emanates from the traumatic separation from the body of the woman who gave us life—we want to replace that first fatal cut with the remerging of bodies.

Along these lines, we can interpret narcissism in its manifestation in the homosexual male as a strategy for the repair and restoration of the split, unmoored subject. What the homosexual child (in Freud) desires is to preserve the intensity of the bond between his mother and himself, the feeling of wholeness, of oneness, when he was his mother's own object of desire. Freud doesn't mention, in his treatments of male homosexuality, the concept of parental narcissism, but we do well to remember his discussion of it in "On Narcissism."

The mother's own narcissism implicitly drives the process whereby the child learned about desire, how to desire himself, and developed his sustaining fantasy of *preserving the scene of maternal desire* that was so influential and affecting for the mind and heart and life of the child. The child acutely experiences, one could theorize, the force of the mother's own investment in the child's success in mirroring back her own desires, needs for self-reflection, and fantasies of self-perpetuation; the child experiences her own desires, needs, and fantasies so acutely that he begins to imagine that they are *his* desires, needs, and fantasies. Installing his mother's psychic life into his own mind, the child develops a kind of double vision that, on occasion, becomes one: he sees the world both through his mother's eyes and through his own; he seeks to find the same rapturously satisfying image that his mother saw in him; he wishes for the opportunity to see as *she* saw, to find the fulfillment of his own desire reflected in another's face, body, eyes.

One of the problems with the ways in which Freud's theory has been interpreted over the years is that homosexual narcissism's investment in gendered sameness has been taken as an interest in finding oneself replicated, another version of the self. Surely, if Freud has taught us anything, it is that this craving for self-sameness is the *universal* condition of human desire, since we all experienced the state of primary narcissism. Behind an interest in gendered sameness lies a radical otherness—the mother's desire behind the gazing eyes of the desiring boy, the fantasy that the mother's desire has been incorporated into and enmeshed with one's own.

Because patriarchy insists upon the perpetual reenactment of the Oedipus complex—far from some natural, inherent process, it is the narrative of socialization, the patriarchal script that Freud decoded—the erotic affiliations a male may feel with his mother's desire are never valorized. Given the patriarchal cast of our culture, the only male desire which culture valorizes is that which replicates the father with whom one has properly identified.

Feelings for mothers; the mother's own feelings; a woman's sexual drives and desires, what motivates her own erotic life: historically, all of these aspects of human life have been suppressed, repressed, and subordinated. The chief problem the homosexual male has encountered in terms of his desire—and this is to speak of it only within the Freudian context of our discussion—is that his desire falls precipitously and disastrously out of the patriarchal, oedipal loop. Sexism, therefore, accounts just as powerfully and poignantly as homophobia for the pathologization of male homosexuality. (The Freudian girl is at such a loss during the Oedipus complex and its aftermath because of the essentially paralytic nature of her social position. Were she to identify with the father to too great an extent, she might become masculinized in a way threatening to and for her in social terms; she cannot easily identify with her mother because the mother has not only failed to protect her but represents a reified version of the misogynistically determined subordination of women. One wishes, in exasperation, that Freud had more sensitively explicated the misogynistic social construction of femininity, rather than femininity's biological "inferiority." But, at the same time, Freud's account of female social experience is also unflinchingly realistic, at least for his own era.)

The male homosexual's strategy for preserving the scene of maternal desire resists patriarchal oedipalization, but, as Freud describes it, it is also a different kind of oedipal tragedy; it is a different kind of destruction of the erotic mother–son bond that enables desire even as it demands to be eradicated. Just as the heterosexual male child must abandon the mother as an erotic object, using her as a model for exogamous erotic attraction, the homosexual male must leave behind the mother to proceed with his desiring life; the difference is that the homosexual child devises a brilliant strategy for preserving the mother's role in his desire. This is, of course, only one difference among many.

What drives homosexual desire is what drives *all* desire: an attempt to repair loss, the lack of something we believe we once possessed, somehow, somewhere. "They proceed from a narcissistic basis, and look for a young man who resembles themselves and whom *they* may love as their mother loved *them*." If Freud draws upon the terror and violence of the Oedipus myth to describe our first confrontation, when we are very young, with adult sexuality, which is to say normative heterosexuality—most evocatively and provocatively drawn, in all senses of the word, in his case study of "The Wolf Man" in which he develops his theory of the primal scene, in which the child literally observes parental intercourse—he draws upon the incomparable frustrations and the plangency of the Narcissus myth to describe homosexuality.[27] Both are tragic myths that mirror each other, providing alternative scenarios of the same theme of impossible desire—they reveal, as does Freud's treatment, that desire is as paradoxically absurd as it is irresistible.

Given that homosexuality has so often been seen as the Oedipus complex gone awry, as a failure to complete the process and be normalized by it, it behooves us to reconsider oedipal conflict. Specifically, we should reconsider any stable notion of the Oedipus complex in Freud's work, for his views on it are characteristically inconsistent; moreover, the Oedipus complex and its narcissistic-homosexual foil bear far more similarities than are commonly acknowledged. If we can demonstrate the similarities that exist between heterosexual and homosexual development, narcissistic sexuality can be seen as an alternative form of identity to an oedipalized one rather than its stunted inferior. As Kenneth Lewes puts it in his superb study *The Psychoanalytic Theory of Male Homosexuality*, "there is no straight line from preoedipal constitution to postoedipal result." Instead, there is only a "bewildering series of transformations": "the mechanisms of the Oedipus complex are really a series of psychic traumas, and all results of it are neurotic compromise formations."[28] If it is absurd to see the transition through the Oedipus complex into heterosexuality as a normal, inevitable, natural process, it is also absurd to view narcissistically inclined, mother-identified homosexual childhood development as stunted, counterfeit, unnatural. Though it has been deployed in resolutely homophobic ways throughout American psychiatric history, and though it bears the traces of Freud's inconsistent views on homosexuality (certainly far from an exclusively inconsistent Freudian topic), Freud's theory in and of itself seems as plausible a way of theorizing male homosexuality as any other; moreover, it movingly captures the emotional complexity of being a mother-identified male in a patriarchal culture. But perhaps the larger topic here involves what I call Freud's subversive children: children who devise all manner of resisting, thwarting, eluding, and generally mucking up, for distinct reasons, the course of their sexual development, normative or otherwise. The homosexual child is far from the only subversive agent in the Freudian field of childhood sexual development. The masochistic male and the phallic girl join the homosexual child in contesting the consolidation of normative sexual roles into which we must all ostensibly fall.

I now turn, at last, to Hawthorne's short story "The Gentle Boy." I read the story from a Freudian perspective, though not the one influentially limned by Frederick Crews. Crews saw the story as a rather unwieldy indulgence on Hawthorne's part in masochistic fantasy.[29] What I will suggest, instead, is that Freud's theory of male homosexual narcissism here serves as *a general allegory for male sexuality* rather than a minor myth for a sexual minority, and as such provides key insights into Hawthorne's story. In turn, Hawthorne's tale explores the fate of a mother-identified male desire in a male-dominated social order.

"THE GENTLE BOY"
HAWTHORNE'S 1830 MASTERPIECE

Nathaniel Hawthorne sets his short story "The Gentle Boy" (written in 1829, first published the year after) in 1650s Puritan New England.[30] The titular boy, a Quaker named Ilbrahim, is adopted by a Puritan couple, Tobias and Dorothy Pearson, after Tobias discovers the boy mournfully keeping vigil at his father's fresh grave. At this time, the Puritans were actively persecuting the Quakers. Ilbrahim had been in the same jail cell as his imprisoned father and has watched him being hanged. Not only have the Puritans killed his father, but they have sentenced his mother to death as well, leaving her to die of exposure in the wilderness. Bereft, abandoned Ilbrahim occupies a liminal state between life and death. Ilbrahim's tremendous tenderness and delicacy of spirit are commingled with a "premature manliness," a gravitas born of suffering.

The Quakers match the Puritans' punitive zeal with an ever-increasing proselytizing passion: "The fines, imprisonments, and stripes, liberally distributed by our pious forefathers; the popular antipathy, so strong that it endured nearly a hundred years after actual persecution had ceased, were attractions as powerful for the Quakers, as peace, honor, and reward, would have been for the worldly-minded" (9: 69). The strange, delicate, remote child Ilbrahim will be the battleground for contending forces: the sadistic Puritan desires to quash rebellion and the masochistic Quaker avidity for their own persecution. But the most resonant battle rages within Ilbrahim himself, between his desire for his biological mother, the wild, enflamed, visionary Catharine, who evades death in the forest, and for the care and concern of his strong, subdued, steadfast adoptive mother, Dorothy. When the two women meet in a dramatic scene in the church and decide with whom Ilbrahim's fate lies, they form "a practical allegory," "rational piety and unbridled fanaticism, contending for the empire of a young heart" (9: 85). Evincing her quiet strength of will throughout the tale, Dorothy unflinchingly withstands the Puritan opprobrium that the Pearsons' adoption of Ilbrahim engenders, whereas her husband Tobias much less steadily stands by his adopted son. Nevertheless, by the tale's close, as Ilbrahim, the boy too gentle for this world, lies dying in his bed, Tobias will embrace the boy's faith.

Let me state the obvious: Hawthorne didn't read Freud and knew nothing of psychoanalysis; when Hawthorne was writing the term "homosexual" did not exist; any overlaps between Hawthorne's work and Freud's theory of homosexual childhood development are coincidental (I have found no evidence that Freud read Hawthorne, though it is not impossible that he did). These disclaimers out of the way, I find remarkable correspondences between Hawthorne's and Freud's depictions of a feminine and female-identified male child. At heart, Freud's theorization of male childhood homosexual development is an account of the process of the development of a male who identifies with the mother rather than the father. Hawthorne allows us to experience the affectional and social ramifications of Freud's theorization of this form of male childhood desire. Hawthorne locates in patriarchy an unyielding refusal to tolerate deviance of any kind and a rapacious drive to destroy the most vulnerable and defenseless in its midst. In his delicacy and, most acutely, in his desire to love, Ilbrahim exquisitely embodies Freud's theoretical construction of the homosexual child, emulating the mother's love for him in his love for another male. In Hawthorne, however, the child emulates a maternal love only haphazardly and incoherently given, and attempts to bestow this love on a wholly inadequate and unworthy object. The love Ilbrahim bestows on others is a phantasy enactment of a love he craves but never receives from his biological mother (and perhaps cannot accept from his adoptive one).

Hawthorne uses all of his already considerable skill in this early tale to create in Ilbrahim a figure of strangeness and beauty, qualities that set him apart from the rest of the characters in the story. With his "pale, spiritual face, the eyes that seemed to mingle with the moonlight, the sweet, airy voice, and the outlandish name," Ilbrahim seems more like a visitor from a distant planet than a seventeenth-century New England child: "He was a sweet infant of the skies, that had strayed away from his home" (9: 79). By representing Ilbrahim as alien, Hawthorne establishes that a feminine, mother-identified male has no place in this world; Ilbrahim chafes against the masculinist, patriarchal Puritan order because the values he embodies can never be affirmed within it. "Quaker" identity in this tale emerges as a broad allegory for phobically perceived differences of all kinds. When Tobias learns that the young, mourning child he attempts to help is Quaker, the "Puritan, who had laid hold of little Ilbrahim's hand, relinquished it as if he were touching a loathsome reptile" (9: 73). Difference dissolves human kinship, renders the other a different species altogether.

"Do we not all spring from an evil root?" Tobias then asks himself, allowing his reason to overcome his prejudice. The specificity of this imagery makes a decisive point: Ilbrahim, a queer child, opposes the destructive phallic power of patriarchy. What can be the fate of a "little quiet, lovely boy, whose appearance and deportment were indeed as powerful arguments as could possibly have been adduced in his own favor," in such a grimly oppressive world (9: 77)? The stern old man—representative of the pattern of intergenerational male conflict that informs all of Hawthorne's work—who will turn his "repulsive and unheavenly countenance" against this boy as if he has "polluted" the Puritan church, synecdochically stands in for the Puritan community, "a miserable world" toward whom Hawthorne feels a repulsion he can barely contain (9: 79).

Dorothy, who immediately takes in the new child as her own, asks Ilbrahim if he has a mother, and "the tears burst forth from his full heart" (9: 75); Dorothy tells him to dry his tears "and be my child, as I will be your mother" (9: 75). Ilbrahim longs for the oral mother, the original mother with whom he experienced, or wanted to experience, the greatest intimacy; Dorothy represents the oedipal mother, custodian of the social order. While Ilbrahim submits open-heartedly to his adoption, it is clear that he never relinquishes his love for Catharine, shown to be almost entirely unsuitable for the role of parent. With her wild, unkempt appearance and feverish, fanatical speeches of condemnation to the Puritans who destroy her and her people, Catharine commands great pity but evokes greater fear; abused, victimized, condemned, her rage and wrath against her oppressors, Hawthorne makes clear, galvanizes as much as it depletes her.

Catharine calls to mind Freud's indelible portrait of the Medusan mother, who represents the terror of adult sexuality. In the iconography of the Medusa, Freud located a metaphor of castration and the child's attendant revulsion—the writhing snakes being representations of pubic hair and also compensatory substitutions for the castrated penis. If the Medusa's head represents the female genitals—and specifically the "terrifying genitals of the Mother"—it isolates "their horrifying effects from their pleasure-giving ones" (SE 18: 274). Catharine, looming before the Puritans in their church, condemns those who have condemned her: "her raven hair fell down upon her shoulders, and its blackness was defiled by pale streaks of ashes. . . . Her discourse gave evidence of an imagination hopelessly entangled with her reason. . . . She was naturally a woman of mighty passions, and hatred and revenge now wrapped themselves in the garb of piety . . . her denunciations had an almost hellish bitterness" (9: 81).

With disorienting urgency, Hawthorne anticipates Freudian themes. He directly pits this Medusan mother against the community that calumniates her; he also matches her against a different kind of phallic maternity, the coolly rational (though also deeply feeling) oedipal mother Dorothy, who represents the reason and rectitude the community claims to possess but obviously sorely lacks. But indirectly Hawthorne also opposes Medusan Catharine with narcissistically inclined Ilbrahim. Ilbrahim's tender, feminine disposition can in no way correspond to the phallic, vengeful fury of the wronged but wrathful Catharine. Nor can Dorothy's courageous and inspiring moral orderliness satisfy Ilbrahim's needs. Ilbrahim roams this inhospitable world in a state of authentic loneliness, in a no man's land of oedipal deprivation; the mother he loves loves her own appropriated phallic power, her rage, above all else, and the mother who loves him loves him from a position within the patriarchal order that the boy, in his very essence, opposes. The most positive embodiment of the feminine in the story, the gentle boy provides a stark contrast to the myriad representatives of phallic power—phallic mothers, phallic Puritans, phallically aggressive children—that dominate the tale.

One of Hawthorne's 1837 revisions of the story uncomfortably clarifies *parental* narcissism as one of the major themes of the work.[31] In the original version, when Tobias brings Ilbrahim home for the first time, Dorothy prepares a meal for him which the boy, with tearful tentativeness, manages to eat. But in the revised version of the story, Ilbrahim never eats and Dorothy never makes him a meal. Dorothy and Tobias have lost all of their children; the implication Hawthorne now makes is that the *role* Ilbrahim serves, that of replacement or substitute for their deceased children, for Dorothy in particular, is more important than his actual, living, breathing, needing, person. Even Dorothy, shown to be of far greater courage than her husband and greater benevolence than their community, in the revised version attends to her own needs before that of the child; Ilbrahim's appeasement of her hunger for a child takes the place of the appeasement of his own hunger. Dorothy, therefore, in a far more muted way, resembles Catharine in her ego-absorption. Tobias, shown to be faltering in his resolve to claim Ilbrahim as his own child despite the scorn of his community, seeks to repair his own lack of a spiritual life; his primary goal seems to be to find a religious conviction, and so it makes sense that the wild, almost antic religious zealotry of the Quakers would be seductive to him. In any event, Hawthorne doesn't seem especially interested in Tobias's portions of the narrative. What chiefly interests Hawthorne is the fate of a gentle boy in an ungentle world; I argue that this was Hawthorne's most personal work, and it is for this reason that the themes of the mother–son relationship are central to it.

Hawthorne wrote of his relationship to his own mother that "there has been, ever since my boyhood, a sort of coldness of intercourse between us, such as is apt to come between persons of strong feelings" (8: 429). Nevertheless, as Hawthorne's astute contemporary biographer Brenda Wineapple observes, the feelings between son and mother "reached deep."[32] Catharine, Ilbrahim's mother, can be seen as a nightmarish version of Elizabeth Manning Hawthorne; like Catharine, the author's mother had "raven-dark hair," a trait she shared, along with "fine gray eyes," with her son. Both Hawthorne and his mother dreaded separations, several of which they were forced to endure during Hawthorne's fatherless childhood. (Hawthorne's maternal Manning family, who ran a stagecoach business, divided their time between Maine and Massachusetts.) During one separation in 1819, Hawthorne despondently wrote, "I am extremely homesick. Why was I not born a girl that I might have been pinned all my life to my mother's apron?" (15: 117).

Juliet Mitchell has revised Freud's theory of the Oedipus complex through her focus on the role that sibling relationships play in childhood development.[33] Along these lines, it is also important to remember that Hawthorne had passionate and complex relationships with his two sisters, Elizabeth and Louisa. "No wonder pairs of women," observes Wineapple, "frequently haunt his fiction. . . . One of the two is usually an exotic beauty, dark-haired, brilliant, and eccentric, like his older sister, Elizabeth; the other, like Marie Louisa, is more overtly conventional, self-effacing, and domestic."[34] Along these sisterly lines, Catharine can be seen as an Elizabeth figure, Dorothy as a Louisa. Further enhancing the biographical valences of the story, Hawthorne's own father, a sea merchant, died in Surinam when Hawthorne was very young; moreover, his childhood health was extremely worrisome to his family. And like the unworthy boy that Ilbrahim will care for in the story, the young Hawthorne also suffered in 1813 a foot injury, one that kept him indoors for several months. The correspondences between Hawthorne's own childhood and Ilbrahim's are too acutely obvious to be ignored.

The greatest point of overlap between Hawthorne and his tale lies in Ilbrahim's beauty and the disturbance it creates. Hawthorne came of age in Jacksonian America, a culture that valorized hypermasculine traits and saw effeminacy as a trait associated with degenerate Europe.[35] Hawthorne's own physical beauty, remarked upon by many people throughout his life, was a trait that most likely caused him discomfort, in that it made him the object of the gaze and therefore placed him in a feminine, passive position against which he no doubt chafed. Quoting Hawthorne's son-in-law George Lathrop's biography of Hawthorne, Henry James recounts in his famous critical book on Hawthorne an episode in which Sophia and Elizabeth Peabody,

> desiring to see more of the charming writer, caused him to be invited to a species of conversazione at the house of one of their friends. . . . Several other ladies . . . were as punctual as they, and Hawthorne presently arriving, and seeing a bevy of admirers where he had expected but three or four, fell into a state of agitation, which is vividly described by his biographer. He "stood perfectly motionless, but with a look of a sylvan creature on the point of fleeing away. . . . He was stricken with dismay; his face lost colour and took on a warm paleness . . . his agitation was very great; he stood by a table, and taking up some small object that lay upon it, he found his hand trembling so that he was obliged to lay it down." It was desirable, certainly, that something should occur to break the spell of a diffidence that might justly be called morbid.

Many fascinations abound here, not the least of which is Hawthorne's own deep discomfort with being the object of visual fascination. (James makes his own specular fascination with Hawthorne palpable in this book.)

James provides another similar anecdote from Lathrop about what would become the famous evening in which the purportedly shy and reclusive Hawthorne sisters brought, at the invitation of Elizabeth Peabody, the New England activist who was the sister of Sophia, who would become Hawthorne's wife, their even shyer and more reclusive brother with them to the Peabody home. "'Entirely to her surprise,' says Mr. Lathrop . . . 'entirely to her surprise they came. She herself opened the door, and there, before her, between his sisters, stood a splendidly handsome youth, tall and strong, with no appearance whatever of timidity, but instead an almost fierce determination making his face stern. This was his resource for carrying off the extreme inward tremor which he really felt.'"[36] In life, Hawthorne strenuously attempted to overmaster the tremendous anxieties, figured in trembling hands and inward tremors, the gaze stimulated in him. As Wineapple writes, Hawthorne's sense of his own masculinity was "unstable"; early on, Hawthorne saw himself as "one apart, marked and wounded, a victim with a special destiny who was, at the same time, as angry as the lame boy in the story 'The Gentle Boy.'"[37]

That Ilbrahim's beauty makes his life more difficult Hawthorne makes quite clear. "Even his beauty," the narrator tells us, "and his winning manners, sometimes produced an effect ultimately unfavorable; for the bigots, when the outer surfaces of their iron hearts had been softened and again grew hard, affirmed that no merely natural cause could have so worked upon them" (9: 77). With remarkable insight, Hawthorne describes the difficulties the feminine male encounters in a masculinist society: the beauty he possesses, while not a curse, is certainly no gift; unsettling the onlookers, it forces them to punish, at least in their own mind, Ilbrahim for having triggered feelings—of longing? of desire? or simply of confusion?—in them. The male child of beauty encounters the same kinds of phobic treatment suffered by women; he is despised for his witchlike powers to seduce and enthrall through "unnatural" means.

Hawthorne, a male who physically and emotionally resembles his mother, who writes fiction from a position of "rivalrous identification" with women, as Millicent Bell puts it, acutely understands the experience of the narcissistic mother-identified child who wishes to bestow upon someone else the love his mother gave him, or that—here we must add to Freud—he wished that his mother *had* given him.[38] Ilbrahim's name associates him with the exotic and with the Far East (where Catharine and other Quakers proselytize); the Orientalism of his name intersects with the homophobic ideologies that associated the East with loucheness, gross sensualism, abandon, and effeminacy. Effeminate, beautiful, tender, and relentlessly persecuted by both other children and their parents, Ilbrahim nevertheless wants nothing more than to bestow his as yet "unappropriated love" on someone else. The someone else that Ilbrahim finds reverses his traits in every respect; duplicitous where Ilbrahim is sincere, ugly rather than beautiful, and violently cruel rather than tender, the boy with a leg injury whom Ilbrahim cares for leads Ilbrahim to premature death rather than to shared love.

The Pearsons take in and care for a young, male Puritan child who has suffered a leg injury; that his parents are so willing to let another family care for their own child indicates something of this boy's nature. Hawthorne takes pains to let us know that this boy is as physically ugly as he will prove to be spiritually. While this conflation of spiritual with physical character commonly appears in Hawthorne's work and in Victorian literature generally, here it has a deeper significance when considered in light of the story's psychosexual themes.

Ilbrahim, normally adept at decoding physiognomies, fails to read the evil in this boy's physical nature. But we, however, are more than encouraged to do so. He has a disagreeable countenance, slightly distorted mouth, an "irregular, broken" near uni-brow; "an almost imperceptible twist" characterizes his "every joint, and the uneven prominence of the breast." Overall, his body, though "regular in general outline," is "faulty in almost all its details"; moreover, he is "sullen and reserved . . . obtuse in intellect" (9: 90). Nevertheless, Ilbrahim nestles "continually by the bed-side of the little stranger, and, with a fond jealousy" assiduously nurses the boy. Deepening biographical valences, Hawthorne depicts Ilbrahim as a storyteller who recites "imaginary adventures, on the spur of the moment, and in apparently inexhaustible succession," to the convalescent child of "dark and stubborn nature," who responds to Ilbrahim's airy fantasies with remarks of precocious and disturbing "moral obliquity" (9: 91). The force of love emanating from him makes Ilbrahim believe that this love will be returned. One day, seeing the boy he cared for playing with a group of other Puritan children, Ilbrahim approaches them, "as if, having manifested his love to one of them, he had no longer to fear a repulse from their society." But Ilbrahim could not be more mistaken about the lack of reciprocity in matters of love: "the devil of their fathers entered into the unbreeched fanatics," and, shrieking like banshees, they hit Ilbrahim literally with sticks and stones, displaying "an instinct of destruction, far more loathsome than the blood-thirstiness of manhood" (9: 92).

The worst part of this brutal assault occurs when the ugly, lame boy whom Ilbrahim cared for lures Ilbrahim toward him with an offer of protection; without hesitation, Ilbrahim complies, only to have the "foul-hearted little villain" lift up his staff and strike Ilbrahim on the mouth, "so forcibly that blood issued in a stream." Ilbrahim had valiantly attempted to protect himself against a "brood of baby-fiends," but after this brutal version of Judas's kiss he wholly submits himself to the bashing crowd, an act of supplication that only intensifies their frenzied fury as they "trample upon him" and drag him by his "long, fair locks" (9: 92). It is impossible not to think of the contemporary crisis of bullying in our own era when reading such depictions of phobic and collective violence.

Some older Puritans happen to rescue him, but Ilbrahim never recovers. Indeed, when Dorothy attempts one day to amuse the utterly withdrawn child, Ilbrahim yields "to a violent display of grief," and during the middle of the night cries "Mother! Mother!" (9: 93). Later, on the night that the child Ilbrahim lies dying in his bed, Catharine returns from her world missionary travels and imprisonments, flush with news that Charles II has repealed the hostilities against the Quakers. Ilbrahim dies in her arms, a relief for him and a punishment for Catharine, now wild with grief. Catharine is ultimately a pitiable figure. Yet she has also been "neglectful of the holiest trust which can be committed to a woman" (9: 95). Like many of Hawthorne's most morally ambiguous figures, Catharine, though grievously victimized, has more grievously erred by placing her ideological commitments above her emotional ties, even above her own offspring.

One of the reasons why Hawthorne's story is especially relevant to thinking about modern queer identity is its depiction of male homosocial violence and the inexpressibly precarious nature of queer identity in the face of it. Ilbrahim confronts the full violence of group male mentality, a confrontation with resonance for modern queer identity but certainly not it alone. As I attempted to make clear earlier, I am not arguing that Hawthorne was either himself homosexual in orientation or that he represented consciously a same-sex-desiring child; rather, I argue that Hawthorne provides us with an allegory of childhood sexual otherness that is especially useful for the study of various forms of queer childhood development (gay, lesbian, bisexual, trans). But the issue is larger still: between Hawthorne and Freud, whatever historical slippages are necessary to make such a statement, the homosexual male child emerges as the model for feminine-identified masculine identity, the model that pertains with greatest significance to those who most clearly match up with it but also relevantly captures the experiences of those whose experiences fall within the paradigms of the model. In other words, Freud's model of the homosexual male child illuminates Hawthorne's depiction—written before the fixing of sexual identities through new taxonomical categorizations that emerged after the American Civil War, if one adheres to Foucauldian paradigms—of a male child who does not conform to the gendered and social standards and practices of his day. (I would argue that *The Scarlet Letter*'s wild, intransigent, phallic Pearl is the female version of the same, and also the gentle boy's avenger, punishing his enemies, at least before her own gender normalization by the end of the narrative.)

Hawthorne himself was a heterosexual man, married with children, whose gender-bending qualities provoked discussion, concern, even awe, as his supporters rallied around a view of him as a sensitive artist who therefore had a poetic, feminine side, and his detractors criticized him for precisely these qualities. I believe that he was quite aware of the reactions he provoked. In constantly conflictual responses himself to these reactions, he wrote fictions, such as "The Gentle Boy," that addressed, problematized, defended against, and mournfully recorded his own difficult experience of gendered identity. As Kenneth Lewes reminds us, identification with the "castrated mother" of the Freudian Oedipus complex can occur in the development of both heterosexual and homosexual males, "since it is quite possible for a male with a primary identification with the castrated mother to make heterosexual object choices."[39]

Ilbrahim, it would appear, dies of a broken heart, a heart broken by two indistinguishable traitorous loves: the boy who returned his love with hate, the mother who returned his love with absence. With exquisite economy and pathos, Hawthorne makes vividly clear that Ilbrahim reproduces a fantasy of *being loved* by the mother whom he loves with an equally illusory fantasy of loving and being loved in return by a boy who resembles Ilbrahim, not physically but in his position within Ilbrahim's own fantasy of having been loved and cared for by his mother. Hawthorne enlarges what Freud imagines to be the psychological basis of same-sex desire by representing another dimension to it, that it can also be an enactment of a *fantasy* for connection between mother and son on the son's behalf, an expression of longing for maternal love as much as a projection of having been its recipient onto another male. Ilbrahim's grief suggests why narcissism is so directly enmeshed with the grievous heart of all desire, which flows from loss: he mourns for something he has already lost, the mother's love so haphazardly and transitorily given, a time in which he and his mother were one. (While one could argue that Ilbrahim, found at the site of his father's murdered body, mourns his dead father as well, this dead parent plays no role in the story beyond the initial mention of him, and Pearson seems more involved in his religious conversion than in Ilbrahim's life or passage to death.) I do not in any way mean to reduce homosexual desire to a kind of misplaced desire for a mother's love. My chief effort here is to make the case that what Freud theorized as homosexual development retains its validity as one pathway to homosexual orientation. Moreover, it retains its validity as a model of the emotional urgency of mother-identified desire and the difficulties faced by a male who identifies with mother rather than father.

HAWTHORNE AND SHAME

"The Gentle Boy" would appear to be, on the face of it, the height of representations of masochistic male sexuality. Certainly, this is the view of Frederick Crews, whose famous (and then famously repudiated, by the author himself) Freudian study of Hawthorne theorized that oedipal conflict is the chief psychoanalytic paradigm at work in Hawthorne's writings. Without disputing the importance of masochism to the story, I would argue that it is narcissism, and specifically homosexual narcissism, that informs the tale. If Ilbrahim desires the ugly, lame boy, what he also desires is to reproduce the scene of maternal desire that undergirds his phantasy life; he wants to love this boy "as his mother loved him," as Freud puts it. But, as we have seen, given that it is never clear that Catharine showed Ilbrahim the love he craves, and that Catharine has been largely absent from Ilbrahim's brief life, this narcissistic process does not reproduce Ilbrahim's own childhood experience of maternal desire but enacts a fantasy of its experiential fulfillment.

And herein lies perhaps the deepest poignancy of the tale. Ilbrahim's lavish bestowal of affection on this ugly child—the descriptions of whom as such border on the gratuitous at first blush—reveals a great deal about how he has felt about *himself*. If he attempts to make real his mother's desire for him through his desire for and expression of love toward another male, that the object of his affections is so deeply, clearly, irredeemably unworthy suggests that Ilbrahim sees himself as ugly, base, unworthy and wishes that his mother would have loved him despite these onerous traits. The disturbing disjuncture between Ilbrahim's actual beauty, readily (if ambivalently) perceived by others, and his fantasy of what he actually is or at least appears to be—if the ugly and violent boy does indeed symbolize Ilbrahim's shameful self-conceptualization—communicates a great deal about the ways in which social, cultural, and other kinds of experiential messages that convey hatred and revulsion against one's own person affect—shape—one's own image of self. Moreover, Ilbrahim blames himself for his mother's failure to love him or to love him adequately.

Mary Ayers has eloquently written about the role that mother–infant attachment plays in shame. "When the maternal intrapsychic conflicts that influence the mother–infant relationship become impingements that in turn become a pattern, the details of the way in which the impingement is sensed by the infant are significant, as well as the infant's reaction to them." The ways in which a child can respond to such emotional abandonment are myriad, and gender and culture will shape the response. Aggression is usually associated with the masculine response, shame with the other. I would argue that Ilbrahim clearly reflects the latter, feminine response, literally dying of shame—shame at public humiliation and betrayal and shame at his mother's behavior, which he internalizes as behavior he himself caused.[40] In the end, the enduring value of Hawthorne's and Freud's depictions of the mother–son bond lies in their evocations of the plangency and the urgency of the bond. It would appear that a desire not to perpetuate stereotypes has led modern commentators to eschew if not altogether do away with homosexual narcissism as a way of theorizing queer identity. When contextualized, updated, and freed from pathologizing impetuses, it remains a profound and meaningful way of thinking about some of the varieties of human emotional experience.

As I will be elaborating throughout this book, particularly in chapter 4, shame is one of the principle affects of Hawthorne's work. But unlike other critics who have also located shame's centrality in Hawthorne, I link shame to narcissism and to Hawthorne's interest in the visual, an interest that becomes only more ardent, perhaps even obsessive, as his career develops. In order to make most sense out of the complexly intricate connections among shame, the visual, and narcissism, it will be helpful to explore further why narcissism, as well as the Oedipus complex, provides an illuminating perspective through which to examine Hawthorne's work, an effort I take up in the next chapter.

CHAPTER 3

Revising the Oedipal Hawthorne
CRITICISM AND THE FORMS OF NARCISSISM

IN ADDITION TO reorienting the psychoanalytic treatment of narcissism and homosexuality, one of the chief goals of this book is to demonstrate why psychoanalytic theory, albeit significantly revised, remains useful for questions of gender and sexuality, male embodiments of both especially. Shaped both by the rise of New Historicism in the 1980s and by the backlash against theory that stems, arguably, from the mid-1990s, Americanist literary criticism has emphasized archival work and material history. While this approach continues to yield insights of lasting value, it also runs the danger of eschewing more intimate matters, such as sexual desire and emotional experience. In my view, some real losses are incurred when we primarily treat these topics from a historical, rather than an affectional, perspective. While developing more of an understanding of the ways in which the expression of sexuality and the lived experience of gender were shaped, curtailed, or determined by cultural and social contexts is crucial to our reconstruction of gender and sexual history, the issue of desire is a more challenging one because it cannot be solely illuminated by even the most scrupulous historical research. As I will elaborate below, psychoanalysis's central premise of an unconscious—a part of ourselves that we cannot rationally know, understand, or access, and that reveals itself only fitfully or metaphorically—makes it a valuable means of considering the paradoxical and contradictory nature of desire. Current Americanist critical practice largely eschews the methodology of psychoanalysis (which is not to suggest that it is absent, only that it is de-emphasized), but it does so at the cost of overlooking certain dimensions of literary experience, specifically those related to the emotional aspects of subjectivity, its gendered, racialized, and sexual components, and the relationship all of these aspects have to desire and the unconscious. Historical and psychoanalytic approaches can have a complementary relationship to one another that is simultaneously mutually reinforcing and productively destabilizing—the historical approach revises and challenges psychoanalysis's reliance on mythic dream structures and generalities; the psychoanalytic revises and challenges history's emphasis on material evidence, which at times borders on a mania for certainty. In any event, my effort here—one mirrored by my attempt to argue for a place for the narcissistic within the oedipal structures associated with Hawthorne's work—is not to replace one critical methodology with another but to enlarge our critical purview to include both. To be as clear as possible, it is my contention that an approach that is both psychoanalytic and historically attentive will yield the richest insights into historical texts.

As I argued in chapter 2, there are very good reasons for regarding psychoanalysis with suspicion; it has had a tendency, in its American contexts especially, to pathologize individuals for failing to live up to the normative standards it has itself either devised or upheld. Psychoanalysis must often be read and used against itself, which queer theory inflections of psychoanalysis make possible because queer theory, at its best, refuses normative programs of identity and subjectivity and promotes productively resistant reading. (I do mean queer theory does this at its best; at its worst, it has a tendency toward the normalizing all its own, especially in terms of political attitudes.)

It is Freud's very inconsistency as a thinker that makes his work valuable for my efforts to reimagine psychoanalytic theory for queer theory purposes and for the purposes of gaining greater understanding of Hawthorne's work, especially in its capacity to critique the normative constructions of gender and sexuality in the United States. Freud's tergiversations; his inconsistently held views; his footnotes that provide a radical counterargument, at times, to his own main text, all evince his habit of revising his opinions. This self-revisionary quality—when matched to the radicalism of Freud's vision of sexuality as essentially a maddening, troublesome, even destructive force, the antithesis, in other words, of heterosexist culture's ennoblement of sexuality as a normalizing, benign phenomenon when properly tied to regimes of reproductivity and heterosexual marriage—gives his work an appealing, exciting looseness.[1]

It is precisely this quality that Frederick Crews, a self-revisionary thinker himself, entirely misses out on in his revisionist work on Freud. Thinking through Crews's positions since the Freud backlash, of which Crews was instrumental, began in the 1980s allows us to gain insights into the ways in which critics have often missed out on what remains valuable in Freud, namely the variability and the resistant pessimism of his vision especially in relation to gender and sexuality, a political pessimism that Hawthorne shares. Interestingly, Crews has also played a significant role in the trends of Americanist literary criticism since the late 1980s, albeit as someone who has steadily critiqued them. (Americanists, for their part, have largely proceeded in comfortable defiance of his positions.) Making sense of Crews's positions, then, will help us to situate this book within Americanist literary studies as well as psychoanalytic theory. This chapter moves from a re-examination of Crews's views of both Freud and Hawthorne to close readings of two key Hawthorne stories, "Roger Malvin's Burial" and "My Kinsman, Major Molineux," both of which, I argue, are more illuminatingly read through narcissism than the oedipal paradigms through which criticism, following Crews, has traditionally framed them.

THE SINS OF THE CRITICAL FATHERS
FREDERICK CREWS, FREUDIAN LITERARY THEORY, AND FREUD-BASHING

By now, everyone knows the story of the once passionately Freudian critic who became an even more passionate, self-described Freud-basher. We know the story well because Frederick Crews has been obsessively telling it since the 1980s. Crews's 1966 *The Sins of the Fathers,* a Freudian study of Hawthorne, remains an important, sharply written and observed work, while also one very much in need of updating. Though quite influential, it has rarely been imitated, its closest equivalent being Gloria Erlich's excellent *Family Themes and Hawthorne's Fiction.* Also of significance, in her book *The Anatomy of National Fantasy,* Lauren Berlant discusses Hawthorne's *Scarlet Letter* in the Lacanian terms of the "National Symbolic." Though I do not concur with all of her readings, especially of Hawthorne's depiction of Hester Prynne (which Berlant frames as a catalogue of biblical misogyny), her study of Hawthorne's relationship to the national construction of subjectivity remains extremely relevant.[2]

Because *The Fragility of Manhood* is the first avowedly Freudian study since Crews's *Sins,* it is important to take a moment both to acknowledge Crews's significance to Hawthorne studies, my own included, and to establish the quite wide gulf between my own approach and his, beginning with his 1966 treatment. One of the vexations of the later Freud-bashing phase of Crews's career is that it proceeds from the implication that his own earlier work was compromised only by its Freudianism, an orthodoxy which, as he claims in his 1989 afterword to a republished *Sins,* he finds himself relieved to discover managed to be tempered even in 1966 by his admirable skepticism: "my only goal was accurate knowledge about Hawthorne" (285). In other words, the Freudian methodology was hopelessly faulty, but the essential Crews probity somehow managed to save the work from its theoretical sensibility. Crews *is* probing, and *Sins* remains an expert and incisive treatment of Hawthorne's work. At the same time, it approaches Hawthorne from a Freudian perspective that is conventional in the extreme.

Crews is a critic whose tendency to scornfulness can overshadow his insights. He works most effectively when he can critique other critics, and part of what drives *Sins* is his disdain for the moralistic critics of Hawthorne's work of the "Christian revival" of the 1950s and 60s. (One of the implications of re-examining Crews's earlier work is that we also re-examine the theologically oriented Hawthorne criticism that he dismissed.) As Crews himself makes clear, *Sins* continues to be worth reading despite Crews's much-publicized rejection of Freud. I believe that a more responsible, generous critic would have revaluated his early argument from a position of self-revision but also in an effort to enlarge, rather than entirely debunk, the earlier critical paradigms, to add new perspectives and current concerns to the dated but still useful methodology. But Crews sees nothing dated or limited in *his* application of Freud to Hawthorne's art; he only sees the limitations of Freud, not of his own *use* of Freud. So determined is the later Crews to exculpate himself from any complicity with Freud that he ingeniously jettisons any investment in Freud, focusing only on the valiant bits of his earlier self that managed always to temper his youthful Freudian idolatry.

We can usefully compare Crews with another critic who revaluated his 1960s Freudianism, Robin Wood. Having written, in the 1960s, a famous Freudian study of the films of Alfred Hitchcock, Wood began, in the 1970s, to revaluate his own work, sternly critiquing his insufficiently feminist earlier views and reliance on a faith in the redemptive power of therapy (although this last remains a stubbornly persistent facet of Wood's work). Updating, critiquing, but also building upon his psychoanalytic principles, Wood was able to offer a powerful new feminist, proto-queer theory critique of Hitchcock.[3] Whereas Wood's self-revisionary work enlarges Freudian critique to make vital interventions in misogyny and homophobia, Crews's revisionism elevates only Crews and, if anything, casts his work generally in an only more indelibly conservative light than his 1966 study did. Ultimately,

Crews's defensive scornfulness becomes the point, rather than a component, of his work.

Crews holds Freud responsible for the rise of poststructuralist theory, for the reign of the "apriorists" for whom a "theory is worth exercising if it yields results that gratify the critic's moral or ideological passions" (285). This argument is incoherent. It is precisely poststructuralist theory, heavily influenced by Michel Foucault and his profoundly committed challenge to Freudian theories of culture, particularly what Foucault calls "the repressive hypothesis," that began to deconstruct and dismantle the Freud legend in the 1970s.[4] (Very briefly put, for Freud, society functions through repression, specifically repression of the sexual; for Foucault, the opposite is true: society, far from repressing sexuality, endlessly incites it and promulgates the idea of its centrality to human life through discourse.)

Crews in 1989, as he will do from then to the present, aligns himself with the noble "empiricists" rather than the dread poststructuralists. It is the empiricists for whom "justification for a theory must reside in its combination of logical coherence, epistemic scrupulousness, and capacity to explain relatively undisputed facts at once more parsimoniously and more comprehensively than its rivals do."[5] One might suggest that considerable biases can inform the empiricist view behind which Crews rallies here. Throughout this book, I attempt to demonstrate the considerable potential of literary Freudianism for "epistemic scrupulousness"; but I also approach Crews's desire for "logical coherence" and "relatively undisputed facts" with suspicion. To my mind, those terms reveal an underlying, and, I hope, unwitting heterosexism. Crews appears to associate the empirical with properly masculine values, emphasizing as positive virtues the factual, the concrete, the tangible, the verifiable. Crews's valorization of the empirical betrays a bias against the qualities that would appear to oppose it: the liquid, the amorphous, the intangible, the obscure, the opaque. In essentialist terms, these values connote femininity; if found in males, they connote effeminacy. Crews's insistence on the supremacy of empiricist approaches proceeds from an attitude of revulsion toward the feminine and effeminacy. "Logic" in the later Crews emerges as the kind of ironclad vehement dogmatism that Hawthorne critiques in the Puritan elders that infiltrate his fictions. Logic is the masculinist ethos that rigidly polices gendered decorum, that relies on the Cartesian model of a human being's value lying exclusively in her rational nature, not in her bodily and affectional dimensions.

I actually share with Crews a profound dislike of theoretical orthodoxy. I write this study neither with a desire to conform to psychoanalytic principles nor to confirm the validity of psychoanalysis for its own sake. I, too, am interested in a real Hawthorne, if only in the sense of discovering an authentic and sound set of insights into his work. (The Hawthorne of Crews's view is a weak, faltering man energized by his disdain and scorn. Given that this is not my own understanding of Hawthorne, I would say that the "real" Hawthorne remains unfound in Crews's work.) But it remains my challenge to make a case for a Freudian literary criticism—and, some would say, for psychoanalytic theory, generally—when many commentators other than Crews have also repudiated the form.

Psychoanalysis is valuable precisely as a means of deriving insights into the emotional and psychic experience of gendered, sexual, and racial identity. What is enduringly valuable about psychoanalysis is its rejection of a faith in, to say nothing of an orthodoxy of, rationalist order at the exclusion of the arbitrariness, perversity, and instability of subjectivity, of the limitless and inscrutable range of our unconscious life. Its belief in an unconscious, a part of ourselves we cannot determine or fully know, makes psychoanalysis extremely useful for thinking about questions as vexed and enigmatic as sexual desire, which cannot be "covered" by context and historical research alone. As I attempted to show in chapter 2, the importance of perversity in Freud's thought is extremely important to any understanding of the value his work retains for the study of gender and sexuality. The Freudian theory of perversity allows us to recognize the enormous reserves of sexual potentialities that are necessarily squelched by the social order to ensure its normative function. As Valerie Rohy puts it in her *Anachronism and Its Others,* "Freud's understanding that the normal is pathological and the pathological is normal may be his greatest and most humane insight: everyone fails at development, everyone is subject to sexual perversity, everyone falls back in time."[6] Theories of arrested development, Freud's included, lose any coherence when such a view is properly considered.

In a fairly unflinching critique of Freudian theory, Marcia Ian succinctly and persuasively defines the value of psychoanalysis. This value lies in Freud's radical refusal of one of the central tenets of classical philosophy, the law of noncontradiction:

> If I were asked . . . to say what is to me the most useful gift of the many psychoanalysis has offered us, I would answer that it is Freud's definition of the psyche as the realm where the law of noncontradiction does not apply. In the psyche, both any idea p and its opposite not-p are true, and may either together or separately cause or prevent, animate or agitate, signify or deracinate, inspire or terrorize—or deaden.[7]

It is precisely in the way in which opposite but equally urgent, felt, meaningful ideas do *not* cohere in Freud that makes psychoanalytic theory so affectingly useful for the study of Hawthorne. It is precisely the ways in which Hawthorne's work complicates, deepens, and challenges psychoanalysis's own pathologizing tendencies toward its own compulsive desire for system and logic that makes Hawthorne's work so relevant for psychoanalysis.

To return to Crews in 1966: in Crews's index, under Oedipal, we find *passim*. The chief limitation of his study is one he shares with Freud, a persistent insistence on the explanatory function of the Oedipus complex, which Crews sees as the central problem of Hawthorne's work. In Crews's version of Hawthorne, the Oedipus complex manifests itself in a fearful apprehension of horrifying incestuous desire on the part of male characters toward sister and mother figures, hostility toward the father, whom the protagonist wishes to see degraded, like Major Molineux, and a desire ultimately to conform to the father's law. Certainly, Hawthorne's work is rife with oedipal tensions. But, as I argue throughout this study, his work is equally, if not more urgently, a conflictual engagement with the phenomenon of narcissism, which manifests itself in recurrent treatments throughout his career of divided selves, reflected selves, beautiful and unattainable selves, bifurcated or hollow or chimerical or fatally masked, veiled, and hidden selves; of paintings, portraits, miniatures, daguerreotypes, and other images of selves within a literary evocation of the visual the intensity of which prefigures the cinema; of the self split off from itself, of the self contemplating itself as another self, of the self cut off from and longing for itself, of the self self-mesmerized, of an essentially conflictual relationship between the self and the image of the self within a body of work whose chief concerns parallel Lacan's theory of the mirror stage. *Pace* Crews, and in agreement with James K. Folsom, I argue that Hawthorne found oneness inscrutable and made its myriad perplexing fascinations his subject.[8]

To demonstrate both the ways in which Hawthorne explores the significance of male beauty and its potentially conflictual experiential and social implications, I will now turn to two famous tales that, while subject to innumerable critical exegeses over the years, have rarely ever been viewed as exercises in narcissistic self-representation and exploration of the dynamics and effects of looking relations. My purpose in this analysis will be to demonstrate the importance of Hawthorne's narcissistic themes even to works that ostensibly seem far removed from them. I will then turn to a discussion of the ways in which Hawthorne's personal experiences may have shaped his attitudes toward the narcissistic visual desire foregrounded in his work.

MURDEROUS NARCISSISM
"ROGER MALVIN'S BURIAL"

Hawthorne's indelible 1832 tale commences in the year 1725, during the battle known as Lovewell's Fight (which Hawthorne names Lovell's Fight), a real event of the French and Indian Wars. A young man and an old man lie depleted and wounded in a forest on their arduous journey home from a battle with Indians.[9] This matched/mismatched pair of young and old man, I argue, is the *locus classicus* of male anxiety in Hawthorne's work.[10] Though tormented as to which decision to make, the young Reuben Bourne agrees to let old Roger Malvin die alone in the forest after the old man has entreated him, despite Reuben's protestations, to do so. But when Reuben returns home to his fiancée Dorcas, who is Roger Malvin's daughter, he finds himself in a panic when Dorcas assumes that her father had already died and been properly buried, with funeral rites, by Reuben when he was rescued by a search party. Tormentedly accommodating himself to her inaccurate belief, Reuben turns into a secretive, inwardly tortured, hostile, and ungiving man as he lives out his life as husband to Dorcas and father to their son, Cyrus. One day, many years later, in the forest with Dorcas and the now teen-aged Cyrus—the same forest in which Roger Malvin's body was left to rot—Reuben and Cyrus go out hunting, and Reuben accidentally—or anything but—shoots Cyrus instead of a deer. As he contemplates the bizarre coincidence that Cyrus's dead body lies beneath the same oak where Roger Malvin died alone, Reuben tells Dorcas that "Your tears will fall at once on your father and your son" (10: 360).[11] So many complex ideas circulate here that to assign the tale one thematic program is quite limiting; yet I wish to demonstrate that its oedipal surface hides a narcissistic depth.

Crews does not simply assert that the tale is a version of the Oedipus complex; his style is to reinforce by qualification. He considers several different reasons for his reading, systematically weighing these pieces of evidence: Roger relates to Reuben as a son, calling him "my boy"; Roger is depicted as a sexual rival to Reuben, who will profit from the older man's death by getting to have his daughter all to himself; the incest themes in other Hawthorne works, as Crews reads them, deepen the incestuous suggestion that Dorcas is a sister to Reuben as well as his wife, being the daughter of Reuben's figural father. "But let us return to less tenuous evidence," writes Crews, now clinching his oedipal case. Hawthorne, Crews cites, writes that Reuben "could no longer love deeply except where he saw or imagined some reflection or likeness of his own mind. In Cyrus he recognized what he had himself been in other days . . ." Crews not only fails to consider the narcissistic valences here (reflections, likeness) but also stops the quote from the story right there, or rather isolates one piece of it.[12] The full passage problematizes Crews's oedipal interpretation of the work.

> The only child of Reuben and Dorcas was a son, now arrived at the age of fifteen years, beautiful in youth, and giving promise of a glorious manhood. He was peculiarly qualified for, and already began to excel in, the wild accomplishments of frontier life. His foot was fleet, his aim true, his apprehension quick, his heart glad and high; and all who anticipated the return of Indian war spoke of Cyrus Bourne as a future leader in the land. The boy was loved by his father with a deep and silent strength, as if whatever was good and happy in his own nature had been transferred to his child, carrying his affections with it. Even Dorcas, though loving and beloved, was far less dear to him; for Reuben's secret thoughts and insulated emotions had gradually made him a selfish man, and he could no longer love deeply except where he saw or imagined some reflection or likeness of his own mind. In Cyrus he recognized what he had himself been in other days; and at intervals he seemed to partake of the boy's spirit, and to be revived with a fresh and happy life. (10: 351)

Gray Kochhar-Lindgren writes, along Freudian lines, of narcissism as a wound: "unless we break out of the magic circle of the ego, unless the self-reflecting mirror of Narcissus is somehow shattered . . . there is no hope that the wound may be healed. And even if it is healed, the scar that marks the place of struggle will remain."[13] Hawthorne's Reuben Bourne cannot break out of his ego's magic circle; he can only love what reminds him of himself, "some reflection or likeness of his own mind." No doubt Reuben loves himself for his mind, but it's Cyrus's body, not mind, that Reuben regards so rhapsodically. Hawthorne's elaborate evocation of the beauty of Cyrus (beautiful youth, glorious manhood) exceeds the parameters of the tale's themes at this point. We know that Reuben is closed off and can love only the son who memorializes his own lost youth, but Hawthorne deepens this memorialization by suffusing it with an ardent beauty, one made more palpable by the Hellenic details of Cyrus's athletic qualities. Reuben's love for him is deep, strong, and silent, expressed entirely through visual contemplation; it displaces almost entirely his love for his steadfast wife, Dorcas. What Reuben seems to love in the boy is his own lost youth, before war and the terrible compact he forged with Roger Malvin took it away; but Cyrus is also an idealized figure, endowed with attractive physical qualities that were not attributed to Reuben. (Hawthorne adds little detail to his description of the young Reuben save his youth and anxiety.) Cyrus exemplifies visual identity, being knowable to us almost exclusively through his physical qualities, his visual design. So we have to ask, what is this beautiful youth who could be a sculpture from classical antiquity doing in the filial forest of Hawthorne's oedipal themes?[14]

To begin the work of challenging the stronghold of Oedipus, we must begin by defamiliarizing the Oedipus complex itself. While it is the process whereby normative sexual identity is, ostensibly, produced—the process that makes us properly heterosexual, no longer seeing the same-sex parent as sexual rival but as the figure with whom we identify; no longer seeing the opposite-sex parent as object of sexual desire but as model for a proper, exogamous sexual object outside the bloodline—it is not some kind of narrative of sexual origins but, rather, itself a late stage in the psychosexual development of the child; it occurs after numerous other stages in which desire and identification take place. Even in its most normative cast, the Oedipus complex is produced through a prohibition on an original homosexual desire (for our discussion, the boy desiring the father before the mother): it does not produce heterosexuality out of thin air so much as it produces it through a repudiation of a prior homoerotic disposition. Judith Butler, writing of the "melancholia of gender identification," draws out the implicit Freudian point that "it would appear that the taboo against homosexuality must *precede* the heterosexual incest taboo; the taboo against homosexuality in effect creates the heterosexual 'dispositions' by which the oedipal conflict becomes possible."[15]

For Steven Bruhm, these queer theory reformulations of classical psychoanalysis illuminate Romantic sexual and textual politics. Bruhm, drawing on Butler's rereading of Freud, argues that "Romantic male desire is structured by a same-sex narcissism that it must continually repudiate." The successful resolution of the Oedipus complex for the male involves identification with the father who had been a rival for the oedipal sexual object, the mother—but it is important to remember that the father, before this rivalry, was the original erotic object. As Butler argues, identifications, which take place in phantasy, express a wish to recover "a primary object of a love lost—and produced—through prohibition." A desire to identify with the father is a desire, we can argue, to preserve some portion of that lost, repudiated desire *for* the father. If, as Butler argues, we mourn for a lost object specifically produced by the prohibitions of the Oedipus complex, that lost object, suggests Steven Bruhm, "can only be seen in a Romantic male optic as a desiring and desired male other whom the . . . subject desires to possess and be possessed by," a complex welter of identification, repudiation, and homoerotic desire.[16]

If the Romantic author/figure cannot acknowledge the homoerotic object of his desiring gaze but must repudiate it, Reuben's desire for Cyrus is met with two repudiations, the inability of Reuben to recognize Cyrus as autonomous, as anything more than a reflection of his father—which suggests that Reuben in his own phantasy imagines himself as a gloriously beautiful youth—and, more intensely, the murder of Cyrus in the forest. I agree with Crews entirely, but for different reasons, that the accident is no accident at all. Reuben kills his own reflection in killing Cyrus, his *own* memory of a lost object, his unruined, earlier self, killed by war and the "Father." In other words, the lost object that Reuben mourns is not the repudiated, repressed father-as-object-of-homoerotic-desire, but, instead, an image of his own prior perfection, which may or may not have ever existed but was produced from the wartime trauma and oedipal betrayal. Reuben mourns his own lost narcissism.

Kochhar-Lindgren's reading of Narcissus illuminates Hawthorne's tale:

> It is otherness as language, person, the unconscious, and death that Narcissus refuses to open himself to as he stares at himself, reflected and unattainable, in the pool. He longs to be both subject and object of his own desire and not to be riddled by the necessity of symbolization and the desire of an other.[17]

The actual living, breathing body of beautiful Cyrus both reflects Reuben's own phantasy vision of himself and disrupts and thwarts it by remaining stubbornly autonomous, other. In other words, as poignantly and erotically as Cyrus reflects, realizes, and extends Reuben's self-image, Cyrus will always remain Cyrus, not Reuben; Cyrus will always be himself, will always elude the totalizing grasp of Reuben's narcissistic projection. Cyrus cannot be contained, subsumed, by Reuben's desire; for each day he exceeds and eludes it, threatening to leave behind his most significant function, to be Reuben's self-reflection. For these reasons, even the stirring promise of Cyrus's future as a military leader is threatening: his increasingly accessible adulthood and mature manhood threatens to dissolve his resemblance to Reuben's phantasy-image and to confirm the inescapable truth of his autonomy, his difference from Reuben, that he is *other.* Liberating, cathartic tears gush from Reuben's eyes as he contemplates his son's freshly dead body lying upon the ashy dead body of his wife's father. Reuben experiences cathartic relief because he is now freed, from memory, from himself, from the binding logic of his own narcissism. The murder of narcissism is simultaneously the murder of homoerotic desire; perhaps this accounts for the orgasmic nature of Reuben's tears, which seem forced out of him, as if they were an *involuntary* orgasm: "Then Reuben's heart was stricken, and the tears gushed out like water from a rock" (10: 360). The father's orgasmic release is tied to death, to the destruction of the son. But this murdered narcissism is itself also a memorial to Reuben's lost narcissism, captured in the perpetual frieze of death agonies; Cyrus can now always remain the beautiful youth of fantasy, and never grow into the older or old man of recrimination and physical decay. Reuben preserves his self-image in his son's glorious manhood, now forever intact in memory.

I CALL what Hawthorne evokes here *murderous narcissism*—the killing projection of one's own phantasies and desires onto another that refuses to recognize another person as an *other*, not part of the self. As noted in chapter 2, Freud describes even parental love for children as a manifestation of their own narcissism. Hawthorne takes this idea, if you will, to diabolical heights here. The particular kind of murderous narcissism at work in this tale may be subclassified as *patriarchal narcissism*, the father's inability to recognize the son as anything other than a reflection of himself. Reuben would appear to view himself as a victim of this force as well, killed off in the prime of his manhood by the troubling ghost of his father-in-law. With chilling cyclical sureness, Reuben kills off his own son, both the older man's future and his (imagined) memory of youth, in the prime of *his* manhood.

The schism between the young man and the old man that informs Hawthorne's work—present in tales such as "My Kinsman, Major Molineux," "Young Goodman Brown," "Rappaccini's Daughter," it becomes only an ever-more pronounced theme in all of the long romances, including the unfinished *Septimius Felton*—can be read as a perpetual acting-out of this narcissistic crisis. The old man threatens to destroy the younger, and the younger resists him. So far, so oedipal. Yet this conflict heavily involves both the logic of the visual and the threat of the homoerotic: who sees whom and *how* seeing occurs become thematic concerns. The young man is almost always described as rapturously beautiful, while the old man's physical decrepitude and ugliness are emphasized and amplified. Robin Molineux is a surprisingly comely youth whose comeliness is in especially marked contrast to the tarred-and-feathered spectacle of his terrified older kinsman (I discuss this story at length in the next section); Young Goodman Brown is fixated on the old man-Devil's writhing snakelike staff, a perversely funny reminder of the homoerotic dynamics of the father–son rivalry in the Oedipus complex; the beautiful Giovanni Guasconti is matched up against the cadaverous, dark Rappaccini; beautiful, tremulously sensitive Dimmesdale against the grotesquely misshapen Chillingworth; Coverdale, said by Zenobia in *The Blithedale Romance* to be "quite the handsomest man," against the ghastly, faded Old Moody; beautiful, lithe, primally sexy Donatello against the sinister Model; multiracial Septimius Felton, who possesses "a certain dark beauty," against the ominous, spider-loving Dr. Portsoaken. These oedipal dynamics are disrupted by and suffused with an ardent, mystifying emphasis on the corruption of a beautiful male youth by an old and ugly one. I argue that this dynamic is at least as resonantly narcissistic as it is oedipal because of the recurring, increasingly incessant focus on both male beauty and the visual, the desire for self-reflection tied, so resolutely, to destruction, sometimes of self, more often of other. What the father seems to want to kill off is not the son but the father's *own* reflection; in so doing, he both destroys and memorializes his own lost beauty or his fantasy of having possessed it. On the part of these beautiful young men, these older male figures are a distorting mirror image for their own bodily perfection, reflecting back a grotesque self. Given that almost all of these young men are revealed to be as morally shallow, dubious, and corrupt as they are comely, youthful, and desirable, Hawthorne appears to suggest that the old man functions as the corrective mirror to the younger. The author employs the cautionary nature of the Narcissus myth as a stern corrective to beautiful young males, forcing them to acknowledge the interior ugliness a beautiful surface camouflages, themes that Oscar Wilde will make famously his own in *The Portrait of Dorian Gray*. Yet why would this be so? Why does Hawthorne regard the young man so skeptically? Another key Hawthorne story raises these questions.

THE NARCISSISTIC GAZE
"MY KINSMAN, MAJOR MOLINEUX"

An awareness of the presence of narcissistic themes in Hawthorne's work makes possible fresh readings of works rarely considered in such a context, such as the famous tale "My Kinsman, Major Molineux" (1832). "Molineux" provides the template for Hawthorne's major narcissistic themes: fraught, painful, violating looking that maims the viewer's vision; the simultaneous pleasure and terror of being looked at; shame and the threat of public exposure; the simultaneous attractiveness and moral dubiousness of the figure of the young man; the rejection of perceived ugliness and fastidious adherence to standards of beauty best exemplified by the youthful, morally callow male. As the discussions of the Lacanian mirror stage (the aggressivity inherent in a fascination with one's image), Mulvey's theory of the male gaze (the desire and ability to subjugate another through the eye), and shame in "The Gentle Boy" (related in no small way to how Ilbrahim looks and is perceived by others) have suggested, for Hawthorne masculinity is inseparable as a psychic as well as social experience from the experience of vision and the harrowing possibilities it raises for violation—either of another person or of one's self. Adding to the complexity of this welter of anxieties is the issue of homoerotic and narcissistic desire—the beauty of youthful male figures makes them simultaneously a gender and sexual threat that intensifies the inherent fears and dangers of images and of looking.

"My Kinsman" depends upon the ambiguous moral nature of its protagonist. But what is the relevance to "Molineux" that its protagonist, Robin, is exceedingly handsome? Moreover, why does Hawthorne reveal Robin's beauty through the perspective of a ferryman's appraising look: "the ferryman lifted a lantern, by the aid of which, and the newly risen moon, he took a very accurate survey of the stranger's figure"? We are introduced to Robin not by name but by body. "He was a youth of barely eighteen years, evidently country-bred. . . . He was clad in a coarse grey coat, well worn, but in excellent repair; his under garments were durably constructed of leather, and sat tight to a pair of serviceable and well-shaped limbs. . . . Brown, curly hair, well-shaped features, and bright, cheerful eyes, were nature's gifts, and worth all that art could have done for his adornment" (11: 209). The contours of Robin's leather-clad body are suggestively eroticized; like those of an athlete in classical marble, his limbs and his features are both strong and "well-shaped." Echoing the Narcissus myth, the ferryman transports this New England Narcissus to the underworld, the nighttime city of political revolt and oedipal confusion.

Robin is primarily characterized through what I call *visual identity*. His outward appearance is the *basis* from which everything we subsequently learn about him—including his morally dubious and climactically revealed disloyalty to his kinsman—proceeds. One could argue that Hawthorne, deeply familiar with the tradition of the romance, merely borrows the form's techniques of idealized figures here. But the references to Robin's beauty surpass the needs of convention. By depicting Robin from the start as a magnet for the eye, Hawthorne foregrounds themes of looking as they relate to the figure of the young man. While Robin would appear to be the chief *subject* of the gaze—looking constantly at multiple others, scrutinizing situations (however strained his powers of discernment)—he is in fact the chief object of the gaze. Robin's own act of looking at his grievously humiliated "tar-and-feathery" kinsman, while the climactic, decisive moment in this famous story, is merely one stage in a series of spectatorial encounters. The tale dramatically engineers and stages Robin's climactic reunion with his kinsman as, essentially, a profound act of *looking,* his kinsman rendered a baroque visual object for the purpose. Yet at the same time, and perhaps even more emphatically, it is *Robin* who is the object of the crowd's fearsome gaze: as he gapes at his uncle, the crowd—verging on assimilating him into their own ranks or submitting him to his uncle's cruel, bitter fate—fixes its collective eye on him. Robin's encounters with dubious and alarming figures, which reach their height in his confrontation with his tarred-and-feathered uncle, rendered an alien figure, occur within a structural field of vision that I refer to as the *narcissistic gaze,* in which Robin is as much watched as he is a watcher—and as much watched by his fictional creator as he is by his fellow fictional denizens.

As we established in the introduction, for Lacan the gaze is indifferent to the subject, for Foucault it is deeply invested in monitoring the subject, and for film theory it constitutes the subject. Finding an ameliorative middle ground in all of these views, I return, albeit from a queer theory perspective, to Laura Mulvey's view of the gaze as active, individually directed, and capable of making an impact that is often quite injurious on a person or persons. Hawthorne's narcissistic gaze is just such a personal, direct, but also overarching and socially structured field of vision in which individual desires intersect with those of a collective as well as those of other individual persons. I call this fictional gaze narcissistic for several reasons. In his avid desire to look and in his frustrated ability to possess what he looks for, Robin enacts the most telling action of the Narcissus myth. Robin is always only one among several lookers competing for the power of the gaze. Hawthorne depicts the limited perspective afforded Robin's look, but, as noted, he also makes Robin the figure around whom disparate acts of looking in the tale rotate. We can say that what Hawthorne literalizes, in the most paranoid but also the most satirical form imaginable, is the narcissistic subject's belief that all eyes are no less fixated upon him than are his own. The most charged desiring perspective evoked through this schema is, I would argue, Hawthorne's own. In looking at his handsome young protagonist, the handsome young author looks at a textual mirror image. Even more intriguingly, as the author, Hawthorne looks upon a mirrored image of his *own* looking self in the figure of the mysterious stranger, lately entering the narrative, who provides Robin with his only useful guidance.

Robin Molineux's nightmarish nighttime encounters with various troubling figures have been repeatedly analyzed over the years, with the chief readings, as with all of Hawthorne's work, classifiable under the general headings of historicist or psychoanalytic-mythic. In the anti-psychoanalytic view of Michael J. Colacurcio, Hawthorne is a writer exclusively devoted to the study of American history. Though he notes the "strong hints of voyeurism" in "My Kinsman," Colacurcio cautions that "some political motive is even more obvious."[18] For Colacurcio, any "psychologistic" reading of this "perfectly crafted" tale reduces "politics to passage."[19] I take Colacurcio's point that we should challenge simplistic psychoanalytic readings that compress the story into a rite-of-passage narrative that reveals some immutable oedipal law of filial overthrow of the "Father." Yet to discuss voyeurism in the story *is* to discuss politics: the gendered politics of vision. Hawthorne's disorganization of gendered and perceptual hierarchies—his refusal to grant his protagonist mastery over the field of vision, his interest in making Robin and other male figures as much the object as the subject of the gaze—makes a radical break with conventional conflations of masculine and visual dominance. Moreover, I argue that Hawthorne's sexual politics is narcissistic rather than oedipal—focused on the rigors of self-consciousness and self-desire and the image of the self rather than a perpetual conflict with the father, which is not to suggest that oedipal themes are in any way unimportant in Hawthorne, only that they are not necessarily preeminent. In his Freudian phase in *The Sins of the Fathers*, Frederick Crews wrote, "Even critics who denounce literary Freudianism have recognized that Robin's real search is for an idealized father—a figure of benevolent power who will shield him from the world and lend him prestige." For Crews, the story transforms "the crisis of late adolescence" into the achievement of "a healthy independence from the paternal image."[20] In his incisive but also conservative readings of Hawthorne, Crews reduces most of the author's work to filial struggles, male quests for independent identity, and heterosexual closure. A much broader range of desires and conflicts can be considered in Hawthorne's work through psychoanalytic paradigms.

Scanned by the ferryman as if he were Narcissus on the River Styx, Robin proceeds, in his search for his kinsman, to scan others. Discerning an approaching figure as a periwigged old citizen, Robin asks for his help; the citizen then rebukes him ("Let go my garment, fellow!.... I have authority, I have—hem, hem—authority"), Robin only discovers after the old man hurries away that he has been observed in his encounter by the "barber's boys," who emit an "ill-mannered roar of laughter" at Robin's embarrassing and fruitless encounter (11: 211). Before being lured into a tavern by its "fragrance of good cheer," the suddenly hungry Robin beholds the "broad countenance of a British hero," whom he follows inside. In the tavern, Robin observes various homosocial groupings occupying the wooden benches, with whom he feels a "sort of brotherhood" (11: 212). Just as Robin seizes upon one figure in particular, "striking almost to grotesqueness," with a "forehead" bulging out into "double prominence," to emerge as a still yet more grotesquely fiendish face later in the story, the innkeeper reveals that he has been observing Robin as the youth has been observing the grouped men and the grotesque figure. Coming up to Robin, the innkeeper presumes that Robin is from the country and asks what his supper plans are (11: 213). By this point, all "eyes were now turned on the country lad," appraising him and his attire (11: 214). Looking at the male group transforms into being looked at by *them*. Intensifying the palpable embarrassment of the scene, the innkeeper, apparently contemptuous of frugal Robin's declining of supper, proceeds to compare Robin with the description of a fugitive servant, which leads the innkeeper to make "occasional recurrences to the young man's figure" (11: 214). It is not clear whether the innkeeper truly believes Robin to be the escaped thief in the "Wanted" poster, or is, on some level, taking the opportunity to make a kinsman of Molineux as uncomfortable as possible, having possibly, as Robin conjectures, discerned a family resemblance. In any event, the overall effect of the episode is to make Robin, a perpetual observer, himself the site of glares from countenances with a "strange hostility." Repeatedly, Robin is shown to be as looked at as he is a looker, and, when looked at, rendered a vulnerable visual object.

Strangely, Robin's avid desire to look decreases not at all even as he somatically registers the psychic effects of the scenes of shame he has endured. He walks "slowly and silently" up the street in his search for his kinsman, the gait I locate as Hawthorne's marker of male shame, as I will elaborate in the next chapter. But he also "thrusts" his face "close to that of every elderly gentleman, in search of the Major's lineaments." The aggression of his looking results not in mastery over the objects of his look, but in the "dazzling of his optics," as a riotous pageant of "gay and gallant figures" whoosh past and bedazzle him. Again, where Robin exerts visual mastery, others overpower him visually. Next, Robin encounters the pretty young woman with the "strip of scarlet petticoat" (11: 216), the Major's housekeeper, who finds in him a "handsome country youth" in whose appearance "nothing [was] to be shunned." Her "dainty little figure" deceptively obscures the heights of her visual power over Robin—her petticoat's hoop lends her the appearance of "standing in a balloon," and her bright eyes possess a "sly freedom, which triumphed over those of Robin" (11: 217). Interestingly, the power of her look transmutes into a seductive power "stronger than the athletic country youth" (11: 218), whom she nevertheless abandons to race into her own domicile when the opportunity arises. The scarlet-petticoated woman's visual mastery over Robin intensifies through displacement: "the sparkle of a saucy eye" catches Robin's own, accompanied by "drowsy laughter," "pleasant twitters," and the beckoning of a "round" arm above him. Good clergyman's son that he is, Robin flees the suddenly lascivious scene (11: 218–19).

The grotesquely double-faced man now reappears in even more grotesque form, his doubleness of visage redoubled in the "infernal" hues of red and black on each side of his face, a harbinger of the full climactic release of accumulating chaotic energies and the fullest intensification yet of the conjoined themes of strange faces and visual dread. By this point in the story, Robin's powers of vision simply falter: just as he appears to "define the form of distant objects," they start away with "ghostly indistinctness" (11: 221). Perhaps it is his inability clearly to see, and thereby achieve mastery over the scene, that leads Robin to present *himself* as a visual object, gaining power from being seen as an impressive figure: to the gentleman who is the first to treat him with "real kindness" (11: 224), Robin describes himself as "well grown, as you see," proceeding then to raise "himself to full height" before the stranger; visual evidence reifies identity, truthfulness, the factual. The stranger reveals his own ambiguous desires to co-opt Robin into the story's gaze, calmly informing Robin "I have a singular curiosity to witness your meeting" (11: 225). G. R. Thompson argues that the gentleman who appears near the end and waits with as he watches Robin waiting for his kinsman should be understood as Hawthorne's authorial stand-in, an argument relevant for our present purposes.[21] The narcissistic gaze of the story directly involves the author, whose own figure and desire to look insert themselves as they are incorporated into the workings of the tale. I argue that Hawthorne stages his own desire to look at *his* figural presence, a desire to look treated no less ambiguously than any other in the narrative.

Hawthorne depicts the gaze as all-sided as he describes the tumult that Molineux's humiliating procession provokes: "many heads, in the attire of the pillow, and confused by sleep suddenly broken, were protruded to the gaze of whoever had leisure to observe them." The double-faced man, now revealed as the processional leader on horseback, assumes the Mars-like guise of "war personified," the red of one cheek flaming like an emblem of fire and sword, the black of the other signifying mourning. He leads a fiery crowd of both men and women, "a mass of people," curiously inactive save for their power as "applauding spectators." "The double-faced fellow has his eye upon me," Robin mutters, apprehensively imagining that he "was himself to bear a part in the pageantry." With a nightmarish theatrical flourish, what Robin fears is precisely what occurs, as the leader turns around in his saddle and fixes "his glance full upon the country youth." The leader's "fiery eyes" exemplify the menacing aspects of vision (11: 228).

In what is perhaps the most widely analyzed moment in a Hawthorne tale, Robin does finally find his kinsman, Major Molineux. What is the significance of this meeting, and of Robin's bizarre, maddening, frightening, and funny decision, if it can be called one, to join in with the cruelly laughing revelers who have tarred and feathered Robin's unfortunate Loyalist kinsman, Robin's laugh the "loudest there"? Pledging allegiance neither to the typical psychoanalytic nor to the historical traditions of readings of this moment, I do not see this climax as either hostile oedipal rejection of the father or as momentous historical allegory (the Revolutionary birth of the United States). Rather, I see it in the terms with which the story has consistently dealt, as the climactic confrontation of the looker and the gaze, and, more specifically, that between Narcissus and a mirror image that, like most in Hawthorne, reflects not a coherent, reassuring reflection of the idealized self, the longing for the reassurance of beauty, but, instead, the reflection as damning, distorted, frightening, ugly.

The tarred-and-feathered spectacle of Molineux reflects Robin, but reflects him inaccurately. For Leo Bersani, desire, homoerotic desire in particular, is desire for "inaccurate self-replication."[22] For Hawthorne, however, desire is desire for perfect likeness, resemblance, self-sameness, in Aristotelian terms, for mimesis. We can translate Robin's shocking laughter into these words: *This old, humiliated, profoundly ugly man does not resemble me.* Hawthorne's personal hatred of ugliness, a recurrent theme in his life as well as fiction, relates to his anguished narcissism: the beautiful young man chiefly seeks an affirmation of his own beauty, remaining perpetually frustrated in this quest.

Fulfilling the obsession with the visual with which every question of identity and every pursuit of mastery in it intertwines, the story makes its most decisive moment of narrative tension a question of complicity with visual spectacle. For Robin to admit that Molineux is really his kinsman is to admit to complicity in the gaze, to admit that he is as horrifyingly vulnerable to its most violent aspects as Molineux now is. Repudiating Molineux, Robin repudiates the entire question of visual mastery, of subject and object, look and gaze, of any complicity in the desire for visual power, as he avidly trades in ego for group psychology. If the gaze has threatened to consume Robin, and by consuming him acknowledge him as desirable object, Molineux's predicament now collapses such questions into the useful pandemonium whereby any intricate questions of desire and identification get lost in the riotous, scapegoating crowd. In joining in with the crowd's boisterous calumniation of the figure who stands in, as site of visual fascination, for himself, Robin effectively cancels out knowledge of his own susceptibility to the gaze, of his own status as desirable visual object.

In this story, the young man successfully displaces his own anxieties about being a visual object onto an old man who, victimized, lends himself all too readily to such uses. But in several Hawthorne works such a strategy is met with far less certain success. His participation in a collective rite of taboo vision in the forest leaves Young Goodman Brown eternally bereft, withdrawn and spiteful; Aylmer's displacement of visual anxieties onto his beautiful wife Georgiana, whose titular "Birthmark" he unceasingly attempts to erase, results in her death. Hawthorne's final story, "Feathertop," provides the most persuasive rationale for Robin Molineux's avoidance of complicity with the visual: once the self recognizes itself as a visual spectacle, it meets its own death. As Slavoj Žižek writes, "'seeing oneself looking' . . . unmistakably stands for death. . . . in the uncanny encounter of a double . . . what eludes our gaze are always his eyes: the double strangely seems always to look askew, never to return our gaze by looking straight into our eyes—the moment he were to do it, our life would be over . . . ."[23] Robin Molineux and others like him in Hawthorne's oeuvre extend Narcissus's phobic campaign against self-knowledge—which carries death with it—yet Hawthorne, in his frequent attempts to grapple with the difficulties of the Narcissus myth and in his frequent creation of a narcissistic double through which he can conduct his own conflictual desires, seems as compelled by a need to look straight into the eyes of the self as he is to look and be looked at askew.[24]

As Lacan argues in his theory of the mirror stage, we are always locked in a relationship with our own image, the "small other" or *autre,* that is our counterpart in the mirror. (Lacan uses the lowercase *a* for the term *autre* to contrast it with the *Autre* of the Big Other, the Symbolic order, which exceeds our understanding and ability to identify with it.) I call this beguiling and illusory mirror image the *specular self,* an *embodiment* of cohesion and bodily perfection that haunts the subject while also connoting an uncanny, magical power. Hawthorne devises a theory of the subject's relationship to the visual sphere that is similar to Lacan's theory of a self irreparably at odds with, even as it is constituted by, its own image.

In his famous study of the double in psychology, folklore, and literature, Otto Rank argued that the double is a transformation of one's own narcissistic self-love into the *doppelgänger,* "the feared and loathed other of one's own desires."[25] Steven Bruhm notes that Rank associated the narcissistic double with paranoia and homosexuality, which is certainly of relevance to Hawthorne's work, and reads Rank through Eve Kosofsky Sedgwick, likening the paranoid terror that the double provokes to cultural regimes of homophobia.[26] Also drawing on Rank, Dennis Bingham, in a study of Hollywood masculinity, notes that Rank theorized the double as a "disastrous wish-fulfillment apparatus that acts out the darkest repressed desires of the subject"; in Rank's words, the classic *doppelgänger* plot is resolved by "the slaying of the double, through which the hero seeks to protect himself permanently from the pursuits of his self." The slaying, however, "is really a suicidal act." To apply Bingham's insights to our discussion of Hawthorne, we can say that the "difference between the classical double and" those in Hawthorne's works "is that they are granted a recognition. In the other they recognize the dark instincts they themselves repress . . . [when the male protagonist] finally confronts himself in the mirror, [he illustrates] the Hegelian notion that the need to change is motivated by self-disgust."[27] As I will be considering at length in the next chapter, Hawthorne repeatedly stages a fateful, fatal moment of self-confrontation—the young man looking at his uncanny double, and grappling with feelings of shame and fear.

IN A CONSIDERATION of the philosophical implications of Hawthorne's notorious shyness, Clark Davis asks what Hawthorne means "when he tells readers of 'The Old Manse' that he veils his face." Hawthorne, Clark theorizes, "chooses an image of public or external identity to figure the private or internal self. He then offers to 'veil' that public/private self by presumably withholding one set of information and simultaneously offering another. In this way 'veiling' is not so much hiding one's 'face' with a blank mask as it is refusing to show one face by showing another in its place. And what is this 'face' but the 'veil' itself . . . Thus, when Hawthorne 'veils his face' he is assuming the general characteristics of human personality; he is displaying his private self in order to receive and perceive the thoughts and feelings of others."[28]

Davis astutely observes the effects created through Hawthorne's rhetoric of veils and masks. I would put the matter differently, however: Hawthorne's constantly threatened unveiling and reveiling function as a kind of authorial striptease for an audience presumed to be hungering for a glimpse of the "real" Hawthorne. This real Hawthorne is not merely the teasingly unyielding private celebrity author but the actual person writing the fictions who can be perceived by others in real life. In other words, Hawthorne transmutes his own felt experience of the gaze—his position within it, its impact on him, his own gazing agency and concomitant powerlessness—into a fictional performance of seeing and being seen that, while it covers a range of effects and feelings, places its chief emphasis on the dangers of vision, the pain of being seen, the violating tendencies of seeing. Hawthorne's veil-dance circles around the concerns of an intensely self-fixated authorial self—no less legitimate a topic for fictive exploration than "the thoughts and feelings of others." In the next chapter, we will explore this self-fixation and its affectional dimensions in depth.

CHAPTER 4

Struck by the Mask

NARCISSISM, SHAME, MASCULINITY, AND THE
DREAD OF THE VISUAL

*I*N CHAPTER 2, I suggested that Hawthorne identified with the gentle boy, an identification that stems from his experience of shame. It is important to establish the cultural as well as psychological contexts for why Hawthorne may have associated shame with the feminine beauty of his Narcissus-like males, a quality that he personally embodied. Hawthorne's gentle boy provides an enduring template for his representations of masculinity. His friendship with Franklin Pierce, his best friend since their college days together at Bowdoin, is a good place to start in thinking about the ways that larger cultural forces intersected with representations of masculinity and homosocial relations. Written shortly before Franklin Pierce's 1852 election and just after Hawthorne wrote *The Blithedale Romance*, Hawthorne's campaign biography *The Life of Franklin Pierce* is certainly not one of his several masterpieces of the 1850s. Nevertheless, it remains a fascinating document in the history of American letters. Part of its fascination, as many scholars have shown, lies in its naked exposure of Hawthorne's agonizingly ignorant view of slavery. Another part lies in its naked exposure of the ways in which white male homosocial relations in this period conducted all of the major ideological, social, and cultural questions of its moment. Indubitably, Hawthorne and Pierce were on the wrong side of the slavery question; Northerners who were surrounded by people who campaigned against the Southern slavocracy should have known better. Pierce, born in New Hampshire in 1804, accommodated Southern interests at every turn, infuriating Northern abolitionists, Despite his best efforts to assuage and accommodate proslavery forces, Pierce may be said to have mobilized the gathering momentum of abolitionist rage against the continuing and expanding might and means of the Southern slavocracy.

Less attention has been paid, however, to the gendered and sexual implications of Hawthorne's campaign biography. In a welcome and revelatory essay, Leland S. Person has argued that Hawthorne endows Pierce with a "physical appeal" that recalls Hawthorne's "ambiguously gendered male characters." Person reminds us that Harry Truman considered Pierce the best-looking of all U.S. Presidents, noting that Hawthorne would probably have agreed.[1] For Person, that Hawthorne wrote this campaign biography after *The Blithedale Romance* and its exploration of same-sex love and gender ambiguity is significant; Hawthorne, notes Person, evokes his gender-liminal male characters Ilbrahim and Own Warland in his depiction of Pierce at various points as "beautiful boy," "sweet," "delicate," "cordial," "soft." Person argues that "the delicate challenge for Hawthorne is marketing such a 'delightful' boy to the 'whole country'—to arouse desire for the 'boy' without transgressing normative boundaries of adult male relationships."[2] Person also helpfully alerts us to the anxious machismo of Pierce's political climate. He discusses a series of political cartoons that depict Pierce in an inferior, unmanly position to his Whig opponent for the presidency, Winfield Scott.

> Finally, in a coup de grace, Pierce and Winfield Scott appear together, with Pierce riding a goose and Scott riding a gamecock. "What's the matter, Pierce?" the caption reads, "feel faint? Ha! Ha! Ha! Lord what a 'goose!' Don't you wish you had my 'Cock?'" Political attacks on a candidate's manhood do not get more political than that.[3]

Though I will not have the opportunity to explore *The Life of Franklin Pierce* further in this book, it is instructive to consider this largely overlooked work as yet another example of Hawthorne's interest in gender liminality, perhaps especially in males, within a context of masculinist standards of gender that emphasized, in the Jacksonian era and beyond, competitiveness, self-sufficiency, and a lockdown on feeling, while also confusingly insisting that men as well as women feel "properly." Homoerotic explorations of male sexuality were especially challenging in this era of homoeroticized homophobia (a description one could apply to all subsequent eras of American life, of course). Moreover, Hawthorne's love for Pierce, with its homoerotic overtones (emphasized by the fact that both men were exceptionally attractive), suffuses his evocation of Pierce's physical appeal, one that sometimes daringly blurs gendered lines. The gentle boy who endures within adult men solicits

Hawthorne's imaginative engagement, leading him to draw out the phantom presence of the feminine boy within his depictions of adult men, who are often youthful. But this phantom presence also provokes fear and even horror. Thinking through the forces that shaped and the implications suggested by this simultaneous desire and repulsion in Hawthorne's depictions of masculinity will be the chief aim of this chapter, in which I move from personal and cultural contexts to psychoanalytic theories of narcissism, shame, vision, and the "fear of looking."

PERSONAL BEAUTY

Though biographical readings are not without their dangers, in Hawthorne's case some elements of his personal history seem not only relevant to his work's central themes but indistinguishable from them, the sources of shame in his life and work chief among them. As an author whose sex appeal became a legendary aspect of his celebrity, Hawthorne could be called the American Byron, though in this regard he certainly pales in comparison to his Romantic predecessor, not only famously handsome but also sexually infamous, linked in his lifetime to both homosexuality and incest.[4] Yet references to Hawthorne's beauty on the part of both female and male commentators recur throughout myriad accounts of him and convey an atmosphere of heightened awareness of beauty as part of the Hawthorne package. His son Julian Hawthorne's description of him, synecdochic of many such appraisals, is perhaps the most sustained:

> He was the handsomest young man of his day . . . His limbs were beautifully formed, and the moulding of his neck and throat was as fine as anything in antique sculpture. His hair, which had a long, curving wave in it, approached blackness in color; his head was large and grandly developed; his eyebrows were dark and heavy, with a superb arch and space beneath. His nose was straight, but the contour of his chin was Roman. . . . His eyes were large, dark, blue, and brilliant, and full of varied expression.[5]

There's a good deal more to this lengthy description, including the tale (most probably apocryphal, but no less suggestive for being that) of an old gypsy woman stopping the young Hawthorne in the forest to ask whether he were "a man or an angel," for seldom was a man so beautiful.[6] Hawthorne's physical beauty is another dimension of the unsettling of gendered norms presented for many people by his writing; it physically evinced the same qualities inherent in his "gentle," "sweet" literary efforts, which many assumed had to be written by a woman. Given the transformation of American masculinity in the Jacksonian era, with its enforcement of codes of frontier toughness and policing of effeminacy, is it possible that Hawthorne's notorious shyness resulted from his anticipation of being a magnet for the eye of the spectator?

If we recall from chapter 2 the incidents of Hawthorne's experience of the desiring gaze noted by both George Lathrop and Henry James, this would have been an anticipation corroborated by frequent and predictable favorable response. These responses could be experienced as pleasurable, a filling up of the libidinal tanks, and therefore no mean achievement for the self-critical Hawthorne. But they would also have been threatening, a public exposure of his own socially unstable gendered identity. I speculate that Hawthorne used writing to negotiate anxieties about his own personal appearance and its incitement of the gaze, anxieties that are one node in a network of far broader, related social and cultural ones. Writing also allowed him to negotiate a wide range of responses to beauty in both women and other men, and in himself.

"The self-doubts, the uncertainty, the sense that even his best gifts were not entirely admirable did little to enhance Hawthorne's confidence in his own masculinity," writes Gloria Erlich in her psychobiographical study of the author.[7] Hawthorne's gendered intermixture was both deeply appealing and vexing for many, including himself. Moreover, male beauty, to the extent that it was thought to effeminate manhood, would have been a quality Jacksonian America deemed decadent.[8] Given Hawthorne's conflictual, simultaneous embrace of his feminine qualities and the very codes of Jacksonian toughness that routed them out, the recognition of his own beauty may have triggered in him the antithetical yet entirely coexistive responses of pleasure and scorn at male beauty that also characterize the fictions.

Hawthorne's physical description of Robin Molineux—his "brown, curly hair, well-shaped features, and bright, cheerful eyes, were nature's gifts" (11: 209)—is remarkably similar to that given by his lifelong friend Horatio Bridge of the young Hawthorne himself. As Bridge described the Hawthorne he knew as a classmate and chum at Bowdoin College in the 1820s, "Hawthorne was a slender lad, having a massive head, with dark, brilliant, and most expressive eyes, heavy eyebrows, and a profusion of dark hair."[9]

Richard Millington's splendid 2011 Norton Critical Edition of Nathaniel Hawthorne's 1852 *The Blithedale Romance* includes several new supplementary materials.[10] One of the freshest and most telling of these is the excerpt from an essay by Ora Gannett Sedgwick, who lived at Brook Farm when she was a teenager. (Brook Farm, which lasted from 1841 to 1847, was a utopian experiment in communal and self-sustaining living that took place in West Roxbury, near Boston. Hawthorne participated in this experiment, famously failing to recoup his financial investment in the project; despite his demurrals, Hawthorne clearly draws on his experiences there in *Blithedale*.) "A Girl of Sixteen at Brook Farm," which Sedgwick published in the *Atlantic Monthly* in 1900, contains several highly interesting firsthand impressions of the real-life Hawthorne, whom the shrewdly observant Sedgwick presents as simultaneously enigmatic and slyly knowing, aloof and genially playful. Her delightful and oddly poignant portrait of Hawthorne confirms the sense that develops in other accounts of Hawthorne as someone who maintained a certain social distance but was also capable of being wooed into sociality (no doubt a quality that appealed to Herman Melville, whose own efforts to woo Hawthorne into intimate friendship are not only a legendary antebellum myth but also widely considered a crucial biographical intertext for *Blithedale*).

Sedgwick adds to the widely documented portrait of Hawthorne as physically arresting:

> One evening he was alone in the hall, sitting on a chair at the farther end, when my roommate, Ellen Slade, and myself were going upstairs. She whispered to me, "Let's throw the sofa pillows at Mr. Hawthorne." Reaching over the banisters, we each took a cushion and threw it. Quick as a flash he put out his hand, seized a broom that was hanging near him, warded off our cushions, and threw them back with sure aim. . . . Through it all not a word was spoken. We laughed and laughed, and his eyes shone and twinkled like stars. Wonderful eyes they were, and when anything witty was said I always looked quickly at Mr. Hawthorne; for his dark eyes lighted up as if flames were suddenly kindled behind them, and then the smile came down to his lips and over his grave face.[11]

Whether it was his dark good looks, the starry shine in his eyes, or simply his very imperturbability, Hawthorne seemed to provoke the attention of others, and their desire to provoke him. Throwing the pillows at Hawthorne, it would appear, was a means for these girls to express their own increasing fascination with this unusual older man, but their impudence also appears to have appealed to Hawthorne. One wonders if he saw in their antic enthusiasm something of the charm that Coverdale reports that he sees in Priscilla, who nevertheless remains one of Hawthorne's most pallid creations (though pointedly so, I think). The ways in which Hawthorne's enigmatic, aloof, reserved beauty provoked the troublesome and tantalizing desires of others, especially young women and other men, while also leading Hawthorne to attempt to control and manage not only these provoked desires but also his own responses to them, which ranged from fear to revulsion to pleasure—these dynamics inform his fiction repeatedly and with increasing intensity.

THE WRETCHED SIMULACRUM
SIGHT AND SELF

If we take Horatio Bridge's description as an accurate one, Hawthorne gives characters such as Robin versions of his own physical traits. He makes sure that we understand that they are beautiful. But he also makes us understand that they are just as morally dim. Beatrice Rappaccini's question to handsome and callow Giovanni goes to the heart of the matter: "O, was there not, from the first, more poison in thy nature than in mine?" (10: 91). Given the moral ambiguity that recurs in Hawthorne's young men along with their beauty, we can posit that they reflect not only Hawthorne's own self-awareness of his attractiveness and his investment in it, an investment that would be the natural result of the constant recognition of his own beauty that Hawthorne experienced throughout his life, even into his later years (in which it admittedly underwent a significant erosion), but also a skeptical view of this surface attractiveness. (That the cult of Hawthorne's handsomeness continues to thrive is amply reflected in the "Hawthorne is a Hottie" T-shirts on sale in gift shops in Concord, Massachusetts, and elsewhere.)

I argue further that Hawthorne's responses to the young men he created went beyond moral skepticism. He views the beautiful young man with an empathetic fearfulness at the power of the gaze—not an avaricious desire to wield it but rather a desire to avoid falling under it.[12] As "My Kinsman, Major Molineux" reveals, for Hawthorne narcissism is a welter of anxieties that revolve around the figure of the young man, anxieties that become especially intense if the young man is also pleasing visually. The disjunct between exterior and interior self Hawthorne consistently thematizes extends the Narcissus myth and its phobic, cautionary associations with the disparity between surface and depth. Hawthorne further intensifies the implications of the Narcissus theme by combining it with his ongoing concern with vision. This concern leads, in turn, to Hawthorne's development of *shame*. Shame is a crucial component of Hawthorne's work, perhaps because it is the affect that he chiefly associates with vision, the sense he most exhaustively examines in all of its psychological and aesthetic complexity. The shame that proceeds in Hawthorne from vision relates, in my view, to the gendered anxieties at work in the Narcissus myth, which renders vision such a vexed and troubling phenomenon. Vision in Hawthorne can signify either shame or an attempt at sadistic visual mastery, such as, if we follow Freud, voyeurism and other forms of visual violation. In the figure of the young man, Hawthorne collapses shameful and sadistic forms of looking: the young man experiences shame at both looking and being looked at, but also sadistically exerts power over the other characters through his eyes.

Hawthorne's work abounds with sight metaphors and visual media—paintings, portraits, mirrors, miniatures, sculptures, carvings—and with lookers, most often ambiguous male figures, whose desire to see others invasively crosses the line into voyeurism. In addition to those already mentioned, such figures include the titular protagonist of "Wakefield," who installs himself as a perpetual watcher of his own life in his absence; Chillingworth, who spies on Dimmesdale, just as Coverdale spies on his fellow Blithedalers from his "inviolate bower" up in a tree; and the Model, who spies on Miriam in *The Marble Faun*. These fictional males participate in voyeuristic schemes that are illuminated by Mulvey's theory of the male gaze, in which she argues that the male protagonist in classical Hollywood cinema dominates the woman through vision, either voyeuristically (investigating the woman and solving her mystery) or fetishistically (breaking her up into idealized components, eyes, faces, and so forth) Moreover, Mulvey argues that the spectator, also gendered male, joins in with the screen protagonist in a shared experience of narcissistic omnipotence.

Yet in Hawthorne's work the male figure, as we have discovered, is as likely to be the object of the gaze as its subject—for example, spying on Beatrice Rappaccini, Giovanni Guasconti fails to realize that he himself is the object of her scientist father's spying eyes, as well as Baglioni's, Rappaccini's rival in more ways than one. Moreover, the *sight* of the male, perhaps especially when he is a handsome figure, causes pain. When the heroine Ellen Langton first gazes at Fanshawe, the doomed, young titular protagonist of Hawthorne's first novel, the "result of her scrutiny [is] favorable, yet very painful" (3: 346). When his fiancée, Elizabeth, finally as overcome by the maddening horror of the black veil as the agitated townspeople in one of Hawthorne's most famous tales, stops to give one last look at his darkly obscured form, Minister Hooper mournfully asks her, "And do you feel it then at last?" (9: 47). The question urgently communicates the gendered and perceptual anxieties Hawthorne fuses in his representation of masculinity. In the midst of hellish visions in the nighttime forest of Satanic seduction, visions that strip away the false appearances of his seemingly pious but secretly evil townspeople, Young Goodman Brown must acknowledge that "he was himself the chief horror of the scene" (10: 83). Learning of the horrifying hypocrisy of *others* seems to trigger in Brown a much deeper revulsion toward him*self*, as if they function as outward manifestations of his own depravity. Brown's recognition reveals the essential conflict at the core of Hawthorne's representation of masculinity, a conflict between the self and itself that is then endlessly outwardly projected to all social relations. For Hawthorne, anti-relation begins with the self; self-regard generates anxiety and dread; and vision is inherently painful and wounding, indicative of the problematic nature of male sexuality.

Psychoanalytic theory helps us to develop a richer understanding of these patterns in Hawthorne's fiction, its tripartite monster of narcissism, shame, and tormenting sight. Shame has come to be a key topic in psychoanalytic Hawthorne studies. Joseph Adamson has written eloquently on the subject, and Benjamin Kilborne's essay "Shame Conflicts and Tragedy in *The Scarlet Letter*" admirably illustrates the multivalent levels on which shame informs this novel. Clearly, I am in agreement that shame is of great importance to Hawthorne's work, in which so many characters must endure the tyranny of another's, or several others', vision. Following Andrew Morrison, however, I see shame as "the underside of narcissism," a component of it. Shame stems from what I term the *narcissistic crisis* at the heart of Hawthorne's fiction, in which young men endlessly confront the desiring looks of others. These visual intrusions intersect painfully with the young man's opposing and equally fervent desires to see and not to *be* seen. As I develop below, Hawthorne's works foreground the fear of looking, or, to use the psychoanalytic term, *scopophobia*.

Narcissism functions in Hawthorne as a crisis on several levels. Being looked at, held by the mastery of another's vision, threatens normative masculine identity because it puts the male in the feminized passive position of not only being under another's power but also of being the object of the look. Looking at oneself, especially if that self-regard provokes pleasurable feelings, crosses the lines of seemly gendered identity and moral standing at once, in that to look desiringly at oneself suggests, on the one hand, either a regressive sexual preoccupation with one's own body or a sexual interest in one's own gender, and, on the other hand, pride, one of the seven deadly sins, and its synonym, vanity. Both of these highly charged signs of the self run amok were culturally scorned in Hawthorne's era, and hardly in his era alone.

Historically, the Narcissus-like male has been considered the effeminate male. "We find," writes Shadi Bartsch in her study *The Mirror of the Self*, "the self-indulgent male gaze demonstrated in artistic representations of Narcissus, who, as he gazes winsomely at his image in the water in" several classical representations "sprouts small but feminine breasts."[13] Hawthorne falls within the continuum of representations of Narcissus as effeminated that extends to Freudian psychoanalytic paradigms of narcissism as principally characteristic of female sexuality. In this regard, Freud follows longstanding tradition. "One of the major motifs through which [the] construction of the feminine has been transmitted in art is the woman holding, or standing in front of, a mirror. What happens to gender identity—and to cultural authority—" asks Thaïs E. Morgan, "when a man poses before and looks at himself in a mirror"?[14]

Sarah Rose Cole writes that in Thackeray's novel *Vanity Fair*, a relevant Victorian intertext for Hawthorne, the "most obvious provocation offered by male vanity is the transgression of gender boundaries; the very act of coupling the words 'male' and 'vanity' implies a gender reversal, 'turn[ing] the tables' on the stereotype of female vanity."[15] For Cole, Thackeray plays with gender stereotypes as a means of negotiating class anxieties. Considering the character of Captain George Osborne, whom she describes as "that paragon of military glamour," Cole writes that "his apparently happy self-objectification—his concentration on his own remarkable good looks—takes on an anxious, even desperate quality when he solicits the gaze that is supposed to certify his class status."[16]

Hawthorne deepens these themes, reaching a level of feeling that far exceeds any specific kind of anxiety—or, to put it another way, that questions the very meaning of identity, which cannot be distinguished from appearances.[17] For example, when his character Feathertop—literally a construction of masculinity, having been assembled from random scraps by the witch Mother Rigby—presents himself as a dandified nobleman and solicits the gaze of the girl he attempts to woo, Hawthorne creates an arresting scene of visual desire with implications for female as well as male sexuality.

> By and by, Feathertop paused, and throwing himself into an imposing attitude, seemed to summon the fair girl to survey his figure, and resist him longer, if she could. His star, his embroidery, his buckles, glowed, at that instant, with unutterable splendor . . . The maiden raised her eyes, and suffered them to linger upon her companion with a bashful and admiring gaze. Then, as if desirous of judging what her own simple comeliness might have, side by side with so much brilliancy, she cast a glance towards the full-length looking-glass, in front of which they happened to be standing. It was one of the truest plates in the world, and incapable of flattery. No sooner did the images, therein reflected, meet Polly's gaze, then she

shrieked, shrank from the stranger's side, gazed at him, for a moment, in the wildest dismay, and sank insensible upon the floor.

What impels Polly Gookin's solicited gaze is a desire to survey her *own* attractiveness as much as Feathertop's apparently splendid figure: his narcissism and self-objectification goads her own, though hers is more tentatively sought. His own gaze solicited by the gaze *he* solicited in Polly, Feathertop follows the track of Polly's vision and also looks into the mirror. What he sees in the mirror—here not a deceptive surface but a properly cleansed door of perception—is not the "glittering mockery of his outside show, but a picture of the sordid patchwork of his real composition, stript of all witchcraft" (10: 243–44).

"The wretched simulacrum!" the narrator laments. "We almost pity him." In a vivid depiction of male anguish with an undertone of dark comedy that deepens the anguish, Hawthorne describes Feathertop's reaction to his own image: "He threw up his arms, with an expression of despair, that went farther than any of his previous manifestations, towards vindicating his claims to be reckoned human. For perchance the only time, since this so often empty and deceptive life of mortals began its course, an Illusion had seen and fully recognized itself" (10: 244). Feathertop's self-recognition exemplifies such encounters in Hawthorne, in which self-perception is fraught with danger and filled with despair. But even if it is in no way redemptive, this experience also defines the human, as it does for Feathertop, whose anguish vindicates his humanity. If looking at oneself causes disturbance, a psychic torment with physical manifestations, what does that say about the self that regards itself—what levels of self-disgust or personal awareness of moral turpitude make the experience of self-regard so loathsome? Can looking at the self lead to self-knowledge, or does it, as in the writings of the Latin Stoic philosopher Seneca, actually function as "an impediment to self-knowledge"?[18]

In Ovid's version of the Narcissus myth, the seer Tiresias cautions that Narcissus will be happy so long as he *never knows himself.* In the myth, to know oneself is to *see* oneself, to recognize that the person one desires is, in fact, an image of oneself. In the myth, this recognition does nothing to reduce the maddening nature of Narcissus's absurd and heartbreaking predicament. In Hawthorne, the sight of one's self provokes deep anxiety, if not horror. As Shernaz Mollinger wrote in a 1983 study of narcissism in Hawthorne and Emerson, "When Ethan Brand sees in himself the sin that he has been looking diligently for in everyone else, he kills himself." As Mollinger concludes, "the underlying self is experienced as overwhelmingly negative—

wretched, sinful, mean, and empty."[19] Yet the paradox here is that very often this cataclysmic revelation of the ugly actual self occurs *within* the spectacle of male beauty. One of the questions demanded by the fusion of ugly depth and beautiful surface—the formula for so many cautionary narcissistic tales, from Ovid to Wilde's *Portrait of Dorian Gray* to Anthony Minghella's film version of Patricia Highsmith's novel *The Talented Mr. Ripley* (1999)—is why it mattered so much to Hawthorne. If in the Narcissus myth self-recognition is self-knowledge, but a self-knowledge that brings one neither relief nor sexual fulfillment, in Hawthorne the Narcissus theme conveys the ambiguity of identity and of desire as well as the terrifying potentialities of both.

Hawthorne's males maintain an attitude of deflection, the chief components of which are averted vision (refusing the eye of others, deferring any encounter with the gaze) and a demurral of physical authority (an abashed, circumspect stance, a bent gait). They refuse or forfeit conventionally masculine attitudes: directness, forthrightness, boldness, in other words, the hallmarks of male authority. Abashed male attitudes form a pattern that extends into Hawthorne's late work, as this description of Septimius Felton evinces: "As for Septimius, let him alone a moment or two, and then you would see him, with his head bent down, brooding, brooding, with his eyes fixed on some chip, some stone, some common plant, any commonest thing, as if it were the clue and index to some mystery; and when, by chance startled out of these meditations, he lifted his eyes, there would be a kind of perplexity, a dissatisfied, wild look in them, as if, of his speculations, he found no end" (8: 6). This attitude of deflection is, I argue, a manifestation of the shame that informs Hawthorne's narcissistically drawn male characters. (In *Septimius Felton,* as I discuss in the last chapter, this shame is tied to anxieties over racial identity.) Cynosures of desire, they deflect, avoid, elude, and refuse the appetites of the eye they have themselves incited.

The deceptively light-hearted "Little Annie's Ramble" (1835) is no longer a well-known story but, as Jane Tompkins points out, was one of the most critically acclaimed of the author's own day.[20] Despite its frolicsome tone, it is a tale of a young man who abducts a little girl in order to take her on that titular ramble. Hawthorne depicts the first-person narrator as a man who "walks in black attire, with a measured step, and a heavy brow, and his *thoughtful eyes bent down,*" here alongside "a gay little girl." The pedophilic relationship suggested in this story is deeply unsettling. What makes Hawthorne's depiction of the narrator particularly jarring is that he assumes these attitudes of submission, but is nevertheless in a position of undeniable masculine dominance. In the famous story "The Minister's Black Veil" (1837), "good Mr. Hooper walk[s] onward" through the gathering crowd gawking at his appearance, "at a slow and quiet pace, *stooping somewhat and looking on the ground*" (my emphasis, 9: 38). As will be increasingly clear, these attitudes of abashed masculinity relate, at once, to an alienation from the conventional codes of heteromasculinity—embodied in Hawthorne's work by characters such as the rival who gets the girl in "The Artist of the Beautiful," the pitiless father of the crying boy in "Ethan Brand," and the most conventional aspects of Hollingsworth in *The Blithedale Romance*—and an ambivalence over heterosexual relationships generally.

In life, Hawthorne himself wore "conservative garb," "a long black jacket, shawl-colored vest, and a black silk bow-tied stock worn with a high-collared white shirt," evincing both his frugality and his propriety. Not only the darkness of his clothing but his "indifference to style" (he requested a friend to buy him "stout dark" cloth from a "cheap clothing establishment") may have signaled Hawthorne's desire to deflect attention from his appearance.[21] Wearing Hawthorne's own customary attire, these dubious young men avert their eyes from the gaze in a manner also reminiscent of the author's. As Horatio Bridge describes Hawthorne's deportment, "Hawthorne's figure was somewhat singular, owing to his carrying his head a little on one side; but his walk was square and firm, and his manner self-respecting and reserved."[22] The anxious conjunctive reassurance of Bridge's "but" may reveal a truth about Hawthorne's relationship to looking: the singular quality of the way Hawthorne looked, keeping his head to one side, troubles Bridge to the extent that he must reassure us that Hawthorne walked with and maintained an air of personal dignity and manliness ("square and firm"). Something slightly abashed—feminine—in Hawthorne's deportment caused, to whatever extent, alarm. The possibility that Hawthorne anticipated his ability to incite the gaze and that this anticipation—and the results that confirmed it, as so many favorable accounts of Hawthorne's appearance attest—caused Hawthorne alarm and discomfort, leading him to protect himself against the looks of others, but also a certain degree of pleasurable self-fascination, finds textual support in his work, which also suggests that he possessed an awareness of the visual compulsions he promoted. Given the moral ambiguity that recurs in Hawthorne's young men along with their beauty, we can speculate that they reflect Hawthorne's own self-awareness of his attractiveness and his investment in it, an investment that would be the natural result of the constant recognition of his own beauty that Hawthorne experienced throughout his life, even into his later years (in which it underwent a significant erosion).

All of these thematic fictional concerns as well as elements of Hawthorne's own life and the ways he was perceived by others have a relevance for the larger question of masculinity and what haunts it, homosexuality, and what haunts homosexuality and masculinity both, homophobia. Hawthorne lived the bulk of his adult life as a man married to a woman with whom he had children, and certainly there is little evidence to suggest that he did all of this under duress at the level of sexual premise. I make no claim about Hawthorne's sexuality in terms of same-sex desire. The claim I do make is that narcissism was a way for Hawthorne to negotiate whatever sexual interests he had and in whatever capacity. The concepts of sexuality and sexual desire in Hawthorne's own cultural era were undeniably distinct from our own; we are no longer dominated, for instance, by a pervasive anxiety about the destructive effects of onanism. Yet, in my view, overlaps do exist between the antebellum period and our own era in terms of sexual matters. In particular, Jacksonian ideologies of gender—man-on-the-make male aggressiveness and self-reliance; the ideal of "true womanhood"; an abhorrence of weakness in men and toughness in women—have lost little of their binding power, though a great deal of their presumed accuracy. Hawthorne's depiction of a shame-informed, narcissistic masculinity has deep relevance for the study of American masculinity, for homosexuality, and for homophobia, which Hawthorne's critical view of normative masculinity can greatly assist us in dismantling.

As T. Walter Herbert observes,

> Homophobia imagines that men animated by same-sex desire are themselves not "real men," but embody an opposite of manhood all the more loathsome because secretly alluring. Hawthorne himself was prominently characterized by such "non-manly" traits. His notable shyness and preference for solitude resulted in good measure from that fact that his emotional life, like that of Arthur Dimmesdale, was exceptionally turbulent, so that he found routine interactions difficult. Talking to Hawthorne, said his college friend Henry Wadsworth Longfellow, was "like talking to a woman."
>
> Hawthorne was also a man of extraordinary physical beauty, who was well aware—and uneasily aware—of awakening sexual desire, both in women and in men. Even if Hawthorne had not been artistically inclined, to say nothing of leading the life of a writer, his familiar social relations would have made his manhood "suspect." The factors that converged to give Hawthorne a "feminine" identity had a paradoxical result: they led him to insist all the more compulsively on his commitment to the conventional ideal of masculine self direction.[23]

Though in agreement with Herbert here generally, I demur on one point: while certainly it is true that in life Hawthorne did insist on proclaiming his allegiance to such commitments, it is also true that his work, far from promoting this allegiance, actively, consistently, emphatically, movingly, angrily contests it. While there were many aspects of Hawthorne's own life and personal views that demonstrate a commitment to the conservative values that found outward form in conventional, female-phobic, queer-phobic masculinity, it is also true that his work evinces a remarkable capacity for empathy for shunned sexual others as well as a penchant for stringent analysis of the foundations of masculinist power. In this respect, Hawthorne's work makes for an interesting point of comparison with Martha Nussbaum's, equally committed to a study of the effects of shaming, especially in public form, on abnegated others, emotions, and bodies.[24]

Moreover, in his book *Devils and Rebels: The Making of Hawthorne's Damned Politics*, Larry J. Reynolds has also done a salutary job of reframing the personal Hawthorne's dispositions toward the political issues of his time—which we generally view as ideologically suspect today—as an unconventional, if often misguided, pacifist politics. Indeed, the term that most of Hawthorne's critics most frequently employ when disparaging his politics, "passivity," emerges in Reynolds as a valiant attribute of this pacifism. Admirably, Reynolds does not overlook the racism in Hawthorne's views, but in his reframing of pacifism and passivity in Hawthorne, he does a heroic job of restoring proper cultural contexts to Hawthorne's thought while alerting readers to the gender biases of their own critiques, such as the easy recourse to passivity as a term of abuse in criticism since the late 1980s.[25]

I would argue that Hawthorne's passivity is an aspect of the shame he incorporates into his depictions of masculinity. (If Reynolds's astute work has a weakness, it is his insufficient attention to matters of gender and sexuality that impinge directly on his project.) Hawthorne's passivity is a response to many things, such as the activist furor he abhorred in abolitionist campaigns against slavery; I would argue it was also his attitude toward the Judge Pyncheons of the world, males in power who exert their wills upon the less fortunate, including those whose gendered performance was seen as faltering, not fully realized, suspect, much like Hawthorne's own at times (he did, it should be noted, always have his champions). Passivity in Hawthorne's case is a political stance *derived* from shame, though distinct from it; if shame is the result of social relations that have proven injurious, passivity can be seen as an attempt to keep potentially injurious social relations—such as those between Hawthorne and New England abolitionists, many of whom were eager for a direct confrontation with a man whose views infuriated them—at bay. Which is to say that shame—the product of relation, the sign of social relation's impact on the individual—

when reformulated as passivity can have a surprisingly useful capacity as self-protection.

EYES OF SHAME
FREUDIAN THEORIES OF VISION AND THE FEAR OF LOOKING

Despite the undeniable difficulties presented by Freud's treatment of the subject, difficulties to which we attend throughout this book, the psychoanalytic thinking on narcissism that I have found to be most suggestive for reconsideration of Hawthorne's writing proceeds directly from Freud. Theoretical treatments that, expanding and revising Freudian paradigms, link narcissism to shame and drive theory, specifically the focus on, in Léon Wurmser's description, "the two major sexual drives of exhibitionism and *Schaulust,* the wish to look (curiosity, voyeurism, or—using the Greek word stem *scop-* for 'spying, watching'—scopophilia),"[26] shed especially illuminating light on Hawthorne's gendered themes and visual sensibility. Hawthorne shares with other Romantic authors such as "Wordsworth, Coleridge, and Keats" (and I would add Shelley) "an abnormal fascination with and fear of the eye as an instrument of public self-confirmation and definition."[27]

At this point, we should refine our understanding of the role shame plays within Hawthorne's narcissism. In his study of shame in Hawthorne's work, Joseph Adamson writes of what is perhaps the "ultimate wish of all human beings perhaps: to be recognized for what one is, by a loving eye from which the need to hide or cover oneself, with all of one's flaws or defects, imagined or otherwise, is absent, without the fear of judgment or shame. . . . One of the signs of psychological and emotional health is to be capable of intimacy, and one of Hawthorne's central themes is the barrier that shame puts up between the self and the other, thus estranging us not only from other human beings, but from our genuine selves."[28] In Hawthorne, this barrier of shame becomes the extruded essence of his characters—their black veils, black clothing, slow and ponderous gait, circumspection, and distrustful looks.

As Andrew Morrison has described it, shame is the "underside of narcissism."[29] In a valuable study that considers numerous psychoanalytic treatments of both concepts, Morrison, noting the lack of consensus about the nature of the relationship between shame and narcissism, points out that while some "maintain that shame functions ultimately to remind the self of its failure to meet perfectionistic demands for worthiness to attain fantasied merger with its" ego ideal, others view shame as "a response to the wish for merger itself": if what the self wants is autonomy, separateness, independence, "any suggestion that it falls short," through a dependence on others, a dependence experienced as regressive, "generates shame. 'To need,' itself, is frequently experienced as shameful."[30] Intervening in these debates, Morrison suggests "that both of these positions are correct—that there is an ongoing, tension-generating dialectic between narcissistic grandiosity and desire for perfection. . . . Thus, shame and narcissism inform each other, as the self is experienced, first, alone, separate, and small, and, again, grandiosely, striving to be perfect and reunited with its ideal."[31]

Léon Wurmser argues that the "perceptual functions affected by shame are predominantly visual": the drives to look (*scopophilia*) and to be seen (*exhibitionism*).[32] The "combination of aggression and libido in these component drives manifests itself particularly and most typically in [a] power struggle" alternately marked by "feelings of powerlessness, helplessness, and passivity or a triumphant sense of power or at least of mastery."[33] Wurmser expands here on Freud's influential and provocative theorization of the roles of these component drives in sexual desire in his *Three Essays on the Theory of Sexuality*, which Freud wrote in 1905 but continued to expand until 1924. Freud observed that infantile sexuality "from the very first involves other people as sexual objects." Scopophilia, exhibitionism, and cruelty, linked "instincts," dominate the early lives of children, who exhibit a great "satisfaction" in exhibiting their own bodies before others. Children can revel in both exhibitionism and in acts of cruelty because they do not yet experience shame (SE 7: 157–60).

As a fraught, resistant object of this gaze who nevertheless perpetually solicits it, and as a textual figure who experiences traumatic pain within spectacles of seeing and being seen, the male of Hawthorne's fiction represents neither scopophilia nor exhibitionism but, most consistently, a psychic response that fuses them: *scopophobia*, or the fear of looking or being looked at. Considering the ways in which this densely complex fear may inspire creativity, David W. Allen theorizes that it may have root causes in "hidden emotional injuries, such as early object loss, with consequent attempts to repair the ruptured union."[34] Allen emphasizes that "the attempt at repair of self-image or repair of the lost relationship takes place within the looking-showing modalities. The repair of the self-image also involves an attempt at repair of the image being exhibited to others. 'You see that I am all right or worthwhile' is an unconscious step in the progression to 'I see that I am all right and unimpaired.'"[35] If we consider Hawthorne's depiction of masculinity as both scopophobic and scopophilic in nature, we can theorize that the intertwined conflicts of narcissistic self-valuing, male beauty, and anguished seeing in his work emerge from a project of self-repair with no attainable success, only capable of producing, at most, a partial, momentary respite from anxiety, and that all of these efforts are heightened and rendered more arduous by the equally incessant desire to look while avoiding being seen—precisely Coverdale's conflictual aim in *The Blithedale Romance*.

In Hawthorne's work, the desire to see and be seen is concomitant with a fervent desire to avoid being seen, either by the self or another person. In every way, desire is balked; whichever way the eyes turn, they seize upon a prohibited, unsatisfactory, or retributively assaultive vision. The self seeking to know and to fulfill itself through the eye is itself subsumed by the power of the other's eye; the self enthralled by self is also subject to the thralldom of the other's gaze, with potentially disastrous consequences and even murderous intent. The traumatic narcissism of Hawthorne's male characters enmeshes them in the gears of their own desires but also those of the other characters. Drawn to others whom they watch, they primarily crave the sight of their own image, powerfully alluring but also potentially deeply dangerous. For all encounters with looking, whether from the position of one's own desire or from that of the other, are profoundly fraught, linked to the potential annihilation of the self and the crucial divide between self and other.

Scopophobia informs several aspects of Hawthorne's fiction. Though not Hawthorne's most famous work, the "Oberon" stories are among Hawthorne's most explicitly autobiographical (Oberon was the nickname Hawthorne used in his post-college correspondence with Horatio Bridge), and they provide telling insights into some of Hawthorne's concerns about himself as an author, his appearance, and his appearance *as* an author.[36] In "Fragments from the Journal of a Solitary Man" (1837), the faithful friend (suggestive of Bridge) who reads, with mingled feelings of interest and guilt, the dead Oberon's journal comes across this record of one of Oberon's dreams:

> "I dreamed that one bright forenoon I was walking through Broadway. . . . By degrees, too, I perceived myself the object of universal attention, and, as it seemed, of horror and affright. Every face grew pale; the laugh was hushed, and the voices died away in broken syllables; the people in the shops crowded to the doors with a ghastly stare, and the passengers on all sides fled as from an embodied pestilence. The horses reared and snorted. An old beggar woman sat before St. Paul's church, with her withered palm stretched out to all, but drew it back from me, and pointed to the graves and monuments in that populous church-yard. Three lovely girls, whom I had formerly known, ran shrieking across the street. A personage in black, whom I was about to overtake, suddenly turned his head,

and showed the features of a long-lost friend. He gave me a look of horror and was gone."

Oberon then notes that he stopped moving and "threw my eyes on a looking-glass . . . *At the first glimpse of my own figure I awoke, with a horrible sensation of self-terror and self-loathing.*" Little wonder, Oberon notes, that he caused the town to flee in fright: "I had been promenading Broadway in my shroud!" (my emphasis, 11: 317–18).

Hawthorne extends the shock effect of this Poe-like ejaculation for the duration of "The Minister's Black Veil," in which the enshrouded minister of a Puritan-era New England town provokes fear and wonder, "just by hiding his face." "The Minister's Black Veil," a voluminously critiqued story, might seem an odd example of narcissistic themes. After all, its protagonist veils his face, not wanting his face ever again to be seen on earth, and succeeds at his goal, though not without cost. Yet this story perhaps most resonantly communicates the anguished heart of Hawthorne's visual and sexual themes. "The veil is the type and symbol of the fact that all signs are potentially unreadable, or that the reading of them is unverifiable," writes J. Hillis Miller.[37] The veil exposes and thematizes the hermeneutical problem of reading: "In order to demystify, 'unmask,' I must forget that I am using as the 'tool' of unmasking the thing I am unmasking, the trope of personification." The story foregrounds the "stubborn presupposition that behind every mask there is a face, and behind every face, as behind every sign or configuration of signs, there is somewhere a personality, a self, a subject, a transcendental ego."[38]

Though I agree that the tale exposes our utter dependence on the "figure of prosopopeia," or personification, I would pull back from the philosophical broadness of Miller's eloquent reading and focus in on the specificity of the particular mask upon which the story fixates. "The Minister's Black Veil" certainly lends itself to many interpretations, but it is also quite simply a work about an ambiguous young man who decides to veil his face from his community and even from his "plighted wife." Much more adamantly than other Hawthorne characters, Hooper, both phobic site and cultic goad of the visual, refuses inclusion in the gaze by barring his face from others; but he thereby simultaneously makes himself a perpetual incitement *of* the gaze. Struck by the mask, the story's townspeople shudder and quake in Hooper's presence even as they endlessly peer at his cordoned-off visage. Even at the end of his life, Hooper adamantly fends off demands that he take off his veil, at last; his veil provokes an unending desire to see him unveiled. His refusal to take off the veil even on his deathbed—and even after death, as the narrator shudders to imagine his body rotting beneath his eternal veil—emerges as a strategy for control of the visual field, both acquiescence and resistance to the ravenous public glare.[39]

In the work this tale most closely prefigures, *The Scarlet Letter,* another young minister, his "tremulous" beauty vividly described, endures even more strenuous bouts with his own reflection, and his desirability as a visual object. Adulterer Arthur Dimmesdale's nightly self-flagellation rituals include terrifying encounters with a "looking-glass" in which he sees images that torment him. In one of the most famous episodes of the novel, Dimmesdale's exposed chest, upon which the dread titular symbol may or may not be engraved, emerges as a site of visual wonder for the villain, the cuckolded and vengeful old physician Roger Chillingworth.[40]

Other works also fuse visual ardor and dread within narcissistic self-mesmerization. In Hawthorne's final tale "Feathertop," discussed earlier in this chapter, a handsome young dandy, who is in reality nothing more than a heap of rubbish given the illusory appearance of a young man by Mother Rigby, a salty-tongued, salaciously lively old witch, enraptures a young woman with his apparently handsome form. But when this Adonis in feathers looks at himself in the mirror, initially as enraptured by the spectacle of his own beauty as she, he discovers the traumatic truth behind his sham surface handsomeness, almost literally crumbling at the sight of his revealed self. He discovers that, once it is shorn of artifice and nakedly revealed, his true self is unbearably hideous. "Feathertop" vividly depicts self-recognition as traumatic; I can think of no more acutely affecting depiction of spectrophobia, the fear of looking at oneself in the mirror, in literature. In *The Blithedale Romance,* which we examine closely in the next chapter, Coverdale finds the odious mesmerist Westervelt both the handsomest man he has ever seen and a humbug whose handsomeness hides a true and abiding ugliness. It is in *The Blithedale Romance* that the narcissistic gaze—in the form of voyeurism—most vividly emerges as a strategy for negotiating homoerotic feelings that verge on explosive crisis. The meeting between Coverdale and Westervelt indexes the homoerotic and homophobic themes linked throughout Hawthorne's work.

SELF-OVERSEEING

To make the sense of vision the central topic of our discussion of Hawthorne threatens to impose this most imperialistic of senses—imperialistic and often critiqued as such—on Hawthorne's work. That is certainly not my intention; rather, I am attempting to respond to the pervasive scenes of looking and being looked at, of vision enacted, that he makes central, and to think through their implications. There are numerous senses at work in Hawthorne (think of those overpoweringly odiferous flowers in "Rappaccini's Daughter," which are also such tactile objects; the resplendent visual beauty but also the tactility of Hester's embroidered A; the stone flesh of his faun). Nevertheless, it is the visual that is privileged. One of the effects Hawthorne derives from his privileging of the visual, in terms of his equally insistent preoccupation with masculinity, is that the visual becomes the key to male subjectivity, the rubric through which it makes sense of itself. If this claim has any validity, we have to acknowledge that men in Hawthorne don't like what they see. But more importantly, they learn something about themselves that they otherwise may not have—or, more properly, *we* learn something about them.

To begin with, we learn that men attempt to control others through their eyes. Men's eyes, however, betray them. Agents with the power to turn back the gaze upon the viewer, men's ocular organs reflect the inner darkness of men. At a wedding for a young couple, the black-veiled Minister Hooper catches "a glimpse of his own figure in the looking-glass," and when he does, "the black veil involved his own spirit in the horror with which it overwhelmed all others" (9: 43–44). What makes this scene chilling is that Hooper has, before his donning of the veil, been especially beloved for his shyly sweet presence at such gatherings. Now, he is an emblem of fear and a source of unease. A potential terror lurks within the genial and the unassuming; the veil is this potentiality made literal, tangible, visual.

Though Michael J. Colacurcio's approach is quite different from my own, his observation is apt: "The terrifying discovery, just as everywhere recorded and predicted, is that no human self will . . . bear very much looking into." Colacurcio links Hooper's traumatic self-encounter in the looking-glass to Puritan theology as it followed Saint Paul and what these theologians referred to as the "looking-glass of the law."[41] As I will have further occasion to discuss in the last chapter, this moment alerts us as well to the thematic of race that gains in intensity and preoccupation in Hawthorne's late work. Hawthorne's creation of a *dark white identity,* "ten times black," to wax Melvillean, in figures such as the black-veiled young man Hooper has relevance for masculinity and increasing relevance for race, especially in that this darkness connotes sexual anxiety and ambivalence, gender disturbance, and racial anxiety at once.[42]

In one of the most penetrating points he makes in *The Western Canon,* Harold Bloom, characteristically reading Freud through Shakespeare, observes, "When [Shakespeare's] characters change, or will themselves to change on self-overhearing, they prophesy the psychoanalytic situation in which patients are compelled to overhear themselves in the context of their transferences to their analysts."⁴³ I suggest that Hawthorne's males have the same gift for prophesy. They also possess the analogous potential to be self-over*seeing*. Just as Bloom's self-overhearing Shakespearean characters, such as Edmund in *King Lear,* do not often absorb the perceptions into their own conflicted psyches that they have themselves uttered but only do so on rare occasions of self-insightfulness, Hawthorne's males, catching on rare but piercing occasions the "true" sight of their own conflicted, divided, tormented natures, for a moment glimpse their interior darkness and confront the harrowing knowledge of their own fragility.

These shocks of self-recognition, however, occur infrequently and are actively avoided: "he never willingly passed before a mirror," the narrator tells us of Minister Hooper's subsequent strategies of avoidance, "lest . . . he should be affrighted by himself." Little wonder, then, that "love or sympathy could never reach him" (9: 48). The last time that his faithful though forever excluded fiancée Elizabeth saw Hooper was in "the comeliness of manhood"; implicitly, Hawthorne suggests, the sight of Hooper unveiled was enough to keep Elizabeth loyal to him (9: 51). This detail comes late in the story, but the confirmation of the male's beauty must be there, somewhere, like an artist's artfully camouflaged but always discoverable signature. (Similarly, very late in *The Blithedale Romance,* Zenobia calls Coverdale "much the handsomest man," and ruefully wonders why she didn't just take up with him instead of pursuing the emotionally unavailable Hollingsworth.) Hooper's self-veiling is the most extreme form of scopophobia in Hawthorne, but it is a strategy also marked by scopophilia, the ravenous desire to look. By donning the veil, Hooper paradoxically both deflects the gaze and endlessly incites it, one of the many predicaments of Hawthorne's visually obsessed and obsession-inducing men. Hooper's eerie, almost malevolent smile, a trope that attends the conclusion of his breakup scene with Elizabeth and other moments, suggests an erotic self-satisfaction in his refusal of the gaze, a desire to *be* seen which, in donning the veil, he has himself so skillfully incited and which his apparent self-camouflaging would appear so adamantly to negate.

HAWTHORNE'S VOYEURISM

If many of Hawthorne's males avoid the gaze, many of his males also attempt to wield it. Their ravenous looking leads not to self-confrontation but to more avid attempts to look at others, a voyeuristic quest that is, ironically, motivated by a hunger to see the self, albeit one that can never be acknowledged as such. Vision becomes an increasingly, even obsessively, important theme in Hawthorne's mature work. Though the visual preoccupations have many different implications and components, even thinking of them in terms of masculinity alone is revealing. The obsessive spying of "Rappaccini's Daughter" transforms into the onanistic voyeurism of *The Blithedale Romance;* the Narcissus-like young men of the tales transform into the once beautiful, now ruined Clifford of *The House of the Seven Gables,* a character who is a veritable index of traumatic narcissism in that his ruined beauty is linked to his failed promise, his having been entombed in a prison right at the moment of his blooming into adulthood (which continues the theme from *Fanshawe* onward of youthful male promise destroyed by blight[44]), his oppression by patriarchal power; moreover, the novel foregrounds an interest in the ethics of the visual (the Pyncheon portrait, uncannily lifelike, with its strange power to extend the patriarchal gaze; Holgrave's role as daguerreotypist, treated ambivalently). In *House of the Seven Gables,* Alice Pyncheon's startlingly speculative, desiring gaze at Matthew Maule unnerves his masculine subjectivity to the extent that he feels he must punish her, using his sorcerer's skills to turn her into a zombie and eventually destroying her, to his later horror. When the woman looks at male bodies, as she often does in Hawthorne, the results can be harrowing. *The Marble Faun* makes masculinity and the visual a central theme right from the first chapter, in which the titular sculpture is presented and discussed and the character of Donatello is depicted as both sexually desirable and as someone who conceals a visual wonder, his purportedly faunlike ears. The feral but feminized Donatello is the object of the collective gaze, threatened with exposure of his hidden attributes, whatever they may be. In his late, unfinished manuscripts, Hawthorne's career-long interest in a masculinity that blurs the lines of gender and sexuality expands to include increasingly urgent concerns over race, concerns implicitly present throughout Hawthorne but now made much more explicit. These topics will be the focus of the last chapter. As I will develop in chapter 7, Hawthorne's thematization of what I call "visual identity" reaches a new level of mature development in *The Marble Faun,* in which the narcissistic crisis in his work achieves a kind of closure. Hawthorne's responses to classical male beauty recorded in his French and Italian notebooks, specifically to the homoerotic cult icon Antinous, open up the question anew of Hawthorne's fundamentally conflicted relationship to male beauty.

Tied to male subjectivity, vision in Hawthorne emerges, finally, as invasive and injurious, in other words, as voyeurism.[45] In turn, voyeurism emerges as the default mode of male subjectivity. Hawthorne's work teems with obsessive male lookers, ambiguous figures whose desire to see others crosses the line into perversity: the titular protagonist of "Wakefield" installs himself as a perpetual watcher of his own life in his absence; Chillingworth spies on Dimmesdale, just as Coverdale spies on his fellow Blithedalers from his "inviolate bower" up in a tree; the Model spies on Miriam in *The Marble Faun*. Spying becomes the way males coordinate social relations, however one-sided such relations must necessarily be. The relationship of narcissism and shame to voyeurism opens up our discussion considerably. In his depiction of voyeurism, Hawthorne evokes the narcissistic and shame-filled nature of the voyeuristic gaze. Moreover, he ties these affective responses to the appeal and the fear of same-sex desire. These themes will be our central focus in the next chapter.

CHAPTER 5

In a Pig's Eye

MASCULINITY, MASTERY, AND THE RETURNED GAZE OF
THE BLITHEDALE ROMANCE

*W*ITH ITS erotic themes, obsession with law and conformity, and fascination with their psychic effects, Hawthorne's work provides an interesting opportunity to consider the ways in which narcissism and voyeurism imbricate one another. In Hawthorne's 1852 novel *The Blithedale Romance,* both modes coalesce in Blithedale's "amorous New World," a realm of apparent sexual license in which each member of the utopian community is seemingly given free rein to act on his or her desires. Wielded by Hawthorne's famously first-person protagonist Miles Coverdale, the male gaze of this novel indexes a range of Hawthorne's concerns: narcissism and voyeurism, autoeroticism and onanism, sexual tourism and self-display, sadism and masochism, self-pleasure and shame, and the established codes of sexual appreciation, the heterosexual, the homoerotic, the bisexual, even the pansexual. But the gaze of *The Blithedale Romance* is varied and multiple: female as well as male, homoerotic as well as heteroerotic, nonhuman as well as human, and Coverdale just as much its object as its subject, as my discussion of "the returned gaze" will demonstrate.

One could argue that Coverdale transforms his fellow denizens of a Brook Farm–like reformers' community into the actors of a pornographic film, which he believes he can watch from afar, maintaining an illusion of mastery through his visual desire. In a discussion with a surprising relevance to this novel, Berkeley Kaite uses pornography as an opportunity to discuss the similarities between narcissism and voyeurism.[1] Kaite helps us to understand the narcissistic core of voyeurism. While the voyeur seems compelled by an aching need to see the other and possess the other by seeing, he chiefly longs for a sight of the self, longings that are also illuminated by Lacanian theory. Pornography emerges as a site in which the plangency and the sadism of this narcissistic voyeurism has full reign. While it endows the spectator with the sustaining, heady illusion of autoerotic plenitude, it proceeds from the logic of prohibition: homoerotic desire is banned, and femininity must conform to the demands of the male gaze. When voyeurism is understood as a kind of narcissism, we can fully appreciate the ways in which an obsession with looking at others reveals a profound ambivalence over how one looks at oneself.[2] Indeed, *The Blithedale Romance* may be said to be one of the first American literary satires of the genre of pornography. In an extraordinarily modern manner that anticipates the films of Alfred Hitchcock and Brian De Palma, and films such as Michael Powell's *Peeping Tom* (1960) and Martin Scorsese's *Taxi Driver* (1976), the novel rigorously interrogates the fantasies of male mastery inherent in voyeurism.

HAWTHORNE AND THE GAZE

The young Ellen Langton stares at Fanshawe, the eponymous protagonist of Hawthorne's first novel, marveling at his beauty; the Minister Hooper prevents anyone from seeing his face, hidden behind a black veil; Feathertop, believing he cuts a dashing figure, stares at himself in the mirror, discovering, to his horror, that he is merely the mirage of a man, a witch's illusion; Giovanni stares at lush, poisonous Beatrice Rappaccini in her equally beautiful and deadly garden, little realizing that her father is all the while staring at him as he stares at her, or that Rappaccini's own scientific rival, Baglioni, is spying on them all; Chillingworth triumphantly stares at the exposed flesh of sleeping, guilt-ridden Dimmesdale: these examples of the function of the gaze in Nathaniel Hawthorne's work metonymically symbolize numerous important issues that inform his oeuvre. Hawthorne's intensely, provocatively visual literary work invites cinematic comparisons. Throughout the book so far, I have been evoking Laura Mulvey's well-known theory of the male gaze. While her theory remains crucial to my understanding of male visual desire, I also challenge her work here, as have numerous critics in the field of film studies, using Hawthorne's cinematic novel as an example of representation that complicates gendered subject positions vis-à-vis the gaze.[3] In his work, Hawthorne makes it impossible to assign clear positions of dominance and submission. In so doing, he offers valuable contributions to our understanding of the construction and organization of gender and sexuality in the antebellum United States. By rendering male subjects just as often the objects as the wielders of the gaze, Hawthorne insists that we view men as possible objects of erotic contemplation, thereby beckoning queer and feminist analysis.

If I am arguing that the radical nature of Hawthorne's work lies, in part, in his insistence on rendering male figures the object of multiple gazes, *The Blithedale Romance* poses a theoretical dilemma, since its protagonist, the cynical poet Miles Coverdale, clearly wields the gaze: one might even say his chief agenda is eluding the gaze of others by gazing at them first. In this chapter, I examine the psychic costs of wielding the gaze, arguing that Hawthorne demonstrates the considerable potential personal risks involved in the avid desire to look, which he never treats as an act or symbol of power but, instead, as the very evidence of the debilitated fragility of the gazer.[4] To be clear, I am not arguing that Hawthorne depicts the phallic gazer as a victim who should be pitied for the patriarchal power he must embody and enact through gazing; this chapter eschews any special pleading for the anxious condition of aggrieved American manhood. As Suzanne R. Stewart, in a study of late-nineteenth-century masochism and manhood, writes, "The problem with so many postmodern theories of the subject is the elevation of the failure of subjectivity into a general condition of all subjectivity, a failure that is then celebrated as subversive."[5] The subversive energy of the novel lies in the manner whereby Hawthorne exposes Coverdale's act of seeming masculine dominance—wielding the gaze, voyeuristically devouring what he sees—as indicative of a hopelessly unsuccessful embodiment of male power. In so doing, I argue that *The Blithedale Romance* can be read as a critique of developing antebellum forms and theories of American masculinity; an evocation of queer threats to it; and as a phobically defensive treatment of the issues of effeminacy that personally plagued Hawthorne. Moreover, and more pressingly, I will argue that *The Blithedale Romance* provides a particular theorization of heteronormative masculinity's *relationship* to the male gaze.

As I established earlier, while I am influenced by Lacan's theory of the gaze as a visual field in which the subject is only one figure and the object looks back at the subject, but at a position from which the subject cannot see itself being looked at by the object, I follow Mulvey in seeing the gaze as an act with real effects on those who look and those who are looked at. In other words, I accept and find useful for my own purposes—though I am not in agreement with many of Mulvey's claims in her 1975 essay "Visual Pleasure and Narrative Cinema"—her literalization of the Lacanian theory of the gaze. Mulvey theorizes the gaze as *the male gaze,* the act of looking at others on the part of the male subject. While I disagree with her reading of the classical Hollywood cinema as being dominated by this male gaze and of the consistent effects of its power as she describes them, and while I aim to show that Hawthorne's work destabilizes her views, I nevertheless orient my own thinking around Mulvey's argument.

Mulvey argues that the male protagonist of the classical Hollywood film as well as the spectator, gendered male, have two strategies for avoiding a defining fear of castration: voyeurism and fetishism. (As an example of my disagreement with Mulvey, I believe that many of the artists she discusses as exemplary of the defensive uses of these strategies actually depict the strategies in a critical way, exposing them as urgent and destructive defenses. Hitchcock's 1958 *Vertigo*, which Mulvey reads an *example* of these effects, is a rigorous analysis of them.) Along these lines, I compare constructions and theorizations of the voyeuristic gaze in Hawthorne, Freud, Lacan, and Hitchcock, artists and thinkers who all use the voyeuristic male gaze as a means of both establishing and deconstructing normative models of patriarchal power. These psychoanalytic and cinematic perspectives illuminate the ways in which Hawthorne's ineluctable conservatism competes with a potential radicalism—his phobic demonizations of male deviance with a genuinely probing inquiry into the nature of male dominance, especially as organized around vision. I argue that the voyeuristic male gaze allows Hawthorne first to spy on and then to confront normative forms of manhood and masculinity. While I focus on the queer implications of Hawthorne's work, especially in terms of the gaze, this focus hardly exhausts the potentialities of Hawthorne gaze-theory.

The feminist implications of the desiring gaze in Hawthorne's work are just as rich, complex, and tantalizing, and demand further analysis than I can provide in this chapter. In chapter 6, I will turn to issues of female sexuality within the context of the gaze. For now, let me establish that these issues are deeply embedded within the core themes of Hawthorne's work. Ellen Langton's desiring appraisal of Fanshawe's troubled beauty; Hester's ardent desire for Dimmesdale; seemingly meek, wan, sweet Alice Pyncheon's frank physical appraisal of Matthew Maule are among the many examples of the female desiring gaze in Hawthorne's work. As I argue in my book *Men Beyond Desire,* the figure of the inviolate male (such as Fanshawe, Natty Bumppo, Dimmesdale, Stowe's Tom, Billy Budd), opposed to both female and homosocial/homoerotic desire, recurs throughout nineteenth-century texts. This man beyond desire, in his emotional, physical, and sexual unavailability, transforms fictional worlds into fields of erotic play in which female and queer desirers both discover opportunities to gaze, a surprising agency to roam the inhospitable expanse of beautiful and undesiring men. In this chapter, I am considering the implications for queer theory of the complex version of male subjectivity we find in Hawthorne, one that oscillates between spectator and object positions. But the fuller understanding of these questions can only come through further work on the implications for feminist literary theory of Hawthorne's representation of masculinity, femininity, sexual difference, and the gaze.

Nina Baym writes that "gay/queer criticism is male-centered by definition. Homosocial and homoerotic moments are excavated and attributed either to Hawthorne's own suppressed sexual inclinations or to the sublimated, affect-laden idealizations of male–male relationships in antebellum culture."[6] Baym's description may be an accurate one for most queer readings of Hawthorne's work, and the present chapter does indeed focus on Hawthorne and manhood, largely because any queer reading of any author's work that does not contextualize itself within the larger question of gender construction is, in my view, unintelligible. But certainly a queer approach to Hawthorne can and should include a consideration of his representation of active female desire. Certainly, one could at the very least read the transgressive desire of his fiery heroines such as Hester Prynne, Zenobia, and Miriam Schaeffer as allegories for transgressive desire of all kinds; moreover, the issue of queer male identification with the desiring woman is crucial though often overlooked.

In her important study *Domestic Individualism,* Gillian Brown discusses voyeurism in the novel and Freudian theory in relation to it. Brown places, however, more emphasis on fetishism, particularly in terms of Coverdale's misogynistic reduction of women, such as the fiery Zenobia, to literal objects, such as her shoe, discovered separately when the drowned Zenobia's dead body is dragged from the water at the climax. One could establish, then, that both Brown's and my readings proceed from the basis of Mulvey's argument, with my own reading emphasizing voyeurism, hers fetishism. For Brown, fetishism, when seen itself as a form of visual pleasure, defends against homoerotic attraction here. It also allows, through a series of displacements, Coverdale to remain safely a consumer—of objects, of women, of men. "In the consumerist pleasures and anxieties of looking that Hawthorne explores," she writes, "homophobia and misogyny proscribe not specific sexes and sexualities, but the visibility of specificity: they prohibit the possibility of the spectator being static enough to be seen."[7]

I discuss fetishism at length in the next chapter, and specifically in relationship to femininity and female sexuality. Here, however, my interest is in the ways in which the spectator is, actually, constantly in the act of *being* seen within his presumed scenes of invisible visual mastery. Hence my focus on the returned gaze. I share Brown's feminist concern for the treatment of the female characters as fetishistic objects, and am in agreement with her reading that Coverdale uses his voyeurism and also his fetishistic regard for people-as-objects in an effort to avoid spectatorial exposure himself. And, though it is not my focus, I also agree with her reading of Coverdale as a nineteenth-century consumer and the importance of the novel to middle-class consumer culture generally, especially in its fantasies of consumerist visual impunity. But in my view the novel more directly engages with Coverdale's "strategies for safe spectatorship," as Brown puts it, in part to expose the homosexual panic, to use an anachronistic, perhaps, but nevertheless irresistible term, at its core. The novel itself incorporates homophobic anxiety into its representation of Coverdale's gaze, but at the same time, it exposes and critiques it as such. Moreover, the women, transformed into fetish objects, at times return Coverdale's gaze, and with a saucy, derisive aplomb at that.

A GREAT DEAL OF EYE-SHOT

Unlike Fanshawe, Minister Hooper, Feathertop, and Dimmesdale, Miles Coverdale, *Blithedale*'s cryptic first-person narrator, occupies the position of watcher, the bachelor onlooker, or "third man," who observes male–female love triangles.[8] Alternatively, he also represents the "the fourth side," as writer, reader, and also participant in the dramatic action.[9] Characters such as Fanshawe and Dimmesdale occupy the position of being the object of the desiring gaze, recalling classical figures such as Endymion, a young man so beautiful that the moon goddess Selene insisted that Zeus cast a perpetual sleep over him so that she could forever gaze upon and caress him.[10] But in contrast, Coverdale *wields* the gaze, albeit surreptitiously, almost as hidden a voyeuristic viewer as James Stewart's Jefferies ("Jeff") in Hitchcock's *Rear Window* (1954).[11]

Coverdale enjoys a "rare seclusion" in his "hermitage," a "leafy cave" high up in the branches of a pine tree. The "decay" of branches "lovingly strangled" by "vine" forms this "hollow chamber." Within his little bower, Coverdale counts "the innumerable clusters of my vine," and forereckons "the abundance of my vintage."[12] Like Fanshawe, the protagonist of Hawthorne's first novel, he is a ruler in an autoerotic world of his own. "This hermitage," reveals Coverdale, "symbolized my individuality, and aided me in keeping it inviolate" (3: 98–99). Coverdale's declaration firmly establishes that, while he fantasizes about Hollingsworth, Zenobia, and Priscilla, his first thoughts tend toward his own "vine" and "vintage," and the hermitage merely extrudes the interior inviolate individuality into which Coverdale burrows.[13] And from this vantage point, Coverdale "peeps," for his position is "loft enough to serve as an observatory," from where he can observe Hollingsworth, Priscilla, the Blithedale goings-on. Coverdale transforms his inviolate sanctuary into a theater in which his scopophilic spectatorship has full voyeuristic reign and range—the self as Panopticon (3: 99).[14]

If Coverdale fetishistically gazes at those around him, the way he looks at Zenobia triggers her to call him on it: "I have been exposed to a great deal of eye-shot . . . but never, I think, to precisely such glances as you are in the habit of favoring me with" (3: 47). If, in Mulvey fashion, Coverdale objectifies women through the power of his vision, Zenobia unflinchingly returns his gaze, a topic to which we will return. Coverdale's anguished appreciation of Hollingsworth's beauty—coming, as it does, along with a sense that Hollingsworth is neither terribly kind nor trustworthy—appears to translate into onanistic fantasy with self-flagellating (shades of Dimmesdale) repercussions, "exemplifying the kind of error into which my mode of observation was calculated to lead me":

> In my recollection of his dark and impressive countenance, the features grew more sternly prominent than the reality, duskier in their depth and shadow, and more lurid in their light. . . . On meeting him again, I was often filled with remorse, when his deep eyes beamed kindly on me. . . ." He is a man after all!" thought I—"his Maker's own truest image . . . not that steel engine of the Devil's own contrivance, a philanthropic man!" But, in my wood-walks, and in my silent chamber, the dark face frowned at me again. (3: 71).

One is reminded of the fiendish figure of the young man's "Shame" who stands before him between consciousness and sleep in the tale "The Haunted Mind." Sophia Hawthorne knew very well that when Hawthorne referred to a solitary chamber, he evoked onanistic pleasure, one reason why she obliterated references to such "filthiness" in her husband's writing.[15] Like the onanist of antebellum health and sexual reformer Sylvester Graham's perfervid imaginings, Coverdale feverishly retreats into private "recollection" in his "silent," secret chamber, where reproduced images of Hollingsworth take on a lurid luster of almost explicitly onanistic and homoerotic fantasy, solidified even in negation by the phallicized quality of what Hollingsworth supposedly is *not,* a "steel engine."[16] It is little wonder that when Coverdale sees Hollingsworth after his solitary imaginings, he feels remorse—even less wonder that this paragraph precedes both Coverdale's declaration that he finds Hollingsworth beautiful and the description of Blithedale as a Golden Age that promotes polyamorous amativeness, that authorizes "any individual, of either sex, to fall in love with any other, regardless of what would elsewhere be judged suitable and prudent" (3: 72).

The inviolate male in Hawthorne (and other authors' works) overlaps with the construction of the onanist in the theories of myriad antebellum sexual and health reformers such as Sylvester Graham, John Todd, and Mary Gove Nichols.[17] In this chapter, my focus will be not on onanism as a discursive category, but on Hawthorne's fusing of an onanistic with a voyeuristic persona in Coverdale, and the various effects such a fusion has on the novel. Contemporary critics have linked Hawthorne's concerns in *The Blithedale Romance* to the science-fiction author and literary theorist Samuel Delany's in *Times Square Red, Times Square Blue*, a study on peep shows, pornographic theaters, and social regulation in New York City.[18] I take these claims to their logical conclusion, seeing Coverdale as an onanistic Peeping Tom in the ever-illuminated pornographic theater of the Blithedale community. If Coverdale is a Peeping Tom, it is a subject position that implies onanistic sensibility. Admiring the beauty of both men and women at Blithedale, Coverdale roams this utopian space as onanistic voyeur, tourist of erotic possibilities.[19]

In chapter 1 we outlined Lacan's theory of the gaze, which has elicited many critical treatments.[20] Focusing specifically on forms of the gaze most relevant to *Blithedale*—the voyeuristic and the returned gaze—we come to some suggestive points toward our fuller understanding of the gaze in Hawthorne. I will first consider the voyeuristic gaze. Because of the sadomasochistic quality of Coverdale's simultaneously anguished and merciless voyeurism, I find Freud's treatment of voyeurism particularly illuminating. Archeologically excavating "the early history of the sexual instinct," Freud observes that infantile sexuality "from the very first involves other people as sexual objects." Scopophilia, exhibitionism, and cruelty, linked "instincts," exist somewhat "independently" from erotogenic sexual activity, dominating the early lives of children. In Freud's view very young children are, crucially, not plagued by shame, and because of this they exude a great "satisfaction" in exhibiting their own bodies before others. (As I suggested in chapter 2, however, children are hardly immune to shame.) Onanistic children, fascinated by their own genitals, also develop an interest in the genitals of others. Such children most often develop into "voyeurs, eager spectators of the processes of micturition and defecation," activities likeliest to satisfy eyes hungering for a glimpse of hidden genitals. After repression sets in, this desire to see others' genitals becomes a "tormenting compulsion." Even more independent an impulse than scopophilia, cruelty comes easily to the child, for the affect of pity, like shame, develops late (SE 7: 191–92).[21]

In his conflation of scopophilia, exhibitionism, and cruelty, Freud appears to suggest that these drives, rather than depending on sexual identity or feeling, manifest themselves as forces with their own agency, onerous demands, power. Moreover, these drives' interrelated qualities hinge on pitilessly attempting to exert dominance over the entire exhibitionistic spectacle. Voyeurism curdles into a desperate sorrow, forever attempting to outwit more powerful repressive forces, while never relinquishing its essentially pitiless agenda to force the gaze-object to submit to the gazing subject. In terms of Coverdale's gaze, the masochism of his own onanistic voyeurism never mitigates the cruelty inherent in his own relentless desire to possess through his ravenous eyes.

Important valences unite *Blithedale* and Freud's *Three Essays on the Theory of Sexuality*. Both works relentlessly assign zoological "types" to sexual and gendered categories while perpetually insisting on the fundamental cruelty of desire's self-propagating exertions. Both works also insist that, far from signifying mere isolate self-regard verging on solipsism, onanistic activity only incites desire for the incorporation, through scopophilia, of the desired other; in fact, onanistic voyeurism becomes an ingenious strategy not only for connecting to others but for possessing and memorializing them, pressing them permanently on the mind's unblinking "inward eye," to lift from Wordsworth's poem "I Wandered Lonely as a Cloud" (written in 1804, first published in 1807, and published in revised form in 1815), where they can be made to "flash" at will. The chief relevance in Freud's work here for the present inquiry lies in its insistence on seeing cruelty *and* torment as inherent aspects of scopophilia generally, voyeurism specifically.

The curious gendered politics of Lacan's theory of the gaze demand some attention. Lacan's theoretical formulations of the gaze are as redolent of gendered anxieties as they are insightful about them. For Lacan, writes Robert Samuels in a Lacanian reading of Hitchcock films, the "ego is pure nothingness. . . . the subject is narcissistically invested in all of its external representations . . . the subject represses any awareness of its own nothingness or its own lack of representation." Desperately attempting to avoid any confrontation with its own lack, the ego projects it "into the place of the Other," then using "this nothingness, or what Lacan called the 'object' (a), as a cause of its own desire or anxiety. In our current civilization and social structure, this dialectic between the Imaginary state of consciousness and the projected object of nothingness is most often played out in gendered and racial terms."[22] Like Jefferies in Hitchcock's 1954 film *Rear Window,* Coverdale perpetually seeks to elude knowledge of his own insubstantiality by forever busying himself with the "external representations" of his own narcissism, that is, the other Blithedalers, who also conveniently provide him with an external cause for his own marginalization ("How little did these two women care for me . . .!" [124]). But rather than projecting his own nothingness exclusively on female characters, who can then conveniently embody the fearsome lack/castration he disavows in himself, Coverdale projects his own nothingness onto male characters as well, most strikingly the mesmerist Westervelt, who embodies Coverdale's "lack" in a vividly homophobic manner. Inadvertently or otherwise, slippages between homoeroticism and homophobia characterize Lacan's treatment of the gaze, in a manner, as we shall see, similar to Hawthorne's. The subject of the gaze seeks to see the "object as absence."[23]

As Lacan himself writes,

> What the voyeur is looking for and finds is merely a shadow, a shadow behind the curtain. There he will phantasize any magic of presence, the most graceful of girls, for example, even if on the other side there is only a hairy athlete. What he is looking for is not, as one says, the phallus—but precisely its absence, hence the pre-eminence of certain forms as the objects of his search.[24]

Lacan's formulation excludes potential feminine and/or queer voyeuristic desire. Continuing to keep our focus on queer desire for the purposes of this study, we may wonder what would happen if this voyeuristic subject were queer. If the queer voyeuristic subject seeks a literal phallus rather than a phantasmatic ideal, symbolic one, the phallus of the hairy athlete who is no goofy, farcical booby prize but the actual focus of the male subject's fantasy (by making him hirsute, athletic, Lacan makes this masculine object especially homoerotic), what might he find on "the other side"? If Lacan is unable here to imagine actual male fantasy for another male, he nevertheless provides a means whereby homoerotic voyeuristic fantasy may be considered. If Coverdale, as moved by Hollingsworth's as he is by Zenobia's or Priscilla's beauty (perhaps even more so), projects his own nothingness upon Hollingsworth, and upon Westervelt, does he find merely the shadow he seeks, the absence in which his own nothingness may be projected?

In the provocative relays among subject, gaze, gender, and otherness that organize *The Blithedale Romance,* Hawthorne parlays his own gendered and sexual anxieties into the only first-person narrator of his novels, who then projects his own anxieties into the beckoning void of the other characters whom Coverdale voyeuristically fetishizes. In Lacanian terms, Hawthorne may be said to project his own sense of gendered nothingness into Coverdale, who then projects his own onto Hollingsworth and Westervelt, freeing himself of it, even more successfully freeing *Hawthorne*—now at an even greater, safer remove—of it. Yet the uncannily unexpected occurs: the text—the void, the shadow that ostensibly marks an absence—will swerve about to reveal another set of eyes, its *own;* they look back on the subject desperately attempting to escape its own insubstantiality through its projected gaze.[25]

MEDUSAN MANHOOD

If Coverdale describes himself in a manner that suggests the self as Panopticon, or figures his mind as a pornographic theater in which he can play recorded erotic images, the novel's interest in evoking images of the Medusa take on a special relevance. The head of the panoptical self, the head-as-pornographic theater: Medusan references corroborate the head as a site of danger and excitement but also one of pollution and contagion. If thine head offend thee, cut it off.

Hawthorne referred to himself as the "Decapitated Surveyor" in "The Custom House," thus associating himself with both Perseus, slayer of the Gorgon, and with Medusa herself (as Joel Pfister also argues), a mythological story he retells in his 1852 *A Wonder Book,* a work of children's literature.[26] (In chapter 28 of *Moby-Dick,* Melville makes reference to Cellini's famous statue of Perseus holding the decapitated head of Medusa, comparing Perseus to Ahab. Elsewhere, he associates the Whale with Medusa.) Hawthorne explicitly uses Medusa—a spectacular subject of the gaze, the ultimate example of the terrible effects of looking, a prime example of male gazing with potentially fatal results—as a symbol in *Blithedale.* Coverdale obliquely associates Zenobia with Medusa and himself with Perseus, who can see the Gorgon only in a mirror (reflected in his shield) lest he be turned to stone: "Zenobia had turned aside. But I caught the reflection of her face in the mirror" (3: 167). When she, as *raconteur,* entertains the Blithedalers, Zenobia likens the Veiled Lady to Medusa (3: 110). Given Freud's eloquently shocking formulation of the Medusa myth as representative of the terror of the primal scene, these references to Medusa clearly associate Zenobia with a threateningly vivid, voracious female sexuality.[27]

But what are we to make of Westervelt's equally Medusan manhood? Coverdale also associates the mustachioed, bearded, and odious Westervelt with the Green Man, "hirsute and cinctured with a leafy girdle," whom Marjorie Garber, in a different context, has described as a *Male* Medusa (91).²⁸ Zenobia, the Medusan harlot, Westervelt, the Male Medusa, and Coverdale, the onanistic voyeur—these three conform to the triptych of Victorian social monsters, as Jonathan Ned Katz puts it, the prostitute, the sodomite, and the onanist, all enemies of the properly reproductive and normative family.²⁹

The Veiled Lady and the Coverdale–Westervelt episodes are exemplary and complementary scenes of spectatorial ambivalence centered in gendered and sexual anxiety. With the Veiled Lady, the veiling of a woman's face functions as a metaphor for the sexual mystery of Woman, and emphasizes vision as the key to this mystery: unveiling her may reveal the face of beauty and sexual desirability or the Medusan face of ugliness and death. (As Richard Brodhead has persuasively shown, the Veiled Lady is an acute metaphor for the paradoxical possibilities of the "public woman" in antebellum culture.³⁰) The Coverdale–Westervelt episode stages an encounter with masculinity's sexual mystery. Unveiled, male sexuality is both desirable and horrifying, and, again, vision functions as key to all sexual mysteries.³¹

Coverdale immediately, instinctively despises Westervelt, who presumptuously hails Coverdale as "friend" (3: 90). Coverdale's appraisal of Westervelt significantly relates to several themes in our discussion of Hawthorne: Westervelt is "young," "well-developed," "as handsome a man as ever I beheld." Coverdale, however, does not like Westervelt's style of beauty, "*though* a masculine" one (my emphasis). The problem with it? "He had no fineness of nature . . . [in his eyes was] the naked exposure of something that ought not to be left prominent" (3: 92). Coverdale hates him, he thinks, because Westervelt's "foppish" garb outdoes his own "homely" one (3: 92). But this revelation clinches Coverdale's appalled appraisal:

> In the excess of his delight, he opened his mouth wide, and disclosed a gold band around the upper part of his teeth; thereby making it apparent that every one of his brilliant grinders and incisors was a sham. . . . I felt as if the whole man were a moral and physical humbug; his wonderful beauty of face, for aught I knew, might be removeable [*sic*] like a mask; . . . [there was] nothing genuine about him. . . ." (3: 95)

If Hawthorne ambivalently regards Fanshawe and Dimmesdale as beautiful young men blighted by onanism, no ambivalence, only a complete hatred, characterizes his response, through Coverdale, to Westervelt. In a provocative essay, Benjamin Scott Grossberg discusses the chief impasse between Coverdale and Hollingsworth as the incompatibility between Hollingsworth's homoerotic desire and Coverdale's queer desire, which encompasses all of the Blithedale community, male and female alike. Yet Grossberg does not grapple with the intensely phobic manner in which Coverdale describes Westervelt—surely, a disruption of a marvelously omnivorous queer sensibility.[32]

When unveiled, Westervelt's monstrous, artificially constructed mouth yawns open like a technologically engineered *vagina dentata*, with mechanized teeth and drawbridge flexibility. Through his representation of Westervelt as all mouth, and by making this somatic zone the prime feature of his Medusan manhood, Hawthorne equates effeminate males such as the "foppish" Westervelt with an alarming artificiality that suggests the consistent Hawthorne theme of physical blight, moral depravity, and "contagion." If Hawthorne previously treated the effeminate male with a certain degree of sympathy, in Westervelt he throws him to the wolves. (Coverdale continues to see Westervelt-types—at the hotel, he spies on a "young man in a dressing-gown, standing before the glass and brushing his hair, for a quarter-of-an-hour together" [150].) From a *critical psychoanalytic perspective*—which critiques psychoanalytic theory's ideological conservatism while also appreciating psychoanalysis for its value and making use of its insights—Hawthorne may be said, however anachronistically, to return the "homosexual" to the oral stage, the first stage of human psychosexual development, as Freud theorizes it in *Three Essays*. Such a return has homophobic implications, associating the nonnormative male with a regressive, stunted, "primitive" stage of human sexuality.

Not only does Hawthorne's depiction of Westervelt homophobically correspond to Jacksonian mythologies and cultural dictates about European dandyish, effeminate artificiality versus sturdy American naturalism—Coverdale fears "the contagion of his strange mirth"—but it also reveals a great deal about Hawthorne's own anxieties about his manhood, under constant threat from those in his circle.[33] Hawthorne frustrated people who associated him with feminine qualities. "Oliver Wendell Holmes complained that trying to talk to Hawthorne was like 'love-making.' Hawthorne's 'shy, beautiful soul had to be wooed from its bashful pudency like an unschooled maiden.'"[34] Emerson's relationship to Hawthorne is also suggestive. Hawthorne and Sophia lived in the Old Manse, the home in Concord, Massachusetts, that had been built for Emerson's grandfather and in which Emerson wrote his famous chapter, *Nature*.[35] Though often in close proximity to each other, the men appeared to regard each other with suspicion and maintained a strange, jangly relationship.[36] Emerson, for his part, once remarked (in an 1838 journal entry) that Bronson Alcott and Hawthorne *together* would make one man.[37] Much more paradoxically, Hawthorne suffered the slings and arrows of charges of effeminacy *after* his marriage to Sophia. Sophia—not only as Hawthorne's wife but also as a fellow artist (she created a memorable illustration for Hawthorne's tale "The Gentle Boy") who appreciated Hawthorne's sensitive, "feminine" qualities—was forced to defend her husband against charges of "womanish weakness" from her own family after their marriage in the summer of 1842.[38]

Hawthorne imbues Westervelt with the calumniating qualities lobbed against the writer himself—foppishness, artificiality, effeminacy. A scapegoat, Westervelt bears these socially undesirable, deviant traits with a smirking gruesomeness that physically manifests his inner depravity.[39] Hawthorne therefore presents himself as an ornery subject for a queer theorist to handle. His repulsion at effeminacy and at male–male bonds—while potentially antipatriarchal—carries a deeply homophobic charge as well.[40] Yet his idealization of male beauty—which amounts to a refracted narcissism, an autoerotic/homoerotic relay between author, fictive mirror-image, and, if present, a spectator (usually, but not always, a woman) who acts as conduit—charges his work with considerable homoerotic power. As Robert K. Martin and Scott Derrick have each observed, Coverdale seems as drawn to as he is freaked out by Westervelt's disconcerting erotic spectacle.[41] (In this chapter I am also only focusing on one aspect of the continuum of sexual modes represented by Westervelt's almost ectoplasmically multivalent sexuality. Westervelt as dandy would be one place to start examining numerous ricocheting sexual valences of his character: Westervelt is both the dandy as effeminate fop and the womanizing "diabolical dandy," who leaves ruined women in his Valmont-like wake. The misogynistic and predatory aspects of Westervelt must not be forgotten and need further analysis.)

Coverdale's loathing of Westervelt can be read as a specific feature of a general erotophobia that seemed to characterize Hawthorne's reactions to Fourierianism. Hawthorne left Brook Farm, the famous, failed utopian communal experiment, before it adopted Fourierian philosophy in 1843; *The Blithedale Romance* is, of course, Hawthorne's roman à clef depiction of his Brook Farm experiences. Despite considerable efforts on the part of Albert Brisbane, an American who tried to reimagine and reshape the Fourierian phalanstery system to make it more palatable to American tastes, Fourierian projects, such as Brook Farm ultimately became, received stinging criticisms that centered around the beliefs that Fourierian communities abolished marriage and promoted polyamorous relations.[42] Certainly, Fourier's own theories provided a deeply radical alternative to conventional middle-class morality. Hawthorne and his wife Sophia both read Fourier's writing and expressed disdain; Hawthorne, reported Sophia, was left "thoroughly disgusted" by what he read.[43] Reading deeply in Fourier himself before writing the novel—Sophia quite adamantly insisted that they both read Fourier in his original French[44]—Hawthorne reacted, in *Blithedale,* to the unadulterated, un-Americanized version of Fourierian utopianism, which promised polyamorous potentialities ranging from "'vestalic' virginity" to "complete promiscuity, both heterosexual and homosexual." In other words, Hawthorne cringed at the possibilities suggested by the seemingly imminent realization of Fourier's "New Amorous World."[45]

Another factor may account for the homophobic depiction of Westervelt. A great deal has been written about Hawthorne's relationship with Herman Melville. Meeting Melville set the stage for writing *The Blithedale Romance.* While the history of commentary on the relationship between these wounded men is too complex to address in this chapter, it is fair to say that *The Blithedale Romance*'s extraordinarily push–pull relationship to male–male desire eerily resembles the dynamics of the Hawthorne–Melville relationship. Certainly, Hawthorne's own feelings toward same-sex intimacies deepened over time—into a genuine disgust. In his first experiences visiting the Shaker communities, Hawthorne found them odd but rather quaint. But, visiting them again—significantly, with Melville—in the period in which *The Blithedale Romance* was written, Hawthorne expressed contempt, and a genuine revulsion, for same-sex Shaker sleeping arrangements.[46] In chapter 7, I will return to a comparative analysis of both authors' treatment of masculinity and male beauty in terms of their distinct reactions to classical sculpture and in the larger context of Melville's late masterpiece *Billy Budd.*

While Hawthorne's depiction of Westervelt as a bionic fop reeks of homophobic disgust, as a whole the novel's depiction of manhood radically critiques national enforcements of masculine identity which were themselves founded on homophobic ideologies. The fears about his effeminacy surrounding Hawthorne especially around the time and the site of his marriage were one dimension of homo-threat in Hawthorne's life. Others came from national currents in the construction of American manhood. The 1850s are a significant decade in the conflation of masculine character and physical strength. "In the three quarters of a century after the American Revolution, bourgeois Northerners showed the deepest concern for manhood in its moral, social, and political meanings, while placing a lesser emphasis on the male body," writes E. Anthony Rotundo. "Then, in the second half of the nineteenth century, this relative emphasis began to change." Middle-class men began paying "assiduous attention to their bodies." Beginning in the 1850s, a "vogue of physical culture" became a mania that would be a fully entrenched aspect of American masculinity by the end of the decade.[47] The novel's critique of this newly hypermasculinist model of American manhood involves two seemingly unrelated yet, upon reflection, perfectly overlapping metaphorical themes: zoological allusions and the male/tourist/voyeuristic gaze.

IN A PIG'S EYE

The dangers of the gaze perpetually confront Coverdale. Interrupting their *Comus*-like masque in the forest, Coverdale gapes at the Blithedalers garbed as Indians, Arcadian shepherds, Shakers, the goddess Diana, and other oddly assorted figures, suggestive of the hellish forest orgy of "Young Goodman Brown" in its decadence. When these revelers spot Coverdale, they give chase, making him feel alternately like Actaeon, the young hunter who accidentally spied on the naked goddess Diana bathing in a pool (after she turns him into a stag, his own dogs kill him), and a "mad poet hunted by chimaeras (3: 211) (inverting the usual order of *people* chasing chimeras). The forest frolic in which Coverdale observes the Blithedale masque suggests another—Pentheus spying, in Euripides' *The Bacchae,* on his mother reveling orgiastically among her fellow Maenads, female worshippers of Dionysius who become wildly drunk and tear animals apart with their hands. Discovering Pentheus, they decapitate him; his own mother, still in a mad bacchic haze, walks around with his head on a stick. Unmentioned yet suggested by the episode, the Pentheus story corresponds to the Medusan theme of castration/decapitation.

The Blithedalers' retaliatory chase after Coverdale opens up an extremely important theme in this work: the returned gaze. No mere passive spectacle, the Blithedalers look back at Coverdale—at us—violently forcing us to account for the spying sacrilege of our gaze, much as the murdered Marion Crane's eye in Hitchcock's 1960 *Psycho* unflinchingly looks back at us for having so long looked at her. I borrow the term "the returned gaze" from Wheeler Winston Dixon's study *It Looks at You.* Drawing on the work of Marc Vernet and Paul Willemen, this study covers such topics as the returned gaze, surveillance, and the trans/gendered gaze as "seen" in a very wide-ranging array of classically mainstream and independent films. Dixon is primarily interested in the process whereby a film "acts upon us, addressing us, viewing us as we view it, until the film itself becomes a gaze, rather than an object to be gazed upon."[48] The returned gaze can produce moments in which "film structure watches us," when we "feel the look of the image being turned against us, surveilling us, subjecting us to the 'look back' of the screen."[49] Discussing the films of Wesley E. Barry and Andy Warhol, Dixon argues that

> the film itself constitutes a body, a living being . . . that . . . views its potential audience, holds them in its gaze, subjects them to the same sort of reciprocal surveillance that is experienced between prisoners and guards [a nod to the Foucauldian Panopticon], a state that leads the viewer, inevitably, to look with her/himself.[50]

The returned gaze is a highly ambivalent phenomenon, capable of both radical effects and reactionary forms of discipline. It is a perfect device, then, for an analysis of Hawthorne's work. Surprisingly, Dixon does not engage with Mulvey's theory of the male gaze. Instead, his primary focus is on the ways in which the camera's own "chorascular" purview over the image becomes a gaze directed at—returned to—the audience.[51] Taking his argument in a different direction, I argue that the returned gaze can be a moment of radical resistance to the domination of the patriarchal male gaze, as theorized by Mulvey, in that the objects—women, sexual deviants, the racial other—at times squashed beneath it return the subject's gaze, occasionally with a defiance that can be read as counterattack. Admittedly, this is a rare occurrence—but that makes instances of it all the more noteworthy. When Zenobia calls upon Coverdale's voracious gazing of him—his excessive "eye-shot"—she is both questioning and undermining the structure of patriarchal power that enables Coverdale to *believe* he can gaze unabashedly. I am interested in the returned gaze's capacity to function as a form of the gaze *within* narrative forms such as novels and films.

In terms of Hawthorne's critique of 1850s hypermasculinity, the gaze, specifically the returned gaze, makes a surprising intervention. In order to understand the manifestation of the returned gaze in terms of the novel's gendered project, we must link it to another aspect of this project, Coverdale's zoologies of gender and Hawthorne's parodistic treatment of gendered stereotypes.

Throughout the novel, Coverdale, a zoological categorizer of people by sex, relentlessly "pegs" his fellow fictive figures—and by implication, us—with broad essentialist generalizations. These generalizations crucially relate to conservative impulses in Hawthorne, especially regarding constructions of gender. But they have a radical side, too—through them, Hawthorne critiques, intentionally, consciously, or otherwise, American hypermasculinity and its concomitant misogyny. Though Coverdale likens Blithedale to the

"Golden Age," the first age in Greek myth and a time *before* women were created (3: 72), he bristles at and buckles against male dominion.

"I hate to be ruled by my own sex," reveals Coverdale, for it "excites my jealousy and wounds my pride" (3: 121). Young or old, man is "prone to be a brute" (3: 73). Men with an "over-ruling purpose" such as Hollingsworth have "no heart, no sympathy, no reason, no conscience," are "not altogether human" (3: 70). Perhaps this is the fault of the male species itself—"we really have no tenderness" (3: 42). Again, confirming what men "are" through negation, Coverdale observes that men naturally contemn those weak, diseased unfortunates who "falter and faint" in the "rude jostle of our selfish existence" (3: 41). Coverdale suspects that Hollingsworth has come among them only because, having no "real" sympathy, he is as estranged from life as they now are (3: 54). While girls, despite their Pearl-like wildness, play with a "harmonious propriety," boys play "old, traditional games," "according to recognized law"—this may not sound so very terribly ominous, but Coverdale concludes: "young or old, in play or in earnest, man is prone to be a brute" (3: 73). (I am reminded of the ad campaign for Anthony Minghella's 1999 film version of Patricia Highsmith's novel *The Talented Mr. Ripley:* "Why is it that when men play they always play at killing each other?") Though highly conventional markers of femininity bestrew the novel—Zenobia's hothouse flower, associating her with Beatrice, Rappaccini's ill-fated daughter (3: 44); Priscilla's purse (intriguingly, Coverdale reveals that he, too, possesses one) (3: 35)—especially sharp spikes line the markers of manhood.

Though a seeming radical, Hollingsworth reveals himself to be a traditional male in the worst sense. Hollingsworth emerges as a great spokesman for domestic violence. Violently aghast at Zenobia's suffragist philosophy, Hollingsworth, all but explicitly assigning them a sapphic identity, deems women who strive for equal rights "poor, miserable, abortive creatures," "petticoated monstrosities." "I would call upon my sex," rails Hollingsworth, "to use its physical force, that unmistakeable [*sic*] evidence of sovereignty, to scourge them back within their proper bounds!" (3: 123). Hollingsworth decries women for failing to adhere to normative gendered stereotypes while fully adhering to those of his own sex. Crucially, Hawthorne puts a strident testimonial to "physical force" as the chief evidence of natural male "sovereignty" in the mouth of an increasingly contemptible, misogynistic character.

Coverdale's sympathies seem firmly in the women's camp—after Hollingsworth threatens Zenobia, Coverdale shares in what he presumes to be her rage at this "outrageous affirmation of . . . the intensity of masculine egotism" (3: 123). Self-pityingly wounded Coverdale transmutes his empathy, though, into rancor at the women for failing to care for him, while brutal Hollingsworth, "by some necromancy of his horrible injustice, seemed to have brought them both to his feet!" (3: 124), leaving Coverdale "to shiver in outer seclusion" (3: 126).

Given Coverdale's nearly misandrist contempt for masculinity, certain passages reek of an especially redolent Hawthornean irony: "After a reasonable training, the yeoman-life throve well with us. Our faces took the sunburn kindly; our chests gained in compass, and our shoulders in breadth and squareness; our great brown fists looked as if they had never been capable of kid gloves" (3: 64). Given the emergent antebellum cult of hypermasculinity, and the critical drubbing that Hawthorne's own performance of masculinity received, this description throbs with satirical and political significance.

Coverdale conjectures that Hollingsworth views mankind as "but another yoke of oxen, as stubborn, sluggish, and stupid" (3: 100), and yet his own theories of manhood correspond symmetrically to Hollingsworth's. The apotheosis of the novel's demythologization of male power—achieved precisely by associating it primarily with "brute" strength—is the passage on the pigs.

Sadly yet bitterly leaving Blithedale after his refusal of Hollingsworth's hand in friendship, Coverdale passes Hollingsworth, as if both were "mutually invisible." What follows is perhaps the most coarsely, palpably visual image in the novel, when Coverdale visits the pigsty before his departure:

> There they lay, buried as deeply among the straw as they could burrow, four huge black grunters, the very symbols of slothful ease and sensual comfort. They were asleep, drawing short and heavy breaths, which heaved their big sides up and down. Unclosing their eyes, however, at my approach, they looked dimly forth at the outer world. . . . They were involved, and almost stifled, and buried alive, in their own corporeal substance. The very unreadiness and oppression, wherewith these greasy citizens gained breath enough to keep their life-machinery in sluggish movement, appeared to make them only the more sensible of the ponderous and fat satisfaction of their existence. Peeping at me, an instant, out of their small, red, hardly perceptible eyes, they dropt asleep again; yet not so far asleep but that their unctuous bliss was still present to them, betwixt dream and reality. (3: 143–44)

The authentically masculine farmer Silas Foster impresses upon Coverdale that he must return to dine on spareribs—"I shall have these fat fellows hanging up by the heels, heads downward, pretty soon, I tell you!" Appalled,

Coverdale responds that only these "four porkers" are happy in Blithedale, and that it would be better "for the general comfort to let them eat us; and bitter and sour morsels should we be!" (3: 144). Hawthorne's dark humor comes through forcefully in such moments—and the joke is entirely on Coverdale.

While some critics might argue that this brief moment in the text does not deserve sustained attention, and that, moreover, the pigs merely peep at Coverdale for an instant, thereby largely constituting slothful sleep rather than assaultive looking, I argue that this passage with the pigs is one of the novel's most significant, especially because it foregrounds by thematizing the issues of gender, voyeurism, zoological typing, and the returned gaze in the work. The pig-passage reveals that, despite his efforts at sadistic voyeuristic mastery, Coverdale's own subject position is resolutely one of enforced, abiding masochism, one that is no match for the pigs' "unctuous bliss." As I suggested in chapter 2, theories of masochism are relevant to Hawthorne's work, and never more so than in this novel.[52]

FLYING THE BOAR

Confirming their allegorical significance as males, these almost oneiric beasts are called "fellows." "Fellows" echoes Coverdale's earlier analogy between the pigs—who need to be acquired shortly after Coverdale arrives in Blithedale—and "the swinish multitude," the masculine world of commerce and industry, the "greedy, struggling, self-seeking world" that Blithedale ostensibly rejects and defies (3: 20).

In his 1853 *Tanglewood Tales,* another collection of classical myths retold for children, Hawthorne recounts the tale from Homer's *Odyssey* of Circe and the pigs. The powerful sorceress Circe turns Odysseus's men into pigs, just as she has transformed other hapless male victims into the various animals that pace around her haunted palace. Admittedly, Homer often depicts Odysseus's hungry men, who make the fatal error of eating the sun god Helios's cattle (Book 12), as stupid and foolish. But Hawthorne extravagantly emphasizes the men's innate beastliness to a degree that bears closer investigation.

As Ulysses' (as Hawthorne Victorianizes "Odysseus") men marvel at their luck at being in the beautiful Circe's beautiful palace and their impending feast, they whisper and "wink" at each other, little realizing Circe's contemptuous plans for them. "It would really have made you ashamed to see how they swilled down the liquor and gobbled up the food," the narrator sighs.

"They sat on golden thrones, to be sure; but they behaved like pigs in a sty." The squeamish narrator remarks, too, that it "brings a blush into my face to reckon up, in my own mind, what mountains of meat and pudding, and what gallons of wine, these two and twenty guzzlers and gormandizers ate and drank" (7: 281).

Disgusted by the men's behavior—which she has herself enabled and orchestrated—Circe calls them "wretches," saying it will take little magic to transform them into the pigs they have *already* emulated.

> They would have wrung their hands in despair, but, attempting to do so, grew all the more desperate for seeing themselves squatted on their hams, and pawing the air with their fore trotters. Dear me! what pendulous ears they had! what little red eyes, half buried in fat! and what long snouts, instead of Grecian noses! (7: 283)

The descriptions of the men as pigs, "buried in fat," seeing "red" as the Blithedale pigs do, corroborates and extends the metaphorical implications of the peeping pigs in *Blithedale*.[53]

In the 1852 novel, the pigs gaze at Coverdale with an oddly, uncomfortably serene and uncanny knowingness; though being prepared for slaughter, these pigs look out from a zone of almost godlike imperturbability. By "Circe's Palace," however, the metaphorical pigs have lost any authority, power, indifference—their association with men and manhood takes on a cursed quality, an air of desperation and despair as these pigs now *see themselves* for what they are, a particularly hideous example of what I called, in the previous chapter, self-overseeing. What is metaphorical in one text becomes literal in the next: pigs that resemble men become pigs *as* men.

As suggested by the knowing looks exchanged among Circe and her staff as they supply the men with fodder for their porcine obscenities, Circe already views the men as pigs before using her magic to make them actual pigs. Her own avidity for transforming men into beasts, these beasts in particular, symbolically extends Zenobia's appalled disappointment at Hollingsworth's animalistically brutish behavior. But Hawthorne's Circe adds what vulnerable Zenobia did not, a retaliatory, indeed a vengeful, campaign against mankind. *Tanglewood*'s Circe acts as Zenobia's avenging sorceress-angel. And if "Circe's Palace" functions as sequel to *Blithedale*, as I argue it does, it is significant that Hawthorne must reach into the recesses of classical literature to "solve" the modern erotic problems of this antebellum utopian community and of antebellum feminism. Rather than using mythic reference to underscore contemporary issues, Hawthorne infuses a retold myth with topical gendered anxieties.

Lee Edelman, writing about W. E. B. Du Bois and African American manhood, thusly critiques Du Bois's statement that he "simply wishes to make it possible for a man to be both a Negro and an American":

> the self-consciousness of the "manhood" he envisions as the fulfillment of that wish suggests that such a manhood must be the *enactment* of a masculinity whose distinguishing characteristic is its power . . . to occupy the place of . . . master of the gaze. If the fantasy of masculinity . . . is the fantasy of a non-self-conscious selfhood endowed with absolute control of a gaze whose directionality is irreversible, the enacted—or self-conscious— "manhood" . . . is itself a performance for the gaze of the Other . . . always the paradoxical *display* of a masculinity that defines itself through its capacity to put others on display while resisting the bodily captation involved in being put on display itself.[54]

Flawed and flagrantly theatrical, Coverdale's performance flails about in its desperate attempts to convince us, himself, the Blithedalers that he is indeed master of his gaze. Coverdale's fantasy of masculine control never convinces, being always transparent as such. Directly challenging any attempt to prove that he controls the directionality of his pseudo-masterful gaze, the pigs return his gaze, stopping his eyes dead in their tracks with their porcine own. They put *him* on display.

Discussing the returned gaze of Andy Warhol films, Dixon notes, "When watching *Vinyl* one gets the continual and uneasy feeling that one is being watched, being *judged*, by Warhol's returned gaze, a gaze that is almost solely a product of the performance space of the film, rather than the 'look' of the actors. . . . [*Vinyl* leaves] the viewer viewed, the gaze returned."[55] Just as Warhol's films seem to look back at the viewer with a life of their own, with a strange air of *judgment*, the pigs return Coverdale's gaze and our own, resisting any facile notion of pity. If we recall Coverdale's seeming concern for their imminent fates, their returned gaze suggests that it is Coverdale who should be worried. A faint undercurrent of hysteria marks Coverdale's words to Silas Foster as he half-mockingly offers himself and his fellow Blithedalers in their place. The pigs, comfortable in their "unctuous bliss," seem to respond with their eyes, "I'd worry about myself if I were you." Dreamily returning his gaze, the blissful pigs reject Coverdale's feeble offer of pity, the only means whereby he might have been able to achieve even a fleeting sense of mastery. With their eyes, they mock Coverdale, just as his own eyes mock themselves.[56]

Moreover, the pigs, in debunking any notion of Coverdale's mastery of the gaze, also debunk any notion of a masculine power out there, somewhere, that Coverdale can tap into, exploit. It is worth remembering that, on a symbolic level, the pig has been closely tied to cultural fantasies of fascist masculinity.[57] If these porcine "fellows" are clearly representative of manhood in Hawthorne's work, the male power they symbolize is also truly and terrifyingly other. Freighted with their own gendered typing, Hawthorne's pigs represent a primordial, chthonic form of manhood and masculinity. When Coverdale stares at them and they look back at him, the authority they wield would appear to depend upon their tie to some form of essential, gendered knowledge, an essential masculinity both base and debased. To reformulate the theories of the Kristevan film theorist Barbara Creed, the pigs embody the monstrous-masculine.[58] When they look back, they are not so much a Greek chorus of eyes, sorrowfully reflecting back Coverdale's own inadequacy and desperation, as they are the godlike power of "gender" itself, a sort of oozing pool of "original," essentialist masculinity. Within their perverse psychic and corporeal plenitude, the pigs need only peep at Coverdale, a mockery through diminution of his large-scale attempt to overmaster by sustained looking.

SHAKESPEARE'S PLAY *Richard III* held a strong fascination for the young Hawthorne, who was prone to quote the line "My Lord, stand back, and let the coffin pass."[59] *Richard III* provides the antecedent for Hawthorne's symbolic imagery of men-as-pigs. In *Richard III,* the misshapen, murderous king is likened to a hedgehog and a boar. (In the 1996 film version, directed by Richard Loncraine and set in a fascist state, Ian McKellen's Richard, in terrifying boar-face, stares and snarls directly at us.) Hastings, who will soon be beheaded at Richard's behest, scoffs at Lord Stanley's dream of a boar—that is, Richard—pursuing him, saying,

> To fly the boar before the boar pursues
> Were to incense the boar to follow us,
> And make pursuit where he did mean no chase. (III.2. 28–30)

Hastings fails to heed the warning of Stanley's dream, ending up beheaded. Coverdale similarly flees the boar, albeit one always on the chase and eternally incensed to follow him.

If, in this peeping-pigs passage, Hawthorne is rewriting the Odyssey episode in which Circe turns Odysseus's men into pigs, this writer normally as interested in the plight and the power of women erases Woman in Melvillean fashion. Hawthorne rarely paints a nakedly homoerotic tableau; rather, he suffuses his work with an erotic awareness of the intense beauty of both men *and* women, a sensibility that anticipates Freudian bisexuality. Yet, as Coverdale stares at these hypermasculine pigs, Hawthorne erases Circe and her role as avenging enemy of male power. It's as if Odysseus were forced to confront the actual animality of his men without the exculpatory hex of an erotomaniacal sorceress.[60] What Hawthorne constructs here, then, surprisingly resembles Marlowe's queer retelling of the Diana–Actaeon myth in *Edward II*, which homoeroticizes the story and removes Diana, transformed instead into "a louelie boye in Dians shape."[61] It is of interest that Hawthorne also includes a retelling of this myth in the novel.

In Hawthorne, myth becomes a means of metaphorizing manhood and male anxieties. Coverdale confronts his own anxieties about being a man in this polyamorous setting, which includes his homoerotic attraction to and disgust toward Hollingsworth and Westervelt, not to mention the effeminate young man he sees from his city window. Beautiful, desirable young men haunt his fiction alongside lushly beautiful women such as Georgiana (with her high-fashion flaw/mole) and Beatrice Rappaccini. Removing the equally pressing beauty of women from this passage, Hawthorne stages a confrontation between a man and *maleness*—with all of its attendant complexities—itself. If homoerotic desire and homophobic disgust equally influence Coverdale's relations with men, which culminate in or are synthesized by the pigs, the novel suggests that homosexuality causes a breakdown of all conventional standards that maintain identity, down to the level of species. Coverdale likens Hollingsworth to a "polar bear" (3: 26). Mingling his desire and disgust, Coverdale says, "I loved Hollingsworth," Coverdale confesses. "But. . . .[h]e was not altogether human" (3: 70). In this manner, Hawthorne anticipates Hocquenghem.[62]

HAWTHORNE'S HITCHCOCKIAN GAZE

In my view, both Hitchcock and Hawthorne consider similar material, especially two interrelated themes—the plight of the independent, headstrong, sexually aware woman in patriarchy and the often murderous rivalry between men within patriarchal capitalism. Both Hawthorne and Hitchcock—in a manner concomitant with their misogyny—express a romantic, anguished interest in and identification with the wronged woman. Hester Prynne, Zenobia, and *The Marble Faun*'s Miriam resemble Hitchcock's embattled, troubled, and determined heroines such as *Notorious*'s Alicia Huberman, *Psycho*'s Marion Crane, and *Marnie*'s titular protagonist. Much like Coverdale, Cary Grant's Devlin in *Notorious* (1946) treats the "bad woman" Alicia Huberman (Ingrid Bergman) with contempt, yet maintains a hidden sympathy for her—he is in love with her, a secret he assiduously hides, until the climax. And his sympathy toward her manifests itself in his contempt for the bureaucratic men who put her to work as a government spy infiltrating a Nazi stronghold in Brazil. In a meeting with his fellow government men, Devlin defends Alicia's honor to one odious man who calls her a "woman like that." Yet toward Alicia Devlin remains aloof, until it is almost too late. At odds with the homosocial, treating women with an ambivalence that borders on sadism, Devlin resembles many Hawthorne men, especially Coverdale.

Rear Window also circulates and examines many of the same tensions and themes in *The Blithedale Romance*. James Stewart's "Jeff," an incapacitated photographer with a broken leg, temporarily wheelchair-bound and peeping on his neighbors, suffers and wounds in Coverdale fashion. Jeff wrangles with his war buddy the detective Tom (Wendell Corey), who refuses to believe that Jeff has uncovered the murder of Mrs. Thorwald by her husband Lars (Raymond Burr) and mercilessly satirizes Jeff's sleuthing. "How did we stand each other in that plane for three years?" Tom asks Jeff, referencing their former intimacy as war comrades while also articulating the essential enmity that defines male–male relationships in patriarchy in modern America no less than in the antebellum period. Much as Hawthorne does, Hitchcock also thematizes heterosexual ambivalence. Jeff's girlfriend Lisa Fremont (Grace Kelly), who works in the fashion industry, is introduced through an overwhelming, denaturing close-up of her face, which casts an ominous shadow over the sleeping Jeff's. "There's only one problem," Jeff says as she plants strategic kisses on his lips. "Who are you?" Jeff's sadism toward Lisa and her wounded responses to it provide a good deal of the film's drama; much like Hawthorne, Hitchcock, though not without ambivalence, maintains a sympathetic identification with Lisa, whose pain we are made to share as Jeff repeatedly rejects her.. In the closest parallel to *Blithedale,* Jeff's apartment is his inviolate bower, the murders and other perversities of his neighbors his questionably distilled vintage. The song that permeates the film (sung by Bing Crosby) could also be applied to Blithedale's world, albeit with severe qualifications, such as the violent tensions the sentiment evokes: "To See You (Is to Love You)."

There is a famous sequence in *Rear Window* that corresponds to the peeping-pig episode in *The Blithedale Romance,* of particular relevance to the issue of masculinity and the returned gaze. Desperate to impress the reticent, cynical, sexually reluctant Jeff, who claims they've no future together, Lisa boldly—a bit maniacally—ventures into Lars Thorwald's apartment to find incriminating evidence, Mrs. Thorwald's wedding ring especially, the logic being she would never have, as her husband claims, gone off on a trip without it. As Jeff and hard-bitten nurse and masseuse Stella (Thelma Ritter) watch, Lisa makes her way through Thorwald's apartment, Jeff on the verge of calling the police and getting Lisa out of there. Jeff and Stella are suddenly distracted by the imminent suicide of the sad woman in a first-floor apartment whom Jeff has dubbed Miss Lonelyhearts. (Stella recognizes the pills she is about to take as lethal in large doses.) But Jeff's phone call to the police to report Miss Lonelyhearts's suicide attempt transforms into his frantic call to rescue Lisa. "The music's stopped her!" cries Stella, discovering that the musical efforts of the equally lonely composer above have stalled Miss Lonelyhearts's desperate act. As Jeff and Stella stare at the transfixed Miss Lonelyhearts, Thorwald returns to his apartment. Shortly afterward, he discovers Lisa, who attempts to convince him that there's a perfectly good reason why she's in his apartment. Thorwald grabs her, they struggle, and then—in one of the most terrifying and precisely engineered suspense moments in Hitchcock's considerable arsenal—the lights are knocked out, and darkness fills the screen, as Jeff, his face contorted in helplessness and guilty despair, says, "Oh, Stella, what am I going to do?" In a moment no Foucauldian could love, the police arrive and restore order. (With Hitchcock's established phobia about the police, one wonders how he could, either.) The lights come back on. Triumphantly, the now rescued Lisa, her back to all of us, taps her finger, upon which glints in merry light Mrs. Thorwald's wedding ring.

As the finger taps and the ring flashes, Thorwald realizes that he is being watched. He stares back at Jeff staring at him, returning Jeff's gaze.[63] It is little wonder that guilty Jeff frantically attempts to elude Thorwald's gaze, which penetrates him with shared knowledge, complicity, understanding, recognition, and that curious air of judgment. "You're no different from me," Thorwald seems to be saying to Jeff. "I may have killed my wife, but since you sent your girlfriend to my apartment, where I could have easily killed her and nearly did, you have no right to judge me." In my view, in these distinct yet thematically linked episodes, Hawthorne and Hitchcock both use the gaze as a means of recording male anxiety about masculinity itself, as a means of looking at masculinity through male eyes, truly a sight hateful, sight tormenting. Thorwald invades Jeff's apartment; Jeff, in self-defense, attempts to blind him with camera flashes that suffuse the screen with a red glow. This confrontation between deeply ambiguous men fuses the homoerotic with homophobic violence, an eerie complement to the Coverdale–Westervelt encounter. Both Hitchcock, as the expressionistic red suffusions and Jeff's phallic telephoto-lens camera evince, and Hawthorne mark the visual as the field for these fierce exchanges between desperate and devious mirror men.

It is precisely within the returned gaze of *The Blithedale Romance* that Hawthorne's conservatism and radicalism coalesce. Clearly, Hawthorne describes in phobic fashion ambiguous male sexuality: his Westervelt is a triumph of sodomitical/effeminate typing. Yet his analysis of normative forms of masculinity—all of those asides about the essentially brutish natures and increasingly regularized bodies of men, not to mention the possibility that what Coverdale seeks is in fact Lacan's hairy athlete; and Coverdale's uncanny confrontation with a terrifyingly chthonic form of manhood in the peeping pigs, peeping back at him; tinged with the author's own anxieties about his gendered identity and how it was perceived—does provide an important critique of the construction of gender in Hawthorne's America.[64]

CHAPTER 6

The Gaze in the Garden
FEMININITY, FETISHISM, AND TRADITION IN
"RAPPACCINI'S DAUGHTER"

THOUGH MY focus has thus far been on Hawthorne's representation of manhood, narcissism, especially in its anguished aspects, also informs Hawthorne's considerable interest in the representation of women, a set of issues that demand a discrete study. No more harrowing and exact transmutation of Hawthorne's anguish over vision exists than the spectacle of Hester Prynne on the scaffold, the object of innumerable pitiless glares. Yet Hester also uses her pride as a shield against their awesome assault, while it is left deeply ambiguous whether Dimmesdale ever acknowledges himself as an equally guilty party in adultery even at the climax of the novel, when the minister finally stands with Hester and Pearl on the scaffold. Hawthorne suggests that his female characters can withstand the gaze far more unflinchingly than his male. In Hawthorne's 1839 tale "The Gentle Boy," examined in chapter 2, of the Puritan couple who adopt the abandoned, persecuted titular Quaker child, it is Tobias Pearson who finds "it difficult to sustain [the] united and disapproving gaze" of his fellow Puritan churchgoers as he and wife walk into a church with little Ilbrahim; his wife Dorothy, however, "whose mind was differently circumstanced, merely drew the boy closer to her, and faltered not in her approach" (9: 78). Georgiana has little worry over her own fatal blemish in "The Birthmark," negotiating with a certain wry humor the various responses it garners from both male and female observers; it is her anxious alchemist husband Aylmer who writhes with discomfort at the sight of the fissure in her visual perfection, "causing him more trouble and horror than ever Georgiana's beauty, whether of soul or sense, had given him delight" (10: 39).

As I have been arguing throughout this book, Hawthorne debunks Laura Mulvey's sense of the stability of the male subject of the gaze, demonstrating that the gaze is indicative of male psychic fragility rather than mastery. Hawthorne also reveals the voyeuristic gaze to be chiefly motivated by the desire to see oneself, and therefore as a subset of the narcissistic gaze. In this chapter, I will explore the ways in which the gaze functions as a structural field for Hawthorne's analysis of gendered relationships in culture. In Hawthorne's version of the gaze, looks not only wound, they kill. Through an analysis of the construction of the gendered gaze in Hawthorne, I will consider the representation of femininity in Hawthorne as well as his ongoing representation of narcissistic masculinity.

My chief argument here is that Hawthorne's fiction is feminist, a disposition chiefly expressed in two ways: his unwaveringly critical view of his male characters' propensity to attempt to dominate women, through the visual and other means, but also, and even more deeply, his allegiance to the women who are victimized by the male lust for control. The chief obstructions to seeing Hawthorne's work as feminist would appear to be the frequency with which many of his female characters fall victim to an oppressive male and the fact that they are powerless to resist or stop their own destruction. I will problematize this view of Hawthorne's work and ultimately dispute it; in my view, we cannot appreciate the feminist sensibility of Hawthorne's fiction if we continue to fault him for failing to envision happier outcomes for his heroines.

My view of Hawthorne's feminism is indebted to Nina Baym, throughout whose considerable body of work on Hawthorne runs a steady argument about Hawthorne's feminism. As her brilliant analysis of *The House of the Seven Gables* demonstrates, Hawthorne's feminism lies in his sympathy and identification with the socially overlooked, such as the elderly, scowling, tender-hearted Hepzibah Pyncheon, and his hostility toward those who sadistically wield their social power against the powerless, such as Judge Pyncheon. Whatever masculinist biases and misogynistic views are present in Hawthorne's work (as well as life), his work is feminist in its disposition toward male power and its abuses as well as its sympathy toward the oppressed, especially in gendered terms.[1]

In a cogent analysis of Hawthorne's representation of women, Alison Easton writes that "while a striking number of his contemporaries commented on his 'feminine' qualities," this "certainly did not mean that [Hawthorne] identified with women." She reminds us that Hawthorne competed against women in one of the few fields in which men and women actually competed, authorship/publishing. "His relationships with women were a confused mixture of the supportive and the competitive," though, Easton adds, "readerly connections with women were undoubtedly important." In a statement that moves from the persuasive to the more debatable, Easton writes, "There is evidence of both feminist and misogynist views in his imaginative and non-fictional writings," but, she adds, "there simply is no certainty about what he believed, and we should be wary when his texts make apparently definitive pronouncements."[2]

Easton is an excellent critic whose nuanced readings I admire. But I would disagree that we simply have no way of knowing how Hawthorne felt about women—at least in his work. His fiction is rife with consistent images of women as courageous, daring, defiant, and authentically true to their feelings, images in stark contradistinction to the equally consistent images of men as duplicitous, fearful, sadistic, weak-willed, hypocritical, and self-hating. Certainly, there is a genuinely autocratic, conservative Hawthorne who fights for the gendered status quo, along with other kinds of sustained normalcy; what I argue is that this Hawthorne is overshadowed by the radical Hawthorne whose views of gender defy and disrupt, along with his heroines, the normative gendered order. I am, in a way analogous to Baym, making a difficult point about Hawthorne's feminism: its power lies in the effort Hawthorne makes to critique normative masculinity rather than in his creation of empowering scenarios for women. Yet, wounded, suffering, and unfulfilled though many of them are, Hawthorne's women are also provocative and stirring, even at their most off-putting.

I feel that I should also explicate anew my own position here. As a gay man writing about a canonical American writer, a writer whom I love, despite his considerable lapses, I am well aware of the awkwardness of my position. On the one hand, this entire study resists and refuses the Foucauldian cast of much of queer theory practice, believing wholeheartedly in such oft-renounced traditional values such as meaning, intentionality, art, and beauty. Freud is specifically valuable to me here because he makes it possible to raise difficult questions about Hawthorne's work while also demonstrating my respect for his imaginative genius. But I have no interest in simply perpetuating the Great Author cults that continue to thrive in certain quarters of academia. Hawthorne is specifically important to me not only because he is a great writer but also, and perhaps more importantly, because I feel that his work offers significant challenges to the normative standards through which gender and sexuality are organized in our culture. I am aware that I seem to be in disagreement with most feminist readings of Hawthorne. I may dispute the specifics of some of these readings, but their principles are my own as well. My hope is that in this chapter, as in this study as a whole, I can offer a reading of Hawthorne as feminist that will also be a feminist reading, which is to say, a reading that is sensitive toward and in tandem with feminist theory and that is also attentive to Hawthorne's misogyny, against which his greater investment in identification with the feminine continuously struggles.

In this chapter, I focus on one of Hawthorne's major works, the tale "Rappaccini's Daughter" (1844), arguing that it emblematizes Hawthorne's feminist politics and interrogation of the male gaze's effects on women. The previous chapter's analysis of the functions of the gaze, voyeurism, myth, and the feminine experience of male visual desire in *The Blithedale Romance* leads me back to the 1844 story. (Rather than seeing this as a regressive move, I believe that it resists the progressive notion of both an author's career and of the typical rhetorical trajectory of the single-author book. Rereading the 1852 novel leads one to rethink, in a nonlinear fashion, certain patterns in Hawthorne generally.)

Though my interest in the gendered gaze informs this chapter, it also moves into a different, though certainly related, area: the issue of Hawthorne's intertextual poetics, the correspondences between this work and sources such as Ovid's *Metamorphoses,* the biblical Genesis narrative, and, especially, Milton's *Paradise Lost.* In this respect, my argument resembles that of Magnus Ullén in the discussions of the tale in his book *The Half-Vanished Structure.* One of the reasons that I will emphasize Hawthorne's intertextuality here is that, in my view, Hawthorne's feminism flows out of the ways in which he reimagines and reframes key texts in the Western tradition, and in this respect, my work takes a quite distinct direction from Ullén's. Like Roy R. Male, Ullén reads Hawthorne's work in biblical terms, reading "Rappaccini's Daughter" as Hawthorne's version of the *felix culpa,* or the "Fortunate Fall." Despite my considerable admiration for both Male's and Ullén's work, I think both critics end up blunting not only the feminist importance of biblical misogyny but also Hawthorne's own critical awareness of this misogyny, which, as I will be arguing, he resists in this tale and elsewhere. Indeed, far from seeing a Christian-allegorical reworking of the *felix culpa* in this work, I believe that Hawthorne quite profoundly challenges this theological reading.[3] At least in terms of Hawthorne's particular version of Christianity, I concur with the view of Hyatt Waggoner that it "repudiated the pagan garden in 'Rappaccini's Daughter.'" For Hawthorne, Waggoner argues, "the Voice in the garden was a real one, and the apple had been the agent of the Fall. As Giovanni in 'Rappaccini's Daughter' had at first failed to see the snaky vines for what they were, so the Puritans could see nothing else. Both views, Hawthorne thought, were unbalanced. Neither pagan nor Puritan himself, he could be described as a Christian humanist."[4]

The question of a feminist Hawthorne cannot be conducted simply by evaluating Hawthorne's views against the dynamics and concerns of his own cultural moment; Hawthorne's engagement with art-making is just as significant to understanding his contributions as are his political stances and his responses generally to his own era's cultural phenomena and social controversies. Hawthorne writes literature with one eye on his own thematic interests and the other on literary tradition. Hawthorne's intertextual poetics are, at present, a largely overlooked aspect of his work that I reinsert into the critical discussion.

VEILING THE MASK

The story begins with a preface in which Hawthorne adopts the persona of Aubépine (French for "Hawthorne"). Aubépine's persona gives Hawthorne an opportunity for self-estrangement, to view himself from a disassociated, yet intimate, position; the preface serves as a drama of self-inspection that will be extended into the story proper. Hawthorne makes himself his own double through his self-figuration as Aubépine. One of the correspondences between this self-doubling and the tale proper is the fascination with doubles, the double as an often distorted if not altogether hideous reflection of the self, that runs throughout the tale, and that has particularly important implications for Hawthorne's representation of masculinity.

Throughout Hawthorne's work, as we have seen, a peculiar figure recurs: a beautiful, callow young man, treated with a certain limited sense of sympathy but always dubiously regarded, who receives a terrible challenge to his masculine composure and almost always fails to rise up to this challenge, irreparably wounding if not killing those around him as he destroys his own life. The protagonist of "Rappaccini's Daughter" fits this bill exquisitely. Giovanni Guasconti is a young man from "very long ago" and the "more southern region of Italy" who enrolls in the University of Padua. He takes lodgings in what might have been once a palace, the home of a noble once "pictured by Dante as a partaker of the immortal agonies of his Inferno." To augment the knowledge of the Dantean plot into which he has fallen, Giovanni will become obsessed with a young woman named after the object of Dante's love in his poem of infinite torment: *Beatrice*.[5] But before we learn of her inevitable beauty, we learn of Giovanni's, through the eyes of the old housekeeper, Lisabetta, who is "won by the youth's remarkable beauty of person" (10: 93). That we are made aware that the young male protagonist is not simply presentable but a youth of *remarkable beauty* signals Hawthorne's interests in this work. The young man who will look, indeed whose looking constitutes the principle action of the story, is himself the object of the gaze.

Installed in "a high and gloomy chamber" that overlooks a garden, Giovanni occupies the structural position of the maiden in the fairy tale, whose plight and lofty remove from the world stimulate the hero below her into action. Giovanni even sighs, maidenlike, heavily and audibly, much to Lisabetta's concern. By placing Giovanni in the tower, Hawthorne creates a schism between two subject positions: the feminine one of fairy-tale tradition and the modern one that endows the viewer from a superior height with mastery over the visual scene, a mastery always associated with masculine power. As subject and object of the gaze at once, Giovanni fuses the familiar feminine and masculine versions of the gaze, connoting to-be-looked-at-ness as he takes on the role of the looker.

Giovanni finds no "better occupation than to look down into the garden below his window" (10: 94). It is not the possible sight of the beautiful woman that impels his desiring gaze but the prospect of joining in with the gaze *itself.* In a kind of sketch for *The Marble Faun,* what Giovanni's eyes light upon are the ruin of a marble fountain, marble urns, and foliage running amok; one plant wreathes itself "round a statue of Vertumnus" (10: 95). The represented figure of Vertumnus is an extremely significant intertextual detail to which I will return below. The significance of the imagery lies in its fusion of biblical and classical references, the garden and the ruins. Hawthorne's settings often fall within the hazy sphere of the merged biblical and classical pasts, his imagery amply partaking in both. Hawthorne creates an environment, highly reminiscent of Milton's *Paradise Lost,* in which he cross-fertilizes Judeo-Christian and classical mythologies. Much like Dante and Milton, Hawthorne contrasts these disparate and equally influential cultures while using them to reinforce thematic concerns: Judeo-Christian morality is jeopardized by riotous pagan sexuality; pagan sexuality is tempered and chastened by Judeo-Christian moral codes. Hawthorne crucially stands at a liminal moment in tradition, between the Renaissance and Romanticism and an incipient modernity; but he does more than stand: he swerves, charging the neoclassical, pagan-Christian register of his allusions with elusive ambiguity, defamiliarizing the expected outcomes of traditional references. This atmosphere of merged references—what I call *compound allusiveness*— reflects, even as it facilitates, Hawthorne's erotics of austerity, which can be described as both the eroticization of the austere and the rendering of the erotic as a form of austerity. In this way, Hawthorne fuses Freud and Foucault—he heightens the erotic in the grim facades of culture as he puts a grim face on the erotic—and therefore definitively heralds and enters modernity rather than remaining a votive Romantic relic. Which is to say, he not only anticipates the crisis of meaning that defines modernity but rises to the semantic and social challenges of this crisis with his own paradoxical sense of terminated traditions and interminable analysis.

THE GORGEOUS beauty of youth needs the misshapen countenance of ugliness, agedness, or a combination of both to counterbalance and reveal it: as we have seen, ugly doubles always counterbalance the rapturously beautiful men and women in Hawthorne's work. The appearance of the titular figure of Rappaccini distorts as it doubles beautiful Giovanni. A "tall, emaciated, sallow, and sickly-looking man, dressed in a scholar's garb of black," Rappaccini, a "scientific gardener," keeps his piercing focus on the plants in the garden; "it seemed as if he was looking into their inmost nature" (95). Beautiful but deadly Beatrice, it should be noted, also has a double in the quietly sinister old housekeeper Lisabetta, a type of the ambiguous nurse familiar from *Hippolytus* and *Romeo and Juliet,* who most likely aids and abets Rappaccini in his schemes.

Rappaccini, in his work and persona, embodies the hierarchization of the senses that achieved its height in the nineteenth century: he privileges vision and associates the other senses with disgust.[6] Utterly eschewing any intimacy with the plants his eyes penetrate, he avoids "their actual touch, or the direct inhaling of their odors . . . [as if he were] walking among malignant influences" (96). Giovanni, deeply uncomfortable with what he sees, locates in Rappaccini an "air of insecurity" as he treads his phobic yet probing path within the ruined yet blooming garden. Rappaccini not only represents the distorted mirror image of ugliness to Narcissus-like Giovanni but also enacts the very same privileging of sight and abhorrence of the other senses that Giovanni himself will enact.

Giovanni's distaste for what he observes in Rappaccini's behavior stems from his perception of Rappaccini's revulsion at the Edenic nature of his environment and toil. Whereas the "unfallen parents of the race" had happily cultivated the wild growths of Eden, this godlike scientist shrinks away from his postlapsarian plants. In Hawthorne's use of *style indirect libre* (the literary technique whereby the character's private thoughts and the narrator-author's own voice merge), the question that now arises is a quiet gasp of horror at the fallen state of the world: "Was this garden, then, the Eden of the present world?—and this man, in such a perception of harm in what his own hands caused to grow, was he the Adam?" (96). In this line, many key themes of the story—and of Hawthorne's art as a whole—converge. Hawthorne's recurring diabolical figures of the horticulturist and the old man merge in Rappaccini; Rappaccini is the anti-father, like Chillingworth in *The Scarlet Letter,* Old Moodie in *The Blithedale Romance,* Judge Pyncheon in *The House of the Seven Gables,* and Miriam's unseen but loomingly threatening father in *The Marble Faun.*[7] Crystallizing the function of the ugly old man as double to the beautiful young man—a function that undercuts the attributes of the latter by suggesting the latter's inevitable fall into a moral and physical decay that *may have already begun*—Giovanni, clearly the closest to an Adam figure in this tale, associates Rappaccini with Adam. This is an unusual suggestion, considering that Rappaccini seems much less Adam-like than he does a Satanic God, presiding, as he does, over the fates of the creatures he has made for his poisoned garden, his daughter and the now entrapped Giovanni. If Rappaccini provides a narcissistic double for Giovanni, then Giovanni beholds in him a paranoid vision of himself—ugly and life-killing, the opposite of the blooming Narcissus whose beauty endows life by enflaming desire and whose youthful beauty is memorialized and immortalized by the flower to which he gives a name. These resonances motivate us to ask, does Giovanni fear his *own* body? Does Giovanni fear that his touch will cause death, that *his* body will produce no life?

As I have argued elsewhere, Hawthorne associates youthful manhood even at its most beautiful with "blight"; he wrote in an erotophobic era in which debates over sexuality and its role in health were public, frequent, and deeply alarmist. The leading voices in health and sexual morality debates (John Todd, Sylvester Graham, Mary Gove Nichols) associated young men with amoral sexuality, chiefly in the form of onanistic practice. One of the common themes in this literature was the young male body succumbing to decay and ultimately to the ravages of death as a result of onanism, or masturbation; of all the forms of sexuality, autoeroticism was among the most phobically regarded, especially in its associations with same-sex sexual practice.

Themes of sterility and death also haunt the Narcissus myth; indeed, they account for its usefulness as a cautionary tale of the dangers of self-love. In Lacanian terms, Giovanni, much as Coverdale will do to his fellow Blithedalers, projects his own nothing onto Rappaccini; though he turns out to be more horribly right than he can possibly know, at this point his understanding of Rappaccini is purely an interpretation. As such, it stems as much from Giovanni's own associations with a male body he repudiates yet also analogously resembles. Milton, who haunts Hawthorne's work, described Woman's "most resembling unlikenes [sic], and most unlike resemblance" to Man.[8] The same, of course, can be said of one man to another. Giovanni and Rappaccini bear unlike resemblance to each other; as a composite portrait, they signify the beauty of the male body and its most loathsome potentialities.[9]

If Giovanni sees Rappaccini as Adam, how does he see himself in this strange non-Edenic Eden? What role could the young man play *other* than Adam? By casting the patriarchal *Rappaccini* in the role of Adam, Giovanni denies himself the role of the generative young hero in a new world and also implicitly declares this world to be God-less, for Rappaccini cannot be both Adam *and* God. Giovanni's view manages somehow to erase both himself *and* the "Father," in a strangely humorous way casting the cadaverous and sinister older man in the role of young hero. What we have come to by this early point in the narrative is a view of the young man as ugly and sinister, death lying at his touch. And Giovanni hasn't even been poisoned yet.

ENTER WOMAN

The entrance of Woman into the story can signal fortuitous change. In *The House of the Seven Gables,* the appearance of delicate but resourceful Phoebe signals a change for the better, a gleam of sunshine in the ancestral gloom. When Beatrice appears in "Rappaccini's Daughter," however, the gears of the story spin into violent motion that accelerates the tale toward its grisly end. In devising Beatrice, Hawthorne drew upon several sources, but one in particular stands out: the myth of an attempted assassination of Alexander the Great, in which a woman, who in the legends tends to be associated with India, is pumped full of poisons and sent to Alexander with the purpose of seducing him and thereby killing him when they exchange bodily fluids through sexual intercourse.[10] Beatrice Rappaccini will be shown to be a genuine fatal woman: her blood and breath mingle with that of her father's poisonous plants, and, like them, she emits a fatal breath and wields an equally fatal touch.

Yet Beatrice never outwardly suggests the poisons that course within her; indeed, she is one of Hawthorne's most poignant creations and a figure of great moral strength. The disjunct between Beatrice's helpless monstrousness and her moral resolve makes her a different kind of mirror for Giovanni. Though Giovanni is her match in physical beauty, Beatrice's moral beauty far surpasses his own, as we will see. Beatrice is reminiscent of the character of Sin from *Paradise Lost,* a pitiable figure caught, as is Hawthorne's Beatrice, between two odious male figures, in Sin's case, her father, Satan, and the child she bore from their incestuous union, Death, who no sooner meets his father for the first time than he attempts to kill him, at which point Sin intercedes. Yet Beatrice is a much more sympathetic figure than the sympathetically treated but ultimately consciously evil Sin, who willfully joins in with Satan and Death to destroy Man. Holding the key that open the gates of Hell, Sin opens Hell's gates to allow her vengeful father and hideous son free rein on Earth.

Hawthorne revisits the hierarchies of sense that had been determined but now blurs them: when Giovanni hears the "rich and youthful" voice of Beatrice, Hawthorne likens the richness of the voice to a "tropical sunset"; it makes Giovanni synesthetically think of colors, "deep hues of purple or crimson," and odors, "perfumes heavily delectable" (97). The depiction of Beatrice denatures the male gaze's visual colonization of women: by emerging first as a riot of sounds and smells and colors, Beatrice defies the imprisoning construction of women as fixed visual objects. Beatrice is initially presented as a prelapsarian image of "Woman," "as beautiful as the day," redounding with health. Yet, immediately upon seeing her, Giovanni's fancy grows "morbid": he sees Beatrice as another flower in the garden, "as beautiful as they—more beautiful than the richest of them—but still to be touched only with a glove, nor to be approached without a mask" (97). Giovanni in his own mind dons the protective gear Rappaccini already wears, thick gloves and a mask, an "armor" in defense against "a deadlier malice" (96). Hawthorne presents us with an intergenerational pair of misogynistic men who don alternately literal and psychic defenses against Woman. No less strikingly than Rappaccini's physical armor, Giovanni's fantasies of prohibition are meant to serve as a defense against any contact with a woman whose image and olfactory properties so easily penetrate his own borders.

In one of the most famous images from Hawthorne's prefaces, those mock-confessions in which the author appears to speak to us directly while goading us into the labyrinth of the mocking, elusive rhetoric where he will remain equally inaccessible, Hawthorne writes (in the essay introducing his 1846 collection of tales *Mosses from an Old Manse*) that, "So far as I am a man of really individual attributes, I veil my face; nor am I, nor have ever been, one of those supremely hospitable people, who serve up their own hearts delicately fried, with brain-sauce, as a tidbit for their beloved public" (10: 32–33). In one of his *American Notebooks*, Hawthorne had also written, "A veil may be needful, but never a mask" (8: 23). Giovanni and Rappaccini avail themselves of both veil and mask; their respective veils obscure their deeper masks. The veil of distance—Giovanni from his lofty chamber, Rappaccini behind his gloves and mask—obscures, shields, the profoundly impenetrable mask of sexual difference. The barriers the men put up serve as flimsy markers of the true impasses separating them from Beatrice and each other.

If woman is conventionally figured as Nature, the garden in a bloom that matches her own, both femininity and the natural world are toxic and deadly here, realms through which male figures make their way behind protective armor. Yet this toxicity entirely stems from male hands. Rappaccini has infused the plants and his daughter with the poison that emanates from his experiments; the fatal poison passes from the hands of the father to woman and through her to other men, a horror-movie version of Eve Sedgwick's theory of triangulated desire.[11] Beatrice and the plant are beautiful "but still to be touched only with a glove, nor to be approached without a mask" (97). Inhaling the odor of woman is no less fatal than her touch. With extraordinary economy and daring directness, Hawthorne indexes the history of misogyny, the bans on women and the male measures taken in phobic defense against them, the gloves signaling a horror of touch, the mask that of smell. Giovanni's lofty visual position emerges as phobic distance that matches the more immediate barriers behind which Rappaccini eludes contact with Beatrice. The *topos* of Genesis—dangerous femininity and the garden—transforms into a controlled site of horrified wonder in which male spectators observe the fatal workings of biology and nature.

Hawthorne's depiction of Beatrice is a feminist reading of the Indian myth of the poisonous woman sent to kill Alexander the Great. Hawthorne decouples his Beatrice from the monstrosity that consumes her by presenting this monstrosity as entirely the creation of patriarchal power. What Hawthorne suggests is that the most enduring misogynistic myths of woman as poisonous, fatal, stem from *male fantasies turned into realities through the exercise of male power:* Giovanni transforms Beatrice into the myth of woman as sexual monster. Yet in so doing, Rappaccini only effects a hideous literalization of what is always already the fate of women *in* patriarchy: to be socialized in patriarchy, especially in the Calvinist theocratical form in which Hawthorne was raised, is to be marked by the stain of human evil, an especially grievous and indelible stain in the case of women, linked with the serpent, original sin, and the corruption of humanity. As Augustine wrote, man is evil from the very moment of conception; indeed, semen itself, from Adam forward, bequeaths original sin upon the newly created human being.[12] What Rappaccini does, then, is to rewrite Genesis, the story in which woman seduced by Satan effects man's fall, as a literal, scientific narrative in which one man programs a woman—in this case, biogenetically engineers a woman—to kill men. If Rappaccini takes Genesis matters into his own hands, transforming the narrative of original sin into his own scientific triumph, he also transforms sexual difference and the problems of gender relations into lab work, recreating the fundamental problems of patriarchy as the stuff of controlled scientific experiment.

Like Hitchcock's indelible *Vertigo* (1958), "Rappaccini's Daughter" exposes the Western image of woman as the product of male fantasy. Beatrice is a sexual monster only insofar as she represents misogynistic fantasies of femininity taken to their logical extremes. If women's bodies are associated with pernicious and mysterious odors, properties, cycles, Beatrice's body literally emanates and causes death. If femininity remains forever trapped in the garden, tethered with the adamantine chains of culture to images of flowering nature and scenes of fatal seduction, this version of femininity has been conjoined to the serpent's poisonous blood. Much like the cloned Ellen Ripley (Sigourney Weaver) of *Alien Resurrection* (1997) in whom human and Alien DNA combine, her blood a seething, acid mixture, Beatrice combines the purity of Eve with the poison of the snake, recalling frequent images of Renaissance art in which Eve confronts the serpent who wears Eve's face. The depiction of nature-bound Beatrice both preserves and revises the Genesis narrative by keeping the woman in the Edenic sphere over which she reigns supreme; her poison nature and the poisoned nature of her garden keep the evil Eden inviolate, impregnable.

One of the strange consequences of this scientific literalization of the Genesis myth—a myth mediated for Hawthorne by the equally relevant intertext of *Paradise Lost,* in which Milton simultaneously submits Genesis to a sensual paganization and uses it to reinforce the most stringent forms of Christian moral code—is that symbols assume the life of characters. Symbols take on human attributes, or suggest them with such intensity that they come to seem human themselves; sign transforms into character. "Rappaccini's Daughter" pushes tensions in Hawthorne's work to their breaking point in the ways in which the tale threatens to explode the confines of its own allegorical form. The "magnificent plant" that symbolizes Beatrice's beauty emerges as "my sister, my splendor," as Beatrice "opened her arms as if to embrace it" (10: 97). The symbols of gendered identity become indistinguishable from what they sign.

Yet Beatrice seems aware of the unseemly tension between sisterly affection for a plant and the unnatural endowment of vegetable life with human qualities. She opens her arms to the plant she calls "my sister, my splendor," but when she does so it is "as *if* to embrace it"—Beatrice recognizes on some level that the plant is a plant, not fully to be embraced as if it actually were a sibling rather than just a sister under the skin. The significance of these seismic tensions lies in what they convey about a character's psychic life in Hawthorne's allegorical narratives in which characters and symbols vie alike for power. Hawthorne's most famous symbol, the scarlet *A,* throbs with life and has more personality than most literary characters; many Hawthorne characters—though certainly not all—function most prominently as symbols in his allegories. Following Sacvan Bercovitch's influential reading in *The Office of The Scarlet Letter,* recent critics of Hawthorne have come to see his once-celebrated technique of ambiguity as a conservative form of political consensus building, the seemingly endless array of interpretive possibilities actually functioning, however counterintuitively, as the denial of interpretive options. But Hawthorne's ambiguity is much more complex, and at times more radical, than Bercovitch would have it. Here, this small instance of ambiguity reveals the intimate knowledge of a character's conflictual feelings. In negotiating anxieties about her relationship to her father's plant, Beatrice struggles over her responses to the enduring symbolic signs and narratives of women in Western culture. The bush symbolizes woman's sexuality, an image repeated and further aestheticized in *The Scarlet Letter*'s rosebush outside the prison, the one gleam of hope in a bed of "black flowers." As a gendered symbol, it synthesizes all of the essentialist markers of Beatrice's beauty—beauty, bloom, and the Edenic garden. What Rappaccini has done is to blur the lines between a woman and the plant-as-gendered-symbol by interfusing their blood; what Beatrice appears to register is the grotesque way in which her own sexuality is delimited and reified by being fused with its own symbolic markers.

FIRST MOTHER, PHALLIC MOTHER

Imprisoned by the gendered symbology that gives her an identity, Beatrice inhabits her closed allegorical world as an Eve without an Adam, unless we view Rappaccini—"was he the Adam?"—as her incestuous father-husband. This is a suggestion the story offers, but more emphatically countermands by presenting the idea of intimacy between lush, floral, deadly daughter and gloved, masked, distant father as unthinkable precisely because the father-figure maintains such a chilly estrangement from the daughter who embodies his most fiendish ambitions while refuting their every import with her own moral code. However we are meant to interpret their relationship, it is redolent of sadomasochism.

In her poison bloom, Beatrice thrives in a state of autoerotic plenitude that anticipates Freud's phallic mother, the mythological construct of male fantasy. As noted in the previous chapter, Gillian Brown has made a strong case for reading Miles Coverdale's incessant looking in *The Blithedale Romance* as a fetishistic maneuver that simultaneously turns women into objects and allows him to remain unperceived as a fetishistic voyeur. I believe that Brown's reading is especially relevant to the present discussion because "Rappaccini's Daughter" is the most fetish-obsessed work in the Hawthorne canon.

In his 1927 essay "Fetishism," Freud explains why "some men" develop fetishes. The fetishist—who privileges a foot, a shoe, a nose, even the shine on a nose as the site of his sexual desire rather than the woman herself—has, through his fetishizing, discovered an ingenious strategy for defending against and coping with a profound childhood psychic trauma that *all* males, in Freud's view, must grapple with throughout their lives: the discovery that their mother, who seemed the embodiment of fullness, presence, oneness, totality, completeness, *does not have a penis*. The fetishist devises a peculiar, specific strategy for coping with the trauma of this discovery, his obsessive endowment of parts of women's bodies with phallic attributes. Men can be divided into three categories: fetishists, homosexuals, and normal heterosexuals. Why some men become fetishists, others homosexuals, and most heterosexuals cannot be easily explained, if at all, but *all* men must cope with the trauma, and these three sexual categories represent the strategies men have for doing so.

If Freud's accounts of female sexuality remain deeply unsatisfying, he nevertheless offers a consistent and provocative view of male subjectivity and sexuality as tormented almost from its inception. Male identity in Freud emerges as a desperate series of ever-mounted psychic defenses, strategies for overcoming, forgetting, and shielding against trauma, all of which fail, and, despite their inherent futility, are perpetually renewed, taken up again as if for the first time. Freud suggests that without his narcissistic reverence for his own phallus, the male's identity would be *utterly* untenable, rather than nearly so. The boy is so traumatized by the recognition that his great and powerful mother has been "castrated" that he, in effect, refuses to acknowledge what he has discovered. "No, that could not be true, for if a woman had been castrated, then his own possession of a penis was in danger; and against that there rose in rebellion the portion of his narcissism which Nature has, as a precaution, attached to this particular organ. In later life, a grown man may perhaps experience a similar panic when the cry goes up that Throne and Altar are in danger, and similar illogical consequences will ensue" (SE

21: 153). In a manner at once subtle and sweeping, Freud explains away here the whole masculine history of war, bloodshed, imperialism, and murderous power—responses to the illogical fears over "Throne and Altar"—as the result of the mythic little boy's silent scream at the thought that his penis, like his mother's, might be taken away. Though this is not the Freudian focus, which is on castration, it is the mother's own sexuality—rather than the idea that it has somehow been taken away—that threatens the boy's narcissism.

While the absence of the mother's penis causes so much consternation for the male child, there is another sense in which that phantom organ remains intact. In the male's mind, "the woman *has* got a penis, in spite of everything; but this penis is no longer the same as it was before. Something else has taken its place, has been appointed its substitute, as it were, and now inherits the interest which was formally directed to its predecessor." As Freud theorizes, "the horror of castration has set up a memorial to itself" through the strategy of fetishism. And as he further argues, "an aversion, which is never absent in any fetishist, to the real female genitals remains a *stigma indelebile* of the repression that has taken place." Nevertheless, his strategy of defense against traumatic knowledge of castration "saves the fetishist from being a homosexual by endowing women with the characteristic which makes them tolerable as sexual objects" (SE 21: 154).

The original, pre-oedipal mother, whom the boy believed to possess a penis and therefore existed *before* the intense need for the fetish arose, ultimately emerges within Freud's theory as the figure of *the phallic mother,* the unity of femininity and masculinity who transcends all fears of castration. This mythic phallic mother exists above, before, and beyond any other version of woman, indeed, any version of man. Rappaccini's daughter Beatrice, in her abundant autoerotic natural plenitude, inhabits the original phallic mother's mythic-psychosexual space:

> Soon there emerged from under a sculptured portal the figure of a young girl, arrayed with as much richness of taste as the most splendid of the flowers, beautiful as the day, and with a bloom so deep and vivid that one shade more would have been too much. She looked redundant with life, health, and energy; all of which attributes were bound down and compressed, as it were, and girdled tensely, in their luxuriance, by her virgin zone. (10: 97)

Lushly beautiful, Beatrice rivals the wonder of Milton's Eve. And yet, as noted, this sight of her nevertheless almost immediately turns Giovanni's fancy "morbid." The phallic mother connotes death as well as generative life. In her sheer vitality, Beatrice suggests the overwhelming, suffocating force of the ancient mother who gives life and death at once. The imagery Hawthorne associates with Beatrice phallicizes her. She emerges *from* a portal, a phallic emergence from a yonic symbol. One shade more of her zestful healthfulness would have been *too much*—she connotes excess. This excess can barely be contained: it must be *bound down and compressed,* and can only be girdled *tensely.* As a figure bursting with her own fleshiness, Beatrice suggests throbbing fullness, a kind of tumescent engorgement. As horrifying as she is beautiful, she fuses the image of the Madonna and the carnal, death-dealing Eve-like seductress, associations that will inform later Hawthorne heroines, especially Hester Prynne (*The Scarlet Letter*) but also Zenobia (*The Blithedale Romance*) and Miriam Schaeffer (*The Marble Faun*). In these capacities, Beatrice occupies the central position in the pre-oedipal realm to which the story returns Giovanni. Giovanni inhabits the realm of *primary narcissism,* in which no distinction was made between the infant and the body of the Mother. The tale proceeds to develop a narrative that parallels the action of Freud's essay on fetishism—the traumatic recognition on the male's part that the looming, all-powerful Mother does not possess the penis, that she has been castrated, and that she will in effect castrate *him.*

In *Remembering the Phallic Mother,* Marcia Ian discusses the cultural politics of Freud's theory of fetishism, and what it reveals about the male biases of psychoanalysis. As she establishes, "Freud has little of use to say about women; but then psychoanalysis is not *about* women."

> Neither is the image of the phallic mother *about* women; it does not *refer* to women or to mothers. It does not refer at all, except to the possible collapse of sign and referent—a collapse represented as and replaced by the fetishization of their phantom connection to the mother. What the phallic mother represents, ultimately, is the "end of contradiction and the end of ambivalence," since she is not two, but one, the mother who "inseminates and lactates." The phallic mother is "neither hermaphrodite nor androgyne, human nor monster, because she is emphatically Mother."[13]

Of Beatrice Rappaccini we can say that she is also neither daughter nor sister, mother nor lover, woman nor nature, but is instead all of these things at once, a super-sign of femininity. The tale allows us, once again, to consider mother-identified narcissistic male desire in terms of an ostensibly heterosexual male sexuality. But it also allows us to consider the potential for misogyny in identification with femininity and, more importantly here, what's at stake in all of this for the woman. The woman's experience—of being identified with, of being made mythological, of being the object of competing fantasies with positive and negative intentions at once, or more properly with intentions put forth as positive that are in actuality inescapably negative—is the chief subject of "Rappaccini's Daughter." Paradoxically, the centrality of femininity in the tale sheds abundant light on its limning of the nature of male subjectivity.

FLOWERING NARCISSUS
VERTUMNUS

We can now return to the image of Vertumnus and make better sense of it. If Beatrice is the Eve-Madonna, the erotic woman of death and the phallic mother, Giovanni is the tale's flowering Narcissus, a self-regarding beautiful man that Hawthorne returns to nature, forcibly and frighteningly. The statue of Vertumnus in Rappaccini's garden synecdochically alludes to the history of masculine Nature that is usually obscured by the preponderance of Judeo-Christian traditions of woman and nature. Vertumnus is a highly charged intertexual sign that marks Hawthorne's negotiation of several key influential texts and the traditions they support—Ovid, the Bible, and Milton's *Paradise Lost*, in particular.

As an Ovidian figure associated with nature—he is the god of seasonal change—Vertumnus provides a link to the classical world and to the trope of masculinity as a force of nature. In Vertumnus, Hawthorne synthesizes several male figures associated with nature, such as the named biblical/Miltonic Adam and the unnamed Ovidian Narcissus. Milton renders the sparsely sketched biblical figure of Adam with an erotic awareness of his beauty that matches that of Milton's lushly desirable Eve; the poet's depictions of the first human couple, both as a couple and as distinct individuals, surges with pagan sexuality. Narcissus emerges as the overdetermined index to these intertextual thematics: the beautiful male figure fuses elements of Vertumnus and Adam, all three being associated with nature (Narcissus is the origin myth for the flower by that name). Narcissus also connotes nature through negation, representing, as a phobic sign of sterility, anti-nature. This anti-nature also informs Milton's representation of Adam, who, in falling from a prelapsarian state, loses his claim to paradisiacal unity with the natural world over which he had presided. (These thematics in Milton require much more discussion than I can provide here.) Like these other figures, Narcissus embodies an ideal of male beauty, but also the possibilities for the metamorphosis of this beauty into a different form: the crone version of Vertumnus in Ovid; the corrupt, fallen, shamed version of Adam in the biblical and, especially, Miltonic contexts; the transformation, through death, of a beautiful young man into a memorial flower (Narcissus, Adonis, Hyacinth, and so forth). Hawthorne funnels this mixture of classical, biblical, and Miltonic associations into a revisionist, secular Christian narrative that imagines Eden as a human male fantasy, organized around the fallible male human gaze rather than God's. Rappaccini, the paradoxically Adam-like figure of death, and Giovanni, the death-haunted new Adam, constitute, along with Beatrice, an Eve whose blood courses with the serpent's poison, a newly ordered, postlapsarian Eden, one suffused with satanic corruptions of flesh, sense, and spirit. (One remembers that Milton's Satan, in his seduction of Eve, hails the Tree of Knowledge as "Mother of Science"; Beatrice, the offspring of masculine science cast as a phallic, deadly anti-mother, embodies this Miltonic-Satanic concept.)

Both Vertumnus and Adam play out the significant action of their story within a garden inhabited by a powerful woman who mesmerizes them: Pomona and Eve, respectively. Eve is the "fair Empress" of her vegetable realm and married to Adam, whereas Pomona, a hamadryad, or wood-nymph, installs herself within the precincts of her garden to *elude* the erotic attentions of various phallically driven male deities: Pan, Priapus, Silvanus. Narcissus, though a figure associated with solipsism, also enjoins a crucial female figure within his myth, Echo, who pines for him and, in the course of his pitiless rejection of her, loses her voice. Similarly, Pomona also never speaks in her myth, though Eve famously does in Milton. Hawthorne disavows the Narcissus themes crucial to his work by refusing to name Narcissus; yet he also fights against or mediates this disavowal. In "Rappaccini's Daughter," he incorporates the narcissistic facets of the Vertumnus and Adam myths into a Narcissus and Echo schema. Giovanni's narcissism flows directly from the Ovidian Narcissus myth, and as it does so it picks up and absorbs those within the Vertumnus and Adam myths, Ovid, the Bible, and Milton. In short, considerable valences as well as differences exist in these myths and the versions of them under consideration here.

The chief relevance to "Rappaccini's Daughter" of the Vertumnus myth lies in these major themes: the display of male beauty, voyeurism, and, as Roxanne Gentilcore has argued, the theme of love as a destructive force. Through various disguises, Vertumnus woos the determinedly inviolate Pomona before settling on one last disguise, that of an old woman, in whose guise he tells her a cautionary tale, that of Iphis and Anaxarete. Anaxarete's hardness of heart destroys both her life and that of her helplessly devoted suitor, Iphis. Iphis hangs himself, and the rejecting Anaxarete turns to stone at his funeral procession. Telling her even this cautionary tale, however, fails to woo and win Pomona, who steadfastly remains sexually unavailable. Seeing that Pomona remains unmoved, Vertumnus resumes his own "Young shape and," as Ovid puts it,

> shed the trappings of old age,
> And stood triumphantly revealed to her as when the sun
> Triumphs in glory through the clouds and rain
> And bright with beams untrammeled shines again.
> No need of force. His beauty wins the day,
> As she with answering love is borne away. (14: 766–71)

Though Ovid appears to suggest that masculinity does not need recourse to violence to secure erotic satisfaction, A. D. Melville points out that "Ovid's text makes it clear that it would have been forthcoming at need."[14] As Roxanne Gentilcore summarizes her argument, "This negative portrait of love is set alongside several other mythological tales which together form patterns of violence and destructive passion" in *The Metamorphoses*.[15]

If Vertumnus signifies the culmination of the list of figures who embody for Ovid "the wild, sexual side of nature," Hawthorne's evocation of him signals an investment in male sexual nature that matches the investment in the feminine sexual nature of Beatrice.[16] Pomona, who has rejected sex with men, is conscripted into sexuality with dramatic force by being forced submit to Vertumnus *as a visual spectacle,* to stare in wonder at Vertumnus's extravagant display of his own beauty. As Hawthorne's contemporary Thomas Bulfinch wrote in his version of the story in his popularization of the Greek myths, Vertumnus, dropping his old-crone disguise, stands before Pomona in "his proper person, a comely youth. It appeared to her like the sun bursting through a cloud. He would have renewed his entreaties," but there was no need: "the sight of his true form prevailed, and the Nymph no longer resisted, but owned a mutual flame."[17] Left out of most critical analyses of Hawthorne's tale (for instance, even Carol Marie Bensick makes no reference to Vertumnus in her book-length study of the story), Vertumnus plays a crucial role here. What makes Vertumnus a figure of vital importance to Hawthorne is his combination of male beauty and sexual menace. Vertumnus is a sign of the erotic masculine and also of the duplicity of male appearances, one of Hawthorne's most consistent themes.[18]

One of the most distinctive hallmarks of the erotic schemes that characterize Hawthorne's fiction is the erotic appeal of his male characters. In other words, Hawthorne does not simply eroticize the feminine, which would be expected, but eroticizes the masculine as well, leaving the reader in the position of experiencing erotic responses to both female and male characters. In this regard, Hawthorne once more recalls Milton, but it must be noted that he does so in an era of increasingly punitive vigilance about such matters, if we see the nineteenth century as moving toward a greater phobic reaction against erotically charged same-sex affiliations. Hawthorne gives us not only Beatrice's ecstatic beauty to contemplate but also that of Vertumnus in his proper guise of comely youth and Giovanni's in his own, which mirrors classical and biblical precedents. If we reinsert the relevance of Vertumnus as a spectacular, overwhelming, nearly obliterating spectacle of male beauty—a spectacle that comes close to scorching Pomona out of existence before it successfully subdues her into acquiescing to his charms—we can better understand the narcissistic themes of the story. For Vertumnus functions as a displacement of the unacknowledgeable, phobic, influential figure of Narcissus in Hawthorne's work.[19]

WILD OFFSPRING

Giovanni wields "the privilege of overlooking" (10: 98); "within the shadow thrown by the depth of the wall," he can "look down into the garden with little risk of being discovered"; he can feast his eyes on the "half-hoped, half-feared" phobic object of his erotic visual frenzy, Beatrice, with what he believes to be the impunity of his gazing male privilege (10: 101). What he actually witnesses, I would argue, is the scene of his own symbolic castration, precisely the fear that his fetishizing ardor is meant to assuage.

A prefiguring of the hothouse flower in Zenobia's hair that signals her overpowering carnality in *The Blithedale Romance,* Beatrice puts a flower on her presumably ample bosom. When Beatrice picks up a small reptile, it appears to Giovanni that "a drop or two of moisture from the broken stem of the flower" with which Beatrice adorns her bosom falls on the lizard's head. "For an instant the lizard contorted itself violently, and then lay motionless"; this phallic symbol then transforms, in Beatrice's hands and in contact with the symbol of *her* sexuality, into a sign of heterosexual failure and male terror over female sexuality at once. "What is this being?" wonders Giovanni: "—beautiful shall I call her?—or inexpressibly terrible?" Combining both his knowing erotic themes and sense of the hideousness that may lie beneath erotically stimulating beauty, Hawthorne thematizes a profound ambivalence over heterosexual relations. This theme will reach only deepening levels in the novel-romances from 1850 forward and also in his late, unfinished *Septimius* manuscripts. As if to compensate for the lack he experiences after witnessing this symbolic castration, Giovanni thrusts "his head out quite out of its concealment in order to gratify the intense and painful curiosity which" Beatrice excites in him (10: 103); Hawthorne, describing the intensity and the pain of Giovanni's curiosity, shares Freud's view of scopophilic impulses such as voyeurism as "tormenting compulsions."

But again, Giovanni's wishes remain unclear: does he wish to see Beatrice or for her to see *him*? At "an impulsive movement of Giovanni," Beatrice "drew her eyes to the window. There she beheld the beautiful head of the young man—rather a Grecian than an Italian head, with fair, regular features, and a glistening of gold among his ringlets—gazing down upon her like a being that hovered in mid-air" (10: 104). This description, I argue, echoes the Vertumnus reference, by depicting Giovanni as someone who commands the woman's gaze and by specifying him as "Grecian." Though Vertumnus is a Roman ("Italian") god, by associating Giovanni with the Grecian, Hawthorne inserts him into the general discourse of Hellenism within which the Vertumnus myth would have been understood; in this way, Vertumnus becomes antitype to Giovanni's type.[20] I will return to Hellenism's significance in the next chapter.

Giovanni's exhibitionism and Beatrice's radical license to wield the gaze and return his look coalesce here. Hardly aware of why, Giovanni tosses a bouquet of flowers to Beatrice, who takes them and passes through the portal back to her home, another hint of sexual intercourse. Yet, in a stunning transformation of the castration metaphor, Giovanni fearfully apprehends, or believes that he does, the bouquet wilting in Beatrice's hand. The phallic lizard she held transmogrifies into the flowers she holds; if we follow the sexual symbolism here, his phallus transforms into *her* flowers, an extraordinary exchange of gendered signifiers that confirms Giovanni's associations with the flowering masculinity of Vertumnus and Narcissus. His phallus blooms in her hands, but then also wilts. This is a poignant nod to Milton, too, if we remember the moment in *Paradise Lost* in which Adam recognizes that Eve has fallen (he notices that the bouquet of roses that he has given her upon her return from her independent labors in the Garden—during which time Satan seduced her—now wither in her hand). Giovanni's phallic sexuality turns into yonic femininity; his looking, his desire, his fear all emasculate him, threaten to turn him into "Woman." But the phallic scopic drive still impels him anew several days later to look again at the perplexing Beatrice, even if as he does so he feels as "if something ugly and monstrous would have blasted his eye-sight" (104). As in the Oedipus myth, eyes, like the phallus, can be castrated. The phallic woman threatens to castrate the male and his gaze.

Like several other Hawthorne males, Giovanni is as motivated by scopophobia, or the fear of looking, as he is by scopophilia, the ravenous desire to look. Even as he consumes her with his eyes when "the wisest course would have been . . . to quit his lodgings," Giovanni attempts to avoid her gaze. To lift, not irrelevantly, from Melville, Beatrice and the visual are both fate and ban. Beatrice synthesizes the anxieties that attend the visual; femininity is the economy that facilitates male visual desire in multiple forms: Giovanni's ravenous looking, her father's engulfing surveillance of her interactions with the youthful stranger, and even the prying, spying looking of Rappaccini's scientific rival, Baglioni (indeed, Baglioni, who watches Rappaccini watching all of the events he engineered unfold, may be the tale's ultimate voyeur). As noted, a palpable ambivalence surrounds the prospect of heterosexual union here. I would suggest that the entire scene of male voyeurism, shot through with conflictual longings between men as well as between men and women, suggests a relationship too terrible to be named, something outside of language, nameless, unrepresentable—in other words, a queer as well as gendered panic. The tale prefigures the terrible mystery, undeniably sexual and criminal at once, that indissolubly links Miriam to the Model in *The Marble Faun*. (As I will discuss in the next chapter, racial and ethnic panic inheres in these mysteries in both works.) The question to ask is, what, exactly, *is* so inexpressibly terrible here?

The voyeur who sadistically attempts to achieve sexual satisfaction through looking at others and possessing them through the look is also the narcissist desperate for a vision of himself. But that self-image, as we have seen, may also itself be a kind of displacement of a desired but repudiated homosexual object: narcissistic desire may be a metaphor for homosexual desire. (Recalling our discussion in chapter 2 of Michael Warner's critique of psychoanalysis, this is to reformulate, in some ways, the homophobic rhetoric, assailed by Warner, that defines queer desire as a desire for sameness. Perhaps narcissistic desire is a metaphor for the queer desire for *different sameness,* for someone who suggests a different version of or alternative possibilities for the self.) Hawthorne suggests that such a displacement may occur for Giovanni. When he closes the lattice as night closes in, Giovanni goes to his couch and dreams "of a rich flower and a beautiful girl. Flower and maiden were different and yet the same, and fraught with some strange peril in either shape." But something else may be deepening his peril. Before closing the lattice and commencing his onanistic nighttime reverie, Giovanni sees Rappaccini take his daughter's arm and retire into their home. There is an ambiguity over what has led Rappaccini to take this action: "Whether Doctor Rappaccini had finished his labors in the garden, or that his watchful eye had caught the stranger's face," we are left to decide for ourselves (10: 98). Such ambiguous moments are, while not definitive, at least suggestive for a queer theory reading of Hawthorne. That Rappaccini may have "caught the stranger's face" is suggestive because of the power of the verb: What does it mean to *catch* someone's face? This is reminiscent of Lacan's theory of *captation,* of being seized by the image. Being seized by the image was our first crucial step toward selfhood, as the image we saw in the mirror captivated us forever. For that matter, if Rappaccini saw and held the image of Giovanni, that also suggests that *Giovanni* saw Rappaccini looking at him and exchanged looks with the scientist. Given this passage's correspondence to the moment in *The Blithedale Romance* when Coverdale imagines seeing the "dark frown" of Hollingsworth before Coverdale commences his "shuddering" nighttime reveries, it may not be implausible to consider that the dark face of repudiated homoerotic desire may frown on Giovanni as well. Such a possibility deepens the resonances of Giovanni's feelings when he awakens the next day: he feels "surprised, and a little ashamed" (10: 98).

But what was a suggestion becomes a reality, in terms of the male–male gaze. Giovanni attempts to avoid Beatrice's sight (10: 105), in accordance with other Hawthorne males, such as Wakefield and Coverdale, who attempt to see while avoiding being seen themselves. But Giovanni cannot escape Rappaccini's invasive, incessant gaze. Rappaccini's eye descends on Giovanni even outside the garden. Baglioni, Rappaccini's scientific rival, keeps trying to explain to Giovanni the terrible danger that he's in, though to no avail. As Giovanni speaks to the Cassandra-like Baglioni, Rappaccini himself appears on the street, "stooping and moving feebly, like a person in inferior health. His face was all overspread with a most sickly and sallow hue, but yet so pervaded with an expression of piercing and active intellect. . . . As he passed, this person exchanged a cold and distant salutation with Baglioni, but fixed his eyes upon Giovanni with an intentness that seemed to bring out whatever was within him worthy of notice." "Nevertheless," adds the narrator, "there was a peculiar quietness in the look, as if merely taking a speculative, not a human, interest in the young man" (10: 106–7).

Giovanni has the privilege of overlooking, but not the privilege to be overlooked. Emblematic of Hawthorne's men, he is as much the object as he is the subject of the gaze. Rappaccini looks at him intently, just as the savagely face-painted horseback rider looks at comely Robin Molineux; ghastly Chillingworth at the splayed-out Dimmesdale, his chest exposed as if he were a character in a nineteenth-century bodice-ripper; the other characters at the earthy, sensual, faun-eared Italian youth Donatello; Septimius Felton and his sister at the handsome young English soldier whom Septimius later kills and mourns over.[21]

Rappaccini is the demonic "Father" here, whose totalizing gaze consumes all narrative space as it fixes upon Giovanni. Rappaccini's gaze subsumes the young man's own puny scopic endeavors. This scene also suggests, again, homoerotic threat, evoking, as it does, a scene of homosexual cruising. That Rappaccini is a debilitated, stumbling figure is significant as well, if we take the older man to be a mirror image for the younger, a mirror image that reveals his interior ugliness. If Giovanni is, like Coverdale, the voyeuristic onanist, Rappaccini, in his debilitated decrepitude, suggests the onanist's fate as foreseen by the sexual and health reformers of Hawthorne's day, such as Sylvester Graham and Mary Gove Nichols, who railed against onanistic practice and created images of the onanist's body as ravaged by disease and of his soul as "ruined."[22] Moreover, Rappaccini walks with the same stooping gait that, as I argued in chapter 4, indicates male shame in Hawthorne, albeit usually associated with the young man. A ghost of sexual ruin, Rappaccini figures the future form of Giovanni, depicted as an onanist, while suggesting that male shame, an imprisonment in the other's judgmental gaze, might descend into voyeuristic sadism, a desire to control others, as one had been controlled, through the cold, pitiless eye.

When the young man's vulnerability, his subjection to the gaze, is considered along with the tale's pronounced bewilderment in the face of heterosexual relations, what we are left with is an overturning of a broad range of presumptions: heterosexual, gendered, sexual, and, of course, racial, as this story's terror in the face of "intermixture" has unmistakably racially charged undertones. The unwieldy, wide-ranging array of anxieties here can only be expressed as something that is itself an expression of the inexpressible. The story thematizes the attempt to express something—perhaps a form of desire—that cannot, ever, be expressed. The only possible vent for an expression of the competing, incommensurate desires in the story is Giovanni's feelings for Beatrice. It is a testament to the utter mystification of normative heterosexuality in this work that Hawthorne can express Giovanni's desire for Beatrice only as the fusion of incommensurate responses:

> It was not love, although her rich beauty was a madness to him; nor horror, even while he fancied her spirit to be imbued with the same baneful essence that seemed to pervade her physical frame; but a wild offspring of both love and horror that had each parent in it, and burned like one and shivered like the other. (10: 105)

With self-preserving defiance, the narrator ejaculates thusly: "Blessed are all simple emotions, be they dark or bright! It is the lurid intermixture of the two that produces the illuminating blaze of the infernal regions" (10: 105). This story's theme of terrible/irresistible looking is a metonymic welter of the anxieties and sexual preoccupations of Hawthorne's oeuvre, fusing the heteroerotic and the homoerotic, the narcissistic with the voyeuristic, all of which produce together this textual wild offspring. Hawthorne's attitude of ambivalence extends beyond gender, nature, race, and the body to the very idea of sexuality itself. It is in this ambivalence that Hawthorne and Freud meet as thinkers who view sexuality as a source of terror as well as beauty.

VOYEURISM AS NARCISSISM

Hawthorne makes Giovanni, with his "Grecian" beauty and golden, glistening ringlets, a poster boy of Hellenism. Succinctly summarizing the sexual import of the discourse, Linda Dowling writes that the "Anglo-Hellenism" of the nineteenth century was "a screen for sodomy."[23] If we recall our discussion of the homoerotic valences of Hellenism in chapter 3, we can understand that Hawthorne's specific attribution of "Grecian," rather than "Italian," beauty to Giovanni has discursive implications for the nineteenth century's homoerotic themes, as does the classically named "Cyrus" of "Roger Malvin's Burial." The Greco-Roman ideal of symmetrical, lithe, and abstracted beauty to which Hawthorne's beautiful males correspond was embodied by the Apollo Belvedere, a central figure and point of celebration for the eighteenth-century German art historian Johann Joachim Winckelmann (1717–68), whose writings on classical aesthetics inspired the nineteenth-century craze for the Grand Tour, an improving journey throughout the great cultural centers of Europe, with a focus on the classical past. The appearance of Hellenic images in the works of antebellum American authors in particular carried with it the dangerous attractions of the homoerotic.

Like Cyrus, Giovanni seems to have wandered from Greek myth into a distinct new realm. Exporting the full weight of Hellenic themes into this neo-Dantean gothic, Giovanni amplifies and extends the associations between classical reference and male sexuality signaled by the reference to Vertumnus. If Hawthorne cannot name Narcissus—the figure that is so crucial to nineteenth-century homoerotic discourse—he *can* evoke his character through a representation of a male figure whose own striking beauty threatens to surpass the female figure who is presumably the focal point of the masculine, which is ostensibly the narrative, gaze; whose own beauty is inextricably intermeshed with his pronounced anxieties over vision and desire.[24] In every way—his excessive beauty, the vulnerability of his body, its susceptibility to penetration, the ease with which the "fierce and subtle poison [that flows] into his system" (10: 105) breaches the borders of his masculine integrity—Giovanni is threatened by homoeroticism and effeminacy, even as he himself carries these threats.

The classical ethical content of the Narcissus myth—its cautionary program of redressing the failure to distinguish surface from depth, true from false value, self from other—is the most audible echo of the myth in Hawthorne's depiction of Giovanni. "Guasconti had not a deep heart," the narrator tells us, when Giovanni resumes his scopophilic vigil. "[O]r at all events, its depths were not sounded now" (10: 105). But there are no depths to sound, save those to be seen in the "haunted verge" of the mirror, as Hawthorne describes it in "The Custom-House" (a thematic I turn to in the epilogue).

What Hawthorne registers most acutely in this scene is the ambivalence over masculinity that suffuses his oeuvre. Beatrice's physical resemblance to Giovanni—she shares his "glistening ringlets" (10: 102)—refracts the narcissistic similarities between them. Resemblances between woman and man signal the threatening infiltration of narcissistic femininity—Eve staring at her own reflection in *Paradise Lost*, the vain woman before her looking-glass in countless works of visual art—into the seemingly staunch, unimpeachably secure masculine character. Males look *at* women in the standard gendered narrative of Western culture and, indeed, of most cultures; the male who looks at *himself* with the same fixation, if not outright prurient intensity, that attends his visual inspection of women threatens to fall into the traditionally feminine languor of self-obsession—and into the even deadlier trap of homoerotic fascination.

In the climactic portion of "Rappaccini's Daughter," Hawthorne finally makes his most explicit statement about Giovanni's narcissistic nature:

> It was now the customary hour of his daily interview with Beatrice. Before descending into the garden, Giovanni failed not to look at his figure in the mirror; a vanity to be expected in a beautiful young man, yet, as displaying itself at that troubled and feverish moment, the token of a certain shallowness of feeling and insincerity of character. He did gaze, however, and said to himself, that his features had never before possessed so rich a grace, nor his eyes such vivacity, nor his cheeks so warm a hue of superabundant life. (10: 121)

Explicating the metaphor that had been suggested earlier, that his phallus transforms into Beatrice's flowers in her hands, Giovanni, momentarily assuring himself that her poison has *not* penetrated him, announces defiantly, "I am no flower to perish in her grasp!" Or, to put it in modern parlance, "You don't own me!"

Yet this assurance is none at all; indeed, it leads to that confrontation with the ugly self on the part of the beautiful male that I have termed *traumatic narcissism*. Giovanni notices that the bouquet of flowers he holds has begun to droop.

> A thrill of indefinable horror shot through his frame. . . . Giovanni grew white as marble, and stood motionless before the mirror, staring at his own reflection there, as at the likeness of something frightful. . . . Then he shuddered—shuddered at himself! (10: 121)

No Hawthorne work more sharply articulates the particular set of anxieties that beset his male characters. Beautiful, they must contend with interior knowledge of a profound ugliness. Loving, they must renounce their love or destroy it. Lonely and longing for connection, they make of themselves a chilly, remote empire which no one else can enter. Giovanni becomes as white as marble and just as motionless—a spectator frozen in place.

Giovanni's exterior beauty masks a shallow heart and a dim soul: he is void of morals and spirit. This scene is a representative example of the theme of scopophobia that recurs throughout Hawthorne's fiction: the fearfulness of returning one's own gaze, the fearfulness of seeing, being seen by others, of truly seeing *oneself;* what makes this fear of looking especially painful and poignant is how closely tethered it is to physical beauty, both in male and female characters. But it is debatable who suffers more, in real-world terms, within the visual regime of Hawthorne's fiction. Hawthorne's beautiful, intelligent, and sympathetic women are all ensnared in the murderous logic of the gaze, be they the center of the assaultive gaze of a sadistic mob, such as Hester Prynne; a woman whose sexual gaze so unmans the desired male that he destroys her in retaliation, such as Alice Pyncheon; the object of a dubious man's "eye-shot," such as Zenobia; or the purveyor of a gaze that literally kills, such as Miriam Schaeffer. But if Miriam's gaze kills, she is also the object of an incessant, injurious, and itself quite murderous gaze, the Model's. Beatrice Rappaccini, visual magnet, is destroyed by the narcissistic male gaze at its most pernicious.

MEDUSA IN THE MIRROR

Giovanni's horrifying self-encounter in the mirror evokes not only the Narcissus myth but also another, analogous mythic figure of equal significance to psychoanalysis and to Hawthorne: Medusa. Turned into "white marble," Giovanni is at once Narcissus and the victim of a woman's killing gaze, a woman in whose image he now sees *himself*. In properly Medusan fashion, she has turned him into stone.

In Ovid's narrative of Perseus's encounter with Medusa, in order to decapitate the infamously hideous Gorgon, whose face turns men to stone, Perseus uses his shield as a kind of mirror in which he can see her reflection, thereby seeing her with no danger to himself before he cuts off her head. The mirror is a type of Perseus's shield; what is fascinating in Hawthorne is that, within it, Giovanni becomes a reflection of *Beatrice*. In other words, he now assumes the position of Medusa, caught in Perseus's shield. Giovanni does not so much recall the figure of the Male Medusa, which we considered in the previous chapter, as he evokes Medusa herself and her structural position in Ovidian myth. If, as I argue, Hawthorne collapses the Narcissus and Medusa myths here, in a significant way Giovanni is also Perseus. Perseus is a liminal figure between Narcissus and Medusa, another male caught up in an anguished relationship toward vision, unable to see properly, but able to kill, a male who destroys woman for his own ends.

If we consider the associations the tale makes between Beatrice and the Medusa myth, we can fully understand the correspondences between the Narcissus and Medusa myths in Hawthorne's works and between Hawthorne and Freudian theory. It behooves us to recall the particulars of the Ovidian myth. As Ovid limns the Medusa myth, she is the victim of both male *and* female oppression. I quote from the translation that Hawthorne would have read:

> Medusa once had charms; to gain her love
> A rival crowd of envious lovers strove.
> They, who have seen her, own, they ne'er did trace
> More moving features in a sweeter face.
> Yet above all, her length of hair, they own,
> In golden ringlets wav'd, and graceful shone.
> Her Neptune saw, and with such beauties fir'd,
> Resolv'd to compass, what his soul desir'd.
> In chaste Minerva's fane, he, lustful, stay'd,
> And seiz'd, and rifled the young, blushing maid.

> The bashful Goddess turn'd her eyes away,
> Nor durst such bold impurity survey;
> But on the ravish'd virgin vengeance takes,
> Her shining hair is chang'd to hissing snakes.
> These in her Aegis Pallas joys to bear,
> The hissing snakes her foes more sure ensnare,
> Than they did lovers once, when shining hair. (Dryden's translation)

The split between Athena-Minerva and Medusa is crucial to an understanding of Freud's treatment of the myth as well as Hawthorne's.

Unpublished in his lifetime, Freud's extraordinary brief paper "Medusa's Head" (SE 18: 273–74; published in 1940 but dated as having been written in 1922) uses this Greek myth as an occasion to defamiliarize at once the oedipal normativity of the family and the pleasures of sexuality.[25] Contemplating the "horrifying decapitated head of Medusa," Freud first associates it with the fear of castration: "To decapitate = to castrate." He then proceeds to make a further linkage: Medusa terrifies because she links castration to "the *sight* of something" (emphasis added). Freud reminds us that castration fear is specifically a *male* fear, a fear that the boy, "who has hitherto been unwilling to believe the threat of castration," is *made* to feel. In an exemplary instance of psychoanalytic theory as the methodology in which the law of noncontradiction does not apply, Medusa's head both signifies castration *and* assuages the male's fear of it, because her writhing snakes-for-hair suggest both the cut of castration and a phallic compensation for it.[26]

This symbol of horror, notes Freud of Medusa's head, "is worn upon her dress by the virgin goddess Athene." "And rightly so," Freud remarks, "for thus she becomes a woman who is unapproachable and repels all sexual desires." She repels them because she "displays the terrifying genitals of the Mother." In her innovative and brilliant study of Freud, *Speaking the Unspeakable*, Diane Jonte-Pace presents Freud's paper on the Medusa—which, as we have made note of, was never published in his lifetime, though he does briefly allude to some of its claims in the 1923 essay "Infantile Genital Organization"—as an example of what she argues is the masterplot/counterthesis tension in Freud. His masterplot is the patriarchal, oedipal narrative, which upholds the Father's law; the counterthesis is the repudiated underside of this paternal law, emblematized by the Medusa myth and its "'horrifying' associations of maternal genitals, female deities, and death."[27] Medusa is an example of the "dead mother" who haunts, in counterthesis form, many of Freud's texts.[28] Jonte-Pace also makes note of Freud's interest in the decisive split between conventionally feminine types and the deadly, "unapproachable woman."²⁹ This split will prove more and more significant to our analysis of Hawthorne's tale.³⁰

What unites the Narcissus and Medusa myths is the theme of vision as trauma (which they share with that other myth deeply significant to psychoanalytic theory, Oedipus). Of the many different ways that we can approach the similarities between these mythic figures, for our purposes the one I will focus on is their relevance to cultural and aesthetic conflations of sexual and visual anxiety. Both Medusa and Narcissus signal a disturbance in sexuality that is manifested in vision and is metaphorical of an essential disturbance within gendered identity. In Medusa's case, she is the beautiful woman made hideous precisely *because* of her sexual desirability; she is forced to carry the burdens of misogyny by being entrapped within the outward display of its horror. Her hideous appearance conveys the horrific misogyny of patriarchy as it also demonstrates the monstrous impact *of* misogyny; in other words, she is both the effect of misogyny and its cause. Moreover, cursed by a female god for a male god's impropriety, Medusa also symbolizes *internalized misogyny:* a woman's self-hatred at her own social, gendered, and sexual subject position.³¹

With Narcissus, the situation is reversed but similar. He is entrapped not within his ugliness but within his own beauty, a beauty that causes a pain to the males and females whose desire he perpetually incites but refuses to satisfy, much like the sexually inviolate males of antebellum American fiction, Hawthorne's especially. No less than Medusa, he must experience the pain his appearance has caused others; if Medusa's beauty "led" Poseidon to rape her—as Ovid's myth constructs it—Narcissus's beauty leads the call to Nemesis for his punishment. His punishment is to pine over the same face that provoked such a frenzy of communal desire, his own face. Once Medusa looks at herself in Perseus's mirror, she herself is subsumed by the horror she embodies; once Narcissus stares at himself in the mirror of the pool, he is subsumed by the beauty he projects but can never possess as his own. These myths invert ugliness and beauty, yet produce the same results.

Tobin Siebers argues persuasively in his study *The Mirror of Medusa* of the parallelism of the Narcissus and Medusa myths. Siebers's study interrogates the culture of superstition that, he argues, extends to our present; the "evil eye" is the powerful superstition that unites Medusa and Narcissus, though in distinct ways. In Medusa's case, she is the evil eye, the look that can kill. But Medusa combines opposites: along with various other apotropaic devices, the image of the head of Medusa can be used to ward *off* the evil eye as well.³²

As Siebers explains, the narcissist takes the place of the figure of the "fascinator," a stranger, most commonly an ordinary male but one with superhuman powers, who fascinates others with *his* evil eye. Like the figure he replaces, the narcissist fascinates, a point Freud echoes in his essay 1914 essay "On Narcissism." Fascination, Siebers notes, is a "communicable disease."³³ Like "the Gorgon, the narcissist seems to enthrall and to stupefy those around him."³⁴ In turn, the "magical familiars of Narcissus reveal their common parentage with the Gorgon. An emblem of fascination, the Gorgoneion directs its fatal glance to catch and stupefy the eye."³⁵ Narcissus and Medusa share this irresistible ability to fascinate. But their erotic predicaments also turn their faces into fearsome masks.

Moreover, each bears the opprobrium of "accusation."³⁶ Narcissus is accused of cruelty, pride, shallowness, vanity, and the failure to distinguish self from other; Medusa's very ugliness is the embodiment of accusation, from others but also the self; the image of Medusa, a welter of rage, violence, victimization, and self-hatred, thematizes both the misogynistic regard in which women are held and the internalized misogyny with which women behold themselves. Narcissus comes to signal the failure of masculinity in his queer affect and his feminine susceptibility to the desiring gaze; Medusa signals not only the apparent horror and terror of female sexuality but also the terrors of a femininity with access to male power. Narcissus and Medusa emerge as symbols of gender and sexual conflict, opposing mirror images of the feminized male and the phallic woman who evoke the prejudices that surround gendered identities.

INTERTEXTUAL POETICS

"What is this being?—beautiful, shall I call her?—or inexpressibly terrible?" Giovanni wonders of Beatrice (10: 103). Giovanni echoes the different traditions of Medusa: both the hideous ugliness she figures but also the "Beautiful Medusa" tradition found in Boccaccio. As Sylvia Huot observes, the latter was "a Medusa based on Ovid's implication that what is dangerous is neither feminine desire nor its effects on men, nor male desire as such, but rather the lack of desire in a woman who refuses to yield."³⁷

Significantly, Milton draws on the Ovidian Narcissus myth for his depiction of Eve's nativity. As Julia M. Walker reminds us, Milton pairs the Narcissus and the Medusa myths in *Paradise Lost,* perhaps the most important intertext for "Rappaccini's Daughter." Walker not only refers to Milton's famous reimagining of the Ovidian Narcissus myth as the scene of Eve's nativity in Book IV, but discusses his reworking of the myth in other ways, such as Adam's recognition of the fallen but still irresistible Eve in Book VIII as "Bone of my Bone, Flesh of my Flesh, my Self / Before me" (VIII. 494–96). Walker argues that Milton fragments and recombines these two Ovidian narratives "to reflect the fallen knowledge of the reader in and from the textual mirror of *Paradise Lost*."[38] Whereas Milton uses classical iconography as a gaudy decoration for his Christian redemption narrative, a redemption as well as a textual project that delegitimates classical myth, Hawthorne writes not a Christian redemption narrative but, rather, an allegorical work in closer allegiance to the despairing view of Ovid. In other words, Hawthorne inserts the redemptive Christian myth into the inescapable strictures of classical myth. But Hawthorne's intertextual *agon* with his literary predecessors is also an engagement with their sexual politics. Hawthorne, ambitiously rewriting the biblical Genesis, Ovid, and *Paradise Lost* in this tale, creates an atmosphere that takes the Genesis narrative to a different level on which the thought of sexual connection is unthinkable. Adam and Eve are severely challenged in their desire, a predicament that Milton dramatically enlarges in his poem of the Fall. But whatever obstacles their desire faces and whatever fateful consequences await it, it is nevertheless always a desire that is sustained, achievable, fulfilled.

In contrast, Hawthorne's version of this tale makes the fulfillment of desire between his new Narcissus-like Adam and Medusan Eve utterly unthinkable, using the full despair and horror of the Ovidian myths to cancel out the generative program of Genesis and the genuine tenderness of marital love in Milton's vision. (Significantly, in Milton's poem it is only after they have fallen that Adam and Eve treat each other with brutality during sex; the Fall makes the first pair treat each other like meat, in marked contrast to their exquisitely erotic prelapsarian sexual tenderness.) Hawthorne may be said, in Beatrice Rappaccini, to fuse the terrible and the beautiful Medusa traditions, palpably registering Beatrice's *Medusan refusal to desire*. These dynamics in Hawthorne's characterization of Beatrice deepen his larger thematic of the ambivalence within—indeed, the unthinkability of—heterosexual relations. This is the aspect of the tale that most resonantly lends itself to queer interpretation.

Hawthorne evokes Medusa when Giovanni makes his way to speak to Beatrice for the first time, making his passage into Beatrice's space: "Giovanni stepped forth, and forcing himself through the entanglement of a shrub that wreathed its tendrils over the hidden entrance, he stood beneath his own window, in the open area of Doctor Rappaccini's garden" (10: 109). Beatrice's yonic portal swarms with tendrils that entangle Giovanni as he "enters" it, imagery that corresponds to Freud's description of the Medusa's writhing phallic snakes as metaphorical of the "terrifying genitals of the Mother." Beatrice, the Daughter, also must represent, in her Eve-like role and status as the only generative woman in this fallen garden, the "Mother." As I have suggested, Beatrice suggests Freud's phallic mother, fetishized by Giovanni as well as Rappaccini. Standing beneath his own window—Giovanni's own sexual symbol, which is appropriately a symbol of gender ambiguation, in that it connotes his phallic vision *and* a yonic portal itself—Giovanni now stands beneath his own mastery, in an effeminated position that reflects his relinquishment of male power.

In Giovanni's fateful climactic confrontation with Beatrice, the overlapping Narcissus-Medusa themes become especially imbricated. If we recall Siebers's interpretation of these myths, *accusation* is a crucial aspect of both. The accuser assigns the blame of the evil eye on the person whose gaze has lingered too long on the object, causing harm. "Accursed one!" Giovanni screams at Beatrice (10: 124), pointedly echoing Adam's rebuke of Eve in Milton's *Paradise Lost:* "Out of my sight, thou serpent" (10: 867). Medusa-like Beatrice—like Hawthorne's later heroines Hester, Zenobia, Miriam—is the accused. Yet it is Giovanni who has sadistically attempted to dominate Beatrice through the gaze; his accusation is a projection of his own guilt and shame. His murderous narcissism reaches its zenith in his denunciation of her: "poisonous thing! . . . Thou hast done it! Thou hast blasted me! Thou hast filled my veins with poison! Thou hast made me as hateful, as ugly, as loathsome and deadly a creature as thyself,—a world's wonder of hideous monstrosity!" (10: 124). This traumatic outburst is specifically traumatic because, in being directed at Beatrice, it reveals both the depth of Giovanni's own self-loathing and his inability to recognize it as such. He can only project it outward at a woman who, if anything, is far more victimized and far more blameless than he. This screed directed at Beatrice explicates the anxieties and tensions that simmer beneath the surface of Hawthorne's placidly beautiful male exteriors—a confessional stream of self-hatred, fatally directed at an unsuitable target, rather than an inward stream of recrimination with the potential to lead to self-recognition and self-knowledge.

Much like Hippolytus's speech in response to the revelation that his stepmother Phaedra loves him in Euripides' tragedy *Hippolytus,* Giovanni's accusation is an index of misogynistic feeling. It also depicts, in the lines that conclude his invective, the idea of heterosexual relations as a monstrous inversion: "Now—if our breath be happily as fatal to ourselves as to all others—let us join our lips in one kiss of unutterable hatred, and so die!" (10: 124). The radicalism of Hawthorne's vision here cannot be overstated: he has re-envisioned the ultimately redemptive Christian version of the myth of Adam and Eve—the origin myth of heterosexuality—as a dead-end narrative of sexual despair, sterility, and futility.

In "Rappaccini's Daughter," Hawthorne presents male-centered heterosexuality as a system suffused with hate, the inverse motivation of Christian love. Emptiness, barrenness, duplicity, and death-fixation characterize the tale's central male and female relationship. In emphasizing the irredeemable fallenness of the first human couple, the tale enacts precisely the outcome that the medieval Christian doctrine of the *felix culpa,* or Fortunate Fall, attempted to avert. The *felix culpa* was the belief that God actually wanted Adam and Eve to sin so that he could demonstrate his goodness by restoring us to a final state that will be "even happier than that from which we fell," as Milton scholar John Leonard explains it.[39] Hawthorne will return to these tragic themes in *The Marble Faun,* but at least that bleak novel has some promise of redemption (however pallid) in the Kenyon–Hilda relationship that may lead to marital union, or, to a lesser extent, the faint belief that sinful Miriam and Donatello may ultimately find redemption through suffering. "Rappaccini's Daughter" provides no compensatory promise of love or redemption, however faint the prospect of either, only the scene of blasted hope. The tale thematizes hatred's triumph over love.[40] It is precisely at this point that I believe I can make a plausible case for Hawthorne's feminism.

MEDUSA'S PROTEST

I can think of few other works that make a more acute case for the Medusa myth as being—like Freud's theory of the phallic mother—entirely a male fantasy, not about women at all. Like Medusa, Beatrice is entirely the victim of different forms of male oppression—her father's cold, inhuman science (shades of "The Birthmark") and Giovanni's sadistic voyeurism, and even Baglioni's rivalrous obsession (he cares nothing for Beatrice, only Giovanni, or perhaps, only for outing Rappaccini's schemes for what they are). Beatrice is imprisoned within a terrifying Medusan identity and narrative, but she is never an *active* part in its construction.

Beatrice is forced to occupy the role of generative mother as well as daughter in this tale, but in this role, she can only be a parodistic version of the mother. The lushly blooming plants and her own lushly blooming body are poisonous, indicative of death rather than maternal nurture. Her Medusan quality—which is to say, the way she fuses Eve, Milton's Sin, and the Gorgon; the numerous symbolic correspondences in the story (for example,

Medusan hair and swarming, poisonous plants)—carry the Freudian associations with "the terrifying genitals of the Mother." Yet these maternal genitals are precisely terrifying not for any inherent quality but because they manifest the overpowering anxieties and phobic defenses against them that characterize male subjectivity in Hawthorne as well as Freud. Freud's misogyny is counterbalanced by his acute understanding of male subjectivity as being anything but what its cultural mythologies purport it to be: solid, rational, impregnable. As Freud represents masculinity, it is dominated from its outset by fears of being ripped apart (castration, decapitation), fears it then, in the broad iconography of misogynistic practice, projects outward, to women, those with nonnormative sexualities, and the racial other. In Hawthorne's case, Hawthorne maintains Freud's skeptical view of masculinity, but he also maintains throughout his career a conflictual but always profound identification with women and the feminine.

If Beatrice represents the full force of the misogyny inherent in Freud's treatment of the Medusa, and a potential misogyny in Hawthorne, it should also be considered that, writing in his Victorian era of True Womanhood, Hawthorne is also offering a defiantly, aggressively satirical response to that desexualizing, domesticating ideal of femininity. Far from a wholesome, life-giving mother, Beatrice is the menace of sexuality and a refusal of the properly generative. While some will undoubtedly argue that this portrait confirms Hawthorne's misogyny, in my view what Hawthorne offers through the tale is a critique of the cultural regime of conformity to normative gendered and sexual standards. Hence the significance of Beatrice as the Medusa who refuses to desire. If True Womanhood constructs women as asexual, the sexually unapproachable Beatrice is both the end of sex and its most luridly monstrous sign. In other words, Hawthorne brings the repressed terrors over female sexuality in the cultural unconscious vividly to the surface. Moreover, and most importantly, it is Beatrice's Romantic nobility of character that makes Hawthorne's identification with femininity most palpable, carrying the full force of his critique of masculinity.

Frederick Crews makes several fine points about the tale in his essay "Giovanni's Garden," especially about Giovanni's character, which he properly recognizes as narcissistic: "Hawthorne shows him to be infatuated with his own 'remarkable beauty of person'" and naively anxious to test out his seductiveness. . . . [He] demands a love-object that will merely flatter his vanity, not make sexual demands of its own. Every hint of Beatrice's complete womanliness is thus a blow to his narcissism. But beyond this, Giovanni displays an abject terror before the whole phenomenon of female sexuality."[41] Crews's conclusion is apt: "Ultimately he has cared only for his attractiveness."[42] Like many Hawthorne works, the tale works hard to keep its male protagonist sexually inviolate. Like Medusa, Giovanni refuses sexual desire; like Narcissus, his desire is arrested at the point between incitement and consummation.

But I think that Crews is quite wrong about Beatrice. Rebutting critics, as is his forte, Crews writes that Giovanni has been accused of shallowness because he rejects Beatrice "as monstrous." But, Crews rebuts, "as a potential bride she *is* monstrous."[43] To Crews, Beatrice is "unaware of her power of enticement." What she really disavows, Crews argues, is that "she has deliberately exploited her attractiveness, which has been enhanced by the mysterious aura of danger attaching to her poisonousness. . . . Her innocence consists in an almost willful ignorance of her sexual power, and this ignorance is the foundation of her claim to spiritual power."[44]

The most hateful aspect of the Ovidian Medusa myth is the way in which Medusa is herself punished for having been raped by Poseidon. Crews accuses Beatrice of knowing innocence about her own sexual magnetism; he creates a portrait of her as a weirdly girlish sexual predator who ensnares Giovanni while all the time coyly camouflaging any personal knowledge of her sexual charms. I do not see any evidence for this reading of her in Hawthorne's portrayal: if she is a monster, her monstrousness stems entirely from the male fantasies that have appropriated her body, though not, entirely, her spirit.

Beatrice has internalized the misogyny in her midst and come to see herself, as Giovanni does, as a monster; in other words, she accuses herself as she has been accused. Unlike Giovanni, however, Beatrice can speak the language of self-recognition, even if she damns herself in the process: "I, it is true, am the horrible thing thou namest me" (124). But why, she asks, does Giovanni include himself in her world of contamination? "Dost thou pretend ignorance?" Giovanni scowls at her. In also condemning her for feigning ignorance, Crews takes a very Giovanni-like view of Beatrice. But Beatrice, we must accept, believes that she is alone in her difference; she truly is not aware of her fatal potentialities to others. She asks Giovanni this question because she does not realize that he now shares in her poisoned nature. Finally, she does come to realize that it is her father who has united her and Giovanni in "fearful sympathy" (125).

> "I see it! I see it!" shrieked Beatrice. "It is my father's fatal science. No, no, Giovanni; it was not I! Never, never! I dreamed only to love thee, and be with thee a little time, and so to let thee pass away, leaving but thine image in mine heart. For Giovanni—believe it—though my body be nour-

ished with poison, my spirit is God's creature, and craves love, as its daily food. But my father!—he has united us in this fearful sympathy. Yes, spurn me!—tread upon me!—kill me! Oh, what is death, after such words as thine? But it was not I! Not for a world of bliss would I have done it!" (10: 125)

Beatrice transforms the emblem of Giovanni's narcissism, his image, into compensation for lovers' loss: she hopes to retain Giovanni's image in *her* heart, assuaging the eventual loss of his bodily presence. Her desire is, ultimately, not a projection of her fixation with her own image but a desire to possess the image of her beloved. Whereas Giovanni and, for that matter, Rappaccini can only see Beatrice as an extension of themselves, as an image of themselves, Beatrice can see that an image of Giovanni is an image of the other, one she can incorporate into her own emotional life, rather than seeing Giovanni as simply another version, copy, likeness, or reflection of herself. As will Sybil in *Septimius Felton*, Beatrice quaffs the potion that promises release from death or that promises death itself, the latter winning out in both cases.

As Beatrice dies, she rebukes both Giovanni and her father, united in their masculinist attitudes if not in their specific positions toward Beatrice. Her father is incredulous that Beatrice is angry with him for what he has done to her. "Wouldst thou, then, have preferred the condition of a weak woman, exposed to all evil, and capable of none?" he asks. Her response is one of the greatest speeches in Hawthorne.

> "I would fain have been loved, not feared," murmured Beatrice. . . . "I am going, father, where the evil, which thou hast striven to mingle with my being, will pass away like a dream—like the fragrance of these poisonous flowers, which will no longer taint my breath among the flowers of Eden. Farewell, Giovanni. Thy words of hatred are like lead within my heart—but they, too, will fall away as I ascend. Oh, was there not, from the first, more poison in thy nature than in mine?" (10: 127)

On the similarities between Georgiana in "The Birthmark" and Beatrice, Alison Easton writes, "Both women protest impotently—Beatrice asserts that she is more than poisonous flesh. . . . Both women die, sacrificing themselves for men demonstrably undeserving of such inordinate devotion."[45] If an impotent protest is one that is defined as a protest that fails to alleviate the misfortune of the protester, than surely that is an apt phrase to describe Beatrice's parting words. Yet I would argue that another way of thinking about Beatrice at this moment is possible.[46] Beatrice stunningly critiques both Giovanni and her father. In being so directed, her dying words are at once a lament and a stinging affront both to heterosexual male privilege and to the "Father": to the oedipal dynamics in which she has lived fatally ensnared, and to patriarchy itself.

While I understand Crews's effort to provide an alternative view to pietistic interpretations of Hawthorne's art, to de-emphasize the religious connotations here, as Crews does, seems to me a large mistake. Beatrice recognizes, and also appoints, herself as a martyr, ascending to an afterlife envisioned specifically as an antidote to both male narcissism and patriarchal misogyny. Beatrice's self-election here may smack a bit of unseemly hubris, but I think its point is that, whereas the males consign themselves to corrupt, worldly values, she embodies true Christian feeling. However one feels about this Christian message, what is significant about it is that it importantly resists not only Giovanni's—and, it should be added, Rappaccini's—calumniation of her sexuality but the misogyny within the long history of Judeo-Christian myth and also of the classical literary tradition. Rappaccini claims that in Beatrice he created a woman who could transcend misogyny by becoming untouchably powerful, far mightier than men; she exposes the underlying misogyny in her father's dark idealism, revealing that he exerts a masculinist privilege that has overridden her feelings and, ultimately, ended her life.

Beatrice's declaration that she would rather have been loved than feared is especially striking. She inverts the Machiavellian maxim that, for a ruler, it is better to be feared than loved, demonstrating a feminine disposition toward such political questions that, I would argue, Hawthorne endorses. (Machiavelli's *The Prince* was published in 1532.) Beatrice makes a declaration for love as a potent force, the true antidote to the tale's regime of hate. This is an affirmation of a redemptive Christian message, but this message is transmitted through a larger network of failure, despair, and death; Beatrice may condemn her oppressors, but she cannot change the logic of patriarchy. I see her predicament as indicative not of Hawthorne's misogyny, but, rather, of his combined empathy for women's situation—allegorical of his own as a "degenerate fellow, a writer"—and pessimistic view of gendered relations.

Most provocatively and movingly of all, Beatrice's own condemnation of Giovanni reveals a great deal about Hawthorne's own views. "Was there not from the first more poison in thy nature than in mine?" Beatrice recognizes that Giovanni is always already "poisoned." Her reference to Giovanni's "nature" synthesizes Hawthorne's textual and symbolic efforts to reinsert masculinity into nature; but this reinsertion only more deeply reveals that it is masculine nature which Hawthorne views as truly poisoned.

"WOMEN HAVE no choice other than to be decapitated," Hélène Cixous wrote in 1976, "and in any case . . . if they don't actually lose their heads by the sword, *they only keep them on condition that they lose them*—lose them, that is, to complete silence, turned into automatons." For Cixous, "women always inhabit the place of silence . . . they remain outside knowledge." If woman could be freed from the shackles of ignorance through which men bind her, she could do the work that would "benefit not only women but all humanity." But in order for that woman to begin her gendered revolution, she must first "*speak,* start speaking, stop saying that she has nothing to say!" Once she does this she may be able to bring man back to an "erogenous field . . . [that] appears shifting, diffused, taking on all the others of oneself."[47]

Beatrice anticipates Hawthorne's strong, resistant female characters of the novel-romances of the 1850s—Hester Prynne, defying the Puritan elders who want to take her child away or telling Dimmesdale that what passed between them, however illicit, had "a consecration of its own"; the elderly Hepzibah, though inwardly timorous, standing up to Judge Pyncheon to protect her spectral brother, Clifford; most strikingly in terms of a woman's voice, Zenobia assailing the solipsistic men around her for their obsession with "self, self, self!" And, most Beatrice-like of all, the dark sexual mystery of Miriam Schaeffer in *The Marble Faun,* a work that could almost be an elaborate sequel to "Rappaccini's Daughter," puts her in a perpetually embattled position. Miriam is a highly ambivalent portrait of femininity, but in her forthrightness, eloquence, and odd courage she demands sympathy even at her most alienating. Moreover, the dark-lady Jewess Miriam far exceeds the pallid, Protestant Hilda in terms of authorial and readerly fascination.

If the position of woman in the West, as Cixous argues, is one of decapitation—the denial of mind and voice—Hawthorne explodes this position, giving the Medusan woman decapitated by misogyny back her mind and voice. Here is the place in which his career-long revision of the Narcissus myth has its most subversive dimension: he gives Echo the power to speak for and as herself and on her own behalf. Nowhere in Genesis, Ovid, Shakespeare, or even Milton does a woman speak truth to patriarchal power more movingly and bracingly, with no hypocrisy or final self-recrimination, than does the dying but resilient Beatrice in "Rappaccini's Daughter."[48] It is in Hawthorne's daring identification with a wronged but valiantly eloquent woman and in his unremittingly skeptical, negative view of the masculine "character" that his feminism makes itself most keenly felt.

CHAPTER 7

Visual Identity

HAWTHORNE, MELVILLE, AND CLASSICAL MALE BEAUTY

> . . . all these marble ghosts. Why should not each statue grow warm with life! Antinous might lift his brow, and tell us why he is forever sad. . . . Bacchus, too, a rosy flush diffusing itself over his time-stained surface, could come down from his pedestal, and offer a cluster of purple grapes to Donatello's lips; because the god recognizes him as the woodland elf who so often shared his revels. And here, in this sarcophagus, the exquisitely carved figures might assume life, and chase one another round its verge with that wild merriment which is so strangely represented on those old burial coffers: though still with some subtle allusion to death, carefully veiled, but forever peeping forth amid emblems of mirth and riot.
>
> —*The Marble Faun*, chapter 2 (14: 17)

IN THE PREVIOUS CHAPTER, I began to explore homoerotic Hellenism and its significance to Hawthorne's work. This topic will be central to chapter 7 along with a comparison that has been hovering, with a certain persistence, as a possibility over my critical narrative. More than any other writer of the antebellum period with the exception of Edgar Allan Poe, Herman Melville shares Hawthorne's preoccupations. Their themes significantly overlap: each author obsessively treats the central idea of the duplicity of appearances; in their work, reality is but a "pasteboard mask" that we must "strike through." Yet, for both, surfaces have depth; they brood upon the beguiling allure of appearances, puzzling out their irresistible and maddening appeal.

While the heady, agonized, enigmatic relationship between Hawthorne and Melville has occupied the minds of scholars for decades well into the present, what I wish to consider is each artist's treatment of Narcissus. In terms of these authors' uses of the myth of Narcissus, I refer not just to this specific myth figure but also to what we can call Narcissus-discourse or a Narcissus-continuum, youthful male figures that evoke qualities associated with Narcissus: great beauty, a tragic early death, flower imagery, and homoerotic associations. These characteristics all inhere in the classical figure of Antinous, whom I treat here as an extension or double of Narcissus.

While the entire premise of this book is that Hawthorne frequently evokes the figure of Narcissus, it is also true that he never names him explicitly. Melville, in contrast, does name him in *Moby-Dick* and makes the figure in all of its explicitness the "key" to his greatest work.

> Why is almost every robust healthy boy with a robust healthy soul in him, at some time or other crazy to go to sea? Why upon your first voyage as a passenger, did you yourself feel such a mystical vibration, when first told that you and your ship were now out of sight of land? Why did the old Persians hold the sea holy? Why did the Greeks give it a separate deity, and own brother of Jove? Surely all this is not without meaning. And still deeper the meaning of that story of Narcissus, who because he could not grasp the tormenting, mild image he saw in the fountain, plunged into it and was drowned. But that same image, we ourselves see in all rivers and oceans. It is the image of the ungraspable phantom of life; and this is the key to it all.[1]

In characteristically haunting and provocative fashion, Melville jams together two thoroughly unlike adjectives—tormenting, mild—to evoke Narcissus and his fundamentally perplexing nature. Melville seizes upon classical myth's iconic power. In his hands, the myth is sent out to float like a phantom of the sea, as if the pool that captured the face of the mythic youth had widened into all of the waters of the world. In Melville's pointed contrast between "the robust healthy" and presumably American youth, even whose soul has similar qualities, and the phantomlike Narcissus, he offers a telling commentary on the gulf between a typical image of youthful masculinity and one associated with the classical world; the latter is inevitably imbued with haunting and uncanny qualities.

I will not attempt to decode the meanings of Narcissus in Melville's epic novel here. Rather, my focus is more disparate. By considering some instances of the reception of classical male beauty in Hawthorne's and Melville's writings, specifically regarding the figure of Antinous, I believe that we can get at something significant about what role classical culture and myth played for antebellum male authors who explored homoerotic themes in an era in which the sexual content of classical literature was generally expurgated. I proceed, after the comparative discussion of Melville and Hawthorne's travel writing and Melville's last major work, *Billy Budd, Sailor,* to a consideration of the titular figure in Hawthorne's 1860 *The Marble Faun.*

While there is much to consider within this extraordinarily dense and rich novel, my focus is on the relevance of the faun to the narcissistic crisis that Hawthorne consistently thematizes and the significance of Hellenism, spectacularly referenced in the ekphrastic appreciation of the faun, to this crisis. Forecasting the concerns of the last chapter, I will also address here the problematic of race and racism. I do so through a critique of the charges of racism that have been leveled not only at nineteenth-century Hellenism generally but also at Hawthorne's deployment of the technique in his uses of the faun. One of my concerns here is the diminishment of issues related to gender, sexuality, and, specifically, queer sexuality that sometimes occurs in critiques of nineteenth-century literary racism. Neither eclipsed nor displaced by these discussions, Freud is alive within them in his study of the homosexual artist *par excellence,* Leonardo da Vinci.

VEXED QUESTIONS
NINETEENTH-CENTURY HELLENISM AND SEXUAL HISTORY

While it is important to note that Hawthorne does not mention Narcissus in print, it is also worth noting that he was not the only antebellum writer working in a mythohistorical context who kept Narcissus and similar kinds of figures unmentioned. Samuel Griswold Goodrich, the editor of the illustrated annual *The Token* (1828–42), which published the younger Hawthorne, and the creator, with his brother, of the *Peter Parley* children's book series, does not mention Narcissus at all in his 1832 *A Book of Mythology for Youth.* And when he does discuss similar figures, he makes no note of their beauty. For example, in a passage from the entry on Venus, Goodrich discusses Adonis, another beautiful youth in the Narcissus tradition who is doomed to an early death and associated with flower imagery. Goodrich makes no mention of Adonis's famed physical splendor, saying only that he is "the son of the King of Cyprus . . . slain by a wild boar. Venus bewailed his death with much sorrow, and changed his blood which was shed on the ground, into the flower *anemone.*"[2] Similarly, the figure Endymion receives a nonerotic reception. A youth so beautiful that Selene (or Diana) the moon goddess rendered him perpetually asleep so that she could contemplate and caress him as he slumbered, Endymion is described simply as "an astronomer." Diana's effort to keep him in eternal amorous captivity is described with similar opacity as "Diana, or the moon, descending from Heaven to visit the shepherd Endymion."[3] When the specific subject of homosexuality comes up, coded language prevails. On the subject of the Thracian women's destruction of the poet-musician Orpheus—triggered by his embrace of homosexual practices and rejection of sex with the women, as described in Ovid's *Metamorphoses* in one of the key instances of same-sex desire in his heterosexually oriented epic—Goodrich writes: "Orpheus fled for ever from mankind. His lyre was silent. The Thracian women, enraged because he avoided their society, attacked and killed him during the feast of Bacchus. They threw his head into the Hebrus . . . ."[4] As still holds true in American culture, violence (the Thracian women's decapitation of Orpheus) remains more safely representable than sexuality. (One recalls the reaction of the late French director Louis Malle to the news that one of his American films would be given an "X" rating: "You can show a breast being cut off and get an 'R' rating, but if you show this breast being kissed or fondled you get an 'X.'")

Goodrich, it should be repeated, is repurposing the classical myths for children, as Hawthorne would in the 1850s. At the same time, his reluctance even to describe the most famously beautiful males from the classical corpus *as such* reveals tensions within the strictures on content in the antebellum period that exceed the category of children's literature. Writing in the 1850s in this genre, Hawthorne also makes no mention of Narcissus, signifying that a shared reticence about the subject was evident two decades after Goodrich's mythology book appeared. At the same time, Hawthorne *does* frequently evoke male beauty in his work generally. The point is not so much that the sexual content of classical mythology was being expurgated in children's literature, but, rather, that children's literature was being chosen as the venue in which to present classical material in order to *keep* its content sexually expurgated.

The homoerotic uses of Hellenism must be understood within the complex relay between the coded and the explicit about sexual matters generally within the period, but especially in terms of classical themes and allusions. Hawthorne's decorum accords with that of his era, as his retelling of the myth of Demeter and Persephone, "The Pomegranate Seeds," in his 1853 *Tanglewood Tales* (7: 296–330) evinces. In the Greek myth, Persephone is a maiden, daughter of the seasonal goddess Demeter, who is abducted by Hades and forced to be his bride. Hawthorne makes Persephone a young girl rather than a maiden, mitigating the force of rape imagery and sexual conquest in the myth. Yet (perhaps unconsciously, but also perhaps not) Hawthorne's representational choices here link his work to the homoerotic tradition from which it emerged: the girl in Hawthorne's retelling evokes the boy, or *eromenos,* of classical pederastic tradition, whose adult male mentor, or *erastes,* initiates him into both intellectual and sexual knowledge, as works such as Plato's dialogue the *Phaedrus* evoke so palpably. This is not to suggest that accurate or even widely available translations of works by Plato were available to Hawthorne; such translations would emerge in print only in the later nineteenth century. But it is also true that the wider reference world of classical reception contained frequent instances of and allusions to homoerotic practices, in addition to other taboo sexual references, in the ancient world. As Louis Crompton observes in his masterly *Byron and Greek Love,* "if Plato was a closed book, the gardens of poetry were open. The classical curriculum in England, as John Stuart Mill was to complain, ignored history and philosophy in favor of philology and poetry. . . . It was a paradox that an age that would have rejected formal sex education as shocking should have prescribed amorous Latin and Greek poetry as a staple of education."[5] Considerable overlaps existed in both the educational practices and the cultural discordances of classical reception in England and the United States. As Caroline Winterer writes, mid-nineteenth-century Americans "wrestled with the problem of representing timeless ideals of transcendent beauty in forms unacceptable to standards of modern social propriety"; the "suspect morality of the ancients became more problematic as the physical and textual remains of antiquity became more numerous."[6] While a fuller consideration of this complex set of historical questions exceeds the scope of this chapter, we can establish that sexual matters related to classical culture were riddled with epistemological inconsistencies, asymmetries, and discordances—in other words, were metonymic of the larger problem of the representation and understanding of sexuality and sexual history in transatlantic nineteenth-century cultural practices. While he observes literary proprieties that were his own as well as his culture's, Hawthorne also at times resists antebellum cultural codes by highlighting the erotic dimensions of classical literature, and sometimes in a homoerotic context, such as in his descriptions of the glorious physicality of the young Cyrus in "Roger Malvin's Burial" and Giovanni's "Grecian beauty" in "Rappaccini's Daughter."[7]

In emphasizing the homoerotic potentialities of Hellenism and classical beauty, I am bringing into clearer focus an underlying theme in this study, though one I have also repeatedly attempted to problematize: the relevance of Hawthorne's work to the question of the presence of same-sex desire in nineteenth-century texts. The determinability of same-sex desire in nineteenth-century texts has been a vexed historical question since the 1980s at least, though one that has been innovated in the past decade. The widespread adoption of the findings of the gay French social historian Michel Foucault, particularly in his influential book *The History of Sexuality, Volume 1*, dramatically reshaped the attempt to recover a homosexual past (the very term homosexual being seen as anachronistic by some) in the 1980s. In *History*, Foucault famously argued that, at a key moment in the second half of the nineteenth century, the homosexual became "a species."[8] The homosexual was a new kind of person, one whose sexual acts were now tied to subjectivity.[9] This new taxonomical identity-category of the homosexual replaced the former category of "sodomite."

What has prevailed since the 1980s, until very recently, is the view that there is no correspondence whatsoever between sexual acts and sexual identities before this taxonomical emergence, identities being the result of classifications such as the naming of the homosexual and the attendant pathologization, in legal, medical, psychiatric, criminal, and religious discourses, of those so named. Significant challenges from certain quarters to the Foucauldian model have been offered in the past decade, however, and as a result debates over nineteenth-century same-sex desire have undergone a remarkable transformation.[10] Even one of the major earlier voices of the Foucauldian positions about matters of sexual history, David M. Halperin, has attempted to challenge the standard view of a sharp distinction between acts and identities before the latter half of the nineteenth century, seeking to reorient Foucault's reception in sexuality studies.[11] My work on Hawthorne reflects my engagement with these more recent approaches to the question of same-sex desire in nineteenth-century texts.

Through the scenes of contemplation of images from the ancient archive within Melville's and Hawthorne's private writings, we can learn more about the meanings that the classical world held for antebellum Americans, an era that was fascinated by simultaneously suggestive and decorous works such as Hiram Powers's sculpture *The Greek Slave*. (It was sculpted by Powers in several versions between 1844 and 1869.) Specifically for our purposes, a historical same-sex desiring presence as well as different styles of masculinity charge these scenes of contemplation with homoerotic and gendered significance for the authors. Comparing Melville's and Hawthorne's reactions to representations of the homoerotic cult icon Antinous reveals some key aspects of the attitudes toward sexuality maintained in their culture and of each author's sensibility.

MELVILLE AND MALE BEAUTY
ANTINOUS, THE APOLLO BELVEDERE, BILLY BUDD

In the course of his travels to England, the Middle East, and Europe in 1856–57, Herman Melville saw a statue of Antinous, the famous young beloved of the Roman emperor Hadrian, in the Capitoline Museum. (The statue is now considered to be of Hermes.) As he wrote in response to it in his journal entry of Thursday, February 26, 1857: "Antinous, beautiful.—Walked to the Pincian hill.—gardens and statuary—overlooking Piazza del Populo.—(Music on the Pincian) Fashion & Rank—Preposterous posturing within stone's throw of Antinous. How little influence has truth on the world!" He goes on to note that fashion is ridiculous everywhere, but especially in Rome. He also writes here that "No place where lonely man will feel more lonely than in Rome," adding parenthetically "or Jerusalem."[12] Two days later that week, he stopped off at the Villa Albani in Rome, where he saw the celebrated bas-relief of Antinous, which had been found in Hadrian's Tivoli villa. In his journal, Melville described the bas-relief this way: "—along the walls—Antinous—head like moss-rose with curls and buds—rest all simplicity—end of fillet on shoulder—drapery, shoulder in the mantle—hand full of flowers and eyeing them—the profile &c. . . ."[13] This entry ends with the line that seems to be a recurring motif: "Silence and loneliness of long streets of blank garden walls." Interestingly placed between Melville's two discussions of representations of Antinous is his report in the *Journals* of visiting the graves of Shelley and Keats. Shelley, in particular, was famed for his feminine handsomeness, and these poets who died young add to the atmosphere of Antinousinian melancholy, of beautiful youth cut down in the prime of life and reverentially immortalized. The cult of Antinous is a variant, one might argue, of the Narcissus myth: both concern the premature death of a beautiful youth whose image galvanizes the spectator.

As Gail Coffler observes in her superb essay "Classical Iconography in the Aesthetics of *Billy Budd, Sailor,*" Antinous was "often assimilated to the fertility god Dionysius, or to his Egyptian counterpart, the underworld deity Osiris, god of the regenerative Nile. Indeed, the erotic, Dionysian impulse informs the identifying facial characteristics of Antinous: the full mouth with curved upper lip; the large, 'melting' eyes; and the distinctive curls extending around his forehead." Coffler proceeds to compare the iconic figure of Antinous to Billy Budd. As Coffler describes, "Billy Budd as a type of the Antinous is clearly adumbrated in that journal description. The rose bud iconography, identifying Antinous with the fertility god Dionysus, also links this journal passage with a Greek youth who anticipates Billy Budd:

the gay Cypriote, whose image appears twice in Melville's poetry. All three figures (Antinous, the Cypriote[s], Billy Budd) are physically alluring and seductively dangerous, like the 'rose' in Melville's 'Naples in the Time of Bomba' . . . For Melville the rose is an emblem of earthly beauty, a reminder that art based on beauty, without the strengthening fiber of transcendent truth, cannot last."[14]

Antinous's backstory, given in Royston Lambert's standard account, bears mentioning. Hadrian reigned for twenty years, from the years 117 to 138. Antinous was a Bithynian slave, Bithynia now being northwest Turkey. While the circumstances of the emperor and Antinous's meeting remain unknown, most sources have described the relationship between the emperor and the famously beautiful youth as a sexual one. It is said that Hadrian wept bitterly and mourned deeply for Antinous after his death in October of the year 130. (Antinous was born in the year 111.) While some reported that Antinous was murdered, it is more generally supported that Antinous committed suicide by jumping into the Nile because of a prophecy that the emperor would die unless someone close to him died in his stead—a voluntary religious sacrifice on Antinous's part. In any event, Hadrian immortalized the young man as the ideal of Greek beauty through all manner of iconography after having Antinous deified, an honor usually reserved for members of the ruling family. While it has been suggested that Hadrian had political motivations for the creation of the Antinous cult—as a means of securing the allegiance of the Greek-speaking East to Roman rule—the lavishness of his tributes to the dead youth suggest that his passion was as heartfelt as his politics were canny. As the cult of Antinous, worshipped as a god, spread throughout the Roman empire, busts of him were rife, and the beautiful young man's face adorned coins, medallions, cut gems and cameos, and even "small collapsible busts" were made for well-off folk to carry with them on their travels. In his honor, Hadrian also founded the Egyptian city of Antinopolis.[15] To flash forward to the period we are examining, busts of Antinous were prominent decorations in the Hellenism-saturated households of the nineteenth century. Hawthorne had a bust of Antinous, kept "in the parlor of his little red house in Lenox, where Melville surely would have noticed it," and Melville kept a bust of the youth in his own home in his later years.[16]

What specifically concerns me here is the way in which same-sex desire and love informed the relationship writers maintained with the classical past. One way or another, many writers, Melville and Hawthorne prominent among them, contributed to the development of a nineteenth-century transatlantic homoerotic aesthetic culture. While many studies have focused on this culture's efflorescence in late-Victorian England, cultivated by figures such as Pater, Wilde, and John Addington Symonds, among others, less work has been done on American artists' participation in this aesthetic culture's development, Henry James being co-opted, as often happens, into English literary traditions for these purposes.

By aesthetic culture, I mean a series of intersections among literary and visual art traditions, with the specific form of Hellenism as their foundation, that together emerged as a language and a tradition, a shared set of references and an index of representations, of homoerotic desire across temporal and geographical spaces. One of the most highly charged precedents for homoerotic aesthetic culture's nineteenth-century manifestation was the writings of Johann Joachim Winckelmann (1717–68), a German art historian and archaeologist who pioneered a new interest in classical art, one that focused on the beautiful male body, albeit as a rejection of the sensual and an embrace of the meditative. Famously, Winckelmann maintained that the Apollo Belvedere, the Laocoön, and the Villa Albani bas-relief of Antinous represented the art of the ancient world at its most glorious. Indeed, by the time Melville and Hawthorne were traveling in Europe in the 1850s, Winckelmann's triumvirate of classical male beauty had become quite thoroughly a cliché, passages in which he extolled these figures' beauty cut and pasted, as it were, into guidebooks for the educated traveler and connoisseur.[17]

From the earliest days of the American republic, a fixation with the classical world was prominent. By the antebellum period, a decisive shift from Rome to Greece (the "Greek Revival") had occurred. During the 1850s, it had become *de rigueur* for educated Americans to embark on an improving voyage to Europe in order to contemplate its endless array of art history treasures. This "Grand Tour" was a central experience of transatlantic nineteenth-century middle-class society. Of chief interest to us here are the possibilities afforded the male viewer of art to register, record, and explore the male form.

The nineteenth century, in terms of the possibilities for the expression of homoerotic desire, was a period in flux. As we have noted, scholars have generally framed the century as a movement from more liquid, amorphous forms of same-sex affiliation to a more rigid, sexually stratified period of modern sexual taxonomies that flowed from the medical and legal discourses that reframed sexualities at the end of the century. This critical narrative has framed the late-nineteenth-century birth of psychoanalysis as the death of free-flowing, unclassified homoerotic relations.[18] While this narrative has its uses, especially for rhetorical purposes, I believe that the question of when and how same-sex desire was regulated—either policed against or allowed a range of public, open, visible expressions—continues to remain an unsettled and enigmatic one. While more strictures were indeed placed on same-sex desire, or more specifically desirers, by the late nineteenth century, it is also true that prohibitive codes of conduct that prevented the public expression of unseemly gendered as well as sexual behavior were well in place in the early nineteenth century. One of the ways of subverting these codes was through coded discourse itself, and nineteenth-century Hellenism was chief among such coded discourses, allowing for the expression of homoerotic appreciation while still within acceptable social parameters of taste and decorum.

From Winckelmann well into the late nineteenth century, classical art, particularly that of ancient Greece as synecdochically embodied by the marble statue, provided a discourse for the male discussion of male beauty with considerable potential for the expression of homoerotic desire.[19] Under the guise of Hellenic art-appreciation, nonthreatening because it was presumed divorced from the sexual and firmly situated on the higher plane of the rational, socially unsanctioned desires, such as same-sex desire, found expressive vent.[20] Though it has come under considerable fire as racist rhetoric from a number of critics who associate it with the promulgation of a white racial ideal, Hellenism had subversive uses within this register. I return to the question of Hellenism and race below.

At the same time, as Hawthorne's responses to the classical representations of Antinous made clear, these responses were in no way predictable or uniform in their effects. In his Italian notebook, Hawthorne described visiting the Villa Albani on May 10, 1858. As he noted,

> I do not recall any of the sculpture, except a colossal bas-relief of Antinoüs, crowned with flowers, and holding flowers in his hand, which was found in the ruins of Hadrian's Villa. This is said to be the finest relic of antiquity next to the Apollo and the Laocoön; but I could not feel it to be so, partly, I suppose, because the features of Antinoüs do not seem to me beautiful in themselves; and that heavy, downward look is repeated till I am more weary of it than of anything else in sculpture. (14: 214)

The narrator of *The Marble Faun* asks why Antinous is "forever sad." But here, the "real" Hawthorne addresses the question with less empathy, focusing on why the statue makes him, as spectator, "weary." Hawthorne's *Passages from the French and Italian Notebooks* was posthumously published in two volumes in February of 1872, edited (and often expurgated) by Sophia Hawthorne before her death in the February of 1871. The 1872 *Passages* included this passage on the weary-making Antinous; Melville, who lived for most of the latter half of the nineteenth century, therefore had access to this and related passages. I will return to Hawthorne's response to Antinous in terms of the larger themes of his work. Before doing so, I want to consider some of the most immediate implications of Melville's encounters with Hellenic art.

Melville's 1857 lecture "Statues in Rome" survives today in reconstructed form. As the editors of the *Piazza Tales and Other Prose Pieces* write, "During his first season as a lecturer, beginning in Lawrence, Massachusetts, on November 23, 1857, and concluding in New Bedford, Massachusetts, on February 23, 1858, Melville discussed the subject of Roman statuary in sixteen cities and towns east of the Mississippi River. He did not publish his lecture in a magazine or book, and no manuscript is known to survive, but contemporary newspapers gave fairly full accounts of the content and even of the organization and style of the lecture" (*Piazza Tales* 723). The consensus of Melville scholars is that he did not attempt to publish his lectures himself; indeed, surprisingly few nineteenth-century authors pursued this option, despite the prominence of the public lecture and the lyceum in the nineteenth century.[21]

In "Statues in Rome," Melville discusses the Apollo Belvedere in the Vatican Museum, for Winckelmann the height of classical Greek art and beauty. He had read Winckelmann's famous *History of Ancient Art* in 1852, and would have been familiar with the high esteem in which the German art historian held the statue.[22] Echoing the German writer, Melville writes of the Apollo Belvedere as the "statue which most of all in the Vatican excites the admiration of all visitors . . . the crowning glory."[23] Further echoing Winckelmann, Melville notes that, in its "divinity," the statue "lifts the imagination of the beholder above 'things rank and gross in nature,' and makes ordinary criticism impossible." He continues: "it gives a kind of visible response to that class of human aspirations of beauty and perfection" that can only be fully experienced, as "Faith" tells us, in the next life.[24] On the dazzling beauty of the Apollo Belvedere, Hawthorne was in agreement. As he wrote in his Italian notebook when in Rome in March of 1858, "I saw the Apollo Belvidere as something ethereal and godlike; only for a flitting moment, however, and as if he had alighted from heaven, or shone suddenly out of the sunlight, and then had withdrawn himself again" (14: 125). Hawthorne goes on to praise the other sculpture that, along with the Apollo Belvedere and the Antinous, represented the height of classical art and beauty for Winckelmann. "I felt the Laocoon, too, very powerfully, though very quietly; an immortal agony, with a strange calmness diffused through it, so that it resembles the vast rage of the sea, calm on account of its immensity, or the tumult of Niagara, which does not seem to be tumult because it keeps pouring on, forever and ever" (14: 125).

Melville's sense of a beautiful art object as *visible* evidence of some kind of divinely perfect beauty—"it gives a kind of visible response to that class of human aspirations of beauty and perfection"—is, in my view, important here for a consideration of the function of art, especially in the context of the ancient archive. Considered by so many, even to this day but especially in the nineteenth century, to be the epitome of human civilization and aesthetics, ancient Greek culture served the role in Victorian America, as it did in Europe at the time, of making aesthetic as well as philosophical, cultural, and social ideals *visible*. While many aspects of this externalization of ideals are important, what interests me specifically is the way in which homoerotic desire could be made visible without being threatening or inordinately obvious. At the same time that Melville could evoke, in his public lectures, the beauty of male forms such as the Apollo Belvedere, the Greek and Roman myths and histories were being expurgated of their sexual content in print, as emblematized by the work of writers such as Goodrich, Thomas Bulfinch, and Hawthorne, who very specifically rewrote the myths as stories for children.

Melville notes that the Apollo Belvedere embodies "the attributes, physical and intellectual, which Milton bestowed on one of his angels, 'Severe in youthful beauty.'" From May 1638 to July or August 1639, Milton went on his own Grand Tour of France and Italy. Melville goes on to call *Paradise Lost* a "great Vatican done into verse."[25] I considered the valences between Milton and Hawthorne in the chapter on "Rappaccini's Daughter." If one thinks of the varieties of male beauty on display in this poem, but specifically the way in which Milton registers Satan's devolution from beautiful near-divine being to fallen angel through highly visualized descriptions of Satan's physical ruination as well as Milton's obsessive plumbing of signifiers from the ancient archive, Milton's work becomes a suggestive intertext for homoerotic aesthetic culture as well.

Hawthorne implicitly registers a kind of discomfort with the visual spectacle of the Apollo Belvedere that I think is also quite suggestive. While he can praise the figure as "ethereal and godlike," he also notes that he only saw it for a "flitting moment." The way the figure shines "suddenly out of the sunlight" suggests a momentary blinding. In contrast, the more reassuringly masculine and patriarchal, however indescribably tormented, Laocoön strikes Hawthorne as, at once, powerful and suffused with a "strange calmness" (14: 125). In Virgil's *Aeneid,* Laocoön, a Trojan priest, is divinely punished for having warned his countrymen against the Greek gift of the Trojan Horse, which is, of course, no gift at all but contains within it Greeks waiting to invade the stronghold of their enemy. The famous Vatican Laocoön—

"Laocoön and His Sons," also known as the "Laocoön Group," a Roman copy, discovered in Rome in 1506, of an ancient Greek sculpture that dates back to 200 B.C.E.—depicts Laocoön and his two sons being squeezed to death by two giant sea serpents. His body horribly twisted into a contorted position, Laocoön cries out, along with his similarly afflicted sons, in silent but palpable anguish. Powerless despite his outsize physical form, Laocoön can do nothing to save either his sons or himself. Laocoön, his sons, and the serpents that intertwine and lock them all together form an exquisite tableau of sorrow, suffering, menace, and helpless human acquiescence to a greater might. For Melville, the Laocoön "expresses the doubt and the dark groping of speculation in that age when the old mythology was passing away and men's minds had not yet reposed in the new faith"; for him, Laocoön, "the symbol of human misfortune," "represents the tragic side of humanity."[26] In psychoanalytic terms, the sculpture thematizes anew what Freud found in the image of Medusa's Head: the Laocoön both evokes castration (male powerlessness and violation) and defends against it with a phallic plenitude (the limbs of the male figures, the invincible, long, coiling serpents).

Hawthorne echoes Winckelmann's famously counterintuitive interpretation, representative of the German art historian's view of classical Greek sculpture generally, of the Laocoön as a serene, *harmonious* work, a view that was famously challenged by Lessing.[27] Even in his "tumult," Hawthorne observes, Laocoön maintains a strange, quiet placidity, one that reassures the spectator. I would argue that a crucial distinction between the youthful male figures Hawthorne discusses and the Laocoön is that the latter is, however tormented, finally a father figure, an older and more authoritarian presence. In contrast, the figures of youthful male beauty, whether Hawthorne disputes or praises their beauty, embody (Antinous's "heavy, downward look") and provoke (the Apollo Belvedere's sudden, blinding brightness) visual disturbance and spectatorial ambivalence. Melville's godlike youth Billy Budd will embody similar qualities and provoke similar effects.

Melville also makes note of a very different kind of male form in the Farnese Hercules who, "leaning on his club," embodies "simplicity and bovine good nature"; indeed, Hercules evokes the "lazy ox, confident of his own strength but loth to use it."[28] Melville's Billy Budd will be compared to Hercules; indeed, in his mixture of both "meltingly" beautiful attributes and animalistic qualities, Billy Budd is a fusion of Antinous and Hercules. One of the most interesting aspects of Melville's literary fusion-technique in his description of the Handsome Sailor is the way it recalls one of Winckelmann's central arguments.

The art historian Whitney Davis, in his 2010 book *Queer Beauty*, discusses Winckelmann's formal doctrine of ideal beauty, achieved when the artist "combines the beauty of many discrete things (or parts of things) judged by him to be beautiful." As Davis describes,

> Winckelmann's implausible doctrine of ideal beauty . . . echoed familiar, banal legends about the practice of ancient artists such as Zeuxis, who supposedly collated the various beautiful aspects (as it were beautiful body parts) of five maidens of Croton in order to compile his depiction of the supremely beautiful Helen of Troy. In this respect Winckelmann's doctrine could hardly have been the radical—the radically *modern*—element of [his method that came to be described by thinkers such as Hegel as "an entirely new organ"].[29]

Davis, parsing late-nineteenth-century critics such as Bernard Bosanquet and Benedetto Croce, writes that Winckelmann's radical modernity and value must lie elsewhere, "in his historical account of the *psychosocial dynamics* and specifically the *cultural erotics* of beautiful artworks, overlaid with his description of their sensible reception on our own part and in this very respect—an eroticized cultural reception that absorbs the original affect and responds to it."[30] Davis's emphasized terms correspond to the kind of approach I have pursued in this study and to the questions I am raising about antebellum authors' apprehension of the classical image.

Near the end of "Statues in Rome," Melville recalls his visit to the Villa Albani. His description of Antinous, at least insofar as the lecture has been reconstructed, is comparatively austere when his description in the *Journals* is recalled. In "Statues in Rome," Melville makes note only of "Antinous with his eye reposing on a lotus of admirable design which he holds in his hand." Melville sandwiches his brief description of the beautiful Antinous, whose beauty would not be guessed, however, from this essay, between descriptions of statues of Minerva, "a creature as purely and serenely sublime as it is possible for human hands to form," and Aesop, "the dwarfed and deformed."[31] The austerely registered homoerotic icon is contrasted against the phallic woman of virginal rectitude (who will play such a key role in Melville's poem "After the Pleasure Party," also written very late in life) and a figure of misshapen manhood who is here also, significantly, a figure of the artist. As I have had occasion to note, Hawthorne frequently contrasts his beautiful youths against grim and unappetizing older figures. And as I noted in the last chapter, Athena, or Minerva, the "unapproachable" goddess, merges with "fatal" woman Medusa, whose image Athena wears as her aegis. What

I want to suggest is not only that a continuum of images, both variously and similarly deployed, runs throughout the works of Hawthorne, Melville, and other nineteenth-century writers, but that this continuum reflects the usefulness of classical iconography for the representation and exploration of otherwise taboo gendered and sexual subjects, precisely because the classical could function as code.

A detail recorded in the editorial notes to the *Journals* regarding Melville's description of Antinous here proves oddly appropriate and suggestive. "The one newspaper report of 'Statues in Rome' to mention this work is obviously garbled: the 'medallion of Antinous,' according to the Montreal *Daily Transcript and Commercial Advertiser* (#8), represents a 'female of crystalline countenance with her eye reposing on a lotus of admirable design, which she holds in her hand.'"[32] Part of the homoerotic threat of Antinous lies precisely in his feminine nature, the "melting" beauty he embodies, the same gender-bending threat associated with Narcissus. The misunderstanding here, the report that Melville was describing a female character, seems to me telling, speaking, as it does, to Antinous's gender indeterminacy. Yet part of that indeterminacy is also Antinous's associations with a striking masculinism, connoted by his large, powerful chest. Antinous's strength is emphasized along with his feminine softness. It is this duality in an icon of male beauty that arrests Melville and which he treats as an endlessly perplexing puzzle.

While, to turn now to *Billy Budd*, left unfinished at his death in 1891 and not published until 1924, many critics have focused on the mystery of the villain Claggart, who embodies the irresolvable conundrum of "Natural depravity, or depravity according to nature?" the short novel's titular figure is no less a mystery. While Coffler links Billy Budd's Hercules-like simplicity of mind and nature back to Antinous, seen as a figure of sensual lassitude and therefore a kind of serene mindlessness, I think the disjunction of both figures within one literary character is a more salient issue.[33] For what Billy Budd represents *at once* is a stereotypically strong, hardy, and murderously powerful form of masculinity and a soft, feminized, and feminizing form of masculinity. Billy Budd's ability to feminize the male gaze—in other words, to elicit responses from other male lookers in a manner customarily associated with the way men look at women—is a key part of the pattern of problems associated with his character.

To switch mythic gears, Margaret Walters's discussion of Michelangelo's *David* in her study *The Nude Male* speaks most directly to the issues at work in Melville's portrait of Billy Budd. As the latest incarnation of the Handsome Sailor, the cynosure who galvanizes male visual appraisal and appreciation, Billy Budd is a figure who embodies the gaze, which as Lacan has famously described is not reducible to the eye or the look of one individual but, instead, encompasses the entire visual field in which the person looking and what is being looked at are only included elements. (Indeed, for Lacan, the gaze is indifferent to the individual subject.) Melville likens Billy Budd to the "comely young David" (78) and also evokes the naked male subject of the sculptor, being a figure "who in the nude might have posed for a statue of young Adam before the Fall" (94).[34] As Walters notes of Michelangelo's famous work, "despite David's size and his defiant nudity—he is stripped for action, and his nakedness is the sign that he is God's warrior—he is not altogether confident. From the front, he looks proudly relaxed; from any other angle, his pose seems more uncertain. . . . The hero is shown, not in his moment of triumph, as is more common, but tensed before the fight. His energy remains petrified, forever unreleased and unrealized."[35]

Melville creates in Billy Budd a figure who represents a similar set of dualities, and it is fair to say, I believe, an idealized self-image on the part of a once hale, handsome author in his final years. What is analogous in Billy to David's uncertainty, as Walters puts it, is Billy's vulnerability, metaphorically registered in his stutter, which further links him to the uncouthness of the stammering barbarian. Indeed, Billy Budd's dualities include his being both David and his foe, the Philistine barbarian Goliath. What I find to be the most telling valence between the David of Walters's description and Melville's beautiful youth is the idea of a banked and potent power—"petrified, forever unreleased and unrealized." He could be a man frozen by Medusa's gaze, frozen, that is, to follow Freud, in phallic rectitude. If this is the case, Melville explodes it—he gives Billy Budd the power to unleash his power. As I argue in *Men Beyond Desire,* Billy Budd transitions from the object of the homoerotic gaze to the disciplinary force that prohibits it—indeed, a murderous force that annihilates it. If Billy Budd is the literary homoerotic icon *par excellence,* his destruction of the queer Claggart (not, to be sure, an innocent character) also makes Billy the icon of homophobic defensiveness.

Billy's ability, as an object of desire, to affect the viewer speaks to the volatility of the work of classical art as a subject of "safe" viewing for the homoerotically gazing spectator. One of Winckelmann's most ingenious strategies for allowing scores of spectators to savor images of beautiful young men was his decisive separation, like the yolk and the whites of an egg, of sexual desire from appreciation of the beautiful. The beauty of young men such as the Apollo and the Antinous could be appreciated, indeed, ecstatically inhabited, while the mantra of nonsexual and idealized response always safeguarded this appreciation against the threat of prurience. But looking at Billy, a kind of living piece of Greek art, does not leave the spectator safe or unimplicated in sexual schemes, points hardly incidental to a work that is so fundamentally obsessed with knowledge and knowledgelessness.

Moving from the "simpler" sphere of the ship the *Rights-of-Man* to the "ampler and more knowing world of" the *Bellipotent,* Billy Budd fails to register the change in his circumstances that is grounded in the change from simplicity to greater knowingness (50). He is a kind of "rustic beauty transplanted from the provinces and brought into competition with the highborn dames of the court" (51), but does not notice this shift in intersubjective relations. "As little did he observe that something about him provoked an ambiguous smile in one or two harder faces" among the "bluejackets," or common sailors, of the *Bellipotent* crew. "Nor less unaware was he of the peculiar favorable effect his person and demeanor had upon the more intelligent gentlemen of the quarter-deck" (51). It is on Claggart that Billy Budd has the greatest power to alter and transform the spectator. This is an effect that Melville produces at times through the alternative route of negation: talking, in a pre-Freudian manner, of Claggart's homoerotic blend of "envy and antipathy," conjoined in him like "Chang and Eng," for Billy, the narrator notes that the envy in Claggart is no "vulgar form of the passion. Nor, as directed toward Billy Budd, did it partake of that streak of apprehensive jealousy that marred Saul's visage perturbedly brooding on the comely young David. Claggart's envy struck deeper" (78). By disputing an outcome that he has himself visualized for us, by telling us that Billy Budd does not mar Claggart's visage in the way that the "comely young David" marred Saul's, Melville is, of course, putting that very image of a desire-marred face in our minds, and therefore recalling not just the homoerotic tradition of Jonathan and David that, as Richard Godbeer has shown in *The Overflowing of Male Friendship,* was one of the central tropes for romantic male friendship in the early American republic, but also the beautiful-ruined face of the fallen Satan staring, with "jealousy, th'injur'd Lover's Hell," at the prelapsarian splendor of Adam and Eve. Perhaps the chief disfiguration that Claggart undergoes is the result of the melancholia that intermittently seizes him when he looks at Billy. Looking at the "cheerful sea Hyperion," Claggart takes on a "settled meditative and melancholy expression, his eyes strangely suffused with incipient feverish tears. Then would Claggart look like the man of sorrows. Yes, and sometimes the melancholy expression would have in it a touch of soft yearning, as if Claggart could have even loved Billy but for fate and ban" (88).

I argue that in *Billy Budd* Melville brings the banned sexual elements in the discourse of Hellenism to a newly articulated and prominently visualized level. While *Billy Budd* is famously unpublished, there is evidence that Melville did not intend it to remain so. In the responses to Billy Budd, especially Claggart's, Melville registered mingled responses to the spectacle of male beauty: feelings of ambiguous regard, of mingled envy and antipathy, and of sorrow, a lingering melancholy. *Billy Budd* is Melville's answer to Hawthorne's question about why Antinous is forever sad. Or, perhaps more to the point, Billy Budd is a figure of the sad young man offered to Hawthorne, whose work teems with such figures, as a tribute from Melville, whose work also teems with such figures. The young man's sadness would appear to be a reaction to the impossible demands of visual identity.

What needs to be disentangled—rethought and reimagined—are the phenomena of a homoerotic tradition coming into greater prominence and decidability and an ongoing fascination with the classical past. As scholars, we continue to ask where the banned homoerotic response begins, and the kind of weariness at looking at a beautiful work of art with unimpressed eyes, as Hawthorne did with the bas-relief of Antinous, ends; where the ecstatic love of the beautiful intersects with an enflamed sexual response; from which source the spectatorial ambivalence with which Billy Budd is regarded flows, homoerotic desire or an essential bewilderment over the unceasing repetition of classical forms in the present.

HAWTHORNE'S ANTINOUS
VISUAL IDENTITY, HELLENISM, AND THE MASOCHISTIC GAZE

Melville still had Hawthorne on his mind when he wrote *Billy Budd* in the late 1880s. "Though our Handsome Sailor had as much of masculine beauty as one can expect anywhere to see; nevertheless, like the beautiful woman in one of Hawthorne's minor tales, there was just one thing amiss in him. No visible blemish indeed, as with the lady; no, but an occasional liability to vocal defect" (53). As he did with such perspicuity in "Hawthorne and His Mosses," Melville isolates here something peculiarly and stubbornly powerful in Hawthorne's writings, and a theme that Melville takes to new levels of complexity in *Billy Budd:* the relationship between men and their own image. The impossibility of "visual blemish" in Hawthorne's beautiful young men ironically alerts us, through negation, to the fact that they are in every other way quite blemished indeed. For Melville, the blemish is located in the body even if it is not on its surface; stuttering Billy's ruptured, impaired voice gives vent to the tensions in the story that are centered in the predicament of Billy's beautiful, feminine form in a world that consists entirely of other men. Hawthorne, generally, establishes a different kind of split: the outward beauty of his young men contrasts with their interior inadequacy, sometimes to the point of moral decay. At the same time, the older men who may be said to prey on these younger men are often described as physically as well as morally inferior, damaged, or downright ugly, like the misshapen Chillingworth, the menacing Model, or, to go back further, the tarred and feathered spectacle of Major Molineux.

In the introduction, I noted the valences between Hawthorne's representation of the male's conflict with his own image and Lacan's theory of the mirror stage, which brilliantly revises Freud's theories of narcissism in ways that dovetail with psychoanalytic film theory. What I want to suggest is that Hawthorne foregrounds a particular understanding of self, sexuality, and the body in his work. His work thematizes what I have called *visual identity*, the conceptualization of the self as a perceivable visual image, something extruded upon the surface of the world as a reflection of a private, interior self the existence of which can be affirmed only through this visualization. Which is to say, selves are known or knowable only through their outward manifestation in physical form. Visual identity is certainly not exclusive to males; indeed, the entire postclassical Western tradition has emphasized the visual aspects of beauty as a female domain. Hester Prynne is first introduced to us in *The Scarlet Letter* as a visual spectacle, the very outward show of her controversial sinfulness, a tableau vivant of her public identity as adulterous woman bearing her adulterously spawned child, a parody of the Christian icon of the Madonna and Child that adds what this icon refutes, a lush, Mary Magdalene–like carnality.

Highly responsive to the beauty of women *and* men in his work as a whole, Hawthorne reinserts masculinity into the continuum of visual desire and concepts of beauty. He extends Winckelmannian aesthetics, preserving their merger of homoerotic appreciation and desexualizing aesthetic distance and adding a fierce, psychologizing, secular-religious moral critique. If Hawthorne's young men are Greek statues come to life, they actively comment on the disparity between a belief in classical perfection and modern forms of beauty, sexuality, and the body: they embody the split by denaturing outward shows of beauty with interior realms of moral depravity.

The distinctions between Hawthorne's disdainful reaction to Antinous in Rome and Melville's transported one make for an extremely telling commentary on how each author imagined "significant personal beauty" in males—and even more saliently why this would be an important issue in representation at all. While one could go in several directions here, and while the comparative discussion of Melville's and Hawthorne's representations of masculinity demands a discrete study, what I want to consider is the disparity between what Hawthorne "said" he liked or disliked in his ostensibly private writing and what he consistently thematized in his fiction. At this point, I would like to introduce into the discussion a concept that I call *the masochistic gaze*.[36]

Melville's reaction to Antinous, though clipped in the manner of all of his journal writing, reflects his ability to respond to an image of aestheticized male beauty with appreciation and something approaching a lack of conflict. In other words, Melville's homoerotic sensibility can come through on the page with greater explicitness and fewer restrictions than could Hawthorne's. Immediately we recall all of the moments in Melville's work in which young men are regarded dubiously (think, for example, of the burly sailors' contemptuous regard of the too feminine and dandified young Englishman Harry Bolton in Melville's underappreciated *Redburn*), none more powerfully in this regard than Billy Budd. But just as Melville can name and poetically evoke Narcissus in his published writing, he can behold Antinous and record his impressions of this beautiful doomed youth with appreciation. In contrast, Hawthorne can only see a drooping, dispiriting attitude in this figure. What makes Hawthorne's response more than simply a matter of opinion, a question of differing tastes, is that Hawthorne continuously thematized in his fiction precisely what the "real" author Hawthorne recorded with disapproval or frustration: an attitude of discomfort on the part of the beautiful young man with male visual identity.

Hawthorne distances himself from received opinion, writing that despite the figure's vaunted beauty, "the features of Antinoüs do not seem to me beautiful in themselves." As he clarifies: "that heavy, downward look is repeated till I am more weary of it than of anything else in sculpture." I call our attention to Hawthorne's admission—or declaration—of "weariness" at beholding that frequently repeated "heavy, downward look." The received opinion to which Hawthorne was aversively responding was Winckelmann's appreciation for the beauty of the Antinous.

Notably well versed in issues of aesthetics and visual representation (as the thematic references to portraits, miniatures, daguerreotypes, statues, and other art objects in his work attest), Hawthorne read Winckelmann's 1764 *The History of Ancient Art* shortly after having completed *The Scarlet Letter*. The English translation by G. Henry Lodge was the one that Hawthorne and Melville read before their trips to Europe in the 1850s.[37] Both writers frequently echo Winckelmann's focus on the classical beautiful male body, such as the famous Apollo Belvedere. Published in 1849, Lodge's translation of the second volume, *Art Among the Greeks,* was the first to be published in the United States, probably precisely because of the second volume's Greek focus. The first volume, which focuses on Egyptians and Etruscans, was published in 1856. It was the first two volumes of Winckelmann's *History of Art*, then, that were available to Hawthorne, since the subsequent two volumes did not come out until 1872–73 (Hawthorne died in 1864). Hawthorne's immersion (along with that of his wife Sophia, a visual artist whose own career and aesthetic interest are finally receiving the scholarly attention they deserve, and his family) in the European art world produced the rich series of commentaries on European culture and aesthetics that are recorded in *The French and Italian Notebooks* as well as in *The Marble Faun*.

While nothing as predictable or rote as a one-to-one relationship between Hawthorne's art and his personal responses exists—to the extent that we can ever really view a famous writer's journal writing as "personal"; it is not difficult to believe that Hawthorne, who had achieved fame a decade earlier with *The Scarlet Letter*, was aware that his private prose might one day be published—what is nevertheless of undeniable interest is the central discrepancy here. As I have had frequent occasion to note, Hawthorne associates youthful male figures in his fiction with precisely the attitude of "heavy, downward" looking that he finds so unappetizing in the Villa Albani Antinous. Generally, the Antinous is associated with certain defining qualities: a sensual, daydreaming lassitude; detachment; a melancholy air; and downcast eyes. Stooping, head bent down, in attitudes that I have associated with shame, passivity, aggression and hostility, and, especially, the fear of looking, Hawthorne's young men share with Antinous, and Antinous as Hawthorne perceived him, a melancholic disposition tied directly to ways of seeing and being seen.

As I have written in another context, masochistic male looking is indicative of the fragility, vulnerability, and powerlessness of the male eye. The masochistic gaze, which renders vision impaired, faulty, or in some other way damaged, is an expression of repressed homosexual voyeurism.[38] What I want to suggest is that—at least to a certain extent—Hawthorne's expression of detachment, skepticism, and disdain toward the highly regarded bas-relief of Antinous was a self-policing maneuver against the homoerotic potentialities of the figure, potentialities suggested within the fame that surrounded it as among the most beautiful of classical works and within Winckelmann's idealization of such figures. (Some critics will inevitably solve the problem by offering that Hawthorne simply didn't like this bas-relief. Based on Hawthorne's consistent themes, I believe that there's more to it than that.)

To speculate, perhaps what Hawthorne found so wearisome about the Antinous was precisely the way in which the attitude of downward-gazing (looking upon the earth and recalling his premature death) thematizes the predicament of his young anguished men, forever caught in a paralytic bind within the gaze, their own desire to look and not to be looked at, their constant vulnerability to the assaultive and ravenous eyes of others. To speculate further, perhaps these afflictions are precisely what safeguard Hawthorne's youthful male figures from a threatening homoerotic explicitness. Were their desirability presented without them, they might be too available as objects of erotic contemplation, too idealized. And yet, at the same time, their afflictions make them more vulnerable and therefore more accessible, as Billy Budd's stutter does him. Sensually feminine and obdurately, stoically masculine at once, Billy Budd becomes an accessible figure through his somatic rupture. And much like Billy Budd, Antinous has the ability to affect the spectator, perhaps, against his will. As looking at Billy Budd on some level deforms Claggart, so, too, does looking upon the Antinous leave Hawthorne wearied—a response that blurs the somatic and the affective.[39] And as the epigraph to this chapter shows, the more explicit the figuration of the young man's melancholia becomes, the more amplified the homoerotic threat. The narrator's question about Antinous's perplexing sadness leads to an almost shockingly explicit homoerotic image of the androgynous wine-god Bacchus bringing grapes to the earthy young Italian man Donatello's lips: "Bacchus, too, a rosy flush diffusing itself over his time-stained surface, could come down from his pedestal, and offer a cluster of purple grapes to Donatello's lips; because the god recognizes him as the woodland elf who so often shared his revels" (14:17). What undergirds this encounter is a knowing, sexually charged kinship between louche god and feral man or "woodland elf," a queer shock of recognition.

By transforming Hawthorne's Georgiana in "The Birthmark," the woman from one of Hawthorne's "minor tales" with a blemish on her beauty, into Billy Budd, a young man without a visual blemish, but with a different kind of somatic flaw, Melville provocatively reorganizes Hawthorne's thematic. The missing figure in Melville's analogy—Hawthorne's male characters—is abundantly supplied by Melville in his most overwhelmingly male-centered and homoerotic work. Melville, in other words, provides a dazzling riff on the beauty of Hawthorne's males while safeguarding the dead author's legacy through an evocation of a flawed female beauty in one of Hawthorne's so-called minor tales. The levels of distancing and detachment at work here paradoxically make it possible for Melville to flood the Hawthorne oeuvre, by implication, with homoerotic valences, embodied in Billy Budd and his own maddening, even wearying incitement of the male gaze.

REFLECTIONS ON THE SIGNIFICANCE OF *THE MARBLE FAUN*

I want to suggest that Hawthorne's last published novel, *The Marble Faun* (1860), represents a certain terminus point, a kind of closure, in Hawthorne's development of his narcissistic themes. Certainly, it is the headiest aestheticization of them, in which Hawthorne offers perhaps the most telling account of his conflicted relationship to male beauty. If narcissism for Hawthorne was a means of both critiquing normative masculinity and mourning for a lost ideal, *The Marble Faun* functions as a kind of narcissistic catharsis, a way for Hawthorne to resolve the maddeningly conflicted anxieties that informed his understanding of masculinity, on a personal and social level. Moreover, Hawthorne's deployment of the titular figure of this novel illuminates the homoerotic stakes in narcissistic self-representation, while also presaging Hawthorne's treatment of racialized masculinity in the late, unfinished work.

As I have been arguing, Hawthorne conducts his inquiry into the anguished nature of gendered identity and issues of power and violation through symbolic reenactments of the Narcissus myth. Yet his aesthetics—as he discusses in "The Custom-House" essay, his view of art as a mirror in whose "haunted verge" can merge the polarities that inform the Narcissus myth, surface and depth, or, in Hawthorne's reformulation, the imaginative and the actual—positively revalues Narcissus. (I turn to the question of Hawthorne's aesthetics, as he presents them in the "The Custom-House," in the epilogue.) I suggest that, towards the end of his career, Hawthorne found a way of resolving his narcissistic crisis, albeit only for a moment. Though *The Marble Faun* is Hawthorne's last "complete" romance, he wrote a great deal after it, including the unfinished *Septimius Felton/Norton manuscripts*, which stage anew the narcissistic crisis at the center of Hawthorne's work, as I will argue in the last chapter. Hawthorne's momentary resolution of this narcissistic crisis in *The Marble Faun* is intimately tied to his anxieties over gender and homoerotic desire, and involves an attempt to mediate them as well as his conflicts over self and self-image. *The Marble Faun* also gives us a valuable opportunity to consider more generally the cultural anxieties over all of these conflicts within Hawthorne's own era.

The spectacle of Praxiteles' faun with which this novel opens is the culmination not only of major preoccupations in Hawthorne's work but also of those in the culture he brought with him to Europe, in which he traveled after finishing his stint as American Consul in Liverpool, an appointment secured for him by his friend, President Franklin Pierce.[40] As we have noted, a decisive shift from Rome to Greece (the "Greek Revival") had occurred in American culture by the antebellum period. The unceasing classical references throughout Hawthorne's work convey the interest in the mythological past in American life, inherited from and cross-fertilized with European Romanticism: the national form of narcissistic relation, in which one nation makes sense of itself by negotiating the effects of its specular image in another.

Hawthorne's interest in Praxiteles' faun, while certainly inspired, flows from the trends Winckelmann set in motion. "The prominence Winckelmann gave to Praxiteles," writes the art historian Alex Potts, along with Whitney Davis one of the key contemporary reinterpreters of Winckelmann, "has remained a feature in modern histories of Greek sculpture ever since." In Winckelmann's wake, a "rash of ascriptions of antique sculptures of beautiful little fauns and satyrs to Praxiteles" occurred, as modern "artists also became preoccupied with this sculptural ideal, and produced a number of interesting renderings of the boyish gracefulness and supposedly 'innocent' homoeroticism that had come to be associated with this great sculptor of antiquity."[41]

Freud illuminates what was at stake for Hawthorne in terms of the sexual relevance of aesthetics generally. In his enduringly controversial study of Leonardo da Vinci, Freud writes with fascination of the homosexual artist's fusion of opposites, particularly of moral opposites:

> Leonardo was notable for his quiet peaceableness and his avoidance of all antagonism and controversy. He was gentle and kindly to everyone . . . He condemned war and bloodshed and described man as not so much the king of the animal world but rather the worst of the wild beasts. But this feminine delicacy of feeling did not deter him from accompanying condemned criminals on their way to execution in order to study their features distorted by fear and to sketch them in his notebook. . . . He often gave the appearance of being indifferent to good and evil. (SE 11: 68–69)

Freud's view of the homosexual artist remains as fascinating as it is problematic. For Freud, Leonardo is the homosexual male artist who sublimates his desires and occupies a strange, anomalous position between love and hate, sexuality and asexuality, good and evil. Morally and sexually ambivalent, he sublimates his sexuality, specifically his homosexuality, into aesthetic endeavor. The homosexual artist emerges in Freud and in popular culture as a beautiful monster, a figure of profound ambivalence. Writing, as he did, of male beauty and the figure of the artist in the period between Winckelmann and Freud, between neoclassicism and psychoanalysis, between the myth-discourse of Narcissus and the classical psychoanalytic theory of narcissism, Hawthorne creates in his marble faun a portrait that combines Winckelmann's aesthetic theory with an uncannily Freudian view of the work of art—and implicitly of the artist—as the merging of opposites.

Discussing the "homoerotic reflexivity operating between image and spectator" in Winckelmann's theories, Alex Potts explains why Winckelmann could not locate the figure of a Zeus or a Hercules as his ideal form of masculine beauty. Only the boyish youth could fill this role, for his "ideal masculinity could be projected while effacing suggestions of any too categorically insistent a masculine identity." Indeed, Winckelmann "suggests that the imperatives of ideal beauty lead ineluctably to the image of the hermaphrodite or castrated figure."[42] In contrast, Melville had no problem doing so, as suggested by his Billy Budd, who fuses Antinous- and David-like beauty with that of the strong man Hercules and with other "barbarian" typings of masculinity.

While a great deal needs to be said about Winckelmann's establishment of a homosexual Hellenic tradition in the nineteenth century, Winckelmann's elevation of a particular figure, "the purified image of the body as a cipher of ideal oneness," most relevantly impinges upon our discussion.[43] For Hawthorne, the faun is just such a unifying cipher, reconciling warring opposites, male and female, human and animal, culture and nature, beauty and horror. The novel's original title (used in England) was *Transformation:* in the faun, the ambiguously beautiful young man in Hawthorne's work transforms into a male figure of beautiful ambiguity. Permanently available to the gaze yet unblinkingly indifferent to it, the faun incites the gaze yet remains utterly invulnerable, the most successful version of a sexually inviolate male in a literary era that teems with such figures. The faun is truly a "man beyond desire," aloof not only from sex but also from the messy complications of the human. Moreover, Hawthorne's representation of the faun intersects with a series of critical controversies concerning race and Hellenism; briefly addressing these controversies will help us to contextualize Hawthorne's more direct interrogation of race in his late work.

Nancy Bentley has reframed *The Marble Faun,* Hawthorne's last complete fictional work, as indicative of Hawthorne's white, imperial disposition toward racial, ethnic, and class otherness. Similarly, Arthur Riss has presented *The Marble Faun* as a chief example of Hawthorne's aesthetics of "anti-black racism."[44] Kendall Johnson's discussion of the racial as well as sexual politics of *The Marble Faun* draws on Bentley's and usefully indexes several concerns relevant to the present discussion:

As Nancy Bentley notes, the faun first appears in Hawthorne's notebook as a "bearded woman" and a link to humanity's "lower tribes." . . . The faun of the notebook seems the product of Hawthorne's anxiety over possibly errant sexual sympathy. Recall [Joseph] Addison's claim that our sense of beauty regulates sexual appetite, directing desire to maintain the proper boundaries between species. In changing the gender of the faun from a woman (in the notebook) to a man (for the novel), Hawthorne bridles the faun's procreative potential with an American brand of impotence, figured through a grammar of noble savagery. . . . Whereas Bentley interprets the faun through Hawthorne's characterization of fugitive slaves in "Chiefly About War Matters" (*The Atlantic Monthly*, 1862), Donatello's story echoes the frame of savage "*doom*," to recall the terms of George Catlin. . . . Donatello's vexed masculinity reflects a logic of racial classification that assumes an impossibly pure ancestry rooted in a pre-national soil outside of history.

In foreclosing the possibility of union and generation between Donatello and Miriam Schaeffer, Johnson argues, Hawthorne echoes the "figurative impotence" of characters such as Chingachgook in *The Last of the Mohicans* (1826): "The exclusive logic of racial ancestry" dooms the Monte Beni family.[45]

Johnson brings many important cultural contexts into the discussion, particularly the legacy of George Catlin (July 26, 1796–December 23, 1872), a Pennsylvanian painter whose "Indian Gallery" was one of the chief antebellum foundations, along with Cooper's novels, of the myth of the American Indian as a romantic figure of lawlessness and a vanished primitive American past. (Catlin used his experience of living among Indians to bolster his own personal mythology.) But Johnson errs, I think, in associating Hawthorne's faun with "impotence"; not only is this a heteronormative argument, relying, as it does, on conventional standards of masculine potency and reproductivity, but it is also a misrepresentation of the faun's properties. Casually teasing and placidly appealing, the faun evokes both the feminine and the masculine, an androgynous figure that synthesizes the kinds of gender-blurring beauty to which Hawthorne is drawn throughout his fiction. Oddly beautiful feminine males abound—Fanshawe, with his scholarly softness contrasted against his jock rival's loping machismo; the gentle boy Ilbrahim; Minister Hooper, with his transvestic black veil; Dimmesdale, as tremulously emotional as he is pleasing to the eye. Oddly masculine while also sensually feminine beauties abound as well—Beatrice, as phallically potent as she is overripely gorgeous; Hester Prynne, a self-reliant woman likened to "man-like Elizabeth" the Queen and the Renaissance Madonna both; Zenobia, with her arresting, Angelina Jolie–like erotic beauty and immense, masculine hands, between which she always threatens to pulverize Coverdale's obtrusive head. The faun's androgynous sexual élan specifically defies the hypermasculine new standards of virility and physical hardness that began to emerge in the 1850s, with the rise of the athletic male body-cult, and that Hawthorne had already satirized, as we have noted, in *The Blithedale Romance*. Far from being a diminution of the queer sexual charge of the "bearded woman," the faun looms above us as a tantalizing queer mystery, one suggestive of an essentially enigmatic quality in Hawthorne's own persona on several levels, the sexual included. None of this is to diminish the problems of race evoked by the figure. The genuinely troublesome issue here is the figure's representativeness as an icon of nineteenth-century Hellenism, to which I now turn.

RACE AND HELLENISM

Sandra Zagarell describes Hellenism as "the celebration of the cultural superiority of Greece that flourished in Europe and the United States in the nineteenth century and that, as Martin Bernal has shown, had strong racist overtones."[46] Martin Bernal's influential and highly controversial *Black Athena*, a study that examines the erasure of the "Afroasiatic" roots of classical civilization, has had the effect of fixing transatlantic nineteenth-century Hellenism as racist practice. In a chapter titled, in a characteristically incendiary manner, "The Final Solution of the Phoenician Problem, 1885–1945," Bernal examines the "consolidation of the Aryan model and the denial of both Egyptian and Phoenician influence on the formation of Greece." By 1898, Bernal argues, the view that a "great mass of Semitic influence" shaped Aegean culture (as the denunciated scholar Robert Brown, who railed against the "Aryanists," argued) "now seemed eccentric."[47] Scholars who have drawn on Bernal's study have, explicitly or implicitly, suggested that writers whose work deploys Hellenism were participating in the erasure of the knowledge of the Semitic and Asian influences on Greek culture and religion.[48]

While a proper discussion of controversies over Hellenism cannot be undertaken in this chapter, it is worthwhile to note them in terms of thinking about the political potentialities of Hawthorne's weird, unsettling meditation on the faun, which has elicited numerous considerations in the past two decades about race and ethnicity but not, however, nearly as many about sexuality.

What the faun represents, if considered from the perspective that Hellenism was racist practice, is idealized whiteness. Yet, and this is both to concur and disagree with Bentley and Johnson, if the faun does indeed embody a confluence of whiteness and otherness, signified by primitivism, it serves as a commentary on the influence and the undeniability of racial otherness, which, in an American context, would most pressingly impinge upon the presence of the Indian and the African. But the wild card in Hawthorne's representation is the figure's mysteriousness. With his vague smile and louche stance, the figure seems to be in on some sexual or cultural or racial joke that forever eludes us.[49] Like the mystery of the faunlike Donatello's hidden ears, the faun's mystery trenches upon sex and race at once, caudal appendages and racial identity presented as similar, teasing questions. The faun simultaneously suggests a masculinity informed by homoeroticism and a whiteness marked by nonwhiteness, by racial difference. As such, it anticipates the intersection of homoeroticism and racial intermixture that so provocatively and disturbingly informs, as we will see, *Septimius Felton*.

THOUGH I have not seen the figure read this way elsewhere, the faun bears a striking physical resemblance to Hawthorne, with his mop of "bright curly hair" and striking eyes and general air of sexual ambiguity, his feminine male beauty. As with Hawthorne, the faun provokes unsettling erotic responses precisely because, though clearly readable as male, he nevertheless infuses the feminine within the masculine form, in fact derives his exquisite beauty precisely from the fusion of masculine and feminine qualities. (Winckelmann was also fascinated by such gender-bending figures, especially hermaphrodites and eunuchs.) In his notebook description, Hawthorne writes of the faun's "voluptuous mouth," of "beautiful and agreeable features" nevertheless "rounded." Much like Freud's Leonardo, the faun has no "principle," yet Hawthorne lays the stress on the faun's truthful and honest "simplicity" rather than his moral ambiguity (14: 191–92). Overall, this bewitching spectacle of the androgynous or hermaphroditic male art object–artist positively rather than diabolically casts its unsettling spell.

In keeping with Winckelmannian theory, Hawthorne designates as his ideal figure a castrated creature: a fig leaf covers his genitals and Hawthorne never makes direct mention of either the leaf or what it covers. Yet Hawthorne carefully alerts us to the sexual potentialities of this teasingly ambiguous figure through his attention to the faun's visible pointed ears and unseen tail, hidden beneath the lion skin slung over its right shoulder, diagonally across its chest, and over its backside. In his notebook, Hawthorne simply states, "a tail is probably hidden beneath his garment," but in the fiction the language becomes more cumbersomely and coyly Latinate: "a certain caudal appendage" would connote the faun's animal nature, and, "*if it exists at all,*" be found under the garment (4: 10, my emphasis). If Hawthorne's self-portrait of the artist eschews the monstrosity Freud added, it is like Freud's in its desire to free the sexually ambiguous artist from the presence of the phallus—Freud's Leonardo is the model of sexual sublimation, and Hawthorne's faun probably lacks a tail.

As we have noted, a key feature of Hawthorne's scopophobia, or fear of looking, is his rendering of vision as violation: masochistic suffering courses through Hawthorne's depiction of narcissistic desire.[50] The faun, looming above observers, fixes the gaze in a timeless frieze of spectatorship over which it presides, the object of the gaze but also its indifferent master. The faun is timelessly indifferent to the ravenous gaze, but the human male is not. Donatello, one of the party of four young people in the Capitoline Museum at the start of this gorgeous and difficult novel (in my view, Hawthorne's greatest work), comes closest to resembling the mythic faun, and the other members of the party—all artists, the exotic, probably Jewish, European Miriam; the Americans Hilda and Kenyon—all tease this apparently peasant-class earthy Italian about his resemblance to the faun, Miriam most mercilessly of all, demanding to see if Donatello's ears are, like the faun's, pointed. (Donatello will later be revealed to be a Count of noble ancestry, exposing the class biases and faulty analytic powers of the group.)

This scene emblematizes our discussion of Hawthorne's depiction of self, manhood, narcissistic desire, and fraught looking, as it stages the narcissistic gaze as desire to see manhood revealed and as the always imminent, inescapable threat of violation. Are Donatello's ears really pointed? Will we see his caudal appendage? As arresting for not being seen as they are for their phallic potentiality, Donatello's ears signify the secret of male sexuality, what lies beneath hair or other veils, what must remain hidden (to most) in order to provoke desire. The ideal male beauty may be castrated, but the human, even if the ambiguously human, male provokes desire by suggesting a lurking phallic potency hidden beneath the beautiful surface. Of most interest here is that Donatello provokes desire from both women and other men (and from androgynous gods), competing, merged desires that always carry with them the threat of violation.

The faun as sexual spectacle provokes a poignant human confrontation with the torments of desire. The faun itself, however, is never violated. In the faun, Hawthorne at last found a figure that could represent his complicity with the gaze and remain invulnerable in the face of it. The faun is a resolution to Hawthorne's crisis precisely because it bears no evidence of Antinous's "heavy, downward" look—the faun looks ahead, and past us, but also at nothing and no one at all, and is thus able to enjoy, or at least to signal, a range of unfettered erotic and even emotional possibilities. The faun is the ultimate figure of the narcissist, the purest, indifferent to all and absolute in his self-regard. As I will demonstrate in the discussion of *Septimius Felton,* this momentary resolution of Hawthorne's narcissistic crisis was, indeed, momentary: the ornery, indeed, the intractable, nature of this crisis would continue unabated. If the figure of the faun signals closure, the concept of closure is parodied from the beginning of *The Marble Faun,* which begins with an evocation of the faun's qualities only to initiate an almost endless series of moral and narrative conflicts and perplexities that will spill out into the unfinished work.

If Billy Budd is a sight that wounds the spectatorial eye, inciting a desire that cannot be fulfilled, the faun also incites the spectator's visual hunger, a desire to denude his human avatar, Donatello. But most resonantly of all, the faun is an apt symbol for the "frozen passionateness" that Hawthorne so eloquently thematizes in this novel. If Billy Budd is, in contrast, a somatic and messily human figure, there is also something nonhuman about him— the silent swiftness of his blow to Claggart's head that suggests a robotic, automaton-response; the lack of any bodily emissions (semen, specifically) once he is hanged; indeed, the bestial quality of his innocence. Perhaps the chief result of so many associations with the classical world and other kinds of mythic parallels is that the human subject becomes indistinguishable from the classical icon. Winckelmann's aesthetic may have allowed a discourse of sexual appraisal that would otherwise have been impossible, but it is also, at heart, an expression of a desire to be freed from sex, one consonant with many trends in nineteenth-century American literature, which often figured sex as violation, for men no less than women.[51] The contemplation of the frozen, blank, beautiful classical form is the expression of a wish for a nonsexual appreciation and even more emphatically *experience* of the body, of one's own and also that of another person. Stasis, nonbeing, is the only real respite from the maddening demands of desire. Yet the faun, in his sexual mystery, remains a perpetual goad to desire. The aging Hawthorne, in contemplating the faun, may have contemplated his own youthful beauty and its ability to incite the gaze; may have recalled the predicaments of his young men and their struggles with self-overseeing, but also, perhaps for the first time, may have imagined the greater possibilities of pleasure within the desiring gaze.

CHAPTER 8

A Certain Dark Beauty

NARCISSISM, FORM, AND RACE IN
HAWTHORNE'S LATE WORK

IN THE PREVIOUS CHAPTER, I considered the overlaps between Hawthorne's and Herman Melville's treatments of classical male beauty. In this chapter, I will consider a theme that has lurked throughout this study as well as Hawthorne's work. The darkness of Hawthorne's young American men is a gender metaphor and a sexual metaphor. It is also a racial metaphor. Melville's famous description of Hawthorne as "shrouded in a blackness, ten times black" blends unsettlingly into the dark white masculinity that Hawthorne himself imagined.[1] Hawthorne's simultaneously appealing and demonic men evoke the fears of the racial other that hovered around New England antebellum culture and became only increasingly more intense as the nation moved ever closer to civil war over slavery. Even as opposition to slavery grew exponentially more heated in the North, particularly in abolitionist centers such as Concord and Boston, fears of a racial other's intrusion into the white homogeneity of antebellum New England intensified. I believe that Hawthorne absorbed and reflected these growing fears of an influx of black bodies. These fears animate his peculiar representation of that iconic American image of the young white man full of promise who is bizarrely afflicted by blight and whose darkness of character belies his pleasing outward show. More to the point, however, his depictions of masculinity reflected his own fears of these bodies and his own racism. That Hawthorne was an artist of supreme moral intelligence makes his racism more vexing, heartbreaking, and infuriating. Without any desire to exculpate Hawthorne for his racist attitudes—which can be summarized as a failure to respond to and empathize with the suffering of the slave—I do nevertheless believe that in his late career, Hawthorne confronted his own racism as well as his culture's and attempted to theorize its psychosexual sources.[2] From within his own aesthetic preoccupations as well as thematic ones, he crafted narratives, most of which remained unfinished, in which race began to play the worrisome, galvanizing near-explicit role that gender and sex had played throughout his work. This is in no way to suggest that racism and race anxiety are not everywhere present throughout Hawthorne's work, but, rather, that in his late phase Hawthorne made these undercurrents something like a current.

In his late work, Hawthorne makes it impossible to distinguish race from sex, sex from race. He makes desire the basis from which *any* question about the self and identity proceeds. All of this makes psychoanalysis helpful to our understanding of the late work. To understand racism fully, we need to consider the sexual logic of all identity formations. Kalpana Seshadri-Crooks urges psychoanalysis to grant race "coevality" with sex: "not to do so," she warns, "trivializes the effects of racial identification."[3] Such a critique could be applied to Hawthorne's work generally, which tended to submerge questions of race beneath those of gender and sexuality. In his last phase, I argue, Hawthorne makes race coeval with gender and sexuality as thematic concerns.

LONG IGNORED by most critics, Hawthorne's late, unfinished work, never published in his own lifetime, is now attracting some new critical interest, the challenge continuing to be the prevailing view of these works as not only uninteresting but also aesthetically inferior to Hawthorne's published, "completed" output.[4] In his superb 1991 study of Hawthorne, Charles Swann had already begun to call our attention to the late work's significance. But only in recent years has it received anything like a sensitive treatment from criticism more broadly, with readings by critics such as Larry J. Reynolds, Rita Gollin, and Magnus Ullén, and, in a more mainstream vein, John Updike in a 2006 *New Yorker* essay.[5] In addition to making a case for its aesthetic worth, I am interested in Hawthorne's late work for its remarkably vivid continuation and revision of Hawthorne's themes of narcissism and homoerotic desire (still underexplored in Hawthorne criticism), which remain deeply relevant and are now much more self-consciously tied to issues of racial identity.

Hawthorne's stance on race and his attitudes toward the Civil War are major preoccupations of contemporary Hawthorne criticism. Belying the view that Hawthorne avoided race in his writing, critics have re-examined Hawthorne's editorship of the 1845 *Journal of an African Cruiser*, written by his friend Horatio Bridge, uncovering far greater contributions to this work than had been previously understood. Larry J. Reynolds's magisterial *Devils and Rebels: The Making of Hawthorne's Damned Politics* makes a concerted effort to contextualize Hawthorne's views toward the Civil War and race as, in part, a pacifist stance against the potential terrors and terrorism of revolution.[6] One of Reynolds's most troubling and eye-opening contributions is his revelation of the extent to which Hawthorne's racist attitudes were shared by many others in his abolitionist New England communities. But the majority of critics take a much more negative view of Hawthorne's attitudes toward race, seeing his racism as indicative of his support of American empire-building.

As we noted in the previous chapter, scholars such as Nancy Bentley, Arthur Riss, and Kendall Johnson have reframed Hawthorne's last complete fictional work, the 1860 novel-romance *The Marble Faun,* as indicative of Hawthorne's white, imperial disposition toward racial, ethnic, and class otherness. In his essay "Nathaniel Hawthorne and Transnationality" in *Hawthorne and the Real,* a collection edited by Millicent Bell, John Carlos Rowe disputes Henry James's assessment of Hawthorne as a provincial writer, but not in a celebratory manner: "Today we are interested in the history of our current global situation and the transnational forces that challenge the nation state and other traditional sociopolitical organizations. In order to understand these phenomena, we would do well to study Hawthorne's fiction, which represents an older world transformed by the new forces of modernization, first announced by the industrial revolution in England and made more urgent and dangerous in the expansionist frenzy of Jacksonian America."[7] Rowe explicitly sees his work as an updating of Bercovitch's influential 1991 study *The Office of The Scarlet Letter.* Bercovitch wrote about Hawthorne's desire to create consensus through the reconciliation of opposing points of view, all of which bolster an ultimate affirmation of liberal individualism. Rowe not only extends the Bercovitchian position but also goes further, arguing that "the abstraction of liberal individualism from its historical and geopolitical possibility in nineteenth-century America is Hawthorne's way of contributing to what today we recognize as cultural colonialism"; indeed, Hawthorne's "romantic regionalism is a trick that serves expansionist political and cultural purposes."[8]

While I certainly share these critics' concerns, and, again, neither wish to exculpate Hawthorne for his racism nor explain away the considerable tensions in his writings related to race and empire, it is my contention that in his last phase the gaps in his thinking on race as well as the biases are precisely what Hawthorne submitted to analysis. This is not to suggest that the late work is entirely antiracist in sensibility or that it thoroughly revises the stances toward otherness that characterize his oeuvre. Rather, I suggest that the late phase marks a new self-consciousness about these stances and a greater sensitivity toward these matters.

The Marble Faun demands a more sensitive treatment, in my view, than many critics have given it. In the previous chapter, I attempted to discuss the novel's sexual radicalism, but clearly a great deal more work needs to be done on this novel. For now, let me establish that, rather than seeing it as the endpoint of his career, I would place *The Marble Faun* at the vanguard of a new direction taken by Hawthorne in which he turns his acute critical gaze upon matters only implicitly or glancingly scrutinized in his earlier work, such as race and racism. None of these critical assessments, for all of the necessary points they make, fairly frame Hawthorne's attempt to make sense of race categories and racial difference in either *The Marble Faun* or the unfinished manuscripts as a *new* phase in his work.

If Hawthorne exudes a deep ambivalence regarding otherness and difference, on racial and ethnic as well as gender and sexual levels, *The Marble Faun* is a case in point of this ambivalence. It is a work with a Jewish heroine that clearly contains negative depictions of Judaism. It is also, at times, poignantly sympathetic toward the history of Jewish oppression. Certainly, it is a work that recognizes the centrality of Judaism to Western culture even within its most avowedly classical and Christian cultural underpinnings. Hawthorne appears to have used fiction as an occasion to work through his personal prejudices while also indulging in them. Donatello's obsession with the dark mystery of Miriam Schaeffer carries over the obsession with Beatrice Rappaccini's dark sexuality on Giovanni Guasconti's part in a tale that many have examined as an allegory of racist fears of miscegenation. What unites both "Rappaccini's Daughter" and *The Marble Faun* is that in these works the racial other becomes a figure of sympathy because embodied by a suffering and embattled female figure, always a figure with whom Hawthorne identifies.

Again, that Hawthorne identifies with the figure does not translate into an uncomplicated feminist portrait, especially in *The Marble Faun*. Resilient, intelligent, eloquent, and admirable a character though she is, Miriam Schaeffer is always highly ambivalently rendered. While it is commonly accepted that Hawthorne's major female characters all proceed from the basis of the dark-lady archetype, it is perhaps more to the point that they each evoke the figure of the Jewess of Hawthorne's 1856 description of Emma Abigail Montefiore Salomons, whom he met in London during his Consulship years.[9] Raven-haired, passionate, darkly mysterious, as well as extremely intelligent, Hawthorne's great heroines Hester Prynne, Zenobia, and Miriam Schaeffer all share with Mrs. Salomons as Hawthorne perceived her an uncanny ability to provoke in the men who behold them simultaneous feelings of attraction and alienation, of desire and "repugnance."

The unremittingly negative portrayal of "dark" masculinity in the depictions of Rappaccini and the Model of *The Marble Faun* make especially significant the fact that, in the *Septimius* manuscripts, the racial other is now the multiracial male protagonist who is also an identification figure meant to solicit at least a certain amount of sympathy from the reader. In that Septimius is such a figure, this late work represents an expansion and development of Hawthorne's figure of the "dark young man," treated here with more sympathy perhaps because of his very "darkness."

The *Septimius* manuscripts, an uneven, often thrilling project, demand renewed critical attention for several reasons. First, they explode the myth that Hawthorne painstakingly avoided race in his fiction, making race not only a major concern but also a decisive theme in the founding of the nation. Second, they foreground same-sex desire, a theme that remains not only underexplored in Hawthorne criticism but also still deeply controversial within the study of nineteenth-century literature. Most importantly, in insisting on the *intersection* of desire and race, the *Septimius* project takes Hawthorne's career-long concerns with male sexuality and its attendant terrors to unexpected places with myriad implications.

The issue of race in Hawthorne's work alone, to say nothing of the antebellum literary period, is deeply vexed and complex. Let me make it clear at the outset, then, that this chapter has a very narrow focus: the relevance of theories of narcissism to an interpretation of the multiracial male subject's relationship to white masculinity. Given that narcissism is so closely tied to male privilege for many—as embodied in Laura Mulvey's treatment of the male gaze—one always raced as white, it is especially interesting to consider narcissism in terms of racialized gender politics. My interpretation of Hawthorne's treatment of this dynamic is informed by the emerging field of whiteness studies, of which Nell Irvin Painter's 2010 book *The History of White People* is exemplary.[10] As we have noted, Hawthorne read some of Winckelmann's *The History of Ancient Art* (1764) shortly after having completed *The Scarlet Letter*,[11] and he applied the German art critic's theories to his own experience of European art in the late 1850s. Winckelmann, as has been frequently discussed, was a pioneer not only in the popularization of Hellenism but in the development of a transatlantic homoerotic Hellenic aesthetic. As Painter elaborates in her book, this Hellenic ideal was also crucial to the cultivation and generalization of an ideal of white beauty.

Hawthorne's previous male characters, such as the Grecian beauty Giovanni Guasconti, evoke this ideal in their Hellenic qualities. In contrast, Septimius Felton embodies the mixed-race mysteries that had been previously associated with Hawthorne's women. In contrast to Septimius, the English soldier embodies the ideal of English-European white male beauty. Hawthorne creates a nationalistic and cultural divide through contrasting styles of masculinity, casting whiteness as the domain of English-European culture, racial tensions and intermixtures as a more distinctively American phenomenon. Lacan argues that the experience of the mirror stage is marked by aggressivity as well as suicidal despair, as we identify with a more perfect, apparently more coherent, miragelike image of ourselves. Hawthorne, in the culmination of his major themes, stages the encounter between Septimius and the English soldier as a confrontation with the specular self, one that produces an appositely violent result, except in real-world rather than psychic terms.

In this chapter, I explore the racial tensions within Hawthorne's treatment of white masculinity while thinking about his depiction of white masculinity as an allegory for race. The linchpin figure in this regard is the multiracial Septimius Felton. I argue that Hawthorne brings an erotic dimension to his construction of racial otherness, one that intensifies the difficulties and the occasional daring in his exploration of race. That Hawthorne's stance on race throughout his career is one of infuriating indifference makes his engagement with the topic in his late career all the more startling. One of the most moving aspects of Hawthorne's career is that his late work—so long denigrated as inferior, evidence of his physical as well as mental and creative enfeeblement—is, in many ways, the most politically radical of his career, which is not to suggest that it is politically radical but, rather, that it represents not only Hawthorne's attempt to grapple with issues of race in the glare of an impending and soon actively fought civil war but also some fresh and surprising thinking on these subjects.

The issue of race in Hawthorne raises an analogous question for psychoanalysis, namely what its relevance to such questions might be. Given how often psychoanalysis has historically ignored questions of race, it is especially important to address this lack in the methodology here. As I will show, Freud's theories of the ego ideal and ideal ego, especially as revised by Lacan, can provide valuable insights into the homoerotic dynamics of race when race is considered in terms of *visual identity*—a making sense of oneself based on visual evidence. Of course, this evidence is so overdetermined by historically shifting and maintained cultural and social standards as to be unintelligible without the context they provide.

Perhaps surprisingly, Hawthorne's late work also allows us a quite welcome opportunity to think about the related and equally vexed topics of Hawthorne's representation of women and Freud's theories of female sexuality. The *Septimius* manuscripts, *Septimius Felton* in particular, offer us a potent account of female agency that makes for a dynamic point of comparison to Freud's frustrating but not entirely irrelevant theories of femininity. Before we can address any of these concerns, however, it is crucial that we establish the grounds for which we can appreciate the late work aesthetically as well as for its considerations of racial identity and sexual politics.

INTERMIXTURES
SEPTIMIUS FELTON

En route to England, where he would be employed as American Consul in Liverpool courtesy of President Franklin Pierce, his best friend since their days as classmates at Bowdoin College, Hawthorne began to write a romance about an American attempting to claim an English estate (*The American Claimant* manuscripts), a project Hawthorne put aside in order to write *The Marble Faun*, his last published novel-romance. He was never able to complete the *Claimant* project; in his final years in Concord, Massachusetts, to which he returned after his years in Europe, Hawthorne took up, among other works, the romance *Septimius Felton*, in a later draft renamed *Septimius Norton*, a tale of a young, multiracial man on a quest for the secret of immortal life.

Betsy Erkkila points out that the America of James Fenimore Cooper's Leatherstocking tales is "spooked by the prospect of a collapse in the distinctions of sexual, racial, and class blood in the America of the future."

> The irony is that the one boundary that remains open—the erotically charged cross-race and same-sex bond among Hawk-eye, Uncas, and, by extension, Chingachgook—is the bond that might seem least threatening by the normative sexual and racial standards of Cooper's time. While the white man and the Indians might share in the phallic rites of guns and blood and sleep with each other in the forest, they would not reproduce a mixed-blood progeny: the love triangle of Hawk-eye, Uncas, and Chingachgook enables the fantasy of blood mixture—of sex and rank and color—without the threat of generation.[12]

What I will be suggesting throughout this chapter is that Hawthorne takes up and continues Cooper's subversive homoerotics of race and race anxiety in *Septimius Felton*. But what Hawthorne adds to Cooper is precisely the idea that "generation"—albeit, a generation of a different kind than biological human reproduction—can indeed result from the intermixture of differently raced male bloods.

Septimius Felton provides evidence that in Hawthorne race and sexuality face each other in a narcissistic relation, each mirroring the other. My claim that *Septimius Felton* is one of Hawthorne's most vibrant and intriguing achievements, which I am aware many readers will find dubious, depends on an even more problematic contention that the most animated and provocative section of this draft version of a never completed work occurs early on: Septimius's encounter with the teasing, haughty, handsome young English soldier whom Septimius later kills in a duel. By exploring this episode in some depth, I aim to make the case that the fragmentary nature of Hawthorne's achievement in these final works both is essential to their special character and has a validity all its own. Moreover, I will use this incident as emblematic of the narcissistic themes that I consider to be a recurring interest in Hawthorne's work.

Prominent among the many links between the *American Claimant* and the *Septimius* manuscripts is the symbol of a bloody footprint. Left on the threshold of an ancestral English home, the bloody footprint marks the crime against innocence, an irremovable sign of indelible guilt. Beyond those familiar Hawthorne concerns, the bloody footprint serves as a poignant trace of Hawthorne's own persistent, painful attempts to craft a romance after his return from England, a return to a transformed America on the brink of fraternal war. Hawthorne wrote with an anguished sense that the romance form he perfected was no longer fashionable, that a new form was needed. As Terence Martin writes of *Septimius Felton,* one can find throughout it "scattered yet provocative evidence that for Hawthorne the literary genre which had served him for years was no longer a viable form."[13] The symbol conveys the somatic pain of Hawthorne's illness-ridden last days. At the same time, the bloody footprint marks the pages of these unfinished late romances with the blood of the slain Civil War soldiers populating Hawthorne's increasingly aggrieved mind. As he wrote, Hawthorne was pondering the human propensity for barbarism and bloodshed in a war he eventually supported but always despised. If a tremendous potential for violence inheres in all of Hawthorne's representations of human relations, especially between men, in Septimius Felton this violence erupts into actual murder. That murder might seem justified during war is the very proposition that Hawthorne complicates and troubles.

Of Hawthorne's late work, Charles Swann, among the most brilliant readers of Hawthorne, writes, "the struggles with his themes and materials is not evidence of imaginative failure but rather of Hawthorne's intelligence, courage and ambition in facing remarkably complex issues at a time of great historical crisis which (had he lived longer) might well have produced a radically new kind of fiction."[14] Swann's 1991 argument, a view I share, was an anomalous one within Hawthorne criticism, which has historically framed these late works as sad indications of Hawthorne's faltering powers. In one of the few earlier studies to consider them, Edward Davidson views the unfinished romances not only as signs of Hawthorne's final ruin but also as evidence that "the seeds of his failure lay back in the years of success. He had at his disposal only a very limited number of plots and an even more limited number of scenes than we have ever suspected. In the short stories and in the earlier novels he had quite thoroughly exhausted his restricted budget." "Old," "miserably old," Hawthorne was "senile," a sad fact reflected in his late writings.[15] Davidson's own critical terminology betrays the sexual register of critical complaint—the supply of the *seeds* of Hawthorne's art was *exhausted* by the end. This is a critical version of G. J. Barker-Benfield's spermatic economy, the spermatic economy of imaginative production.[16] Traditional criticism maintains masculinist standards of productivity that insist on closure as the end result of a literary work; little wonder, then, that the unfinished Hawthorne works have had such a hard time gaining recognition.

Hawthorne repeatedly writes of being unable to finish these romances, often with irritation, sometimes with despair. Yet the sheer persistence of his attempts conveys the urgency of his need to communicate something. One possibility that has not been raised in most critical accounts of late Hawthorne is that the impossibility of completion was aesthetically *necessary* to the nature of these late works, not in the reductive sense that their unfinished nature somehow reflects the impossible, unrealizable goals of the plots, for example the futile quest for the key to immortal life, but, rather, that the unfinishability itself serves as a response to the welter of conflictual, maddening pressures Hawthorne faced—national unrest; shifting literary tastes; his faltering, mutinous body—a statement about the impossibility of *finding* resolution, clarity, closure.

The major source of the opprobrium the late works have inspired in criticism would appear to be Hawthorne's inability to find a workable plot or to carry a plot to its conclusion. It is part of my goal here to demonstrate that, at least to a certain extent, Hawthorne self-consciously thematizes the "failed" nature of *Septimius Felton,* allegorizing the work's very unfinishability through the work itself. Moreover, as I will show, this self-conscious textuality corresponds to and deepens the novel's daring exploration of the intersection of desire and race in male–male relationships, which Hawthorne symbolically conducts through the figure of a maddening text passed from hand to hand from one male to another. If normative standards of male sexual performance appear to have dominated critical practice, these standards nevertheless appear very much to have been on Hawthorne's mind as he wrote *Septimius Felton.*[17] An obsession with potency courses through the *Septimius* manuscripts, as its hero attempts to transform the alternately crimson and purple flowers that flourish above the grave of the young English soldier he kills into the elixir of immortal life.

Ingeniously crafting a Civil War allegory that reminds its still largely undiscovered readers of the historical continuity of war and bloodshed, Hawthorne sets *Septimius Felton* in the Revolutionary War American past. In the Concord of 1775, Septimius Felton, of mixed English and native American stock (and possibly of African stock as well), lives with his fiery, witchlike Puritan-Indian Aunt Keziah (whose name changes throughout the manuscript, finally to Nashoba in the *Norton* version). As he ambivalently pursues the ministry, he commits himself to a life of scholarly toil, much like the titular protagonist of Hawthorne's first romance, *Fanshawe.* His purported love interest, Rose Garland (in later drafts turned, not implausibly, into his sister, given the lack of any sexual ardor between the characters), and his boyhood friend, strapping Robert Hagburn, who joins the fighting, provide the makings of a romantic triangle that Hawthorne barely invests with any interest whatsoever, his concerns lying in quite different areas. The quest that Septimius undertakes for the creation of an elixir for immortal life was derived from a legend that Henry David Thoreau had told Hawthorne about one of his Concord homes, The Wayside: a generation ago, it had been inhabited by a man who believed that he would never die. If the inspiration for this novel was the product of an exchange between two artists, it is interesting to see how this male–male exchange becomes so complexly literalized in the unfinished romance. It is also an elaboration of a Revolutionary War tale that Hawthorne recounted in the preface to his 1846 collection of tales, *Mosses from an Old Manse:* on that famous April morning, a youth is chopping wood behind the Manse residence. He races to the scene of battle, axe in hand. He sees two English soldiers lying prostrate on the ground—one stirs and looks him in the face. Instantly, the boy raises his axe and buries it in the still-living soldier's head. Hawthorne remarks that he frequently wonders about the boy's tortured soul after this wartime act. In the *Septimius* manuscripts, Hawthorne imagines his way through the psychological repercussions of wartime killing.

The sheer wastefulness of wartime carnage loomed large in Hawthorne's mind as he wrote *Septimius,* as his letters, journals, and essays of the time evince. Hawthorne also wrestled with feelings of mingled contempt and longing for England upon his return, as evinced by the essays in *Our Old Home,* the only work after *The Marble Faun* that Hawthorne was able to complete. The English soldier of the early portion of the romance fuses all of these tensions in his surprisingly comely, flirtatious form, appearing as a harbinger of war and imperial menace, yet casually teasing Rose, upon whom he plants a kiss, and charming as much as angering Septimius. *Teasing* emerges as a quality of male sexual appeal in the later Hawthorne: the sexual suggestiveness and mysteriousness of the faun, the arch, playful, erotic mirth of the English soldier. Hawthorne appears to have finally begun to enjoy the appeal of his desirable young male figures in his later career and years.

If the figure of the beautiful young man recurs in Hawthorne's work (Robin Molineux, Giovanni Guasconti, Dimmesdale, the young Clifford), and if he always regards this figure ambivalently, the beautiful, budding young English soldier carries with him the promise of beauty, death, and immortal life all at once. By investing the soldier with a sexual charisma and charm, Hawthorne intensifies our understanding of the pointlessness of his death.

"In an encounter," as John Updike puts it, "that has strong narcissistic and homoerotic overtones," Septimius kills the soldier and "finds on his body the formula for eternal life."[18] Kneeling by his "fallen foe's side," Septimius ponders, watching him die, the magnitude of what he has done and the nature of this loss:

> It seemed so dreadful to have reduced this gay, animated, beautiful being to a lump of dead flesh for the flies to settle upon, and which in a few hours would begin to decay; which must be put forthwith into the earth, lest it should be a horror to men's eyes; that delicious beauty for woman to love; that strength and courage to make him famous among men,—all come to nothing[.] (12: 31)[19]

The young English soldier's allegorical functions are multivalent and substantial. He stands in for the otherness of the soldier on the other side— English or Southern—so alike yet so different; in his maddening appeal he signals secret sympathies and affiliations.[20] Most pressingly, he represents in his fullness the promise of art as well as, in his national identity, the origins of the art-making tradition Hawthorne would emulate. If Hawthorne struggled over the future of the form of the romance inherited from Walter Scott and other English forebears, the deeply appealing soldier who must be killed may be said to represent the form of the romance itself, Hawthorne's awareness of its continuing charms, and the impossibility of its survival. The soldier's scarcely justifiable death allegorizes the transition from one form to another, the transformation of the romance into something else, that *something* that Hawthorne kept trying to get at, possibly the realist novel his conflicted disciple Henry James would fashion as his own, possibly something else altogether.

The scene of the killing of this young English soldier also elegiacally mourns Hawthorne's own lost youth and impending death. As Septimius stares into the soldier's face, he broods upon the awful significance of the waste of youth, but, more specifically, the waste of the soldier's "delicious beauty." Throughout Hawthorne's work, motifs of mirrors, reflections, doubles recur along with the equally consistent motif of the young man the sight of whom causes as much consternation as pleasure (Fanshawe, Minister Hooper, Feathertop, and several others).

A point to which we will return, Septimius is not unbeautiful; indeed, he himself possesses "a certain dark beauty" (40). What I have called Hawthorne's *traumatic narcissism* takes a spellbinding form here. Staring into the dying young soldier's face and lamenting the loss of the beauty it synecdochically signs, Septimius can be said, from a psychoanalytic perspective, to be mourning the loss of a prior state of perfection, specifically his ego ideal, the more attractive, more appealing, and inaccessible version of himself. This literally as well as symbolically traumatic loss suggests implications of all kinds: to begin with, the loss of the aforementioned allegorical notes of beautiful, unrealizable form. But most crucially, given the fraught racial dynamics of the novel, this loss suggests a longing for the apparently more perfect, more beautiful form of European whiteness, a "delicious" versus a "certain dark" beauty, a point which I expand in the next section.

"Sing, goddess"—if the Muse is conventionally gendered female, in the tradition that derives from classical Greek mythological origins of the nine daughters of Zeus and Mnemosyne, in *Septimius Felton* Hawthorne devises the Muse in masculine terms; if we view Septimius as a figure of the artist, it is the slain young soldier who inspires his art. This inspiration takes literal shape in the form of the manuscript that provides in cipher-code the key to the immortality Septimius seeks. In addition, Septimius's bullet shatters the miniature portrait of a woman on the soldier's person. Recalling the myth of

Achilles and Penthesilea, the Amazon warrior-queen he slays, falling in love with her just as she dies on the battlefield, Septimius realizes his heart-stopping ardor for the soldier only when he annihilates him; in especially violent terms, their connection appears to obliterate any sign of conventional heterosexual love by literally smashing in the face of woman, obviously a horrifying implication.

Hawthorne would appear to suggest that art can be passed from one male to another only through the obliteration of woman. Beyond this, art, the search for immortal life, emerges from suffering and death; only the murder of something—a soldier, a literary form, the symbol of love—can bring forth the new life of art. It will be revealed, however, that the young woman of the photograph, Sybil Dacy, far from being dead, is alive and vying for narrative control, a development of great interest to this analysis.

The manuscript—"that weary, ugly, yellow, blurred, unintelligible, bewitched, mysterious, bullet-penetrated, blood-stained manuscript" (58)—becomes a simultaneously fetishistic and phobic object for Septimius. It combines somatic with material properties, turning the page into battered, hateful, yet also irresistible flesh. More than any other Hawthorne work, *Septimius Felton* reveals the wrenching pain Hawthorne experienced within the act of art-creation, suggesting that beneath the elegant, hypercontrolled Latinate prose has lurked a writhing sense of discomfort.

This work oscillates among several thematic concerns, some aesthetic, some psychosexual, and some political and historical. The duel synthesizes these last concerns. Harkening back to the bad old days of the early American republic, the duel symbolizes relations between men in patriarchy, seeking "satisfaction" from each other through the economy of violence.[21] But Hawthorne in this scene returns to a much earlier time, the mythic-Edenic time of the prelapsarian. He returns the male body to nature and to origins; from a psychoanalytic view, he returns masculinity to its disavowed, rejected place in the pre-oedipal world of the mother. In the well-known paradigms of Jacques Lacan, there are three "orders" of human life: the Imaginary, dominated by the mirror stage and its imaginary identifications, specifically the incipient subject's identification with an illusory image of wholeness in the mirror; the Symbolic, the father's realm of language and law; and the Real, that which stands outside of signification and representation. Buried, the body of the soldier produces a field of crimson and purple flowers that will provide the final, decisive ingredient for Septimius's recipe for immortality. As his own body faltered and failed him, Hawthorne fantasized about a generative and blooming, youthful and beautiful male body returned to the time before symbolic subjectivity. In a Lacanian elaboration, the English soldier—

in his whiteness and desirability on both racial and homoerotic levels—is the false but irresistible illusion of wholeness with which the mixed-race Septimius identifies, an image of desirable perfection shattered, along with the triangulated woman, by Septimius's bullet.

Hawthorne's characteristic concerns over the troubling form of masculinity continue to inform his late work. Given the metaphorical world of the novel, the depiction of writing as an extension of the male body, the somatic qualities of the manuscript signal the phobic dimension of Hawthorne's view of this male body, so beautiful in one dimension, so hateful in another. If Hawthorne recalled his own youthful beauty in such stark contrast to his present state of infirmity in the body of the soldier with its multivalently life-giving properties, he also conveyed a sense of this body's grotesque, unseemly physicality. The Elixir of Life recipe, once laboriously decoded by Septimius, reads like a tract written to young men by antebellum sexual reformers such as Sylvester Graham and John Todd exhorting them to practice rigid sexual continence.[22] The yellowish quality of the manuscript links it to the color of the whale oil in the scandalous and joyous sperm-squeezing passage in Melville's *Moby-Dick,* as it also recalls the Creature's lurid flesh in Mary Shelley's *Frankenstein* and the fluid into which M. Valdemar deliquesces at the climax of Poe's story, notable for its particularly grotesque homoerotic tableaux. (In "The Facts in the Case of M. Valedemar," published in 1845, a dying man, surrounded by a homosocial group of male scientists who have hypnotized him, lies suspended between life and death; his one quiveringly lifelike organ is his tongue.) If yellow is the color of male sexual fluids, the written page is steeped in it here.

On the one hand, in the somatic economy of this work, writing suggests ejaculation, in terms that recall the Coen Brothers' film about a maddened writer, *Barton Fink* (1991), with its trope of yellow fluids oozing out behind wallpaper, a failed orgasmic release that mocks the titular character's writer's block. On the other hand, it suggests the "flow" Hélène Cixous associated with *women's* writing, which she links with blood and disengorgement, in stark contrast to masculine writing. Highly essentialist though they are as a schema of gendered writing, Cixous's theories have a great relevance for considerations of the gender dynamics of literary production, especially given the masculinist critical standards that predominate. In his near-final phase, Hawthorne portrayed art-making as the release of fluids. Hawthorne recalls Coleridge's famous description of the essential androgyny of the artist's mind by associating the male body with conventional markers of both male and female sexuality while making the bloody male body generative in conventionally feminine terms.[23]

Matching yellow as a heavily freighted symbolic color in this work, red—a particularly deep, "crimson," red, evocative of the scarlet "A"—also connotes creativity as it emanates from the male form. Hawthorne's use of winemaking metaphors to describe the manuscript recalls both Virgil's Georgics and, as an intercalary note makes explicit, Burton's *Anatomy of Melancholy*. These metaphors liken writing to a vintner squeezing "viscid" juice from "the great accumulation of grapes that it had gathered from so many vineyards" (49). One and the same, the rich blood of writing and the rich blood of the fallen dead produce a "great abundance, a luxuriant harvest," "as if the dead youth beneath had burst into a resurrection of many crimson flowers!" (109). This explosive image connotes a linkage between male sexuality and creativity.

In a very Cixousian way, then, *Septimius Felton* is a work that refuses to finish. If, in Cixous's terms, feminine writing is about flow and disgorgement, *Septimius Felton* bleeds out its contents, its text bursting free of the confines of form and narrative. The finished product always remains willfully and intransigently uncontained. I do not mean to suggest that *Septimius Felton* is—in the manner suggested by Elizabeth Wanning Harries in her study of eighteenth-century fiction *The Unfinished Manner*—a work left *deliberately* unfinished, a statement of defiant incompleteness.[24] Rather, what I wish to suggest is that Hawthorne found the form he was looking for, the elusive form of a work that could be neither completed nor finished, an immortal text that in its exasperating irresolvability refuses to die.

As I suggested earlier, in mourning the dying English soldier, Septimius may be said to be mourning the loss of his ego ideal. The difficulties of Hawthorne's depiction of a narcissistic male sexuality with implications for both same-sex desire and race are encompassed by the juxtaposition the work makes of two forms of male beauty: the English soldier's "delicious beauty" and that which characterizes Septimius, "a certain dark beauty."

Hawthorne inserts Septimius's desire for the solider he kills into his fiction's *topos* of male guilt, a killing in the forest, a crime that must be buried. *Septimius Felton* recalls Hawthorne's superb early story "Roger Malvin's Burial," which we explored in chapter 3. Here, rather than beginning with a tense scene between a young man and an old one, we open, roughly speaking, with a traumatic encounter between two young men that revises the young man–old man split in Hawthorne's work—at least until the enigmatic and creepy Doctor Portsoaken, associated with occult details such as a huge, knowing spider, makes his appearance. Constantly returning to the scene of his crime, the memory of which alternately revivifies and torments him, Septimius develops a much more sustained and passionate relationship with the buried corpse of the soldier than he does with any of the other characters, with the possible exception of his Aunt Keziah, at once, like Mother Rigby in "Feathertop," witchlike and motherly. As the dead soldier's body decays, it paradoxically blooms with life, transforming into the lush field of flowers from which Septimius will extract the key ingredient to the elixir of immortal life.

Hawthorne's own status as a white male writer can hardly be incidental to his depiction of a multiracial young man's ambivalent desire for the "secret" of a comely white European youth. His decision to make Septimius a fusion of his own race and cultural ancestry *and* the fraught and contested racial identities of Indianness and blackness could not have been anything other than a highly self-conscious choice on Hawthorne's part. If a thematic of narcissism with implications for both heterosexual and same-sex desire informs Hawthorne's work, it is through this thematic that Hawthorne imagines race consciousness in *Septimius Felton/Norton*. The question that presents itself here is to what extent narcissism reflects Hawthorne's own feelings toward race, in the sense of complicating, deepening, or scrambling the controversial record of Hawthorne's own recorded views about race, slavery, and otherness. In other words, does Hawthorne view race, racism, and racial consciousness as a set of psychosexual, social, cultural, or historical dilemmas? (Clearly, the answer must be some combination of all of these, the salient question being on which factor Hawthorne places his emphasis.) Related to these concerns is the question of how psychoanalysis helps us to think through such matters, especially given the methodology's historical indifference to them.

PSYCHOANALYSIS AND RACE

In employing psychoanalytic theory to discuss authorial investments in race, I join in recent efforts to challenge psychoanalysis to extend its valuable findings about human subjectivity to theorizations of race as a lived experience. Psychoanalysis is not an end to itself, at least in my view, but an aid to understanding the emotional and psychic underpinnings of our culture and our art. When psychoanalysis, and any other theoretical apparatus for that matter, becomes an end in and of itself, the critic ends up mistaking the tool for the task. To make my intentions clear once again, my aim is to use psychoanalysis as a political maneuver against the prohibitive and silencing voices of our culture that impede understanding of its traumatic knowledges, past and present.

Of chief interest to me here are the valences between Hawthorne's depiction of the Septimius-soldier episode and the psychoanalytic theories of the ego ideal and the ideal ego. In her application of Freudian theories of melancholia to race, Anne Anlin Cheng asks, "How is a racial identity secured? How does it continue to generate its seduction for both the dominant and the marginalized?" As Cheng notes, insufficient attention has been paid to "the ways in which individuals and communities remain invested in maintaining such categories, *even when such identities prove to be prohibitive or debilitating.*"[25] As Cheng continues, racialization in America "may be said to operate through the institutional process of producing a dominant, standard, white national ideal, which is sustained by the exclusion yet retention of racialized others."[26] It also, along these lines, seems to be sustained by the instantiation in these simultaneously excluded and retained racial others of investments in the national ideal that are as urgent psychically as they are outmoded and contestable socially.

In his study *The Color of Sex: Whiteness, Heterosexuality, and the Fictions of White Supremacy,* Mason Stokes equates narcissism with white heterosexual privilege: "for my purposes I understand it as a way of being that requires a consideration of others solely for the purpose of articulating and buttressing the ego, the self.... Although Freud focuses most of his attention on 'perverts and homosexuals,' I want to add whiteness to that category of perversions (though not endorsing his views on the narcissism of homosexuals and women). Doing so allows us to see whiteness as a pathology, as an unhealthy way of living in the world." By "making this leap" to contemporary psychiatric understandings of a "controversial psychological category," Stokes claims that he is shedding light on "a larger ideological presence—whiteness, that 'shadow of a reflected form [that] has no substance of its own,' to borrow once again" from Ovid's version of the Narcissus myth.[27]

I am in ideological sympathy with Stokes's effort to dismantle white heterosexist privilege. The process whereby he employs narcissism in this effort, however, unwittingly exposes a fundamental social and theoretical queasiness about narcissism. This queasiness must be considered if we are to appreciate narcissism's value as a potentially radical sexual disposition that disrupts normative sexual categories. It is neither possible to extricate Freud's view of the perversions from his theory of narcissism nor to apply perversion to a normative category, such as racial whiteness, without jeopardizing the entire structure of Freud's argument. As Jonathan Dollimore points out, "Freud described homosexuality as the most important perversion of all," "as well as the most repellent in the popular mind," while also being "so pervasive to human psychology" that Freud made it "central to psychoanalytic theory."²⁸ In terms of Freud's theory of psychosexual development and perversity's place in it, Dollimore writes, if the value of psychoanalysis lies in its exposure of the essential instability of identity, "then this is never more so than in Freud's account of perversion. At every stage perversion is what problematizes the psychosexual identities upon which our culture depends."²⁹

Stokes obscures the disruptive force of both perversion and narcissism in his conflation of hegemonic whiteness with both. This maneuver has the effect of rearming the categories as pathological diagnoses. Stokes retains the presumed pathological imperative of the Freudian diagnosis while losing the inherent instability *within* this diagnosis. It is this instability that is precisely what makes narcissism an excitingly weird way of thinking about sexuality. The central instability of narcissism is that, like homosexuality, it represents for Freud both a perversion *and* a universal human disposition.

Freud's concepts of the ego ideal and the ideal ego, variations on the theme, allow us to take into further account the value of his theory of narcissism. Freud theorizes love in terms of idealization, a process that involves narcissism and the ego ideal. When we idealize the object of our desire, we treat the object as we do our own ego. When we are in love, Freud writes in *Group Psychology and the Analysis of the Ego*, "a considerable amount of narcissistic libido overflows onto the object." Fascinatingly, Freud even goes so far as to suggest that very often the "object serves as a substitute for some unattained ego ideal of our own. We love it on account of the perfections which we have striven to reach for our own ego"; indeed, being in love is a "roundabout" way of "satisfying our own narcissism"! (SE 18: 112–13). Far from being a minoritizing discourse about desire, the Freudian theory of narcissism claims it as one of the major components of human love.

As Jacques Lacan, reworking these Freudian ideas, explains the relation of ideal ego to ego ideal, it helps us to consider certain key questions: "What is my desire? What is my position in the imaginary structuration? This position is only conceivable in so far as one finds a guide beyond the imaginary, on the level of the symbolic plane . . . This guide governing the subject is the ego ideal."³⁰ In one of his best glosses, Slavoj Žižek explains Lacan's reframing of these Freudian concepts, including the superego:

> Lacan introduces a precise distinction between these three terms: "ideal ego" stands for the idealized image of the subject (the way I would like to be, the way I would like others to see me); Ego-Ideal is the agency whose gaze I try to impress with my ego image, the big Other who watches over me and impels me to give my best, the ideal I try to follow and actualize; and superego is this same agency in its vengeful, sadistic, punishing aspect.

The underlying structuring principle of these three terms is clearly Lacan's triad Imaginary-Symbolic-Real: ideal ego is imaginary, what Lacan calls the "small other," the idealized mirror-image of my ego; Ego-Ideal is symbolic, the point of my symbolic identification, the point in the big Other from which I observe (and judge) myself; superego is real, the cruel and insatiable agency that bombards me with impossible demands and then mocks my botched attempts to meet them, the agency in whose eyes I am all the more guilty, the more I try to suppress my "sinful" strivings and meet its demands.[31]

To consider *Septimius Felton* from these psychoanalytic perspectives, we can posit that the English soldier functions for Septimius as both ideal ego ("the way I would like to be, the way I would like others to see me") *and* as ego ideal. The soldier's cultural heritage—the fatherland England of law and traditional values; the motherland England of generative aesthetic forms—and his racially privileged whiteness provide the foundation for his role as ego ideal to Septimius. The racially charged descriptions of Septimius's possession of "a certain dark beauty" and the handsome, confident English soldier's "delicious beauty" emerge as poles of possession and lack, of longing and excess, of having and not having. The multiracial male longs for the secret to the fecundity of the European white male's overflowing racial *fullness*. This fullness finds explosive metaphorical form in the fecund field of flowers growing over the soldier's grave, flowers that symbolize the soldier's life-giving powers. The voice of Hawthorne's narrator, as always evasive and endlessly evaluative, provides a perverse textual superego, faltering in its occasional empathy, more often more than adequate to its authoritarian task.

If the text would appear to suggest that whiteness is the mixed-race subject's ego ideal, what undermines the racial politics of the scenario, a racial politics that would appear to confirm Hawthorne's status as white writer extending a fantasy of white privilege into the private provinces of sexuality, is Hawthorne's investment in the imaginary life of a mixed-race subject. Of all canonical white antebellum writers, Hawthorne and Harriet Beecher Stowe are among the few to have written a work that attempts to understand the differently raced subject *from within*. (For all of his daring and brilliance generally and specifically in his exploration of race, Herman Melville rarely attempts such an inhabited experience of racial difference. For example, his villain Babo in *Benito Cereno*—serialized in *Putnam's Monthly* in 1855, and then somewhat revised for inclusion in his collection *The Piazza Tales* [1856]—is endlessly fascinating but always a character beheld from the outside, never one given interior personhood.) To be clear, I am not making any evaluation here of the success or failure of these efforts. Rather, what I'm suggesting is that Hawthorne's career-long interests in male sexuality and narcissism, and his personal investments in these themes, are precisely what give *Septimius Felton* its value as a work about race. *Septimius Felton* deepens, in this regard, Hawthorne's attempt to inhabit a Jewish identity in his depiction of Miriam Schaeffer in *The Marble Faun*. In that novel, the heroine's Jewishness is suffused with the same aura of impenetrable mysteries—tied to sexual crime of some kind, most likely incest between Miriam and her father, recalling the famous tragic figure of Beatrice Cenci—that suffuses the novel. *Septimius Felton* is less invested in the "mystery" of its protagonist's racial heritage than it is fascinated by the mysteriousness of his desire, ostensibly figured as the quest for immortal life, but a quest everywhere shown to be inextricable from his desire for a white, English masculinity. Adding to the gendered daring of Hawthorne's conceptions here, this English masculinity is depicted as a generative feminine form, a kind of male mother, on several, mutually reinforcing levels a matrix.

If *Septimius Felton* reveals that Hawthorne's unusually explicit depiction of male beauty depends upon a privileging of a whiteness that is crucial to this beauty, it is nevertheless a perverse, excessive whiteness. It is not a whiteness governed by symbolic law (in Lacanian terms, the realm of the Father, his language and his laws, the social order that upholds sexual difference) but specifically a whiteness in *defiance* of the law. The English soldier's flirting and teasing manner extends as fully to Septimius as it does to Rose, his sister. His appeal seems more deeply registered by Septimius than by Rose, but it is offered freely, excessively, to all.

By suggesting the confusing homoerotic pull of the bond Septimius has with the soldier, Hawthorne implicitly challenges the homophobic desexualization of all male bonds in our culture. The daring of Hawthorne's depiction of this homoeroticism can be seen in Hawthorne's own disavowal of it in the *Septimius Norton* draft. The description of the aftermath of the soldier's death in *Norton* subtly and tellingly alters the fuller intensity of feeling in the *Felton* draft. If we recall the *Felton* description given above, the one in *Norton* evinces a diminution of feeling achieved through revision. Now, Septimius cannot

> help shuddering at himself, for reducing that gay, beautiful boy to a lump of dead flesh, which a fly was already settling upon, and which must speedily be put into the earth else it would grow a sensible horror, that beauty for women to love, that strength and courage for men to fear, all annihilated[.] (240)

Removed from this passage now are the idea that the corpse will be "a horror to men's eyes"; most significantly, that what we have lost is the "delicious" beauty of the soldier. Hawthorne also dampens the phallic charge of the soldier's appeal—the soldier's "strength and *energy*" (31) transmutes now into the more conventional "strength and *courage*" proper to a soldier. Along similar lines, what had been the soldier's "beautiful *grace* of form and *elegance* of feature" (31) transforms now into the blander and more general "This *beauty of form,* and bright *intelligence* of feature" (240, all italics mine).

In the later draft, Hawthorne commits the unexpectedly emotionally intense earlier version of the scene to a more conventional fantasy of autogenesis, the modified language aiding in a more properly desexualized version of male–male relations. If my reading of these shifts has any validity, we have to conclude that Hawthorne retreated from the radicalism of his libidinal investments in *Septimius Felton,* a sexual panic that then has to be, on some level, connected as well to the general sense of "failure"—unpublishability, incompleteness—hovering around both drafts and the period of the late works.

The perversity of *Septimius Felton* is that in it Hawthorne inhabits the consciousness of a multiracial male in order to gaze upon the spectacle of male whiteness that Hawthorne treats not as prohibitive privilege but as site of spectacle and *jouissance,* an excessiveness of pleasure bordering on death. In other words, Hawthorne renders whiteness here a spectacle of wonder in which he himself shares; he puts himself in the removed, alienated position of the other to marvel at the irresistibly compelling spectacle of whiteness. All of this is to say that the white male author remains more fascinated by whiteness and its workings than by any other racial category. Certainly, a potential for racist attitudes and white privilege abounds here. At the same time, Hawthorne imbues whiteness with a Freudian perversity. In other words, whiteness is associated here not with the stifling, crushing, grandiose narcissism of the social order but, instead, with something closer to the polymorphous perversity that, in Freud's view, the social order determinedly represses.

HAWTHORNE AND MIXED-RACE MASCULINITY

Septimius can be read as an ameliorative figure across racial lines, like mixed-race Dirk Peters in Poe's novel *The Narrative of Arthur Gordon Pym of Nantucket.* In that novel, the mixed-race Dirk Peters, initially described as an eye-poppingly grotesque fusion of white, "negro," and Native American races and as a figure that exceeds the boundaries of the animal and the human, nevertheless undergoes a confusing racial transformation by the end of the novel, in which he and Pym, the narrator, emerge as the "only living white men" on a dark-skinned-savage-overrun island. Hawthorne does not relinquish Septimius's racial mixture, as Poe does, to a program of white makeover, even as Septimius's quest may be interpreted as an attempt to transform himself *into* the body of the white man he kills. Hawthorne takes great pains to make us—to *keep* us—aware that Septimius emerges from complex racial lineages. Hawthorne appears to suggest, in his depiction of Septimius, that beauty is the result of a special discernment—a certain slant of light, to wax Dickinsonian, will reveal a "certain dark beauty" in the figure of someone from a race associated in racist thought with physically unattractive qualities that outwardly evince moral and cultural failings. (Native Americans' dark skin and non-European clothing was thought to connote the savagery of their characters; the dark skin of Africans was taken as a literal form of their "benighted" condition as a race and linked to animality and an aesthetically displeasing physicality. Given the sheer intensity of this racist rhetoric, Hawthorne's evocation of beauty in Septimius stands out all the more. Stowe evoked the beauty of both African and mixed-race characters in the 1852 *Uncle Tom's Cabin* as well, and it is possible that Hawthorne may have been inspired by her deeply popular work.)

Septimius should be read, I argue, as a male mulatto. The figure of the mulatto in literature is usually rendered in alternately tragic or sexually threatening terms. Moreover, the mulatto is most usually a woman (Cora Munro in Cooper's *The Last of the Mohicans,* the titular heroine of Frances Harper's *Iola Leroy*). Rafia Zafar notes that James Weldon Johnson's depiction of the mulatto as male in his *The Autobiography of an Ex-Colored Man* in 1921 is a significant break in the tradition of the mulatto as female. Given this significance, it is even more remarkable that Hawthorne represents the mulatto male in the early 1860s.[32]

The appearance of mulattoes was particularly unsettling to many nineteenth-century viewers. As Stephen Talty writes of antebellum Americans, "Most whites looked on blacks with disgust or pity, but, mostly, indifference. It was not that they secretly knew that blacks were human and chose to ignore it. Their blindness was so deep-seated as to be almost a function of brain chemistry; they simply could not look on blacks and see creatures like themselves." Mulattoes, Talty writes, were a "shock to the optic nerve."[33] Septimius's surprisingly appealing—though its appeal is undeniably qualified—appearance suggests a broader capacity to appreciate the range of human "looks" on Hawthorne's part than one would have thought likely, especially given the paucity of direct references to raced subjects in Hawthorne's work before *Septimius* and the general, almost hysterical, abhorrence of "ugliness" he consistently expressed.[34]

The category of ugliness was one of the most potent weapons in the arsenal of anti-black racism. This tradition of thought can be traced in American culture at least from Thomas Jefferson forward. In his "Notes on the State of Virginia" (written in 1781, revised in 1782), Jefferson crystallized white racism's construction of the ugliness of the physical appearance and customs of Africans. "Are not the fine mixtures of red and white, the expressions of every passion by greater or less suffusions of color in the one, preferable to the eternal monotony which reigns in the countenances, that immovable veil of black that which covers all emotions of the other race?"[35]

If Hawthorne's marble faun suggests an attractive white male body tinged with dark racial as well as interspecies otherness, in Septimius he suggests that racial intermixture can produce a white subject with an unusual, offbeat appeal. Hawthorne suggests that the attractiveness of a mixed-race person is a matter of perspective—the anamorphic angle from which Septimius's certain dark beauty can be perceived and evaluated as such—and such a person's appearance is a phenomenon that does not produce an inevitable revulsion in the white spectator, always assumed to be the subject of the desiring gaze. And given that it is precisely from such an anamorphic angle that same-sex desire can be viewed in nineteenth-century texts, as Valerie Rohy has argued, the ability to take an unusual perspectival position comes to be crucial to the late romance's negotiation of the homoerotics of race.[36]

In light of Jefferson's repellent racist aesthetics, Hawthorne's depiction of a darkness blended into whiteness comes to seem a daring exploration of the limits of white identity figured, as ever in Hawthorne's visually oriented fictions, in the physical and the outwardly visible. Indeed, in these terms, before the marble faun and the mixed-race Septimius, Minister Hooper, a white male shrouded by his own self-donned "immovable veil of black," begins to suggest the first in a series of the "dark" white males in Hawthorne's imagination. That Hawthorne could devise in Septimius such an ameliorative figure is notable, given how wrenching all of these issues were in antebellum America and Hawthorne's own conflicted attitudes toward racial difference. Again, none of this exculpates Hawthorne for his lapses in empathy for the condition of the enslaved and racially oppressed. Nevertheless, *Septimius Felton* evinces a shift in Hawthorne's thinking, one registered through his imaginative faculties: his first mixed-race protagonist. In this work, the sexually ambiguous male familiar from Hawthorne's fictions becomes *explicitly* racially ambiguous as well, as opposed to the inchoate racial allegory of Minister Hooper and his black veil. Figures of "black whiteness," such as Hooper and much more pronouncedly Septimius Felton, combine sexual and racial ambiguity.

Though the "delicious" excessiveness of the handsome English soldier is one important aspect of white identity as Hawthorne represents it, throughout both *Septimius* manuscripts, a much more critical view of whiteness prevails. Here is the point at which Hawthorne may be considered authentically daring. Linking white male subjectivity to the histories of imperialism and exploitation of other cultures, Hawthorne repurposes in the *Septimius Norton* manuscript the bloody footprint symbol from the *American Claimant* manuscripts in a revealing manner. The spectral, immortal man known as the Sagamore, who lends guidance to but also tyrannically controls a tribe of Native Americans, is actually the Englishman cursed by the "Bloody Footprint," which he attempts to flee by venturing to the New World.

As Charles Swann writes, "The white benevolent dictator may (quite unintentionally) have made it easier for the Puritans to conquer the Indians by sapping their individual and social independence and aggression. . . . [he] becomes a Tories' Tory, a tyrant[.]"[37] The Sagamore is the embodiment of all of the sinister old white males in Hawthorne's fiction; now, Hawthorne inserts his dubious old white male into the history of colonization and racist oppression through which the United States was founded, and in which the Sagamore plays a central role. It should not be overlooked as well that, while Aunt Keziah in her virulent opposition to white culture conforms to racist stereotypes of the barbarous and uncouth other, her character nevertheless provides an alternative view of Hawthorne's own white Calvinist culture and is, moreover, a figure of considerable sympathy, one who demands far more consideration than I have the space to provide here. She embodies the figure of the savage mother, but she is also a loving maternal presence, and an alternative point of identification for the nonnormative male Septimius. In contrast, the Sagamore represents the negative narcissism of white, colonial power, the textual superego against whom Septimius chafes even as he shares in his fantasies of narcissistic, imperialistic omnipotence. Similarly, Dr. Portsoaken, in his enigmatic and dubious scientific role, and with his familiar, that large, diabolically knowing spider, is a kind of warlock double to witchlike Aunt Keziah.

The abortive romance between Septimius and the soldier looms above *Septimius Felton* as an unfulfilled possibility of connection across racial, national, and sexual lines. Its tender, evanescent memory—and the aesthetic power of the episode as Hawthorne describes it—provides a constant counterpoint to the increasingly obsessive fascination with white morbidity and duplicity, conducted across and seeping into the centuries, in the manuscripts; Septimius's quest enshrines the encounter with the man he kills and whose multivalent textual blood infuses his volatile own. The surprising suggestion Hawthorne makes in *Septimius Felton* is that homoerotic male intersubjectivity disrupts and challenges the ongoing, inexorable patterns of white hegemonic rule.

FEMALE AUTHORITY

One character complicates all of these matters even further: Sybil Dacy, the woman whose image Septimius's bullet shatters. Sybil is the daughter of Dr. Portsoaken and the betrothed of the young English soldier, a decisive fact Septimius learns only in the climactic portion of the *Septimius Felton* narrative. Considering her role in this version of the narrative allows us to consider more broadly the question of female sexuality in Hawthorne and Freud's theories.

Throughout this study, my focus has been on Freud's theory of masculinity and its self-defeating and self-protecting psychic defenses, such as voyeurism and fetishism. In chapter 6, I attempted to make use of these Freudian theories in order to appreciate Hawthorne's critique of misogyny. But I have not wanted to give the impression that Freud's theories are uniformly revelatory or potentially radical—far from it. His views of female sexuality are an especially difficult aspect of his work that demands careful consideration and, I would argue, reconsideration. Altogether, they are hampered by his inability either to understand or to make clear that he understands the social constraints upon femininity. If "penis envy" has any validity at all, it is only when retooled—if I can be excused the term—as desire for a share in social power always already decreed as the privilege of the male. Lacan, in his theory of the phallus, comes closer to doing so than Freud, but I share feminists' frustrations with the treatment of "woman" in Lacan as a "symptom of man." In order to make better sense of the significance of the Sybil Dacy character as well as to establish both the inherent frustrations in and the possible uses that can be made of Freud's theories of femininity, I want briefly to compare Hawthorne's and Freud's views of women before commencing an analysis of femininity in *Septimius Felton*.

In her essay "Bourgeois Sexuality and the Gothic Plot in Wharton and Hawthorne," Monika Elbert speaks to an important issue, "the bourgeois dilemma of exploiting woman's body for public consumption—exposing

Hester in the marketplace—and of exploring class anxieties and allegiances using woman as a battleground for these tensions" (260).[38] Elbert's major argument in this essay is that Hawthorne is disturbed by the spectacle of unlicensed female sexuality, which he works to contain. If this is indeed the case—and despite my admiration for Elbert's work, I am not in full agreement with her—he also questions the socialization of women, suggesting that patriarchy denies girls and women the full range of their sexualities generally. This disposition finds a particularly harrowing exploration in the episode in *The House of the Seven Gables* in which Alice Pyncheon is punished by Matthew Maule because she visually appraised his body and found it desirable. He makes her a zombie slave, and then inadvertently kills her. In my view, Hawthorne is critiquing here the male sexual anxiety that motivates Maule's malevolent vengeance.

Hawthorne problematizes heterosexual presumption and compulsory heterosexuality by repeatedly returning to themes such as bachelor anxiety (almost all of the young males of his short fiction and novels are unmarried and deeply anxious about the prospect of heterosexual intimacy), marital discord (Young Goodman Brown leaving his new wife alone for a dark night in the forest, the husband who walks out on his wife for years in "Wakefield"), and, most importantly, the tendency for men to betray the trust women invest in them (*The Scarlet Letter* and *The Blithedale Romance* are exemplary in this regard). Creating an ongoing ominous atmosphere of tension, anxiety, and even sadism when it comes to matters of sexuality, Hawthorne refuses any view of sexuality as necessarily positive, affirming, or unquestionably appealing. This is, ultimately, the meeting place between his sensibility and Freud's.

The feminist relevance of Hawthorne's work stems from this skeptical view of sexuality and lies specifically in his consistent, ruthless depiction of male inadequacy and tendencies toward both duplicity and domination. By unceasingly exposing the precarious nature of relations between men and women in his culture, Hawthorne sheds empathetic light on the social condition of femininity in patriarchy. Of course, this empathy is in no way a straightforward empathy, intermixed as it is with ambivalence, alienation, and even antipathy. Without denying this intermixture, I nevertheless argue that the empathy is genuine and politically valuable. Of course, the views that Hawthorne expressed in life about women complicate matters further. Hawthorne frequently made derogatory and hostile comments about women in his private writings (correspondence, journals, notebooks). I can only add that his fictional version of Margaret Fuller in *The Blithedale Romance,* the fiery feminist Zenobia, is a far more sympathetically drawn portrait than his scabrous comments about Fuller herself, whom he once called a "humbug," would suggest was a possibility.

With Freud the situation is much more vexed for feminism. After a demonstration of genuine identification with his female patients in his early *Studies of Hysteria* (1895), an identification fraught with difficulty, Freud proceeded to discuss women with an increasingly alarming lack of sympathy, to say nothing of empathy. A desultory tone pervades his discussions of women and female sexuality; Freud is indifferent to the social and experiential ramifications of his theory of penis envy, which, while it has a certain value when his social context is taken into consideration, audibly expresses his competitive hostility toward women. Where, then, is the feminist value in Freud, who differs from Hawthorne in that whereas there's a genuine feeling for the plight of women detectable *throughout* Hawthorne's body of work, Freud's work evinces a greater and greater indifference to women?

The primary feminist value of Freud lies in the general stance he maintains toward the relationship between human beings and culture. As does Hawthorne, Freud overturns positive assumptions about and associations with the two most prominent social roles and functions our culture designates as the responsibility of women: mothering and marriage, woman's social responsibility being, on the one hand, to provide nurture and to domesticate her children, and, on the other hand, to ensure that marital sexuality is full and fulfilling and that men are properly socialized through marriage. Casting, as does Hawthorne, these compulsory roles and the social system dependent on them in an ominous, denatured light, Freud makes sexuality a source of ongoing frustration and even terror. The value of his Grand Guignol version of sexuality is that it renders normative, positive views of sexuality and the assumption that individuals must conform to them deeply suspect. Troubling the socially enforced views of such phenomena as the family, marriage, child rearing, and childhood as inherently positive, Freud offers a pessimistic theory of culture. The feminist value of his theory lies in its implicit critique of the effect culture has on the people who live in and make it. It is the Freudian view of culture and civilization as deeply suspect that enables a feminist view of women's oppression within culture to emerge *from* Freud's work, even if it does not frequently emerge *within* it.

In her discussion of what value lies, if any, in Freud's *Fragment of an Analysis of a Case of Hysteria,* commonly known as *Dora,* Toril Moi puts the matter somewhat differently, but in a way that extends what I mean here: "Freud's epistemology is clearly phallocentric. . . . To undermine this phallocentric epistemology means to expose its lack of 'natural' foundation. In the case of Dora, however, we have been able to do this only because of

Freud's own theories of femininity and sexuality. The attack upon phallocentrism must come from within. . . . We can only destroy the mythical and mystifying constructions of patriarchy by using its own weapons. We have no others."[39] Moi's statement about the usefulness of Freud is hard won, hardly celebratory; I invoke it here because it demonstrates the difficulty of Freudian theory but also what remains useful in it for the purposes of projects such as feminism as well as queer theory. Despite Freud's considerable failures, his theories retain their value as methods for the study of the ways in which we are sexually socialized in patriarchy. Freud's theories of femininity are also not entirely without value. Nancy Chodorow argues that one of the vexations of Freud is that while he is deeply insightful on masculinity, he is equally troubled and troubling on femininity.[40] Despite, as Chodorow rightly notes, the infiltration of Freud's cultural biases into his more clinical findings, Freud nevertheless provides a piercing account of the thwarting of female autonomy and self-confidence by the misogynistic strictures of the patriarchal social order, even if he is also intricately connected to these strictures.

Freud repeatedly returns to an increasingly poignant theme: the condition of femininity is one of loss. Freud shares with Hawthorne a tragic view of gender. Girls *must* relinquish their active, phallic sexuality in order to become *women*. This is the central issue in Juliet Mitchell's brilliant feminist reformulation of Freud's theories of female hysteria in the *Dora* case history especially, in which she argues that one of its major issues is that the young Dora was forced to relinquish her active sexuality, while her brother Otto was allowed to maintain and develop his own.[41] This compulsory forfeiture of women's sexuality has tremendous significance for their subsequent relationships with their mothers and other women, males, and with themselves and their own psychic and corporeal lives. With this theme comes another significant insight: misogyny is the result of the trauma of male socialization.[42] In other words, our culture's socialization of males manufactures misogynists. However blinkered Freud can be, he does at times provide an insightful account of the female experience of patriarchy and, given how both females *and* males are socialized, the inevitability of misogyny. What Hawthorne and Freud share is the sense that women fight for their right to *act* and for their right to *desire* in patriarchy.

WHEN SEPTIMIUS first discovers Sybil Dacy, she is fluttering about in "his" hillside spot where the soldier lies buried by Septimius's own hand. Indifferent to her in a manner suggestive of his likely sexual disposition, Septimius, like the protagonist of classical Hollywood *film noir,* nevertheless becomes hopelessly intrigued by Sybil; in turn, she emerges as an emotionally unstable *femme fatale.* Indeed, Hawthorne may be said to rework the conventions of *noir* by depicting Sybil not as the black widow who lures the protagonist to his doom, but as a wronged woman who takes narrative into her own hands for more ambiguous purposes, including revenge. Hawthorne reveals the tellingly named Sybil as a rival author figure in a work that teems with them: Septimius, the solider, Dr. Portsoaken, Aunt Keziah with her own diluted "elixir" recipe, and the Sagamore who inscribes his own identity upon the tribe he colonizes. Sybil may be said to be the most successful author figure in *Septimius Felton* in that she not only concocts some versions of the elixir herself but overmasters Septimius in the process of his own quest to do so, subsuming his quest into her own stratagems.

Given the number of female characters who become ensnared within if not altogether destroyed by the male quest in Hawthorne's fiction—Georgiana in "The Birthmark," Beatrice in "Rappaccini's Daughter," the wife in "Wakefield"—Sybil's outmaneuvering of Septimius takes on a note of feminine triumph, the nature of which feminist and queer theory revisions of Freud illuminate. Judith Butler, drawing on the work of French feminist Luce Irigaray, describes the prevailing Western fantasy of autogenesis as "a spiritualized and desexualized desire for the form or reflection of a masculine self in another," which produces the "fantastic logic whereby men beget other men, reproducing and mirroring themselves at the expense of women and of their own reproductive origin in women/mothers."[43] As Irigaray puts it in *Speculum of the Other Woman,* "The only men who love each other are, in truth, those who are impatient to find the same over and over again." Unable to find the same in "some other part of man," they must seek out what Irigaray calls "that *mirror of vision* in which they can look at themselves in the very gaze of the other, perceiving, in one and the same glance, their view and themselves."[44] This circuit of male self-reflection depends, writes Butler, upon an excluded third term or medium, "the girl, considered a flawed copy, or the mother, the medium through which procreation becomes possible and who physicalizes and, hence, demeans the higher form of the spiritual reduplication of 'man' that is philosophy." As Butler continues, "For Irigaray, then, there can be no feminine desire inside this economy and certainly no parallel possibility of feminine self-reflection."[45]

If Septimius, the dead soldier, the manuscript, and the abundant field of purple, tumescent flowers that grow above the soldier's body all connote a fantasy of masculine autogenesis, a shared male world of spiritualized male desire and male beauty—what Luce Irigaray critiques as *hommo-sexuality*—

Sybil disrupts, even shatters, the fantasy by insisting upon inserting herself within the circuit of male self-reflection and reordering the logic of the male quest plot. In this manner, if we recall the shattering of her portrait by Septimius's bullet, she may be said to restore her shattered image, insisting upon its solidity and that of her own presence. But Hawthorne, even in his most fantastic plots, is too much of an emotional realist to describe this daring act of feminist agency as being without cost: Sybil immolates herself in the process. Having vengefully intended to kill Septimius because he killed her lover, the English soldier, Sybil realizes that she now loves Septimius herself. She quaffs the poisoned elixir she meant to give Septimius, even as he cries out in horror that she must not do so, and dies.

Hawthorne critiques the male fantasy of autogenesis by enlarging our understanding of what this fantasy means in something like the real world. He does so by making vividly clear this fantasy's costs to femininity. But he also undermines the fantasy by emphasizing the force of female *will*—Sybil's active desire constitutes a parallel quest narrative in this work, even if a quest for revenge. At the same time, Septimius's solipsistic quest for immortal life robs Sybil and also the soldier of their own. The eerie, despairing, and highly frustrating means that women have of demonstrating their agency and acting on their desires is to choose death over subjugation, as happens repeatedly in Hawthorne (Beatrice, Zenobia), and happens, on some level, here. Again, such a theme provides no comfort to anyone. At best, it reflects what I have called Hawthorne's tragic view of gender. In his near-final works, Hawthorne continued to explore the woman's experience in patriarchy, her means of negotiating it, and also the male's investment in women.

Sybil initially recalls Ophelia, Hamlet's would-be fiancée, who, driven mad by Hamlet's own feigned madness, drowns herself. But Hawthorne's Sybil is an Ophelia with the guile of Hamlet: she uses a veneer of madness as a cunning strategy. Hamlet, in fulfillment of his revenge plot, also ends up dead from a poisoned drink, murders his mother in the process, and was, if not the cause of, certainly the catalyst in Ophelia's suicide: if Hamlet manages to defeat his enemies, he does so at considerable cost to himself and those around him, particularly the women he loves. His nearly Pyrrhic triumph haunts Sybil's own ambiguous fate. The interest, in both Shakespeare's and Hawthorne's work (and one inevitably thinks of Melville's ecstatic celebration in his review "Hawthorne and His Mosses" of Hawthorne as nearly Shakespeare's equal) lies precisely in these muddles of gendered representation.

One further point in our consideration of Hawthorne's treatment of femininity deserves amplification. Aunt Keziah-Nashoba is a maternal presence despite her savagery, one that will in no way allow itself to be excluded or repudiated. She is like a Mistress Hibbens or a Mother Rigby who has been endowed with a human complexity, vulnerability, and depth. Moreover, she is, like Septimius, a mixed-race character who ultimately solicits our sympathy and even admiration. As such a persona, she signals a further development in Hawthorne's thinking about gender and race, and the mother–son bond. In his portrait of the depth of Septimius's bond with Aunt Keziah-Nashoba, Hawthorne further develops the theme of mother-identified masculinity that he began to explore in his tale "The Gentle Boy." But here, the bond is constant, lasting, and mutual.

CHARLES SWANN writes that by the 1860s, Hawthorne's "confidence in the realities or truths of world or reflection and in the stability of the relations between world and reflection has, it seems, been replaced by the larger question of whether there is a stable reality to which we can have access." Of *Septimius Felton,* Swann writes, "Ambitious as *The Marble Faun* was, Hawthorne has gone beyond that. While we may only have fragments, they are fragments of a masterpiece."[46] Swann's astute reading of the value of *Septimius Felton* not only recuperates its aesthetic worth but also draws our attention to the ways in which its textual and thematic qualities mirror while deepening the significance of each other: the fragmentary text and the fragmentation of identity it thematizes achieve an exquisite equilibrium.

Gray Kochhar-Lindgren writes of the necessity for the textual Narcissus's transfiguration, which demands that Narcissus "shift the cathexis of his libido from his own self-representation to a textual body that enters the chain of signification. . . . When Narcissus moves from the imaginary register of reflexive mirroring to the symbolic dimension of subjectivity that acknowledges the necessity of otherness, the body emerges from the chrysalis of reflection."[47] Death emerges as the fate Narcissus attempted to elude with his self-mesmerized desire, and acknowledging its inevitable presence provides cold comfort. But it is the very acknowledgment of death that frees the narcissistic subject to experience the larger world beyond the self.

If the heart of Narcissus's tragedy is that he can never recognize an other, in the *Septimius* manuscripts Hawthorne, to whatever extent we can view him as a Narcissus figure, insists upon seeing the other in his depiction of an other-raced protagonist, a character through whom he gazes upon a character whose beauty reflects Hawthorne's vanished own. Septimius's obsession with "undyingness" can be read as Hawthorne's own ambivalence toward acknowledging the increasingly undeniable imminence of his own death.

These late works insist, however, upon grappling with otherness in a way unparalleled in Hawthorne's previous work. Overall Hawthorne's last phase marks his emergence from the chrysalis of self-reflection into a world of difference. These features alone make the late work meaningful and worthy of renewed attention.

The new critical work on Hawthorne and Freud begins rather than ends with this book. The entire question of masculinity in Hawthorne (as well as Freud) needs further analysis. A range of masculine styles animates Hawthorne's work and would benefit from the Freudian queer perspectives that illuminate his dark young men. What is the psychology of the Judge Pyncheons, the Old Moodies, and the Sagamores, the robber barons of their day, who exert their will sadistically on others? Of the Chillingworths, whose desires for vengeance mutate, along the way, into obsessive desires to keep their male quarry all to themselves? Perhaps even more urgently, Hawthorne's feminist poetics and politics need further exploration. In life, though in his "private" writing, Hawthorne said some unforgivably uncharitable things about women. In his fiction, however, Hawthorne exhibits a feminist sensibility in his empathy with embattled women and in his unyielding critique of male dominance, both of which also make his work important to queer theory. That so much work has been done on Hawthorne over the years and that so much more work still needs to be done attests to the significance of his achievement.

EPILOGUE

The Haunted Verge
AESTHETICS, DESIRE, HISTORY

*H*AVING BEEN absorbed throughout this book with questions of gender and sexuality, I want to take the opportunity provided by the epilogue to consider other ways in which Hawthorne thematized narcissism: first, in his aesthetic theory; second, in his idiosyncratic theorization of history. Considering the importance of narcissism to Hawthorne's aesthetics takes my effort to rethink and revalue the question of narcissism to a new level while also further developing our understanding of Hawthorne's writerly sensibility. Considering the question of history—as critics such as Sacvan Bercovitch, Lauren Berlant, Eric Cheyfitz, John Carlos Rowe, and others have demonstrated, a deeply vexed one for Hawthorne—in terms of Hawthorne's narcissistic aesthetic, as evinced by his novel *The Marble Faun*, yields some fresh insights into what, precisely, was Hawthorne's understanding of the historical.

TEXTUAL NARCISSISM
HAWTHORNE'S AESTHETICS

Though it has been frequently framed throughout the Western tradition and well into the present as pernicious—used as the model of the failure to love properly or of an egotism run monstrously amok—narcissism has also proved richly useful in several disciplines for the contemplation of the essentially paradoxical nature of subjectivity and its relationship to desire and language. This book has chiefly considered the insights into male subjectivity offered by Hawthorne and Freud in their thematizations of the Narcissus myth; at the same time, this book has also attempted to establish the value of narcissism as a textual figure and a psychological experience. Toward this end, it is helpful to think through, once again, the various ways in which the concept of narcissism has been theorized, especially by those who have found the concept intellectually productive. Beginning with a consideration of the relationships among narcissism, language, and myth, I proceed to a discussion of an aspect of the narcissistic sensibility in Hawthorne's work that I have not yet explicitly considered, what I call Hawthorne's *textual narcissism*.

NARCISSISM, broadly understood, encompasses the varieties of desire and the most profound questions that pertain to self and other. Narcissus, as Lacan suggested in his influential theory of the mirror stage, is the child fixated on his own reflection, which he mistakes for an image of authentic wholeness that will continue to haunt him as the unattainable ideal of his own bodily cohesion, so radically distinct from the fragmentation of his non-imaged body.[1] We see through Narcissus's eyes when we contemplate our own body, so much ours yet so intangible; when we contemplate the beauty of a person whom we desire yet can't access, much less possess. Narcissus evokes our desire for perfect likeness, to see ourselves reflected in another's eyes; the myth also speaks to the ways we project our will and our anxieties onto another, the ruthless potentiality of this need to see ourselves reflected back to us. Narcissism is longing and power, vulnerability and domination; it is man, woman, both, neither, other.

Narcissism is also nothing. The nothingness of narcissism speaks to the mystery—the void—at the heart of myth and language as well as desire. Eric Gould's concept of "mythicity" importantly draws upon the Narcissus myth. Mythicity, a view of myth as "a metaphysics of absence implicit in every sign," "is the condition of filling the gap with signs in such a way that Being continues to conceal Nothing as a predication of further knowledge."[2] In his study *Narcissus Transformed*, Gray Kochhar-Lindgren writes in response to Gould that the "hidden presence of the nothing necessitates myth, metaphor, and endless interpretive play. But Narcissus refuses to see the insubstantial shadows, the shades of nothingness, that lie so close to his fixed and staring face."[3] As Kochhar-Lindgren theorizes,

> The myth of Narcissus narrates a dialectic of reflection that is internally disturbed by an obsessive desire for immediacy. It is a poetic narrative that

depicts a way of being that wants to destroy the surface of things, the appearances, in order to plunge into the depths and shatter the reflecting mirror completely so that the other of love—which is only apparently other—might be possessed. But a terrible paradox binds any desire that enters into this symbolic topos: If the appearances are destroyed, then the apparent object of love, the image of Narcissus, will also be destroyed. If, on the other hand, the mirror is not shattered, Echo will remain but a desolate voice, and Narcissus himself will die from the grief of love unreturned. How shall we respond to the mirror with which we are so closely identified? How shall we think about myth and the fictions of representation?[4]

The urgency of the questions the Narcissus myth raises about myth and language, and, I would add here, also about gender, sexuality, and identity, arises from the myth's fundamental intimacy with death. "The mirror of fiction," Kochhar-Lindgren argues, "does not naively and mimetically reflect its subject matter. Rather, fiction transforms the writer, the reader, and society by a critical unmasking of the forms of death." This unmasking involves a challenge to orthodoxies of all kinds as well as the ways in which we relate to others and ourselves. "One must reflectively gaze at death before there is a possibility of becoming more free in the face of the glassy-eyed stare of Thanatos." But whatever liberation we may derive from staging such a confrontation can only be partial: "reading, like psychoanalysis, is interminable."[5] Signs, like mirrors, give the illusion of depth, but they are themselves no more than a surface. The Narcissus myth thematizes not only the tormenting disparity between surface and depth—we recall Melville's description of the image of Narcissus as "tormenting, mild"—but the tantalizing, seductive ways in which surface gives the appearance of depth, the ways in which signs signal meaning, a presence rather than an absence.

As Judith Butler glosses Lacan, both she and Lacan appear to be rewriting the Narcissus myth: "Linguistic reference fails in the same way that desire is structured by failure: if language were to reach the object it desires, it would undo itself as language."[6] As I discussed in the introduction, the fundamentally split subject is a creation of language. One of the major paradigms of Lacanian psychoanalysis is that language fundamentally alters a human being: in order to render us a speaking subject, language cuts us off from the pre-oedipal world of the mother and the state of primary pleasure in which our mother's body and ours were one. Language thereby transforms us into a subject of the Symbolic order, the father's world of language and law, a theory of the formation of the subject that has informed this study as well as its revised Freudian methodology.

A colonizing force, language bars access to whatever was part of that being before language transformed it. Desire proceeds from the split between need and demand that heralded the end of our pre-oedipal state of plenitude and pleasure, the moment when we *demanded* the breast even after our biological needs were satisfied. Desire can never be fulfilled, for if it could, we would simultaneously return to that original state of bliss and cancel out our own subjectivity, which proceeds from the basis of our *loss* of that original state. Subjectivity is a form of exile, desire a longing for the lost world of origins, and language the vexed means we have of negotiating the two. The myth of Narcissus metaphorizes the split nature of subjectivity—that it emerges from the split between an original self and a self remade through language—and the split between a human being and language: we can no more access authentic meaning or the primary pleasure of lost origins through language than Narcissus can grasp the image of the boy that beguiles him. The figure of Narcissus illuminates the disparity between the textual and whatever may be the "actual," that term that so plagued Hawthorne as he defensively made a case for romance in opposition to the novel and its penchant for depicting "the actualities" of the "real" world. One of the central debates of psychoanalysis, in its Lacanian cast, is the disparity between a human being and language, the profoundly limited medium that is the only means whereby a human being can communicate.

In his writings, Hawthorne exudes an awareness of the Narcissus myth's relevance to these philosophical concerns. The author playfully prefaces "Rappaccini's Daughter" with a framing device—the other half of which is never provided, as the frame that precedes the story is not returned to at the end—that metatextually serves as autocritique (10: 91–93). Presenting the story as being "From the Writings of Aubépine," Hawthorne both satirizes himself and the more acid among his contemporary critics by assuming the role of the "introducer" of the works of Aubépine, a writer so obscure that "his very name is unknown to many of his countrymen," echoing Hawthorne's own admission of feeling like the "obscurest man of letters" in his own land. French for "Hawthorne," Aubépine fuses Hawthorne's own sense of his authorial persona and how it was viewed by various critics. "As a writer," the anonymous preface writer remarks of Aubépine, "he seems to occupy an unfortunate position between the Transcendentalists . . . and the great body of pen and ink men who address the intellect and the sympathies of the multitude." Aubépine's writings "are not altogether destitute of fancy and originality," but fame has eluded them because of the author's "inveterate love of allegory," which has stolen "the human warmth out of his conceptions."

Hawthorne chides Aubépine throughout, but he also cannot resist the opportunity for defensive self-flattery. On occasion, "a breath of nature, a rain-drop of pathos and tenderness, or a gleam of humor" manages to burst free from the stuffy confines of this inveterate allegorist's oeuvre. His alter ego's fictions are "voluminous," his prolixity "praiseworthy and indefatigable." The author has produced a "startling catalogue of volumes" which, however "wearisomely" perused, nevertheless leave behind a "certain personal affection and sympathy, though by no means admiration[.]" Hawthorne uses the Aubépine persona as an opportunity for self-inspection as well as for playing his usual sadistic, wounded, cunning verbal games with his readers. Hawthorne's prefaces are stripteases in which we're led to believe the author will lay himself bare before our eyes only to see him become more armored against our prying vision than ever before. Behind all the cunning play lies a sense of anxiety betrayed by the indecisive tone that vacillates between smug self-satisfaction and an awareness of faults, limitations, and an uncertain readership (this story was written in 1844, quite a few years before Hawthorne's first major success, *The Scarlet Letter*). Aubépine's persona gives Hawthorne an opportunity for self-estrangement, to view himself from a disassociated, yet intimate, position; the preface serves as a drama of self-inspection that will be extended into the story proper.

HAWTHORNE famously theorized the romance as "a neutral territory, somewhere between the real world and fairy-land, where the Actual and the Imaginary may meet, and each imbue itself with the nature of the other" (1: 36). I argue that as Hawthorne lays out his aesthetic philosophy in "The Custom-House" chapter that prefaces *The Scarlet Letter,* he evokes the Narcissus myth; and in the manner that he evokes it, he intervenes in the dead end of signs, meaning, and interpretation embodied by the myth. Hawthorne makes an intervention by framing the romance as an attempt to find some means of bridging surface and depth, meaninglessness and meaning, desire and the unattainable, life and death: the romance is a neutral space between these polarities, a retrieval of the space from which they diverge. Narcissus is the chief metaphor of the beauty and terror of the mirror image, the desire it instigates and the despair it returns; about the power of reflections over the human mind, eye, and heart. The reflection seems more real, more "winning soft," as Eve says of her reflected image in *Paradise Lost* (IX: 479), than reality.

For Hawthorne, it is the mirror of art where a compromise—the merger that is neutral territory—can take place. Moonlight metaphorizes the imaginative faculty; it casts an uncanny, defamiliarizing light on the objects of a nighttime sitting room, lending all of its contents a "quality of strangeness and remoteness." But the "somewhat dim coal-fire" also plays an important role. Throwing its "unobtrusive tinge," "faint ruddiness," and a "reflected gleam" throughout the altered room, this "warmer light mingles itself with the cold spirituality of the moonbeams," thereby communicating "a heart and sensibilities of human tenderness." Hawthorne suggests that the transforming, uncanny power of art competes against the warm glow, the hopefulness, of human emotions (1: 36). But this competition produces a salutary effect on "the forms which fancy summons up."

> It converts them from snow-images into men and women. Glancing at the looking-glass, we behold—deep within its haunted verge—the smouldering glow of the half-extinguished anthracite, the white moonbeams on the floor, and a repetition of all the gleam and shadow of the picture, with one remove farther from the actual, and nearer to the imaginative. (1: 36)

Hawthorne privileges the imaginative over the actual—presumably, emotions over facts, art over reality—but the mirror emerges as the place where neutral territory awaits, where the imaginative and the actual can exist at once. Hawthorne transforms the dead, dread mirror of Narcissus into a place where disparities, divergences, splits, wounding if not mortal separations—chiefly Narcissus's aching separation from himself, from his desire, his image, his other—and other gulfs can find some respite and perhaps even repair. Hawthorne's "haunted verge" is the space where myth, language, self, otherness, and nothingness can find animating play, a play that, while no resolution, gives empty forms back their vitality, turns ghosts into flesh, allows us to stare Narcissus in the face. Yet if Hawthorne in his aesthetic philosophy positively rewrites the Narcissus myth so that the mirror enables connections and exchange, rather than merely and conventionally presenting itself as the limpid impenetrability of the sign, his fiction's thematic concerns—about illusion, identity, masks, masquerades, and violation, the imposition of personal will that threatens to obliterate the other—much more consistently convey the deep anguish of subjectivity, informed by the implicit presence of the Narcissus myth.

Hawthorne's textual narcissism is the basis from which his larger exploration of "identity themes" proceeds. The fullest account of Hawthorne's work will be one that considers the relationship between his aesthetics and his political concerns—his gender as well as sexual politics. His belief that in art imagination and reality can meet and merge was manifested in his fiction, in which fantasies and social realities confront one another but also have an equal legitimacy. Hawthorne's belief in individual fantasies, in the unconscious urgency of human minds, passions, and lives, makes him a psychoanalytic author. At the same time, I believe that he was also very conscious, and increasingly more so, of the often brutal implications of fantasy's encounter with the "actual." In the end, Hawthorne was an empathetic author. His darkest fictional devisings were tempered always with an awareness of the fragility of human experience. His key insights into the relationship between the visual and gendered identity, and between anxiety and sexuality, make him one of the most significant and prescient theorists of gender and sexual identity in nineteenth-century American letters—maddening and at times limited in his views, but, on balance, bracingly astute and even more bracingly resistant.

HAWTHORNE, NARCISSISM, AND THE HISTORICAL

While often being accused of having actively skirted the issue, Hawthorne has a great deal to teach us about history; indeed, I would say that in his late works, especially, history emerges as a central preoccupation. What distinguishes Hawthorne's version of history is the centrality of desire's role in it. In my view, the question of desire, harder to chart, more difficult to track, is sometimes neglected in Americanist literary criticism, which places its emphasis on material history, cultural context, and the archive, as I discussed in chapter 3. (Several important Americanists certainly do consider desire—Lauren Berlant, Kathryn R. Kent, Valerie Rohy, Dana Luciano, Christopher Castiglia, and Peter Coviello come immediately to mind. I do not want to present a distorted view of the field, only to register that its predominant practice has a tendency to deemphasize the role of desire as well as the concept of the unconscious, a substantial portion of the subject, and indeed of existence, that is unknowable except in dreams, slips of the tongue, and other eruptions of this kind. In my view, any historical inquiry is always already haunted by desire and the unconscious. This is not to suggest that historical inquiry is not necessary—of course it is—but that any such inquiry must proceed in the knowledge of its partial, fragile condition.) Hawthorne, as Freud will do later, insists on making the presumably antithetical fields of history and desire interchangeable, indeed, synonymous. Both Hawthorne and Freud theorize history as an endless battle between the individual and civilization in which desire is the battleground.[7]

IN CHAPTER 45 of Hawthorne's 1860 novel *The Marble Faun,* "The Flight of Hilda's Doves," Kenyon, an American sculptor living in Rome, discovers that Hilda, the young American woman he loves, has apparently disappeared, intelligence that leaves lovelorn Kenyon bereft. Hilda, a fellow artist who makes copies of the great works of Western visual art, had illuminated the "whole sphere" of Kenyon's life, chased out the "evil spirits"; without her, he finds himself "in darkness and astray" (4: 409). Kenyon has already suffered the loss of the intimacy that once existed among himself, Hilda, and their friends Miriam, an artist with a dark, hazy past, and Donatello, initially a carefree handsome young Italian man now rendered morbid and distant by the central traumatic action of the novel. Ardently in love with Miriam, Donatello—at the behest of her eyes—killed the Model, an obscure, loathsome figure who stalked Miriam during the early portion of the novel. Hilda witnessed Donatello pushing the Model over the precipice of the Tarpeian Rock, from which the "political criminals" of ancient Rome were once flung to their deaths. It "was an admirable idea of those stern old fellows," muses Kenyon, to fling such wrongdoers "down from the very summit on which stood the Senate-House and Jove's Temple; emblems of the institutions which they sought to violate," a fall symbolic of the suddenness with which one could plunge from "the utmost height of ambition to its profoundest ruin" (4: 168). But the sudden repetition of such retributive retaliation in the present has disastrous consequences. The hideous sight of not only the murder but also of the female gaze that impelled it drives the deeply pious Hilda into a despair so deep that she puts her adamantly maintained Protestantism aside to seek the solace of the Catholic confessional. An intricate series of later events results in her temporary disappearance from the city. Having spent time after the murder (of which Kenyon is not yet aware) with a transformed, newly somber Donatello, now revealed as a Count, in his Tuscany estate, and having met up again with Miriam, to whom he offers cautious advice when she speaks to him of Donatello's apparent rejection of her, Kenyon needs Hilda's reassuring plainness (as I would describe it) more than ever upon his return to Rome.

It is little surprise that this return inaugurates in Kenyon an awareness of "what a dreary city is Rome." When the gloom cast over one's heart, observes the narrator, corresponds to the city's "spell of ruin," "all the ponderous gloom of the Roman Past" will "crush you down with the heaped-up marble and granite, the earth-mounds, and multitudinous bricks, of its material decay" (4: 410). And so crushed, a melancholy man might supposedly "make acquaintance with a grim philosophy": he "should learn to bear patiently with his individual griefs," which he must endure only over the course of his own brief life, for what are they in comparison to "tokens of such infinite misfortune on an imperial scale," the knowledge that this vast history of ruin memorializes an eternal span of horror and misery. Moreover, these "landmarks of time" bring "the remoteness of a thousand years ago" to bear on the present, all of which might lead the melancholy man of current times to consider the puniness of his own travails, in the awesome light of this history of oppression and oppressing history, a kind of comfort. Yet even this "shrub of bitter-sweetness" cannot be found. For however long a view of history you take, however many "palaces and temples," "old, triumphal arches," or "obelisks, with their unintelligible inscriptions, hinting at a Past infinitely more remote than history can define," you see before you; however aware you become that, "compared with that immeasurable distance," your "own life is nothing," *still* "you demand, none the less earnestly, a gleam of sunshine, instead of a speck of shadow, on the step or two that will bring you to your quiet rest." You *know* how "exceedingly absurd" you are to do so.

> But, even while you taunt yourself with this sad lesson, your heart cries out obstreperously for its small share of earthly happiness, and will not be appeased by the myriads of dead hopes that lie crushed into the soil of Rome. How wonderful, that this our narrow foothold of the Present should hold its own so constantly, and, while every moment changing, should still be like a rock betwixt the encountering tides of the long Past and the infinite To-come! (4: 410–11)

Numerous problems inhere in this passage: Hawthorne's deft, troubling use of *style indirect libre,* the narrator's voice blending into Kenyon's inner thoughts so that we struggle to differentiate the two, wondering whose point of view we should accept, or, indeed, if any point of view is offered at all; more directly, Hawthorne's interesting, for him, use of the second person, here an aggressive way of hailing the reader and interpolating him or her into the action.

Though the delicacy of such textual tensions should not be overlooked (who is speaking and for whom?), I wish to make a broad point. Here, the novel philosophically expresses a problem that Freud will also take up: the essential narcissism of the human disposition, *not* a narcissism that should be typed as pathological but one that should be understood as fundamental, intrinsic, a constitutive aspect of the human mind. This is the narcissism of the kind Rei Terada describes as "an extra you," the kind needed for the "virtual self-difference" required for any emotional experience.[8] Seeing the limitless scope of ruin, of history, makes the melancholy viewer see *himself* seeing—see himself dwarfed by time, himself in time, only himself making time. We can rationally understand that events, structures, and experiences vastly more powerful and far more powerfully vast than our own loom before and beyond us, but we can only process history, life, reality, through the methods of our individual consciousness. We make sense from the self outward.

The view expressed here makes very clear the always already subjective nature of our grasp on reality, the way we focus on self rather than world; yet it also does something more. It emphasizes the individual experience of history, the predicament of aloneness—what Freud calls the "curse of solitude"—that is the irreducible essence of existence, however much love, empathy, hatred, and other forms of relation draw us to others. The obelisks of time loom above us, taunting us to decode their inscrutable messages, but the mystery of our own self-consciousness surpasses theirs. Even as we understand the infinitude of the past, we demand that our own present moment's concerns take precedence. Hawthorne articulates here an understanding of human desire that anticipates one of the major precepts of psychoanalysis, as Octave Mannoni so succinctly summarized it: "I know very well, but even so. . . ." We know that in the face of time we mean next to nothing, but even so we value our time as distinctly crucial.

An individual is history. I would argue for this idea as the major thrust of Hawthorne's philosophical statement in these passages about Kenyon's survey of the past, that we can only process our own experience with any measure of success, and even this success will only ever be partial, delimited, narrow. Yet despite its obvious limitations, an individual's experience has a value equal to that of any other piece of evidence in the survey of human history; what one feels and thinks, what one desires, *makes* history; is, indeed, the historical. Those memories lying in ruins can only be memorialized in the mind of a person thinking and feeling in the present; nothing happens, in the past or in the future, except in the present; the past and the future only connote the boundaries of, the dark borders around, our present view.

Freud and Hawthorne share a view of the parity between individual and cultural history. One of the major and most familiar tenets of the work of Michel Foucault is that the concept of the individual subject has been deployed by "power" to control, conscript, and contain the minds and bodies of beings caught in the meshes of discursivity, and that psychoanalysis, far from a resistant position from which to critique these cultural workings, enables, facilitates, and precisely relies on this construction of the subject. Foucault's own work and Foucauldian criticism have offered one of the most unified and influential challenges to psychoanalytic theory. Given that the crucial contention within the Foucauldian view is its dispute with the construction of the subject and psychoanalysis's investment in it, it is interesting indeed to consider that the radicalism of both psychoanalysis and Hawthorne's psychological literature may lie precisely in their interest in the individual subject. Having attempted to demonstrate that historical and psychoanalytic questions and methodologies are, far from mutually exclusive, mutually illuminating; that Hawthorne's work foregrounds these overlaps and their stirring potentialities; and that narcissism, far from a moribund and deadened fixation on the self, is the key to desire and social relations as well as literary production, I turn, in conclusion, to the very tendency we have, as critics, to insist, even at this point, on the old philosophical law of noncontradiction. It is precisely in their contradictions, their irresolvable conflicts, their sense of the equal legitimacy of antithetical realities, that the enduring value of Hawthorne's and Freud's accounts of human experience lies.

NOTES

INTRODUCTION

1. In contrast to Hawthorne, Herman Melville has the mythic figure of Narcissus making an explicit appearance in the first chapter of *Moby-Dick, or The Whale*. The main source text for the Narcissus myth is Ovid's *The Metamorphoses,* one of the key classical texts for the European-American literary tradition; Hawthorne was familiar with the 1717 translation of the Ovidian Narcissus myth by Joseph Addison. In addition to Ovid's, the volume of mythology that Hawthorne specifically cited as a source for his two children's books of classical Greek mythology, *Anthon's Dictionary,* was published in 1841 and went through several editions. "Not once, however, in either his fiction or journals or letters did he ever mention Narcissus specifically, as did Herman Melville, or others of his era. Yet the presence of the deluded beautiful youth seems to haunt the subconscious world of the New England writer, providing much of his narrative structure and his characterizations," an assessment with which I am in agreement. See MaryHelen Cleverly Harmon's dissertation *The Mirror of Narcissus: Reflections and Refractions of the Classical Myth in the Short Fiction of Nathaniel Hawthorne* (Ph.D. diss., Florida State University, 1981), 27–28; 34; 37–38.

2. Sándor Ferenczi, *Further Contributions to the Theory and Technique of Psycho-Analysis* (1926; London: Hogarth, 1950), 365.

3. Jacques Lacan, "The Mirror-Stage as Formative of the Function of the I," in *Ecrits: A Selection*, trans. Alan Sheridan (New York: Norton, 1977), pp. 1–7. My interpretation of Lacan has been greatly influenced by Tim Dean in his superb *Beyond Sexuality* (Chicago: Chicago University Press, 2000), 37, 44, 46, especially. Dean is particularly useful to me as a rigorous queer theorist of Lacan. Dean places less emphasis, however, on the visual in Lacan's theories of the development of the ego, discussing the "model of the inverted bouquet" as an alternative to the mirror stage (46).

4. To offer an absurdly simplified summary: the other orders are the Symbolic and the Real. The Symbolic is associated with language, law, rationality, and is therefore the order of the father, whose name and law language enacts; it is through the symbolic that we are produced as "subjects." The Real is the unrepresentable, that outside or prior to the

symbolic, sometimes referred to as "the impossible"; it is the material of life that cannot be incorporated into the forms of signification, such as language.

5. Copjec, *Read My Desire: Lacan Against the Historicists* (Cambridge, MA: MIT Press, 1994), 37.

6. Copjec quoted in Edelman, *No Future: Queer Theory and the Death Drive* (Durham, NC: Duke University Press, 2004), 51.

7. Edelman, *No Future*, 52.

8. See chapter 7 of Castiglia's *Interior States: Institutional Consciousness and the Inner Life of Democracy in the Antebellum United States* (Durham, NC: Duke University Press, 2008). This is a rich and provocative discussion of Hawthorne's engagement with the disciplinary culture of interiority through which, in Castiglia's view, the antebellum United States organized the emotional, somatic, legal, and criminal dimensions of its social order. Given that my work, rather than striving for a "post-interiority," attempts to make sense of the lived experience of interiority that Castiglia critiques as a discursive phenomenon, I find his argument quite differently motivated from my own.

9. Joyce W. Warren, *The American Narcissus: Individualism and Women in Nineteenth-Century American Fiction* (New Brunswick, NJ: Rutgers University Press, 1984), 230.

10. Lillian R. Furst, *Romanticism in Perspective: A Comparative Study of Aspects of the Romantic Movement in England, France, and Germany* (London: Macmillan, 1969), 99.

11. Ibid., 64.

12. See Michael Davitt Bell, *The Problem of American Realism: Studies in the Cultural History of a Literary Idea* (Chicago: University of Chicago Press, 1993), 45. The issue of Hawthorne's sexuality overlaps with the sexual ambiguity of the Romantic male author. For a discussion of the linkages between homosexuality and the Romantic male genius, and especially the ways in which homosexuality emerges as pathological in studies of genius, see Andrew Elfenbein, *Romantic Genius: The Prehistory of a Homosexual Role* (New York: Columbia University Press, 1999).

13. Percy Bysshe Shelley, *Shelley's Poetry and Prose*, 2nd ed, ed. Donald H. Reiman and Neil Fraistat (New York: Norton, 2002), 503–4.

14. In contrast to Freud in the pathologizing dimensions of his theory of narcissism and the trends of American psychiatry, Heinz Kohut, in *The Analysis of the Self* and other writings, offered a radically normalized view of narcissism, which he saw as linked to poor early attachment but also as a commonplace, nonpathological aspect of emotional and psychosexual life.

15. Wilhelm Stekel, *Auto-Erotism: A Psychiatric Study of Onanism and Neurosis* (New York: Grove, 1950), 32.

16. Wilhelm Stekel writes, "I consider auto-eroticism, the expression proposed by Havelock Ellis, preferable to the antiquated and abused term, onanism." For Stekel, the psychic aspects of onanism are just as crucial an aspect as any other, hence his preference for "autoerotic." Ibid., 31.

17. Sylvester Graham's writings are exemplary of these concerns. To his horror, as he wrote in *A Lecture to Young Men*, Graham discovered that public school boys who masturbated even engaged in "criminal," "unnatural commerce with each other!" thus belying any critical notion that homosexual relations are never explicitly specified in nineteenth-century texts before the 1860s. Sylvester Graham, *A Lecture to Young Men* (1834; repr., New York: Arno, 1974), 43.

18. See Nissenbaum, *Sex, Diet, and Debility in Jacksonian America: Sylvester Graham and Health Reform* (1980; repr. Chicago: Dorsey, 1988).

19. See, especially, Sacvan Bercovitch, *The Office of The Scarlet Letter* (Baltimore: Johns Hopkins University Press, 1992); Jonathan Arac, "The Politics of *The Scarlet Letter*," in *Ideology and Classic American Literature,* ed. Sacvan Bercovitch and Myra Jehlen (New York: Cambridge University Press, 1986), 247–66; John Carlos Rowe, "Nathaniel Hawthorne and Transnationality," in *Hawthorne and the Real: Bicentennial Essays,* ed. Millicent Bell (Columbus: The Ohio State University Press, 2005), 88–106. Eric Cheyfitz chides Arac and Bercovitch for not going further in their critique of what Cheyfitz views as Hawthorne's "immoral passivity." See Eric Cheyfitz, "The Irresistibleness of Great Literature: Reconstructing Hawthorne's Politics," *American Literary History* 6, no. 3, Curriculum and Criticism (Autumn 1994): 539–58. I critique these ideological positions in my essay "Masculinist Theory and Romantic Authorship: Hawthorne, Politics, and Desire," *New Literary History* 39, no. 4 (Autumn 2008), 971–87.

20. T. Walter Herbert, *Sexual Violence and American Manhood* (Cambridge, MA: Harvard University Press, 2002), 40–41.

21. See in particular the introduction to Greven, *Men Beyond Desire: Manhood, Sex, and Violation in American Literature* (New York: Palgrave Macmillan, 2005).

22. Hofstadter, *Anti-Intellectualism in American Life* (1963; repr., New York: Vintage, 1999), 159.

23. Ibid, 157–59.

24. Ibid, 159.

25. Hawthorne joined in public celebrations of Jackson, much to the surprise of his sister Elizabeth. As Edwin Havilland Miller describes of Hawthorne, "One of his heroes was the greatest Democrat of his era, Andrew Jackson, who was scarcely tolerated or even mentioned in elite circles in Salem. Jackson, however, was in the tradition of the Hathornes: virile, energetic, and more than a little ruthless. When Jackson visited Salem in 1833 after his reelection Hawthorne walked to the outskirts of the town, in the words of his sister Elizabeth, 'to meet him, not to speak of him, only to look at him; and found only a few men and boys collected, not enough, without the assistance that he rendered, to welcome the General with good cheer.' Forty years later Elizabeth was still surprised: 'It is hard to fancy him doing such a thing as shouting.'" As Miller further observes: "Hawthorne's opinion remained fixed. In 1858 he insisted that Jackson 'was the greatest man we ever had; and his native strength, as well of intellect as of character, compelled every man to be his tool that came within his reach; and the cunninger the individual might be, it served only to make him the sharper tool.' He wished in a strange mismatching that 'it had been possible for Raphael to paint General Jackson.'" Miller, *Salem Is My Dwelling Place* (Iowa City: University of Iowa Press, 1991), 89.

26. Holland, *The Dynamics of Literary Response* (1968; New York: Norton, 1975), vii. I will admit to finding that Holland's work lacks bite. But one does occasionally come across a telling insight or analytic passage.

27. Coen, *Between Author and Reader: A Psychoanalytic Approach to Writing and Reading* (New York: Columbia University Press, 1994), 130.

28. Skura, *The Literary Use of the Psychoanalytic Process* (New Haven, CT: Yale University Press, 1981), 242.

CHAPTER 1

1. Robert Graves, vol. 1 of *The Greek Myths* (New York: Penguin, 1985), 287. I find

Graves's summary useful, but I should note that classicists have very little use for Graves's work, which has been discredited within the field.

2. Hélène Cixous, "Castration or Decapitation?" in *Contemporary Literary Criticism,* ed. Robert Con Davis and Robert Scheifler (1976; repr., New York: Longman, 1989), 488–90.

3. Steven Bruhm, *Reflecting Narcissus: A Queer Aesthetic* (Minneapolis: University of Minnesota Press, 2001), 15.

4. Béla Grunberger, *Narcissism: Psychoanalytic Essays,* trans. Joyce S. Diamanti (Madison, CT: International Universities Press, 1979), 108.

5. Ibid., 107–8.

6. Frederick Crews, *The Sins of the Fathers: Hawthorne's Psychological Themes* (1966; repr., Berkeley, CA: University of California Press, 1989), 282.

7. Laplanche and Pontalis, *The Language of Psycho-Analysis* (London: Karnac Books, 1988), 314.

8. Mark Edmunson, *Towards Reading Freud: Self-Creation in Milton, Wordsworth, Emerson, and Sigmund Freud* (Princeton, NJ: Princeton University Press, 1990), 56.

9. See, for example, Nancy F. Cott's essay, "On Men's History and Women's History," in *Meanings for Manhood: Constructions of Masculinity in Victorian America,* ed. Mark Christopher Carnes and Clyde Griffen (Chicago: University of Chicago Press, 1990), 209–13. Cott, providing a summary response to the collection, makes use of Freud's concept of repetition–compulsion to describe the patterns she finds to be recurrent in nineteenth-century masculinity as treated in the collection's essays.

10. R. Horacio Etchegoyen, "'On Narcissism': Text and Context," in *Freud's "On Narcissism: An Introduction,"* ed. Joseph Sandler et al. (New Haven, CT: Yale University Press, 1991), 54–75. Quoted passage on p. 56.

11. Janine Chasseguet-Smirgel, *The Ego-Ideal: A Psychoanalytic Essay on the Malady of the Ideal,* trans. Paul Barrows (1975; repr., New York: Norton, 1985), 232.

12. Jeremy Holmes, *Narcissism* (Cambridge: Icon Books, 2001), 7.

13. It is worth considering here the unsettled nature of the question of the difference between primary and secondary narcissism; from my perspective, the more we understand how frustratingly inconclusive Freud's essay on narcissism remains for many, the better, for it is precisely this inconclusiveness that makes fresh readings of the work possible and resists any normalizing, pathologizing application. As Ruth Leys puts it in her important study of trauma, Freud's concept of primary narcissism is "notoriously problematic." Discussing the incoherencies inherent in this concept, Leys discusses the preliminary definition of it offered by Laplanche and Pontsalis. They "describe primary narcissism as an 'early state in which the child [or ego] cathects its own self with the whole of its libido.' But as they make clear," Leys continues, "precisely the status of the ego is problematic in such a formulation. On the one hand, as a state in which the ego takes itself as its love-object, primary narcissism corresponds to the first emergence of a unified subject or ego. On the other hand, Freud also conceptualized primary narcissism as a primitive state of the infant that occurs prior to the formation of an ego, a state epitomized by life in the womb." In this view, primary narcissism is an "objectless state, implying no split between the subject and the external world. As Laplanche and Pontsalis comment . . . it is difficult to know just what is supposed to be cathected in primary narcissism thus conceived." Jean Laplanche and J. B. Pontalis, *The Language of Psycho-Analysis,* trans. Donald Nicholson-Smith (New York: Norton, 1974), quoted in Ruth Leys, *Trauma: A Genealogy* (Chicago: University of Chicago Press, 2000), 139.

14. Michael Warner offers a valuable critique of psychoanalytic denunciations of homosexuality as narcissistic, but to my mind his argument is deeply hampered by a reductionist view of Freud that does justice to his treatment neither of homosexuality nor of narcissism. The best overview I have found of the radicalism possible in psychoanalytic discussions of narcissism is Dean and Lane's introductory essay to *Homosexuality and Psychoanalysis*. Andrew Morrison collects significant contributions from leading thinkers such as Freud, Heinz Kohut (whose efforts to depathologize narcissism are distinct from many of those of the twentieth century), Otto Kernberg (most notable for his theory of the grandiose self and narcissistic rage), and the overlooked but deeply insightful Annie Reich (wife of the more famous Wilhelm) in his *Essential Papers on Narcissism*. Notably absent from Morrison is Jacques Lacan, whose writing on narcissism is extensive. In his essay "Homosexuality and the Problem of Otherness," Dean provides a helpful unpacking of Lacan's views. While Lacan considers narcissism pathogenic, writes Dean, it is "as a consequence not of homosexuality but, more generally, of the ego's delusional attachment to a mirage" (Tim Dean and Christopher Lane, eds., *Homosexuality and Psychoanalysis* [Chicago: University of Chicago Press, 2001], 127). See Bruhm and Kochhar-Lindgren for particularly interesting reinterpretations of narcissism: Bruhm calls attention to the homoeroticism of the myth, whereas Kochhar-Lindgren focuses on narcissism as an inability to recognize otherness.

15. All quotations from Freud will be taken from *The Standard Edition of the Complete Psychological Works of Sigmund Freud* (SE) and will be noted parenthetically in the text.

16. Etchegoyen. 66.

17. Jacques Lacan, *The Four Fundamental Concepts of Psychoanalysis*, trans. Alan Sheridan (New York: Norton, 1981), 102–3.

18. Kaja Silverman, *Male Subjectivity at the Margins* (New York: Routledge, 1992), 130; 146; 152. Tim Dean also stresses the importance of distinguishing "vision" from the "gaze." Dean critiques Lee Edelman's conflation, in his *Homographesis*, of vision and gaze. Tim Dean, *Beyond Sexuality* (Chicago: University of Chicago Press, 2000), 195n26. Henry Krips notes that the gaze is Lacan's name for "the structural distortions of the visual field, those that are not only seen but are also the source of a look turned back upon the viewer." Henry Krips, *Fetish: Erotics of the Gaze* (Ithaca, NY: Cornell University Press, 1999), 27.

19. Lacan, *The Four Fundamental Concepts of Psychoanalysis*, 84–85 (my emphasis).

CHAPTER 2

1. I want to thank Dr. David Diamond for kindly reading an early draft version of this chapter and generously sending me his responses, which I found to be valuable, challenging, and insightful. Dr. Diamond pointed out to me that Ilbrahim is keeping vigil at the scene of his father's death at the start of the story, suggesting a strong oedipal-paternal identification. This is not a dynamic that I focus on here, but I believe it is one that is worthy of further consideration.

2. For his discussion of the historical emergence of homosexuality in the latter half of the nineteenth century, a theory that has sometimes had the effect of creating a view of homosexuality as an invention datable only from this period forward, see in particular Michel Foucault's *The History of Sexuality*, vol. 1, trans. from the French by Robert Hurley (1988; New York: Vintage Books, 1990). A great deal of work done on both Foucault and the question of nineteenth-century sexual history over the past decade has significantly enlarged our understanding of the latter and usefully clarified the claims of the former.

3. Richard C. Friedman and Jennifer I. Downey, *Sexual Orientation and Psychodynamic Psychotherapy: Sexual Science and Clinical Practice* (New York: Columbia University Press, 2002), 97.

4. Relevant for our study, Friedman and Downey do discuss the mother–child relationship to a certain degree.

5. It should be clearly stated that my project proceeds from the theoretical, rather than clinical, dimensions of psychoanalysis, and that any attempt to rethink narcissism has to take into account that pathological forms of it do indeed exist in severe mental illness, such as schizophrenia and other forms of psychosis. Less severely, but nevertheless painfully, the narcissism of intensely self-involved persons for whom an obsessive interest in the self damagingly limits their emotional lives and intersubjective relationships must be understood as problematic, as a barrier between satisfying relationships with self and other.

6. Michael Warner, "Homo-Narcissism: Or, Heterosexuality," in *Engendering Men: The Question of Male Feminist Criticism*, ed. Joseph A. Boone and Michael Cadden (New York: Routledge, 1990), 190–207. My discussion of Warner here echoes that in chapter 1 of my book *Manhood in Hollywood from Bush to Bush* (Austin: University of Texas Press, 2009).

7. Ibid., 200.

8. Ibid., 202.

9. Ibid., 206.

10. Freud wrote *Three Essays on the Theory of Sexuality* in 1905 but kept adding to it until 1924. This footnote was added by Freud in 1910.

11. Socarides was a pioneer in the movement to "cure" homosexuality through psychiatry. As Ronald Bayer discusses, Socarides was to become, "in the late 1960s and early 1970s, a leading and forceful proponent of the view that homosexuality represented a profound psychopathology." In Socarides' own words, "Homosexuality is based on fear of the mother, the aggressive attack against the father, and is filled with aggression, destruction and self-deceit. It is a masquerade of life in which certain psychic energies are neutralized and held in a somewhat quiescent state. However, the unconscious manifestations of hate, destructiveness, incest and fear are always threatening to break through." See Ronald Bayer, *Homosexuality and American Psychiatry: The Politics of Diagnosis* (Princeton, NJ: Princeton University Press, 1987), 34–38. Socarides quoted in Bayer, 34.

12. Jonathan Dollimore, *Sexual Dissidence: Augustine to Wilde, Freud to Foucault* (New York: Oxford University Press, 1991), 174.

13. Ibid., 181.

14. Freud's difficult treatment of the Oedipal complex for girls remains deeply controversial. Without discounting the problems of Freud's sexism, I would argue that we can say that he exposes the effects of misogyny at the same time as he constructs them. I discuss the uses that can be made of Freud's theories of women at greater length in chapter 1 of my book *Representations of Femininity in American Genre Cinema: The Woman's Film, Film Noir, and Modern Horror* (New York: Palgrave Macmillan, 2011).

15. Judith Butler, *Gender Trouble: Feminism and the Subversion of Identity* (New York: Routledge, 1990), 64.

16. These innovative projects focus on the intersections of melancholia, race, class, gender, and queer desire. See, especially, Douglas Crimp, *Melancholia and Moralism: Essays on AIDS and Queer Politics* (Cambridge, MA: MIT Press, 2001); Anne Anlin Cheng, *The Melancholy of Race: Psychoanalysis, Assimilation, and Hidden Grief* (New York: Oxford University Press, 2001); *Loss: The Politics of Mourning*, ed. David L. Eng and David Kazanjian (Berkeley and Los Angeles: University of California Press, 2003) [the introductory essay

provides an especially helpful updating, for queer theory purposes, of Freudian melancholia theory]; Ann Cvetkovich, *An Archive of Feelings: Trauma, Sexuality, and Lesbian Public Cultures* (Durham, NC: Duke University Press, 2003); Dana Luciano, *Arranging Grief: Sacred Time and the Body in Nineteenth-Century America* (New York: New York University Press, 2007). Luciano's extensively engages with Freud's theories of "mourning and melancholia."

17. Freud often discusses the ways in which the Oedipus complex goes awry for those who emerge as heterosexually oriented. The masochistic male who emerges as heterosexual doubles the homosexual male in his complex maneuvers to reimagine, innovate, and thwart the normative course of the Oedipus complex; though a sustained discussion of this point exceeds the scope of this chapter, the valences that exist between male heterosexual masochism and male homosexual narcissism—both of which processes privilege the *maternal* rather than paternal role in the Oedipus complex—demand a thorough investigation. Indeed, one could make the case that it is Freud's theory of heterosexual male masochism, which involves identification with the mother, that is even more germane to Hawthorne. Certainly, there are masochistic elements in Hawthorne's representation of masculinity, but to my mind the thematization of narcissism in Freud's theory of male homosexuality, when linked to identification with the mother, sheds more light on Hawthorne's work. As Leland S. Person persuasively argues in his review essay "Middlesex: What Men Like in Men," *American Literary History* 17, no. 4 (2005): 753–64, the varieties of male desire for other males, however we define this desire, is wide-ranging. The male-identified homoeroticism in Hawthorne's work, suggested by his idolization of the rough-hewn President Andrew Jackson, would be a compelling subject for future study.

18. Leo Bersani, "Genital Chastity," in *Homosexuality and Psychoanalysis*, ed. Tim Dean and Christopher Lane (Chicago: University of Chicago Press, 2001), 365.

19. Jacques Lacan, "The Mirror Stage," in *Ecrits: A Selection*, trans. Alan Sheridan (New York: Norton, 1977). Lacan's theory evolved over time; he gave the first versions of this paper in 1936.

20. Tim Dean, *Beyond Sexuality* (Chicago: University of Chicago Press, 2000), 198.

21. Jean Laplanche, et al., *Jean Laplanche: Seduction, Translation and the Drives* , trans. Martin Stanton, ed. John Fletcher and Martin Stanton (London: Institute of Contemporary Arts, 1992), 93–120.

22. Bersani, "Genital Chastity," 356.

23. Steven Angelides, "Historicizing Affect, Psychoanalyzing History: Pedophilia and the Discourse of Child Sexuality," *Journal of Homosexuality* 46, no. 1/2 (2003): 79–109.

24. Tim Dean and Christopher Lane, eds., *Homosexuality and Psychoanalysis* (Chicago: University of Chicago Press, 2001), 123.

25. Ibid., 130.

26. Marcia Ian, *Remembering the Phallic Mother: Psychoanalysis, Modernism, and the Fetish* (Ithaca, NY: Cornell University Press, 1993), 21.

27. Freud's Wolf-Man case study, *From the History of an Infantile Neurosis,* was written in the year 1914, but did not appear in print until 1918.

28. Kenneth Lewes, *The Psychoanalytic Theory of Male Homosexuality* (New York: Simon and Schuster, 1988), 82.

29. Frederick Crews, *The Sins of the Fathers: Hawthorne's Psychological Themes* (1966; repr., Berkeley: University of California Press, 1989), 67–72. Masochism in Hawthorne is far from an unimportant issue, but Crews's argument is characteristic of his frequently highly conventional uses of Freud, which at times blunts the effectiveness of his often insightful treatments of Hawthorne. A more thorough and complex treatment of Freud's theory of

masochism would need to be undertaken for real clarity about the issue's development in Hawthorne to be gained.

30. All quotes from Hawthorne are taken from the *Centenary Edition* of Hawthorne's works, and all volume and page numbers will be noted parenthetically in the text.

31. For Hawthorne's revisions to "The Gentle Boy," see *The Centenary Edition of the Works of Nathaniel Hawthorne*, vol. 9, ed. William Charvat et al. (Columbus: The Ohio State University Press, 1962), 613–19.

32. Brenda Wineapple, *Hawthorne*, 16.

33. See, especially, Mitchell's *Siblings: Sex and Violence* (Polity, 2004).

34. Wineapple, *Hawthorne: A Life* (New York: Knopf, 2003), 21.

35. I discuss these issues at length in the introduction and in chapter 2, *Men Beyond Desire*, passim.

36. Henry James, *Hawthorne* (1879; repr., New York: Cornell University Press, 1997), 54–55.

37. Wineapple, *Hawthorne*, 31; 15.

38. Millicent Bell, introduction to *Hawthorne's Major Tales*, ed. Millicent Bell (New York: Cambridge University Press, 1993), 15.

39. Lewes, *Psychoanalytic*, 84.

40. Mary Ayers, *Mother–Infant Attachment and Psychoanalysis: The Eyes of Shame* (New York: Brunner-Routledge, 2003), 76–77.

CHAPTER 3

1. My view of Freud has been influenced by Leo Bersani, one of Freud's most radical and galvanizing interpreters, especially in a queer theory context. See especially Bersani's *The Freudian Body* (New York: Columbia University Press, 1986). For a discussion in which I establish my disagreements with Bersani, particularly his views on queer masochism, see Greven, *Manhood in Hollywood from Bush to Bush* (Austin: University of Texas Press, 2009).

2. There is much to admire in Berlant's invaluable and still-provocative reading. I also feel that it is consistently a distortion of Hawthorne's personal literary investments, especially in terms of his identification with Hester Prynne. See Lauren Berlant, *The Anatomy of National Fantasy: Hawthorne, Utopia, and Everyday Life* (Chicago: University of Chicago Press, 1991).

3. The Wood of 1989 can now write of Hitchcock in ways that reflected a deepening and political expansion of Freudian method rather than an abrasive, near-hysterical rejection of it, as his treatment of Hitchcock's 1956 remake of his own 1930s version of *The Man Who Knew Too Much* evinces: "The two great liberating screams of *The Man Who Knew Too Much* (Doris Day's in the Albert Hall, Brenda de Banzie's 'answering' scream in the embassy) must be read on one level," argues Wood, "as the protests of women against masculinist politics and the cruelty and violence that issue from it." Robin Wood, *Hitchcock's Films Revisited* (1989; repr., New York: Columbia University Press, 2002), 361.

4. For a far sounder critique of these matters, see Eugene Goodheart, *The Reign of Ideology* (New York: Columbia University Press, 1996).

5. Frederick Crews, *The Sins of the Fathers: Hawthorne's Psychological Themes* (1966; repr., Berkeley: University of California Press, 1989), 285.

6. Rohy, *Anachronism and Its Others: Sexuality, Race, and Temporality* (Albany: State University of New York Press, 2010), 128–29.

7. Marcia Ian, *Remembering the Phallic Mother: Psychoanalysis, Modernism, and the Fetish* (Ithaca, NY: Cornell University Press, 1993), 8.

8. Crews wrote disdainfully in 1966 of James K. Folsom's book *Man's Accidents and God's Purposes: Multiplicity in Hawthorne's Fiction* (New Haven, CT: Yale University Press, 1963): "concluding regretfully that Hawthorne considers Oneness inscrutable," Folsom "claims that the concept of 'multiplicity' governs the tales and romances." But Crews seems to share Folsom's view even as he dismisses it: Hawthorne "was aware that in exposing our common nature he was drawing largely on his own nature"; "uneasy with the self-revelatory aspect of his work," Hawthorne with "one arm strikes a pose of cold dignity and holds us at bay, but with the other beckons us forward into the cavern of his deepest soul." Crews, *Sins*, 9; 11–12.

9. "Roger Malvin's Burial" was first published separately in 1832 and was later included in the collection *Mosses from an Old Manse* (1846).

10. One could make the case that the young man / old man split is also fundamental to Edgar Allan Poe's work—one immediately thinks of tales such as "The Man of the Crowd," in which the narrator insatiably follows around an old man with an insatiable desire for crowds, and of "The Tell-Tale Heart," in which the narrator kills an old man whose titular heartbeat drives him mad. Homoerotic valences charge these as well as other Poe works with a disturbing intensity, disturbing because the homoeroticism is indistinguishable—indeed, constitutive of—a deep psychic dislocation. Herman Melville's work is rife with split masculinities. His fictional worlds—especially in his sea fiction but not only there—are dominated by older men who prey on younger men, a form of dominance with often violent sexual implications, that is, implications of real sexual violence.

11. "She heard him not. With one wild shriek, that seemed to force its way from the sufferer's inmost soul, she sank insensible by the side of her dead boy. At that moment, the withered topmost bough of the oak loosened itself, in the stilly air, and fell in soft, light fragments upon the rock, upon the leaves, upon Reuben, upon his wife and child, and upon Roger Malvin's bones. Then Reuben's heart was stricken, and the tears gushed out like water from a rock. The vow that wounded youth had made, the blighted man had come to redeem. His sin was expiated, the curse gone from him; and, in the hour, when he had shed blood dearer to him than his own, a prayer, the first for years, went up to Heaven from the lips of Reuben Bourne" (10: 360).

12. Crews, *Sins*, 86–87.

13. Gray Kochhar-Lindgren, *Narcissus Transformed: The Textual Subject in Psychoanalysis and Literature* (University Park: Pennsylvania State University Press, 1993), 37–38.

14. Fascinatingly, Cyrus's own name-origins seem programmatic of his function in the story. As Herodotus tells Cyrus's story, he is, like Oedipus, another one of those legendary royal children condemned to death who manage to survive (through the kindly intervention of a nonnoble person, such as a shepherd, who rescues and adopts them) and later reclaim their noble ancestry. See Herodotus, Book 1 of *The Histories* (New York: Penguin, 1972), 85–90.

15. Judith Butler, *Gender Trouble: Feminism and the Subversion of Identity* (New York: Routledge, 1990), 64. Though space limitations preclude a discussion of them here, several innovative projects on the intersections of melancholia, race, and queer desire have been undertaken in the wake of Butler's retooled Freudian paradigms, and the fullest treatment of these themes in Hawthorne would have to take them into account. See note 16 of the previous chapter.

16. Bruhm treats Coleridge's 1802 poem "The Picture; or The Lover's Resolution" as a

prime example of Romantic narcissism. The speaker of this poem, Bruhm argues, "holds a desiring male imago as the central phantasm of the poem." "As the speaker falls into the image of youth at the end of the poem, and the youth is absorbed by the speaker (and then, both collapse into the image of the boy in the picture, whose desire for the m/other they imitate), we see the act of identity and identification that this poem is really about." See Steven Bruhm, *Reflecting Narcissus: A Queer Aesthetic* (Minneapolis: University of Minnesota Press, 2001), 30–38; Bruhm references Butler's *Bodies That Matter: On the Discursive Limits of "Sex"* (New York: Routledge, 1993).

17. Kochhar-Lindgren, *Narcissus Transformed,* 121. I admire this theorist's formulations greatly, but I should add that he sometimes too uncritically pathologizes Narcissus for his homoerotic desire to reproduce a blissful heterosexuality within his self-desire.

18. Michael J. Colacurcio, *The Province of Piety: Moral History in Hawthorne's Early Tales* (Durham, NC: Duke University Press, 1995), 144.

19. Ibid., 153.

20. Crews, *Sins,* 74–75.

21. As Thompson writes, "The stranger is, not Hawthorne, but a symbolic figuration of, a substitute agent for, a Hawthorne: that is, an *author figure,* symbolically present in the narrative." The transformation of self into figure has decisive repercussions for the narcissistic gaze, in which the various possibilities for seeing and being seen are constantly explored and negotiated. Turning oneself into a figure—especially here, the authorial figure of the stranger who can watch Robin, another version of the authorial self, being seen as he sees—is a strategy of control of the visual field. G. R. Thompson, *The Art of Authorial Presence: Hawthorne's Provincial Tales* (Durham, NC: Duke University Press, 1993), 156.

22. Leo Bersani, "Genital Chastity," *Homosexuality and Psychoanalysis,* ed. Tim Dean and Christopher Lane (Chicago: University of Chicago Press, 2001), 365.

23. Slavoj Žižek, "'I Hear You with My Eyes'; or, The Invisible Master," in *Gaze and Voice as Love Objects,* ed. Renata Salecl and Slavoj Žižek, (Durham, NC: Duke University Press, 1996), 94.

24. To be sure, vision is not the only sense thematized in the tale. The story's concomitant obsession with the voice demands attention that I do not have the space to elaborate upon here. But to make a brief note of the point, the story is governed by images of the aural/oral, especially the riotous, sybaritic, barbaric laughter that frequently erupts, evoking the Bakhtinian theories of the carnivalesque and the grotesque. This raucous and derisive laughter anticipates the terrible, demonic laughter of the damned Ethan Brand. Slyly, smugly, and coyly, the stranger asks Robin if multiple voices can occur as well as faces (226). In this story, the voice shields the eye; or rather, the voice *is* the eye, coming at Robin from all sides and no less entrapping, enclosing, and imprisoning than the gaze.

Robin's visual face-off with aggrieved Molineux perpetuates the pattern of seeing / being seen that structures the story: Molineux stares back at Robin staring at him, even as the "lantern-bearer" "drowsily" enjoys "the lad's amazement" and that "saucy eye" again "meets his" (228). All the old gazers gather round, having never gone away—the innkeeper, the periwigged old citizen hemming and hawing, the derisive barbers, the guests of the inn, "and all who made sport of him that night," all present, all watching Robin watch his kinsman writhe, all joining in with him, in a defensive denial of rapacious visual desire through raucous mass-laughter (228). I would argue that the shared laughter strategically distracts us from the profound desire to look that engulfs each figure in the story, and in which Robin engulfs his own desire to look.

25. Otto Rank, *The Double: A Psychoanalytic Study,* trans. Harry Tucker, Jr. (Chapel Hill: University of North Carolina Press, 1971), 74; 85.
26. Bruhm, *Reflecting Narcissus,* 44.
27. Bingham, *Acting Male: Masculinities in the Films of James Stewart, Jack Nicholson, and Clint Eastwood* (New Brunswick, NJ: Rutgers University Press, 1994), 214–15.
28. Clark Davis, *Hawthorne's Shyness: Ethics, Politics, and the Question of Engagement* (Baltimore: Johns Hopkins University Press, 2005), 56.

CHAPTER 4

1. Leland S. Person, "A Man for the Whole Country: Marketing Masculinity in the Pierce Biography," *The Nathaniel Hawthorne Review* 35, no. 1 (2009): 4.
2. Ibid.
3. Ibid., 5–6.
4. For a study of Byron's sexuality in the context of the Romantic era, see Louis Crompton's excellent book *Byron and Greek Love: Homophobia in 19th-Century England* (Berkeley: University of California Press, 1985), passim; for a study of narcissism in Byron's poetry, see Steven Bruhm, *Reflecting Narcissus: A Queer Aesthetic* (Minneapolis: University of Minnesota Press, 2001), 20–53. Also relevant is Nathaniel Brown's book *Sexuality and Feminism in Shelley* (Cambridge, MA: Harvard University Press, 1979).
5. Julian Hawthorne, *Nathaniel Hawthorne and His Wife: A Biography,* vol. 1 (1884; Boston: Houghton Mifflin, 1892), 120–21.
6. The son's rapt account of the father's beauty alerts us to the narcissism inherent within oedipal relations. Julian becomes one of the men in Hawthorne's fiction who contemplates the beauty of another man (Rappaccini and the younger Giovanni, Chillingworth and Dimmesdale)—albeit here, in life, it is the younger man who contemplates the older, indeed, the dead, man. But younger only in a relative sense—Julian, who was born in 1846, was thirty-eight years old when *Nathaniel Hawthorne and His Wife* was published.
7. Gloria Erlich, *Family Themes and Hawthorne's Fiction: The Tenacious Web* (New Brunswick, NJ: Rutgers University Press, 1984), 124.
8. For a discussion of the calumniation of effeminacy in Jacksonian America and the treatment of male sexuality in the literature of the time, see Greven, *Men Beyond Desire: Manhood, Sex, and Violation in American Literature* (New York: Palgrave Macmillan, 2005).
9. Horatio Bridge, *Personal Recollections of Nathaniel Hawthorne* (1893; Honolulu: University Press of the Pacific, 2004), 4.
10. Hawthorne, *The Blithedale Romance* (New York: Norton, 2010).
11. Sedgwick quoted in ibid., 200.
12. In psychoanalytic terms, Hawthorne's depiction of male beauty could be called a compromise formation. A compromise formation occurs when the psychic agencies at our disposal, such as the id, ego, superego, confront a split or conflict between what we desire and what has been prohibited from us and work within the confines of reality to produce something like a workable fantasy that a conscious mind can tolerate. Male beauty in Hawthorne points to a desire for an image of male beauty—a desire that we can understand as autoerotic, homoerotic, or both—and a painful apprehension of the terrible repercussions of having this beauty perceived. He allows himself to inhabit this beauty while also registering its dangers and the phobic responses it generates.

13. Shadi Bartsch, *The Mirror of the Self: Sexuality, Self-Knowledge, and the Gaze in the Early Roman Empire* (Chicago: University of Chicago Press, 2006), 31.

14. Thaïs E. Morgan, *Men Writing the Feminine: Literature, Theory, and the Question of Genders* (Albany: State University of New York Press, 1994), 5.

15. Sarah Rose Cole, "Aristocrat in the Mirror," *Nineteenth-Century Literature* 61 (2006): 147.

16. Ibid., 161.

17. Though it is not my focus here, the issue of class in Hawthorne has been underexplored and would make for a resonant complement, I think, to this analysis.

18. Whereas Plato argues that the mutual gaze of lovers leads to self-knowledge, his "trio of eros, self-speculation, and philosophical self-knowledge becomes diluted in Seneca in particular. In Seneca's work the erotic force of gazing at self provides an impediment to self-knowledge." Bartsch, *Mirror of the Self,* 72. A fascinating discrete study could be done of the correspondences between Hawthorne and the ancient writings on these matters.

19. Shernaz Mollinger, "On Hawthorne, Emerson and Narcissism," *Psychoanalytic Review* 70, no. 4 (Winter 1983): 580.

20. Tompkins points out—in a derisive gesture meant to jab at critics who venerate Hawthorne's brooding, darkly themed work—that nineteenth-century critics valorized Hawthorne stories such as "Little Annie's Ramble," "Sights from a Steeple," and "A Rill from the Town Pump," not stories such as "The Minister's Black Veil" (10–11). Jane Tompkins, *Sensational Designs: The Cultural Work of American Fiction, 1790–1860* (Durham, NC: Duke University Press, 1986), 9; 122.

21. Rita K. Gollin, *Portraits of Nathaniel Hawthorne: An Iconography* (DeKalb: Northern Illinois University Press, 1983), 2.

22. Bridge, *Personal Recollections of Nathaniel Hawthorne,* 5.

23. T. Walter Herbert, "Hawthorne and American Masculinity," in *The Cambridge Companion to Nathaniel Hawthorne,* ed. Richard Millington (New York: Cambridge University Press, 2004), 60–78, quoted passage from p. 74. See also Herbert's *Sexual Violence and American Manhood* (Cambridge, MA: Harvard University Press, 2002). Though I admire *Sexual Violence,* I actually find Herbert's analysis of Hawthorne and masculinity sharper in his *Companion* essay; his chapter on *The Scarlet Letter* in the 2002 book reads the Dimmesdale and Chillingworth relationship as a metaphor for male–female relationships and misogyny, which I find blunts the considerable issues involved in Hawthorne's depiction of a bad *male* marriage.

24. Many Nussbaum works speak to these issues, but see, for example, *Hiding from Humanity: Disgust, Shame, and the Law* (Princeton, NJ: Princeton University Press, 2004); *Frontiers of Justice: Disability, Nationality, Species Membership (The Tanner Lectures on Human Values)* (Cambridge: Belknap, 2007).

25. "As Hawthorne drew on his readings in seventeenth- and eighteenth-century American history, he developed the strong pacifism that served as the foundation of his political thought. Although this pacifism wavered at times . . . it nevertheless served as the basic and consistent principle by which he implicitly judged the actions of individuals and nations." See Larry Reynolds, *Devils and Rebels: The Making of Hawthorne's Damned Politics* (Ann Arbor: University of Michigan Press, 2008), 19.

26. Léon Wurmser, *The Mask of Shame* (Baltimore: Johns Hopkins University Press, 1981), 147.

27. As Charles J. Rzepka continues, for Romantic authors, "the self that is engaged in direct confrontation is, on the one hand, individuated and affirmed as real thereby, but

on the other is nearly always felt to be taken away from itself by the eye of the person confronted, especially if that person is unsympathetic or a stranger." Hawthorne's entire body of work thematizes these conflicts. See Rzepka, *The Self as Mind: Vision and Identity in Wordsworth, Coleridge, and Keats* (Cambridge, MA: Harvard University Press, 1986), 27.

28. Joseph Adamson, "Guardian of the 'Inmost Me': Hawthorne and Shame," in *Scenes of Shame: Psychoanalysis, Shame, and Writing*, ed. Joseph Adamson and Hilary Clark (Albany: State University Press of New York, 1999), 73.

29. Attesting to the proliferation of studies of shame in recent years, Morrison wrote another (much more populist) book and edited a collection of essays on the subject, while Eve Kosofsky Sedgwick presented a new edition of Silvan Tompkins's important theories of the concept. The most interesting aspect of the growth of shame studies is its implicit reversal of the emphasis on phallic aggression in earlier Freud-focused discussions. It should be noted as well that David Halperin and Valerie Traub have edited a collection called *Gay Shame* (Chicago: University of Chicago Press, 2009). The volume collects papers from the controversy-filled conference by that name that the editors organized at the University of Michigan in Ann Arbor on March 27–29, 2003.

30. Andrew Morrison, *Shame: The Underside of Narcissism* (Hillsdale, NJ: Analytic, 1989), 65.

31. Ibid., 66.

32. Wurmser, *Mask of Shame*, 160.

33. Ibid., 161.

34. David W. Allen, *The Fear of Looking: Or, Scopophilic-Exhibitionistic Conflicts* (Charlottesville: University Press of Virginia, 1974), 118.

35. Ibid.

36. As Bridge notes, "Soon after graduation [from Bowdoin] we agreed to correspond regularly at stated periods, and we selected new signatures for our letters. Hawthorne chose that of 'Oberon,'" while Bridge (not being a Romantic artist, evidently) chose the more prosaic name "Edward" (55–56). Bridge debunks the idea that Oberon was Hawthorne's college nickname or that "his beauty" had anything to do with the name: "In a letter of Miss Peabody, quoted by Mr. Conway, it is stated that 'his classmates called Hawthorne 'Oberon the Fairy' on account of his beauty, and because he improvised tales.' It seems a pity to spoil so poetic a fancy; but, if truthful narrative is required, the cold facts are these," i.e., that Oberon was a post-college signature (55). Bridge does not, however, dispute the idea that the real-life Hawthorne was beautiful.

37. J. Hillis Miller, *Hawthorne and History: Defacing It* (Cambridge: Basil Blackwell, 1991), 97.

38. Ibid., 124.

39. "The narrator of 'The Minister's Black Veil,'" writes Richard Millington, "notes that Hooper's sartorial orientalism makes him a peculiarly effective clergyman: 'Strangers came long distances to attend service at his church, with the mere idle purpose of gazing at his figure, because it was forbidden them to behold his face' (9: 49). Hooper's strategy has been to make himself a piece of art, a 'figure' instead of a 'face.'" Millington notes that this strategy's one obvious benefit is that it does wonders for Hooper's career. Another obvious benefit is that it allows Hooper (and Hawthorne) to maintain some degree of control over the visual field in which Hooper is an object. Richard H. Millington, *Practicing Romance: Narrative Form and Cultural Engagement in Hawthorne's Fiction* (Princeton, NJ: Princeton University Press, 1991), 30.

40. For Michael T. Gilmore, the title of whose book *Surface and Depth: The Quest for Legibility in American Culture* (New York: Oxford University Press, 2006) bespeaks its relevance to a study of narcissism, *The Scarlet Letter* is a key text in the American quest for legibility, which Hawthorne treats with appositely contradictory impulses because he "at once shares and recoils from the [American] demand for openness" (80). Hawthorne can barely hide his revulsion against the stocks, "a penal technology that immobilizes the culprit before 'the public gaze' and forbids him 'to hide his face for shame.'" (81). Hawthorne "craves truthfulness without" this "pitiless exposure"; he wants "the balm of self-disclosure in a context secure from the 'public gaze.'" (83). Gilmore reads Dimmesdale's ultimate "self-erasure" as an attempt to convert "abasement into narcissistic falsehood" (85). I would place a somewhat different emphasis on what Hawthorne creates here—not narcissism as flight from shame but, instead, an atmosphere of shame in a state of shockingly public exposure that is itself a mediation of essentially narcissistic desire to see the self and control the ways in which the self is seen by others—the shame is the symptom of a fatally conflicted narcissism.

41. As Colacurcio writes, "On this point Jonathan Edwards and Edgar Poe would be in perfect agreement: the appropriate result of a truthful look might be fairly described as 'horror'; the blackness within the self would correspond much more nearly to the darkness outside the wedding into which Hooper rushes ('For the Earth, too, had on her Black Veil') rather than the cheery light inside the [wedding] hall." Michael J. Colacurcio, *The Province of Piety: Moral History in Hawthorne's Early Tales* (Durham, NC: Duke University Press, 1995), 340.

42. Noting that Hooper spills his wine at the wedding, Colacurcio reads this moment as an allegorical evocation of the dread antebellum figure of the onanist. Frederick Crews reads "sexual ambivalence" in figures such as Hooper and Young Goodman Brown: "It is possible that Hooper, who like Goodman Brown is obliged to confront the sexual aspects of womanhood, shares Brown's fears and has hit upon a means of forestalling their realization in marriage. His literal wearing of a veil, like Brown's figurative removal of it to leer at the horrid sexuality underneath, acts as a defense against normal adult love." Immediately upon making these suggestive though heterosexist observations, Crews retreats from their implications ("I do not care to lay very much stress on indications of sexual squeamishness in Hooper") yet also rightly observes that the rumors of a sexual scandal involving Hooper and the young dead woman who is said to shudder when he peers at her corpse are just that, rumors, started by the townspeople and, in a review of *Twice-Told Tales,* Edgar Allan Poe, wearing his critic's hardhat. Crews, *The Sins of the Fathers: Hawthorne's Psychological Themes* (1966; repr., Berkeley: University of California Press, 1989), 109–10.

43. Harold Bloom, *The Western Canon: The Books and School of the Ages,* 1st ed. (New York: Riverhead Trade, 1995), 365.

44. See Greven, *Men Beyond Desire,* chapter 2, for a discussion of male blight in *Fanshawe.*

45. In part such a rendering of male vision stems from Hawthorne's Gothic framework. "Gothic villains," Benjamin Franklin Fisher writes in an excellent study of Poe's "renovations" of the Gothic, "are possessed of a startlingly piercing eye, which functions symbolically in phallic terms in its ability to penetrate its victims' innermost secrets." Fisher, "Poe and the Gothic Tradition," in *The Cambridge Companion to Edgar Allan Poe,* ed. Kevin J. Hayes (New York: Oxford University Press, 2002), 72–91, quote from p. 76. Many of the same themes in Hawthorne powerfully animate Poe's work as well, to say the least.

CHAPTER 5

1. Berkeley Kaite, *Pornography and Difference* (Bloomington: Indiana University Press, 1995), 81–82.

2. What Richard Gray discovers in Faulkner's novels can also be said of Hawthorne's: "voyeurism and narcissism frequently elide, because what the solitary seer sees is a reflection of himself, the imperatives of his own gaze." Richard Gray, *The Life of William Faulkner: A Critical Biography* (Cambridge, MA: Blackwell, 1996), 173.

3. See Laura Mulvey, "Visual Pleasure and Narrative Cinema," *Screen* 16, no. 3 (1975): 6–18, repr. in *Visual and Other Pleasures* (Bloomington: Indiana University Press, 1989), 14–27; "Afterthoughts on 'Visual Pleasure and Narrative Cinema' Inspired by King Vidor's *Duel in the Sun*," *Framework* 15/16/17 (1981), repr. in *Visual and Other Pleasures*, 29–38. I do not mean to denigrate Mulvey's bold and revolutionary work; as much as anything, I am critiquing its continued hold on critical accounts of the gaze. "Visual Pleasure and Narrative Cinema" was a very early Mulvey article, and her *own* views have evolved over time, though this evolution has not resolved their controversial nature. For a discussion of feminism's shifting responses to Mulvey, see Susan White's excellent essay "*Vertigo* and Problems of Knowledge in Feminist Film Theory," in *Alfred Hitchcock: Centenary Essays*, ed. Richard Allen and S. Ichii-Gonzales (London: BFI, 1999), 278–98. I discuss the shifts in Mulvey's thinking and in critical responses to her in chapter 1 of my book *Manhood in Hollywood from Bush to Bush*.

4. "Although the gaze might be said to be 'the presence of others as such,' it is by no means coterminous with any individual viewer, or group of viewers. It issues 'from all sides,' whereas the eye '[sees] only from one point.'" In her delineation of Lacan's theory of the gaze, Kaja Silverman differentiates the eye or the "look" from the gaze, making the analogy that the eye and the gaze are, in psychoanalytic theory, as distinct as penis and phallus. Drawing from Lacan, Silverman elaborates that, far from lending an air of mastery to the subject, voyeurism renders the looking subject "subordinated to the gaze," disturbed and overwhelmed, and overcome by shame. In Lacanian gaze theory, "the possibility of separating vision from the image" is called "radically into question," and along with it the presumed "position of detached mastery" of the voyeuristic subject. This clarification of Lacanian gaze theory has bold implications for feminist film theory, whose proper interrogation of the male look has not, at times, "always been pushed far enough. We have at times assumed that dominant cinema's scopic regime could be overturned by 'giving' women the gaze, rather than by exposing the impossibility of anyone ever owning that visual agency, or of him or herself escaping specularity." See Kaja Silverman, *Male Subjectivity at the Margins* (New York: Routledge, 1992), 130; 146; 152. This view of the voyeuristic subject not as victim but as vulnerable and fragile insofar as he can never achieve the sense of mastery that fantasmatically impels his very voyeuristic project informs my reading of *The Blithedale Romance*.

5. See Suzanne R. Stewart, *Sublime Surrender: Male Masochism at the Fin-de-Siècle* (Ithaca, NY: Cornell University Press, 1998), 10. In this study, Stewart discusses the discourse of the masochistic male in the German-speaking world between 1870 and 1940. Male masochism, she suggests, was a rhetorical strategy through which men asserted their cultural and political authority paradoxically by embracing the notion that they were (and always had been) wounded and suffering.

6. Baym specifically refers to the work of critics such as Robert K. Martin, Scott Derrick, David Leverenz, and Karen L. Kilcup. See her chapter "Revisiting Hawthorne's Femi-

nism," in *Hawthorne and the Real: Bicentennial Essays,* ed. Millicent Bell (Columbus: The Ohio State University Press, 2005), 111.

7. Brown, *Domestic Individualism: Imagining Self in Nineteenth-Century America* (Berkeley: University of California Press, 1990), 131–32.

8. The bachelor has been established as a highly interesting figure in contemporary critical work. In her excellent study *Bachelors, Manhood, and the Novel, 1850–1925,* Katherine V. Snyder writes, "I like to think of the bachelor as the figure who stands in the doorway, looking in from the outside and also looking out from within" (17). Examining first-person bachelor narrators, Snyder argues that "bachelor trouble was gender trouble. While they were often seen as violating gender norms, bachelors were sometimes contradictorily thought to incarnate the desires and identifications of hegemonic bourgeois manhood" (3–4). Bachelors have a "wide variety and sheer intensity" of "erotic and identificatory energies" (5). As Snyder writes in her discussion of the "third man" who observes male–male–female triangles, this "bachelor onlooker is a figure of surplus value, one who is apparently in excess of the requirements of a homosocial market in Oedipalized desire." It is remarkable that Pearl describes Dimmesdale, interrupting her forest fun with her mother Hester, as "the third man" (10). See Katherine V. Snyder, *Bachelors, Manhood, and the Novel, 1850–1925* (Cambridge: Cambridge University Press, 1999).

9. In *The Blithedale Romance,* Coverdale provides the crucial fourth side, "being writer and reader as well as participant in the dramatic action he describes." See Allan Gardner Lloyd Smith, *Eve Tempted: Writing and Sexuality in Hawthorne's Fiction* (Totowa, NJ: Barnes and Noble, 1984), 73–74.

10. As the online journal *Encyclopedia Mythica* reports: "Endymion was a handsome shepherd boy of Asia Minor, the mortal lover of the moon goddess Selene. Each night he was kissed to sleep by her. She begged Zeus to grant him eternal life so she might be able to embrace him forever. Zeus complied, putting Endymion into eternal sleep and each night Selene visits him on Mt. Latmus, near Milete, in Asia Minor. The ancient Greeks believed that his grave was situated on this mountain. Selene and Endymion have fifty daughters" [!]. Micha F. Lindemans, "Endymion," *Encyclopedia Mythica,* http://www.pantheon.org/articles/e/endymion.html.

11. In classically Hellenizing fashion, the walls of the Hawthornes' West Newton home, which Nathaniel rechristened "The Wayside," "were adorned by a bust of Apollo" and "Mrs. Hawthorne's drawing of Endymion." No more perfect emblems of Hawthorne's own enigmatic beauty and personality could have existed, and it is little surprise that they adorned their home, or that Sophia drew the figure so often present—in my view—in her husband's fiction. See Randall Stewart, *Nathaniel Hawthorne* (New Haven, CT: Yale University Press, 1948), 124.

12. Interestingly, the allegorical Hawthorne-figure in Herman Melville's poem *Clarel* is called "Vine." For a wonderful queer reading of *Clarel* in terms of Melville's love for Hawthorne, see Robert K. Martin, *Hero, Captain, Stranger* (Chapel Hill: University of North Carolina Press, 1986), 96–99.

13. Thomas Laqueur has written about the history of masturbation in *Solitary Sex* (Cambridge: Zone Books, 2003).

14. In calling Coverdale the self-as-panopticon, I attempt to evoke Jeremy Bentham's original design for supervision of prison inmates and the now conventional Foucauldian ominousness of social surveillance, but I do not mean to offer a Foucauldian argument in this chapter. Coverdale's panoptical selfhood explodes the idea of a functioning means of surveillance that can in any way control or shape or manipulate what it sees. Along these

lines, see E. Shaskan Bumas's essay "Fictions of the Panopticon: Utopia and the Out-Penitent in the Works of Nathaniel Hawthorne," *American Literature* 73, no. 1 (March 2001): 121–45, which provides insights into early prison reform. Bumas contends that "in *Blithedale*," Hawthorne "shows the virtually historiographic power of a narrator over narrated events and people, and he judges this power as barren but not much different from other forms of power. In Coverdale, the spy, the voyeur, and the observer overlap" (133). I would add that Hawthorne actively critiques and destabilizes Coverdale's narrative subject position of power and mastery.

15. See T. Walter Herbert, *Dearest Beloved: The Hawthornes and the Making of the Middle Class Family* (Berkeley: University of California Press, 1993), 144.

16. As Hortense Spillers writes in her chapter on *Uncle Tom's Cabin*, "negation becomes an alternate route to confirmation." Hortense J. Spillers, "Changing the Letter: The Yokes, The Jokes of Discourse, Or, Mrs. Stowe, Mr. Reed," in *Slavery and the Literary Imagination: Selected Papers from the English Institute*, ed. Deborah E. McDowell and Arnold Rampersad (1987; repr., Baltimore: Johns Hopkins University Press, 1989), 44.

17. For a sustained discussion of inviolate manhood and the antebellum threat of onanism as represented in Hawthorne's first novel, the 1828 *Fanshawe*, see my book *Men Beyond Desire*, chapter 2.

18. See Christopher Newfield and Melissa Solomon, "Few of Our Seeds Ever Came Up at All: A Dialogue on Hawthorne, Delany, and the Work of Affect in Visionary Utopias," in *No More Separate Spheres!*, ed. Cathy N. Davidson and Jessamyn Hatcher (Durham, NC: Duke University Press, 2002), 377–408.

19. Many discussions of the "tourist gaze" exist, most notably in recent examinations of Jewett's 1893 novel *The Country of the Pointed Firs*. For our discussion, I find Katherine Frank's examination of it in *G-Strings and Sympathy*, a theoretical deconstruction of her own experiences as a stripper, particularly interesting (though far too brief). Drawing on the work of sociologist John Urry, Frank discusses the "collective gaze"—in which multiple tourists lend glamour to their surroundings—and the "romantic gaze"—which emphasizes solitude and privacy; obviously, Coverdale embodies the latter, but one could argue that Blithedale as a whole constitutes a collective gaze. See Katherine Frank, *G-Strings and Sympathy: Strip-Club Regulars and Male Desire* (Durham, NC: Duke University Press, 2002), 28–29.

20. Krips offers a stimulating discussion of onanistic voyeurism as treated similarly but also very distinctly in Hitchcock's 1954 film *Rear Window* and David Cronenberg's 1996 film *Crash*. See Krips, *Fetish: Erotics of the Gaze* (Ithaca, NY: Cornell University Press, 1999), 171–83. In addition to Kaja Silverman's *Male Subjectivity at the Margins* and Henry Krips's *Fetish*, see Robert Samuels's *Hitchcock's Bi-Textuality: Lacan, Feminisms, and Queer Theory* (Albany: State University of New York Press, 1998).

21. Freud wrote *Three Essays on the Theory of Sexuality* in 1905 but kept adding to it until 1924. See Freud, *Three Essays*, 58–59.

22. Samuels, *Hitchcock's Bi-Textuality*, 10.

23. Ibid., 113. Samuels reads this desire to see not the presence of the object but its absence as a desire on the part of the [male] subject to dominate the object by pushing it to "the limits of the visible and the sayable," an especially relevant goal for the misogynistic subject.

24. Jacques Lacan, *The Four Fundamental Concepts of Psychoanalysis*, trans. Alan Sheridan (New York: Norton, 1981), 182.

25. Like the uncanny apparitional Green Knight of the great medieval poem *Sir Gawain*

and the Green Knight, the pigs have "red eyes," an odd parallel, to be sure, but, for me, one that corroborates the uncanny quality of these highly odd pigs. Like the Green Knight—who carries a bunch of holly in one hand, an axe in another—the pigs signify gendered anxiety and threat, and much less merrily than the Green Knight.

26. See Joel Pfister, *The Production of Personal Life: Class, Gender, and the Psychological in Hawthorne's Fiction* (Stanford, CA: Stanford University Press, 1991), 101.

27. For Freud, the head of the Medusa suggests part of the terror of accidentally viewing the primal scene that Freud located in the iconography of the Medusa, which he saw as a representation of the male child's attendant revulsion—the writhing snakes being representations of pubic hair and also compensatory substitutions for the castrated penis. The 1922 essay "Medusa's Head" (SE 18: 273–74) was unpublished in Freud's lifetime.

28. As Marjorie Garber writes in her marvelous chapter on the gender indeterminacy of *Macbeth,* the Male Medusa, "the foliate head or leaf mask which gained enormous popularity in England and throughout western Europe during the Romanesque and medieval periods . . . with leaves sprouting from [its face] . . . [is] often sinister and frightening. . . . [This] Green Man . . . embodies a warning against the dark side of man's nature, the devil within" (101–3). It is interesting that this sinister figure represents the union between brutal masculinist power and generative female nature. See Marjorie Garber, *Shakespeare's Ghost Writers: Literature as Uncanny Causality* (New York: Methuen, 1987).

29. Jonathan Ned Katz, *The Invention of Heterosexuality* (New York: Dutton, 1995), 45.

30. See chapter 2, "Veiled Ladies: Toward a History of Antebellum Entertainment," in Brodhead's *Cultures of Letters: Scenes of Reading and Writing in Nineteenth-Century America* (Chicago: University of Chicago Press, 1993), 48–68.

31. For an excellent discussion of the implications of the veil for female sexuality, see the discussion of *The Blithedale Romance* in chapter 4 of Roberta Weldon's *Hawthorne, Gender, and Death: Christianity and Its Discontents* (New York: Palgrave Macmillan, 2008).

32. Benjamin Scott Grossberg, "'The Tender Passion Was Very Rife Among Us': Coverdale's Queer Utopia and *The Blithedale Romance,*" *Studies in American Fiction* 28, no. 1 (2000): 3–25. While I admire Grossberg's highly interesting chapter, I think his approach to Coverdale's queer sexuality verges on a celebratory quality and eschews its problematic, chilling complexities.

33. Jacksonian America was growing increasingly aware of, and hostile to, the image of the European dandy, as historian David G. Pugh points out: "[Jackson could] speak from experience . . . [since he] brought earthy wisdom to Washington rather than esoteric knowledge. . . . Their independence from Europe secure, Americans turned upon themselves and found on their own eastern doorstep the cultivated, effeminate enemy of the true democrat." David G. Pugh, *Sons of Liberty* (Westport, CT: Greenwood, 1983), 18.

34. "Hawthorne's great friend Horatio Bridge wrote that [the author] was invariably cheerful with his chosen friends." But then Hawthorne could relax with companions such as Bridge; with literary celebrities and rival authors he seldom opened up. See James R. Mellow, *Nathaniel Hawthorne in His Times* (Baltimore: John Hopkins University Press, 1998), 28.

35. Ibid., 195.

36. See Renée Bergland's chapter on the sexual and national politics of Hawthorne and Emerson's relationship, "The Puritan Eyeball, or, Sexing the Transcendent," in *The Puritan Origins of American Sex: Religion, Sexuality, and National Identity in American Literature,* ed. Tracy Fessenden et al. (New York: Routledge, 2001), 93–108. In terms of Hawthorne's marriage and the political and historical significance of the Old Manse, Bergland provides

interesting contributions; especially useful are her sympathetic insights into the often misunderstood Sophia Peabody Hawthorne, her own writing, and how the pain she suffered from a miscarriage affected it.

37. Sophia's sister Elizabeth Peabody strove to incite enthusiasm for Hawthorne's work in Emerson, who, after reading Hawthorne's "Footprints on the Seashore," an account of a Salem seashore day-trip, found that it had "no inside to it." See Carlos Baker, *Emerson Among the Eccentrics: A Group Portrait* (New York: Viking, 1996), 210.

38. See Herbert, *Dearest Beloved,* 140, for a discussion of the Peabodys' opinion of Hawthorne's "suspiciously feminine" manhood. Sophia chided her family for failing to recognize that her husband possessed a "divine poetic manhood, into which feminine qualities are incorporated," as Herbert puts it. They needed, felt Sophia, to better comprehend Hawthorne's androgynous Apollonian qualities as such.

39. In the early republic, "European immigrants . . . were increasingly regarded with suspicion, as sources of contamination to the 'democratic' spirit, a suspicion made lawful in the Alien and Sedition Acts." See Dana Nelson's *National Manhood: Capitalist Citizenship and the Imagined Fraternity of White Men* (Durham, NC: Duke University Press, 1998), 38. This anti-European and newly nativist sensibility seeped into manhood as a social category, increasingly reimagined as a decisive break with European decadence.

40. It is of course impossible to discuss the issue of homoeroticism in Hawthorne without mentioning the issue of Hawthorne's relationship with his uncle, Robert Manning. Hawthorne shared an adolescent bed with his uncle after an accident that left the young Hawthorne unable to use one of his legs for several months. See Mellow, *Hawthorne,* 610, n66, for a very interesting discussion of Hawthorne's "animus" toward his uncle. Mellow makes the interesting point that this animus appears to translate itself into the association with horticulture on the part of Hawthorne villains such as Rappaccini, Chillingworth, and Judge Pyncheon: Uncle Robert Manning was also a horticulturist. Whatever their relationship, a wounded quality seems to permeate Hawthorne's depiction of young men, who often flinch against the threat of an older and more powerful male ("Young Goodman Brown," "The Gentle Boy," "The Artist of the Beautiful," "Rappaccini's Daughter," *The Scarlet Letter*). Mellow suggests that this theme may be attributable to a childhood sexual trauma that Hawthorne, who once noted that "an uncle is a very dangerous thing," may have experienced at the hands of his uncle. Though there is, undeniably, a considerable amount of suggestive evidence in Hawthorne's work for Mellow's theory, there is also nothing in the way of concrete evidence for it. I would point out that by placing this information in a footnote, Mellow both makes sure to include it—give it voice—and keep it discrete, if not discreet. I would add that works such as the tale "The Gentle Boy" could be justifiably read as an allegory of childhood sexual trauma.

41. See Robert K. Martin, "Hester Prynne, C'est Moi: Nathaniel Hawthorne and the Anxieties of Gender," in *Engendering Men: The Question of Male Feminist Criticism,* ed. Joseph A. Boone and Michael Cadden (New York: Routledge, 1990), 135–36. My only disagreement with Martin's essay—a superlative tour of the dynamics of gender representation in Hawthorne from a great critic—is his insistence that at the heart of Hawthorne's male characters' gendered anxieties lies an "unacknowledged, or at least denied, desire for intimate companionship" (138). Another fine critic, Scott Derrick, concurs: what motivates Hawthorne's rejection of masculine worlds in "The Custom House" chapter may stem less from a distance toward them than an unsettling erotic attraction. See Scott Derrick, *Monumental Anxieties: Homoerotic Desire and Feminine Influence in 19th Century U.S. Literature* (New Brunswick, NJ: Rutgers University Press, 1997), 43–44. While I definitely

see a problematic, unsettling homoerotic desire as a factor in the anxiety of Coverdale and other Hawthorne males, I think a revulsion against male intimacy—exemplified by Hawthorne's experience at the Shaker community (see n46)—needs to be considered not only as a panicked cover for an actual desire for other men but also as a chafing against compulsory American homosociality.

42. "Fourier's plan for a social system was embedded in a broad philosophical program. Rejecting contemporary individualistic and competitive society, which he called Civilization, Fourier projected a future ideal state of Harmony based on cooperation. He imagined a system of communities, what he termed phalanxes or phalansteries, in which all adults would engage in productive work determined by their interests and be rewarded by a complex scheme of remuneration for both labor and capital." The American Albert Brisbane, who studied in Europe and worked with Fourier before his death in 1837, transmogrified the French philosopher's ideas into an American version that de-emphasized Fourierian irreligiousness and sexual openness, heightening instead Fourierian elements that appealed to "economic and social value." See Helen Lefkowitz Horowitz, *Rereading Sex: Battles Over Sexual Knowledge and Suppression in Nineteenth-Century America* (New York: Knopf, 2002), 261.

43. Engaged in a passionate discussion with her mother about Fourier, Sophia reported finding Fourier's views "abominable"; she noted that while she read a small part, "My husband read the whole volume and was thoroughly disgusted." Sophia slightly exculpated Fourier by noting to her mother that his having written after the French Revolution "accounts somewhat for the monstrous system" Fourier proposes. Mother Peabody responded by saying that the French "have been and are still corrupt." See Mellow, *Hawthorne*, 248–49.

44. "It was not a translation of Fourier that I read," wrote Sophia. "It was the original text." She then passed it onto her husband, who read the whole volume. Ibid., 249.

45. See Horowitz, *Rereading Sex*, 262–63.

46. See Mellow, *Hawthorne*, 378–79. Touring a Shaker village with Melville, interestingly enough, Hawthorne, observing quarters in which men slept in the same beds with other men, called the Shakers "filthy." His hostility toward the Shakers seems only to have deepened over time.

47. See Anthony Rotundo, *American Manhood: Transformations in Masculinity from the Revolution to the Modern Era* (New York: Basic Books, 1993), 223. By the end of the nineteenth century, American men, obsessed with men's bodies, even more obsessed with their own, "treated physical strength and strength of character" as one and the same.

48. See Wheeler Winston Dixon, *It Looks at You: The Returned Gaze of Cinema* (Albany: State University of New York Press, 1995), 2.

49. Ibid., 14.

50. Ibid., 17.

51. Drawing on Kristeva's theory of the "chora," a womb/receptacle, Dixon argues that the camera is the dark womb, the chora, of film, the birthplace of imagery. Ibid., 81–82.

52. Drawing on the work of sex researcher Theodor Reik, Silverman argues that "the male masochist," unlike the female, "leaves his social identity completely behind—actually abandons his 'self'—and passes over into the 'enemy terrain' of femininity." Male masochism can be "disruptive," "shattering." See Silverman, *Male Subjectivity*, 190. Though highly unpleasant for him, Coverdale's masochism does allow him to be critical of the masculine subject position as a whole and to empathize with women and female desire, as his empathy for Zenobia in the face of misogynistic Hollingsworth's freezing idealism evinces. It does

not, however, enlarge his capacity to see dandified Westervelt in anything but phobic terms, though it must be insisted upon that this phobia is indistinguishable from the critique of masculine power and capacity for cruelty that makes Coverdale such an unflinching critic of manhood in the first place. The pig-passage, as I elaborate upon, functions as Hawthorne's authorial critique of the illusion of mastery that Coverdale fantasmatically believes he gains from his phobic calumniation of Westervelt, who is, after all, not essentially read *inaccurately* by Coverdale, given Westervelt's showman's knack for domination and cruelty. We can further interpret Coverdale's apprehensiveness around Old Moody, revealed to be the father who abandoned Zenobia, as further evidence of his skill for discerning questionable manhood.

53. For a characteristically insightful examination of the particular implications of pigs as a beast-metaphor in Homer and elsewhere, see Marina Warner, *No Go the Bogeyman: Scaring, Lulling, and Making Mock* (New York: Farrar, Straus, and Giroux, 1998), 265–67; 277–78.

54. Edelman is, I think, insensitive to the anguished awareness of racial inequality that informs Du Bois's rhetoric. Nevertheless, Edelman's theorization of masculinity as a public performance, one that is *enacted* and wholly self-conscious, is useful. See Lee Edelman, *Homographesis: Essays in Gay Literary and Cultural Theory* (New York: Routledge, 1994), 50–51.

55. See Dixon, *It Looks at You*, 31.

56. In her chapter "The Animal Department of Our Nature," Rita K. Gollin discusses pigs in Hawthorne's work as signifiers of sensual decadence, "types of unmitigated sensuality." The figure of the pig can represent concupiscence in both men and women, female sexuality as well as male. But the strenuously specific nature of the gendered typing of the pigs in *The Blithedale Romance* cannot be underemphasized, nor should be. See *The Nathaniel Hawthorne Review* 30, nos. 1 and 2 (2004): 145–66.

57. "Pig" is a common epithet for police officers; pigs are also the animals who betray their beastly brethren in Orwell's *Animal Farm*, finally indistinguishable from the "men" to whom they sell out their ideals.

58. Barbara Creed—drawing, like Dixon, on the work of Julia Kristeva—theorizes that traditional narrative film thematizes the figure of what Creed calls "The Monstrous-Feminine." As discussed by Creed, this figure evokes "the dread of the generative mother seen only in the abyss, the monstrous vagina, the origin of all life threatening to reabsorb what it once birthed" (54). See Barbara Creed's book *The Monstrous-Feminine: Film, Feminism, Psychoanalysis* (New York: Routledge, 1993), particularly the chapter on *Alien*, 16–31, in which Creed unpacks Kristeva's theory of abjection for feminist readings of the horror film, focusing on the figure of the archaic mother; or her chapter "Horror and the Monstrous-Feminine: An Imaginary Abjection," in *The Dread of Difference: Gender and the Horror Film*, ed. Barry Keith Grant (Austin: University of Texas Press, 1996), 35–65. If the monstrous-feminine represents the primal, archaic mother who threatens to devour, to re-engulf, the subject, the pigs in Hawthorne represent a primal, archaic father, animal and barbaric masculinity unvarnished by language, rationality, culture, the embodiment of a bestial irrational gendered knowledge a return to which is too terrifying to contemplate. One thinks of Cronos, madly and with an unappeasable appetite, devouring his children in Goya's famous painting. Perversely, the pigs can suggest such a bestial gendered state of origins while being themselves fattened up for the slaughter.

59. The "whole of *Richard III* resonated" for the boy Hawthorne. See Brenda Wineapple, *Hawthorne: A Life* (New York: Knopf, 2003), 25–26. Wineapple links Hawthorne's

fascination with the malformed Richard III to his ambivalent feelings about his maternal Manning family and Uncle Richard in particular.

60. Monika Mueller sums up the Hollingsworth–Coverdale relationship this way: "In *The Blithedale Romance,* homoeroticism is finally abandoned in favor of 'frosty bachelorhood' on the part of one character involved in the relationship and a heterosexual marriage, clouded by the outcome of the homosocial exchange of women, on the part of the other" (71–72). See Monika Mueller, *This Infinite Fraternity of Feeling: Gender, Genre, and Homoerotic Crisis in Hawthorne's "The Blithedale Romance" and Melville's "Pierre"* (Madison, NJ: Fairleigh Dickinson University Press, 1996). Overall, Mueller's approach is too simplistic. Some critics, such as biographers James R. Mellow and Edwin Havilland Miller, Robert K. Martin, and Mueller, argue that Hawthorne and Melville both worked out in literature—*The Blithedale Romance* and *Pierre,* specifically—the tortured feelings each eventually developed within the course of their famous friendship. If, as these critics contend, Hawthorne transmuted his fraught friendship with Melville into art with *The Blithedale Romance,* we can look upon Hollingsworth as the Melville figure, brimming with blustery brio, offering his hand to Hawthorne in deep longing promise of friendship, and Coverdale as the Hawthorne figure, cryptic and unresponsive, but secretly filled with unresolved longings. Yet I would argue that Hollingsworth is also an Emersonian figure, in that he represents a social-program-obsessed visionary with huge philanthropic ideals but a lack of interest in the individual human soul. Hawthorne "took aim at his public-spirited neighbors," such as Emerson, when he lived in Concord, surrounded by "poets, reformers, and wooly transcendentalists of the sanguine persuasion." Hawthorne saw Emerson as "pretentious and spoiled," and had little use for his lofty transcendentalist ideals and programs. See Wineapple, *Hawthorne,* 171–72. But I also think Wineapple's wonderfully compelling biography is too dismissive of Hawthorne's own feelings toward Melville. She discusses the famous first meeting between Hawthorne and Melville as " a good story" (222) and focuses primarily on Melville's overheated passion for Hawthorne, never fully exploring Hawthorne's own potential desires for the younger, initially idolatrous author. Wineapple offers a much more considered account in her essay "Hawthorne and Melville: Or, the Ambiguities," *Hawthorne and Melville: Writing a Relationship,* ed. Jana L., Argersinger and Leland S. Person, 51–70 (University of Georgia Press, 2008). See also Robert Milder, "The Ugly Socrates: Melville, Hawthorne, and the Varieties of Homoerotic Experience," *Hawthorne and Melville: Writing a Relationship*, ed. Jana L. Argersinger and Leland S. Person (Athens: University of Georgia Press, 2008), 71–97.

61. At the start of Marlowe's *Edward II,* the King's lover Gaveston, who has just been recalled from exile, describes the erotic entertainments he wants to stage for Edward:

> I must haue wanton Poets, pleasant wits,
> Musitians, that with touching of a string
> May draw the pliant king which way I please:
> Musicke and poetrie is his delight,
> herefore ile haue Italian maskes by night,
> Sweete speeches, comedies, and pleasing showes,
> And in the day when he shall walke abroad,
> Like *Siluian* Nimphes my pages shall be clad,
> My men like Satyres grazing on the lawnes,
> Shall with their Goate feete daunce an antick hay,
> Sometime a louelie boye in *Dians* shape,

> With haire that gilds the water as it glides,
> Crownets of pearle about his naked armes,
> And in his sportfull hands an Oliue tree,
> To hide those parts which men delight to see,
> Shall bathe him in a spring, and there hard by,
> One like *Actæon* peeping through the groue,
> Shall by the angrie goddesse be transformde,
> And running in the likenes of an Hart,
> By yelping hounds puld downe, and seeme to die,
> Such things as these best please his maiestie. (1.1. 51 forward)

Not only does this homoerotic revision of the Diana-Actaeon myth correspond to Hawthorne's masculinization of the Odysseus-Circe-male pigs episode from *The Odyssey*, but it also influences our reading of Hawthorne's own version of the Diana-Actaeon myth in *The Blithedale Romance*. In this manner, Coverdale reproduces or is forced to relive his confrontation with the peeping pigs when he spies on the Comus-like masque of revelers in the forest. I thank Alan T. Bradford for reminding me of the Marlowe passage.

62. In his revolutionary 1972 study *Homosexual Desire* (Durham, NC: Duke University Press, 1993), Guy Hocquenghem discusses homosexual desire as "an arbitrarily frozen frame in an unbroken and polyvocal flux" (50). Hocquenghem's refusal to distinguish homosexual from any other form of desire—which is to say that desire has multiple forms, and cannot be subdivided into homosexuality or heterosexuality, that is, imitative and prior forms—matches, in my view, the polyamorous appreciation of male and female beauty in Hawthorne's work. Significantly for the pig-passage and its breakdown of normative forms of identity, as well as for Coverdale's inability to distinguish Westervelt from man or machine, Hocquenghem writes, "Homosexuality exists and does not exist, at one and the same time: indeed, its very mode of existence questions again and again the certainty of existence" (53). The animal–male references—their interspecies blurriness—contribute to the overall sense of splintering, shaken order, dissolving reality.

63. Surprisingly, Thorwald's returned gaze is not discussed in Dixon's *It Looks at You*, not only because it's a great moment for his thesis but because surely Thorwald stares just as harrowingly at us as he does at Jeff.

64. Precisely because Hawthorne's greatest political accomplishment is his consistent and consistently unflinching critique of conventional, compulsory forms of manhood and masculinity, which has implications not only for heteromanhood but for queer manhood as well, I find the strain of masculinism in treatments of Hawthorne's politics vaguely humorous and largely unsettling. Since the 1980s, in a critical movement spearheaded by Jonathan Arac and Sacvan Bercovitch, a broad critique of Hawthorne's ambiguity—seen as, among other dubious things, an aesthetic maneuver for expressing by camouflaging ambivalence over the slavery issue or for providing a seeming array of possibilities to us as desiring subjects while actually depriving us of all choice, making us complicit with our own deadening socialization—has denatured Hawthorne's aesthetics by seeing it in strictly political terms. The issues in this critique, which extends into the present, as many chapters in the Millicent Bell–edited collection *Hawthorne and the Real* evince, are painfully, pressingly important, but, as I argue at length in chapter 1, the critique in its Arac–Bercovitch cast suffers from an inability to see aesthetics in anything other than ideological terms.

I am left largely mystified by Michael J. Colacurcio's provocative, at times revealingly well-observed, but ultimately quite confused reading of the novel in "Nobody's Protest Novel," *The Nathaniel Hawthorne Review* 34 (2008): 1–39. While this essay deserves a much more elaborate response than I can provide here, I find his thesis—that Coverdale actually murders Zenobia—wildly improbable, especially given the passivity and fragility that defines Hawthorne's sympathetically drawn males even at their most scornful. In other words, I find it vexing that Colacurcio ignores Hollingsworth's declaration of his willingness to beat women into submission—literally, through physical violence—and focuses on Coverdale as a would-be lover so jealous that he's driven to kill the woman his love for whom he cannot explicitly express. Not only does Colacurcio fairly thoroughly heterosexualize Coverdale—in that he is read as a character motivated by sexual passion for a woman he cannot possess—but he also blunts Hawthorne's tragic feminist point: Zenobia's suicide is her only means of real resistance in the novel, at least in her own view.

CHAPTER 6

1. Nina Baym, "The Heroine of *The House of the Seven Gables;* Or, Who Killed Jaffrey Pyncheon?" *The New England Quarterly* 77, no. 4 (December 2004): 607–18.

2. Allison Easton, "Hawthorne and the Question of Women," in *The Cambridge Companion to Nathaniel Hawthorne,* ed. Richard Millington (New York: Cambridge University Press, 2004), 82.

3. See especially the chapter "The Ambiguity of Beatrice" in Roy R. Male, *Hawthorne's Tragic Vision* (New York: Norton, 1957) and chapter 2 of Ullén, *The Half-Vanished Structure: Hawthorne's Allegorical Dialectics* (New York: Peter Lang Publishing, 2004). These are both superb studies, but their insistence on seeing "woman" as the embodiment of man's sinfulness rather than as a thoughtful, resistant agent of her own desires in Hawthorne's work is, in my view, a limitation.

4. Hyatt H. Waggoner, *Hawthorne: A Critical Study,* rev. ed. (1955; Cambridge, MA: Harvard University Press, 1963), 159.

5. The Italian poet Dante, whose works define the early Renaissance, evoked the character of Beatrice in his *La Vita Nuova* and *Paradiso,* the third book of *The Divine Comedy,* in which the figure of Beatrice, embodying the divine grace of womanhood, leads Dante to Heaven. (Figured as one of Heaven's great women, Beatrice takes over the role of Dante's guide from Virgil, author of *The Aeneid.* The Latin poet, because pagan and therefore fallen, cannot lead Dante into paradise.) A significant intertextual overlap for Hawthorne's work generally is the figure of "The Lady of the Screen" in *La Vita Nuova.* Dante anticipates modern theories of the gendered gaze in his thematization of The Lady of the Screen, the woman that Dante used as a substitute object of veneration so that he would not embarrass the real-life object of his desires, Beatrice Portinari, with his unceasing gaze. One also inevitably thinks of the historical Beatrice Cenci, executed for having murdered her powerful, cruel father but venerated as a victim who fought back (her father forced her to have sexual relations with him), a tender soul plunged into a miasmic world of sin who yet managed to retain her poignant, delicate humanity. She became a prominent figure of sympathy in the Romantic era, as evinced by Percy Bysshe Shelley's drama *The Cenci;* Hawthorne centrally evokes her in *The Marble Faun.*

6. For a book-length discussion of this topic, see Jonathan Crary, *Techniques of the Observer: On Vision and Modernity in the Nineteenth Century* (Cambridge, MA: MIT Press, 1990).

7. For a discussion of the diabolical horticulturist, which she ties to the avuncular figures in Hawthorne's life and fiction, see chapter 4 in Gloria Erlich's *Family Themes and Hawthorne's Fiction: The Tenacious Web* (New Brunswick, NJ: Rutgers University Press, 1984).

8. Milton writes of this gendered relationship in his divorce essay "Tetrachordon." See Milton, *The Riverside Milton,* ed. Roy Flannagan (Boston: Houghton Mifflin, 1998), 1033.

9. This is a structuring theme that is not unique to Hawthorne, and nor are its homoerotic as well as homophobic implications. Poe's stories ranging from "The Man of the Crowd" to "The Tell-Tale Heart" also contrast a young man against a frightening older man, although the sources of this fear appear to lie in the younger man's own conflictual feelings. Similarly, Melville frequently contrasts endangered younger men against alternately predatory and brutal older men, while consistently thematizing that the younger man is sexually endangered, if not actively violated, within this intergenerational conflict.

10. As Carol Marie Bensick explains, Hawthorne draws on

> the poison damsel tradition. This tradition was widely circulated in the sixteenth century. The tradition of the poison damsel had entered Europe from the East via the two pseudo-Aristotelian miscellanies, the *Gesta Romanorum,* from which Baglioni's version comes, and the *Secreta Secretorum.* In the legends, the poison damsel tended to be associated with India, as in Baglioni's rendering. Variants included the presence of a characteristic "flowering creeper"; subtraditions dealt specifically with "Poisonous Breath" and "Poison by Intercourse." An especially famous version form the Neapolitan chronicler Costanzo told the story of King Ladislaus of Naples, a retelling of which by Montaigne Hawthorne transcribed in his notebook. In Costanzo's original version the father of the poisonous bride is "a certain unscrupulous doctor of Perugia"—the citadel, we may recall, of the historic Balioni. One version of the Alexander legend was circulated in the sixteenth century under the title of "La Pucelle venimeuse"; this title seems close to Aubépine's supposed original title for "Rappaccini's Daughter," "La belle empoisonneuse." Even earlier, a variant of the legend was circulated by Dante Alighieri's teacher and later fictional inhabitant of the circle of Inferno reserved for sins related to sex, Brunetto Latini.

Carol Marie Bensick, *La Nouvelle Beatrice: Renaissance and Romance in "Rappaccini's Daughter"* (New Brunswick, NJ: Rutgers University Press, 1985), 83–84.

11. See chapter 1 of Eve Kosofsky Sedgwick, *Between Men: English Literature and Male Homosocial Desire* (New York: Columbia University Press, 1985), in which she influentially describes, building on the theories of René Girard, the theory of triangulated desire, the ways that males exchange and circulate their own desires through the traffic in women.

12. See Pagels, *Adam, Eve, and the Serpent: Sex and Politics in Early Christianity* (New York: Vintage, 1989), 109.

13. Marcia Ian, *Remembering the Phallic Mother: Psychoanalysis, Modernism, and the Fetish* (Ithaca, NY: Cornell University Press, 1993), 8–9.

14. Editor's note, Ovid's *Metamorphoses,* ed. A. D. Melville (New York: Oxford University Press, 1998), 458n770.

15. Roxanne Gentilcore, "The Landscape of Desire: The Tale of Pomona and Vertumnus in Ovid's 'Metamorphoses,'" *Phoenix* 49, no. 2 (Summer 1995): 120.

16. Ibid., 112.

17. Thomas Bulfinch, *Bulfinch's Mythology*, vol. 1, *The Age of Fable* (New York: Signet, 1962), 112.

18. Robert Daly mentions Vertumnus in his review of various intertextual valences in the story; his conclusion, that Hawthorne's tale is primarily about a broad battle, one going beyond Christian philosophy, between *fideism* (faith as the ultimate knowledge) and empiricism seems to me to miss out entirely on the provocatively sexually charged nature of Hawthorne's themes. See Daly, "Fideism and the Allusive Mode in 'Rappaccini's Daughter,'" *Nineteenth-Century Fiction* 28, no. 1 (June 1973): 25–37.

19. Vertumnus is a related, complementary figure to Narcissus, not his opposite. If we consider the reference to Vertumnus as Hawthorne's means of exploring his unacknowledgeable interests in the figure of Narcissus, the Freudian concept of *reaction-formation* illuminates this device. In Freud's theorization, a reaction-formation is the psychic defense whereby a desire or image one cannot acknowledge and or wishes to repudiate is replaced by its opposite quality. While Hawthorne's use of Vertumnus is not precisely representative of this Freudian concept, the concept sheds light on Hawthorne's usage of one classical figure to evoke another, at least insofar as I interpret Hawthorne's work. The explicit reference to Vertumnus exposes the absence of a textually named Narcissus as it nods to Ovid.

20. For a discussion of typology in Hawthorne, see Courtmanche, *How Nathaniel Hawthorne's Narratives Are Shaped by Sin: His Use of Biblical Typology in His Four Major Works* (Lewiston, NY: Edwin Mellen, 2008).

21. Though I have not found a discussion of it in print, in a conference paper, T. Walter Herbert made the allusion to the Dimmesdale-exposed-chest scene as a scene reminiscent of the nineteenth-century bodice-ripper.

22. For a discussion of the "debility" caused by onanism, the finest study of sexual reform in the antebellum United States remains Stephen Nissenbaum's *Sex, Diet, and Debility in Jacksonian America: Sylvester Graham and Health Reform* (1980; repr., Chicago: Dorsey, 1988). His primary focus is Sylvester Graham, and there is also a notable chapter on Thomas and Mary Gove Nichols. Helen Lefkowitz Horowitz's *Rereading Sex* is an important new interpretation of sexual morality and its mavens in nineteenth-century America.

23. Linda Dowling, *Hellenism and Homosexuality in Victorian Oxford* (Ithaca, NY: Cornell University Press, 1994), 91.

24. Oscar Wilde called his beloved "Bosie," Lord Alfred Douglas, "Narcissus" among other classical names. "[T]he notion of the male lover as ethical mirror," writes Dowling of the Platonic discourse of same-sex desire in the nineteenth century, "would come to be represented by the figure of Narcissus, a symbol that, emptied of its classical ethical context, would in turn come to represent male love—Wilde and [W. H.] Mallock . . . both deploy it this way." Ibid., 145, 147.

25. Of "Medusa's Head," Freud's standard translator James Strachey writes that "it appears to be a sketch for a more extensive work" (SE 18: 273n1).

26. Freud cited Sándor Ferenczi's discussion of the myth as a goad to his own theorization of the Medusa. Ruth Leys offers an excellent discussion of Ferenczi's views of Medusa (in his *Clinical Diary*) in her book *Trauma: A Genealogy* (Chicago: University of Chicago Press, 2000), 134–38. As Leys observes, Ferenczi gets the details of the myth wrong but comes up, nevertheless, with a fascinating reading of Medusa's hideousness as a mirror for that of her raging, animalistic killer, whom Ferenczi fails to identify as Perseus.

27. Diane Jonte-Pace, *Speaking the Unspeakable: Religion, Misogyny, and the Uncanny Mother in Freud's Cultural Texts* (Berkeley: University of California Press, 2001), 53.

28. Ibid., 54.

29. Jonte-Pace notes that Freud remarked on this theme in print, in a footnote to the published paper "Infantile Genital Organization." As Freud put it, "Athene, who carried Medusa's head on her armor, becomes, in consequence, the unapproachable woman, the sight of whom extinguishes all thought of sexual approach" (SE 19: 144n3).

30. The relationship between Athena and Medusa was certainly well known in the antebellum context. As S. G. Goodrich, who was the editor from 1828 to 1842 of the illustrated annual *The Token*, which published the younger Hawthorne, wrote in his book of mythological stories retold for children, "The countenance of Minerva was generally more expressive of masculine firmness than of grace or softness. She was clothed in complete armour, with a golden helmet, a glittering crest, and nodding plume. She has a golden breast-plate. In her right hand she holds a lance, and in her left, a shield, on which was the painted the dying head of Medusa, with serpents writhing around it." See Goodrich, *A Book of Mythology for Youth: containing descriptions of the deities, temples sacrifices and superstitions of the ancient Greeks and Romans: adapted to the use of schools* (Boston: Richardson, Lord and Holbrook, 1832), 37.

31. For a probing discussion of misogyny in this tale, see Dana Medoro's essay "'Looking into Their Inmost Nature': The Speculum and Sexual Selection in 'Rappaccini's Daughter,'" *The Nathaniel Hawthorne Review* 35, no. 1 (Spring 2009): 70–86.

32. Tobin Siebers, *The Mirror of Medusa* (Berkeley: University of California Press, 1983), 12.

33. Ibid., 44.

34. Ibid., 57.

35. Ibid., 65.

36. Ibid., 85–86.

37. Huot quoted in Julia M. Walker, *Medusa's Mirrors: Spenser, Shakespeare, Milton, and the Metamorphosis of the Female Self* (Newark: University of Delaware Press, 1998), 182.

38. Ibid., 185.

39. John Leonard, introduction to *Paradise Lost*, by John Milton (New York: Penguin, 2003), xxvii.

40. For a fine discussion—and one of the first to make the point—of the overlaps between Hawthorne's tale and *Paradise Lost*, see Liebman, who argues interestingly, especially given that the essay dates from 1968, that Hawthorne figures Beatrice as the New Adam, and Giovanni as the New Eve. Hawthorne inverts the *Paradise Lost* myth, since it portrays "the second fall, the fall from the promised paradise rather than from paradise itself." Liebman reads Baglioni as Satan to Rappaccini's God, and therefore argues that Giovanni is the Eve figure seduced by Satan-Baglioni, whereas the "New Adam"-Beatrice is "fallen but pure." See Sheldon W. Liebman, "Hawthorne and Milton: The Second Fall in 'Rappaccini's Daughter,'" *The New England Quarterly* 41, no. 4 (1968): 521–35; quote from p. 534.

41. Frederick Crews, *The Sins of the Fathers: Hawthorne's Psychological Themes* (1966; repr., Berkeley: University of California Press, 1989), 122.

42. Ibid., 130.

43. Ibid., 117.

44. Ibid., 120.

45. Easton, "Hawthorne and Women," 86.

46. Georgiana's character is a related but distinct one from Beatrice, I think. She seems much more complicit in her own death than Beatrice, although that story is as much a critique of misogyny as "Rappaccini's Daughter." Surely we are never asked to sympathize with

Aylmer's quest to rid Georgiana of the birthmark, and her capitulation to her husband's deranged quest indicates an internalization of his misogyny as well as that of the social order.

47. Hélène Cixous, "Castration or Decapitation?" in *Contemporary Literary Criticism,* ed. Robert Con Davis and Robert Scheifler (1976; repr., New York: Longman, 1989), 486–87.

48. Milton's Eve has many magnificent moments, but the one moment in which she rebukes masculinist authority occurs not only after she has fallen but also in the speech in which she incoherently and vituperatively accuses Adam of not having exerted his masculinist will more forcibly upon her: "Being as I am, why didst not thou the head / Command me absolutely not to go / Going into such danger as thou sadist?" (9: 1155–57). Eve, who so stirringly had explained to Adam why they should divide up their labors in the Garden and work independently, now condemns Adam—who is, of course, condemning her for having been tempted and tempting him in turn—for having treated her with too much respect, for having recognized her self-sufficiency and fortitude.

CHAPTER 7

1. Melville, *Moby-Dick, or, The Whale,* ed. Harrison Hayford, et al. (Evanston, IL: Northwestern University Press, 2001), 5.

2. Samuel G. Goodrich, *A Book of Mythology for Youth: containing descriptions of the deities, temples sacrifices and superstitions of the ancient Greeks and Romans: adapted to the use of schools* (Boston: Richardson, Lord and Holbrook, 1832), 40.

3. Ibid, 45.

4. Ibid, 103.

5. Crompton, *Byron and Greek Love: Homophobia in 19th-Century England* (Berkeley: University of California Press, 1985), 91.

6. Winterer, *The Culture of Classicism: Ancient Greece and Rome in American Intellectual Life, 1780–1910* (Baltimore: Johns Hopkins University Press, 2002), 91.

7. As Laura Laffrado rightly reminds us, in Hawthorne's version of the Demeter and Persephone myth, sexuality has "not been sanitized; instead, it has gone underground. The sexual innuendo in the pomegranate scene is coded sexuality located in little red caves and significant seeds. Sexuality is hidden, not eliminated. . . . [This] is a movement toward denial, not purification. The strategy to desexualize the myth by reducing Proserpina's age fails. The denial of overt sexuality and the lack of a pure world for children remain." See Laffrado, *Hawthorne's Literature for Children* (Athens: University of Georgia Press, 1992), 122.

8. As Foucault quite influentially wrote, in 1870 homosexuality emerged as a psychological, psychiatric, and medical category, as "a certain way of inverting the masculine and feminine in one self. Homosexuality appeared as one of the forms of sexuality when it was transposed from the practice of sodomy to a kind of interior androgyny, a hermaphrodism of the soul. The sodomite had been a temporary aberration; the homosexual was now a species." See Foucault, *The History of Sexuality,* vol. 1, trans. from the French by Robert Hurley (New York: Vintage Books, 1988–90), 43.

9. "The word 'homosexuality' was not invented until 1869 (by the Hungarian, Benkert von Kertbeny) and did not enter English usage until the 1880s and 1890s, and then largely as a result of the work of Havelock Ellis." Jeffrey Weeks, *Against Nature: Essays on History, Sexuality and Identity* (London: Rivers Oram, 1991), 16.

10. Critics such as Graham Robb, George E. Haggerty, William Benemann, Judith Halberstam, Christopher Castiglia, Christopher Looby, Peter Coviello, Richard Godbeer, Heather Love, Regina Kunzel, Valerie Rohy, and Axel Nissen, and others already mentioned, with their attention to historical specificity as well as a new openness, have been opening up the sexual terrain, allowing for fresh connections to be made.

11. David Halperin, *How to Do the History of Homosexuality* (Chicago: University of Chicago Press, 2002).

12. Melville, *Journals,* ed. Howard C. Horsford and Lynn Horth (Evanston, IL: Northwestern University Press, 1989), 106.

13. Ibid., 107.

14. See Coffler, "Classical Iconography in the Aesthetics of *Billy Budd, Sailor,*" in *Savage Eye: Melville and the Visual Arts,* ed. Christopher Sten (Kent, OH: Kent State University Press, 1991), 261.

15. Lambert, *Beloved and God: The Story of Hadrian and Antinous* (London: Weidenfeld and Nicolson, 1984), 5.

16. Coffler, "Classical Iconography in *Billy Budd,*" 257, 259.

17. See Francis Haskell and Nicholas Penny, *Taste and the Antique: The Lure of Classical Sculpture, 1500–1900* (New Haven, CT: Yale University Press, 1982), 146. The authors specifically note Hawthorne's dissent from what had become Winckelmann's "clichéd" view.

18. I discuss this critical narrative and establish the basis for my dissent from it in my essay "The Bonds of Men: A Review of Richard Godbeer's *The Overflowing of Friendship* and Brian Baker's *Masculinity in Fiction and Film,*" *College Literature* 37, no. 3 (2010): 193–202.

19. For discussions of literary male viewing of visual art representations of male beauty as mediated by Winckelmann, see excellent discussions in Brown of Percy Bysshe Shelley's appraisal of male sculpture in classical art, especially chapter 1, and Crompton; and of Henry James's encounter with homoerotic imagery in France in Michael Moon, *A Small Boy and Others: Imitation and Initiation in American Culture from Henry James to Andy Warhol* (Durham, NC: Duke University Press, 1998).

20. For discussions of the considerable homoerotic implications of nineteenth-century Hellenism, see especially Nathaniel Brown, *Sexuality and Feminism in Shelley* (Cambridge, MA: Harvard University Press, 1979; Linda Dowling, *Hellenism and Homosexuality in Victorian Oxford* (Ithaca, NY: Cornell University Press, 1994); Louis Crompton, *Byron and Greek Love: Homophobia in 19th-Century England* (Berkeley: University of California Press, 1985); and Moon, *A Small Boy*.

21. I gratefully thank Tom Rice as well as several on the C-19 e-mail discussion list, especially Robert Wallace and John L. Bryant, for their feedback on the question of the publication of lectures in the nineteenth century and of Melville's lectures in his lifetime.

22. "A number of Goethean references to the writings of Winckelmann were marked, showing an interest that seems confirmed by Melville's reading of Winckelmann's *History of Ancient Art* in 1852." See Douglas Robillard, *Melville and the Visual Arts: Ionian Form, Venetian Tint* (Kent, OH: Kent State University Press, 1997), 35. Given the growing importance of Goethe to the emergent homoerotic aesthetic culture of the eighteenth and nineteenth centuries, further analysis of the overlaps among the German writers and Melville's and Hawthorne's work should prove quite fruitful.

23. Melville, *The Piazza Tales and Other Prose Pieces, 1839–1860,* ed. Harrison Hayford et al. (Evanston, IL: Northwestern University Press, 1987), 402.

24. Ibid.
25. Ibid., 403.
26. Ibid., 403–4.
27. Gotthold Ephraim Lessing, in his famous 1766 *Laocoön: An Essay Upon the Limits of Poetry and Painting,* disputes Winckelmann's view of the serenity of this sculpture, although the chief issue for Lessing is one of genre and its inherent constraints. For example, sculpture should not attempt to reproduce literary narrative (such as the action of *The Aeneid*) but should, instead, capture iconic moments. As Deanna Fernie notes in her 2011 book on Hawthorne and sculpture, "Modern works of sculpture failed, in Lessing's view, because they attempted to incorporate narrative, which sculpture, as a spatially determined form, should not. Where writing builds an impression by word, sculpture presents in material form a complete entity. The sculptural Laocoön succeeds for Lessing because it does not attempt everything that the myth's literary renditions achieve. Although Laocoön's mouth is open, he appears to be withholding or at least subduing utterance rather than shrieking (as he does in Virgil)." In other words, Laocoön's open mouth is *iconic* of suffering rather than a representation of an action in Virgil's poem; it is not an attempt to reproduce Virgil's epic narrative in sculpture. See Fernie, *Hawthorne, Sculpture, and the Question of American Art* (Burlington, VT: Ashgate, 2011), 32–33. My thanks to Brian Glavey for his feedback on the question of Lessing's relationship to Winckelmann.
28. Melville, *Piazza Tales,* 406.
29. Whitney Davis, *Queer Beauty: Sexuality and Aesthetics from Winckelmann to Freud and Beyond* (New York: Columbia University Press, 2010), 13.
30. Ibid.; emphases in the original.
31. Melville, *Piazza Tales,* 407.
32. Ibid., 753.
33. Coffler, "Classical Iconography," 267.
34. Melville, *Billy Budd: The Genetic Text,* ed. Harrison Hayford and Merton M. Sealts (1978; Chicago: University of Chicago Press, 2001). All citations from *Billy Budd* will be from this edition and are documented parenthetically within the main text.
35. Here is Walters's description in fuller form, which I include here because of its dexterity and relevance:

> The great marble David, carved when Michelangelo was not yet thirty, is not just a symbol of Florentine liberty, but the sculptor's idealized self-image. The obscure and youthful shepherd goes out alone to prove himself to his doubting family and countrymen and to carve his place in history: the personal implications for Michelangelo are obvious. David is at once classically ideal, and far more particularized than any ancient hero. The boy has been turned into a giant, but he is as gawky as an adolescent. The enlarged hands, with their swollen veins and muscles, belong to a laborer, or a stoneworker. . . . But despite David's size and his defiant nudity—he is stripped for action, and his nakedness is the sign that he is God's warrior—he is not altogether confident. From the front, he looks proudly relaxed; from any other angle, his pose seems more uncertain. The head turning over the shoulder disturbs David's poise, and his frowning face is both angry and anxious. The hero is shown, not in his moment of triumph, as is more common, but tensed before the fight. His energy remains petrified, forever unreleased and unrealized.

See Margaret Walters, *The Nude Male: A New Perspective* (New York: Paddington, 1978), 138–39.

36. For elaborations on the "masochistic gaze," see my 2010 book *Manhood in Hollywood from Bush to Bush,* particularly chapters 2 and 4.

37. Winckelmann's writings on Antinous were available within the second volume, which was the first to be published in the United States, in 1849. As Alex Potts puts it in his introduction to Winckelmann's *History of the Art of Antiquity,* published in a new translation in 2006,

> The publication history of this translation by G. Henry Lodge, titled *The History of Ancient Art,* is strangely erratic: Volume 1 (Boston: Little, Brown) came out in 1856, volume 2 (Boston: J. Munroe) in 1849 (reprinted with volume 1 in 1856 by Little, Brown), and volumes 3 and 4 (Boston: J. R. Osgood) in 1872–73. The complete four volumes were reissued in Boston in 1880, in London in 1881[.]

See Potts, introduction to *History of the Art of Antiquity,* by Alex Potts and Johann Joachim Winckelmann (Los Angeles: Getty Research Institute, 2006), 38n5.

38. Ibid., 80, 144.

39. For discussions of the American male traveler's response to classical sculpture and its homoerotic implications, see Person, "Falling into Heterosexuality: Sculpting Male Bodies in *The Marble Faun* and *Roderick Hudson,*" in Robert K. Martin and Leland S. Person, *Roman Holidays: American Writers and Artists in Nineteenth-Century Italy* (Iowa City: University of Iowa Press, 2002), 107–40; Robert Milder, "The Connecting Link of the Centuries: Melville, Rome, and the Mediterranean, 1856–57," in *Roman Holidays,* 206–26. For a discussion of the relationship among the melancholia that Winckelmann characteristically associated with the Antinous, pederasty, and the "queer subject in history," see Thomas Alan King, *The Gendering of Men, 1600–1750: Queer Articulations* (Madison: University of Wisconsin Press, 2008).

Milder is very interesting on the eye pains that Melville experienced while gazing at the "stunning" art works in Italy. Unlike Hawthorne, Milder observes, "Melville typically viewed statuary and painting with an eye less to character than to history and the progress (or regress) of civilization. What impressed him most about Rome—ancient Rome—was the ["massive," "majestic," "colossal," et al.] scale of life it evinced." See Milder, "The Connecting Link of the Centuries," 218. It would have been interesting to hear Milder's speculations on what role Melville's distinct view of historical scale played in his appraisal/reception of Antinous.

Person's view of the significance of the faun differs from my own. "Working strenuously . . . to portray the Faun as another 'neutral territory,' Hawthorne's best effort produces a male body that reflects an uneasy truce between desire and its expression—a prison house of desire, sportive and frisky, that threatens to burst forth a monster." See Person, "Falling into Heterosexuality," 116. As I will be suggesting through my comparison of Hawthorne's view of the faun as art object with Freud's discussion of the homosexual artist Leonardo, Hawthorne does not come down on the side of seeing the faun as monster. Rather, Hawthorne frames the faun as representative of the freedom that is made possible only through the aesthetic—a freedom both *from* sex and from sexual restraint.

40. "Immediately after General Pierce's election to the Presidency, in 1852, he offered Hawthorne the Liverpool consulate, an office then considered the most lucrative of all the

foreign appointments in the Presidential gift, and soon after his inauguration he gave him that place. With his family, Hawthorne sailed for England in July, 1853." The appointment lasted for four years. Horatio Bridge, *Personal Recollections of Nathaniel Hawthorne* (1893; Honolulu: University Press of the Pacific, 2004), 150.

41. Potts, *Flesh and the Ideal: Winckelmann and the Origins of Art History* (New Haven, CT: Yale University Press, 1994), 91.

42. Ibid., 165–66.

43. Ibid., 167.

44. Bentley, *The Ethnography of Manners: Hawthorne, James and Wharton*, 1st ed. (New York: Cambridge University Press, 2007); Riss, *Race, Slavery, and Liberalism in Nineteenth-Century American Literature*, 1st ed. (New York: Cambridge University Press, 2009).

45. Johnson, *Henry James and the Visual* (Cambridge: Cambridge University Press, 2007), 57–58.

46. Sandra A. Zagarell, "Country's Portrayal of Community and the Exclusion of Difference," in *New Essays on "The Country of the Pointed Firs,"* ed. June Howard (New York: Cambridge University Press, 1994), 39–60; 53–54.

47. Martin Bernal, *Black Athena: The Afroasiatic Roots of Classical Civilization*, vol. 1, *The Fabrication of Ancient Greece, 1785–1985* (New Brunswick, NJ: Rutgers University Press, 1987), 367–70.

48. Attesting to the controversial nature of Bernal's book, two classical scholars have put forth a collection of essays from classicists who strongly dispute Bernal's claims. See *Black Athena Revisited*, ed. Mary R. Lefkowitz and Guy MacLean Rogers (Chapel Hill: North Carolina University Press, 1996).

49. Considering the productively maddening "perplexity" of the faun, Emily Budick argues that the faun is both childlike and presexual, and also postsexual, signifying the erosion of art and eros. See Budick, "Perplexity, Sympathy, and the Question of the Human: A Reading of *The Marble Faun*," in *The Cambridge Companion to Nathaniel Hawthorne*, ed. Richard Millington (New York: Cambridge University Press, 2004), 241–42. I am not in agreement with Budick here—in my view, the faun represents a sexual tease very much of the present as well. Nevertheless, I think she offers a brilliant reading of the novel. For Budick, the novel is ultimately a critique of Protestantism, "more ignorant in its sternness, more in flight from the realities of human being" than the moral worlds of Judaism and Roman Catholicism, to which the novel offers, in her view, a surprisingly sympathetic response (249).

50. In *Caravaggio's Secrets* (Cambridge, MA: MIT Press, 1998), Leo Bersani and Ulysse Dutoit discuss masochistic narcissism in the context of Freud's 1915 essay, "Instincts and their Vicissitudes" (SE 14: 109–40), an essay "concerning the fundamental antagonism between the ego and the external world. . . . Within the Freudian scheme . . . the ego's profound mistrust of the world can be 'overcome' only by a narcissistic identification with the hated object, one that masochistically introjects that object. This masochistic narcissism sexualizes our relation to the world at the same time that it eliminates the difference between the world and the ego" (40–41). In less cosmic terms, Hawthorne suffuses narcissistic desire with an awareness of the painfulness of looking relations fully enmeshed with their pleasure. The theme of masochistic looking has most thoroughly been explored in feminist film theory; see in particular Tania Modleski's discussion of masochistic female viewing in Alfred Hitchcock's film *Notorious* in her study *The Women Who Knew Too Much: Hitchcock and Feminist Theory* (New York: Routledge, 1988).

51. This is the thesis of my book *Men Beyond Desire: Manhood, Sex, and Violation in American Literature*.

CHAPTER 8

1. Herman Melville, "Hawthorne and His Mosses, *By a Virginian Spending July in Vermont*," originally published in *The Literary World* on August 17 and 24, 1850.
2. While noting that Hawthorne did not condone slavery even "for a minute," Brenda Wineapple in her biography of Hawthorne notes—and it is difficult to disagree—that it is "strange and disappointing" that Hawthorne completely lacked "empathy for the slave. His conscious sympathies lay with the laboring white man who would certainly lose his job to an emancipated black man. And doubtless Hawthorne identified with the southern white slaveholder to the extent that he romanticized an agrarian planter class as more cultured and genteel than its busy Yankee counterpart . . . Yet like most people, Hawthorne regarded himself as well-intentioned and fair-minded, a neo-Jeffersonian patriot" devoted to the preservation of the Union, seen as crucial not just to the American future but to that of humanity itself (264). See Wineapple, *Hawthorne: A Life* (New York: Knopf, 2003), 269. Perhaps *Septimius Felton* allows us to see that Hawthorne's *un*conscious feelings about the slave—or, at least, about the differently raced—were more inclined toward empathy.
3. Seshadri-Crooks seeks to challenge the view, especially prevalent, for her, in psychoanalytic feminism, that "sexual identity precedes racial identity," which she critiques for its dependence on the "feminist axiom that sexual identity is both private and public, while race and class, insofar as they invoke a group or collectivity, belong only to the public domain." Kalpana Seshadri-Crooks, "Psychoanalysis and the Conceit of Whiteness," in *The Psychoanalysis of Race*, ed. Christopher Lane (New York: Columbia University Press, 1998), 356–57.
4. With Magnus Ullén, I have co-edited a special, 2010 edition of *The Nathaniel Hawthorne Review* on Hawthorne's late work. I am grateful to Ullén for his innovative work on Hawthorne's late period. See especially his essay "The Manuscript of Septimius: Revisiting the Scene of Hawthorne's 'Failure,'" *Studies in the Novel* 40, no. 3 (Fall 2008): 239–67.
5. Charles Swann was one of the first recent critics to take Hawthorne's late work seriously in his excellent study *Nathaniel Hawthorne: Tradition and Revolution* (New York: Cambridge University Press, 1991). In the potent collection *Hawthorne and the Real: Bicentennial Essays*, edited by Millicent Bell (Columbus: The Ohio State University Press, 2005), several essays, notably by Larry J. Reynolds, Rita Gollin, and Brenda Wineapple, touch on Hawthorne's late work; Gollin's essay "Estranged Allegiances in Hawthorne's Unfinished Romances," 159–81, makes the late work its specific focus.
6. Larry J. Reynolds, *Devils and Rebels: The Making of Hawthorne's Damned Politics* (Ann Arbor: University of Michigan Press, 2008).
7. John Carlos Rowe, "Nathaniel Hawthorne and Transnationality," in *Hawthorne and the Real*, 88.
8. Ibid., 91.
9. On Sunday, April 13, 1856, Nathaniel Hawthorne attended a banquet in London at the Mansion House, to which he was invited by David Salomons, the Lord Mayor of London. Salomons was honoring Hawthorne in his capacity as U.S. Consul in Liverpool. Salomons was a pioneering activist for Jewish rights. The U.S. President Franklin Pierce,

for whom Hawthorne had written a campaign biography, had appointed Hawthorne, one of his best friends since their days as college classmates at Bowdoin College, to this position in 1853. The description he provides in *The English Notebooks* of Mr. Salomons's brother Philip and of his wife, Emma Abigail Montefiore Salomons, is fascinating on many levels, revealing, as it does, both his deep-seated anti-Semitism and his intense fascination with the figure of the "Jewess" (21: 481–82). Why can so many qualities about the Jewish woman strike Hawthorne as aesthetically and sensually pleasurable, even as he registers the inescapable "repugnance" he feels toward her, while his feelings toward the Jewish man are unremittingly negative? The gendered imbalance in Hawthorne's phobic disposition toward the Jew—the bifurcation of the figure of the Jew into the beautiful, if also disturbing, Jewess, and the wholly displeasing Jewish male—also raises the often unexplored question of the intersection between racist and anti-Semitic attitudes and anxieties over gender and sexuality.

On Hawthorne's uses of the dark-lady archetype, see Philip Rahv's classic essay "The Dark Lady of Salem," *Partisan Review* 8 (1941): 362–81.

10. Nell Irvin Painter, *The History of White People* (New York: Norton, 2010), 61.

11. Rita K. Gollin, *Prophetic Pictures: Nathaniel Hawthorne's Knowledge and Uses of the Visual Art* (Westport, CT: Greenwood, 1991), 31.

12. Betsy Erkkila, *Mixed Bloods and Other Crosses: Rethinking American Literature from the Revolution to the Culture Wars* (Philadelphia: University of Pennsylvania Press, 2005), 19–20.

13. Terence Martin, "*Septimius Felton* and *Septimius Norton*: Matters of History and Immortality," *The Nathaniel Hawthorne Review* 12, no. 1 (1986): 1–4.

14. Swann, *Nathaniel Hawthorne: Tradition and Revolution*, 134.

15. Edward Hutchins Davidson, *Hawthorne's Last Phase* (New Haven, CT: Yale University Press, 1949), 121.

16. Barker-Benfield theorizes the rhetoric of the anti-onanism sexual reformers of antebellum America as the "spermatic economy." See G. J. Barker-Benfield, *The Horrors of the Half-Known Life: Male Attitudes towards Women and Sexuality in Nineteenth-Century America* (New York: Routledge, 2000).

17. The differences between the *Septimius Felton* and *Norton* manuscripts are striking, and they demand thorough textual analysis. My present focus on a certain constellation of thematic and ideological issues in *Septimius Felton* is not in any way a foreclosure of the necessary scholarly work that needs to be done on both texts, and I do mean both texts; though there are obvious and significant overlaps, the *Felton* and *Norton* manuscripts should be considered not homogenous but actually quite distinct works.

18. John Updike, "Late Works," *The New Yorker*, August 7 & 14, 2006, 64–72.

19. All quotations from Hawthorne are taken from *The Centenary Edition of the Works of Nathaniel Hawthorne*, 23 vols., ed. William Charvat et al. (Columbus: The Ohio State University Press, 1962).

20. For a discussion of Hawthorne's sympathy for the Southern soldier during the Civil War, and Hawthorne's overall opposition to violence and to the demonization of those on opposing sides of debates even as vexatious as those about slavery during the antebellum era, see Larry Reynolds's brilliant essay "'Strangely Ajar with the Human Race': Hawthorne, Slavery, and the Question of Moral Responsibility," in Bell's *Hawthorne and the Real*, as well as his *Devils and Rebels*.

21. For a discussion of the evolving significance of the duel in antebellum American life, see Kenneth S. Greenberg, *Honor and Slavery* (Princeton, NJ: Princeton, 1996).

22. For a discussion of antebellum health and sexual reformers and their relevance for literary output in the era, see David Greven, *Men Beyond Desire: Manhood, Sex, and Violation in American Literature*.

23. Coleridge wrote, on September 1, 1832, that "I have known strong minds with imposing, undoubting, Cobbett-like manners, but I have never met a great mind of this sort. And of the former, they are at least as often wrong as right. The truth is, a great mind must be androgynous. Great minds—Swedenborg's for instance—are never wrong but in consequence of being in the right, but imperfectly." See *Table Talk of Samuel Taylor Coleridge* (London: George Routledge and Sons, 1884), 173.

24. In her discussion of *Tristram Shandy,* Harries explains that Laurence Sterne should be seen as a writer who deliberately and self-consciously "*produces* fragments, works that have not become incomplete but have been planned and executed as incomplete." See Harries, *The Unfinished Manner: Essays on the Fragment in the Later Eighteenth Century* (Charlottesville: University Press of Virginia, 1994), 43.

25. Anne Anlin Cheng, *The Melancholy of Race: Psychoanalysis, Assimilation, and Hidden Grief* (New York: Oxford University Press, 2001), 7 (my emphasis).

26. Ibid., 10.

27. To elucidate the rationale for this view, Stokes quotes from the 1980 version of the American Psychiatric Association's *Diagnostic and Statistical Manual of Mental Disorders*' entry on narcissism: "A grandiose sense of self-importance or uniqueness; preoccupation with fantasies of unlimited success; exhibitionistic need for constant attention and admiration; characteristic responses to threats of self-esteem; and characteristic disturbances in interpersonal relations, such as feelings of entitlement, interpersonal exploitativeness, relationships that alternate between the extremes of overidealization and devaluation, and lack of empathy." Mason Stokes, *The Color of Sex: Whiteness, Heterosexuality, and the Fictions of White Supremacy* (Durham, NC: Duke University Press, 2001), 72–73.

28. Jonathan Dollimore, *Sexual Dissidence: Augustine to Wilde, Freud to Foucault* (New York: Oxford University Press, 1991), 174.

29. Ibid., 181.

30. Lacan, *The Seminar of Jacques Lacan,* Book 1, *Freud's Papers on Technique 1953–1954* (New York: Norton, 1991), 141.

31. Žižek, *How to Read Lacan* (New York: Norton, 2006), 79–81. Lacan explains the distinctions himself in *The Seminar of Jacques Lacan,* chapter 11, 129–43.

32. For a discussion of Johnson and the gendering of the literary mulatto, see Rafia Zafar's section, titled "Fictions of the Harlem Renaissance," in *The Cambridge History of American Literature,* vol. 6, *Prose Writing 1910–1950,* ed. Sacvan Bercovitch (New York: Cambridge University Press, 2002); specific reference to the mulatto as usually female can be found on page 299.

33. Talty, *Mulatto America: At the Crossroads of Black and White Culture: A Social History* (New York: HarperCollins, 2003), 6–7.

34. "He would not abide a cracked or broken dish on the table, and he detested anything, or anyone, he deemed ugly, particularly women." See Brenda Wineapple, "Nathaniel Hawthorne 1804–1864: A Brief Biography," in *A Historical Guide to Nathaniel Hawthorne,* ed. Larry J. Reynolds (New York: Oxford University Press, 2001), 14.

35. Thomas Jefferson *Notes on the State of Virginia,* ed. David Waldstreicher (New York: Palgrave Macmillan, 2002), 176. For discussions of the implications of associations of blacks and ugliness for the white desiring gaze, see Hortense J. Spillers, "Mama's Baby, Papa's Maybe: An American Grammar Book," in *The Black Feminist Reader,* ed. Joy James

and T. Denean Sharpley-Whiting (New York: Wiley-Blackwell, 2000), 57–88; Maurice O. Wallace, *Constructing the Black Masculine: Identity and Ideality in African-American Men's Literature and Culture, 1775–1995* (Durham, NC: Duke University Press, 2002).

36. See the last chapter, "Ahistorical," especially, in Valerie Rohy, *Anachronism and Its Others: Sexuality, Race, and Temporality* (Albany: State University of New York Press, 2010).

37. Swann, *Hawthorne*, 239.

38. Monika M. Elbert, "Bourgeois Sexuality and the Gothic Plot in Wharton and Hawthorne," in *Hawthorne and Women: Engendering and Expanding the Hawthorne Tradition*, ed. John L. Idol, Jr. and Melinda M. Ponder (Amherst: University of Massachusetts Press, 1999), 258–71.

39. Toril Moi, "Representation of Patriarchy: Sexuality and Epistemology in Freud's *Dora*," in *In Dora's Case: Freud—Hysteria—Feminism*, ed. Charles Bernheimer and Claire Kahane (New York: Columbia University Press, 1985), 198.

40. See especially Chodorow's *Femininities, Masculinities, Sexualities: Freud and Beyond (The Blazer Lectures)* (University Press of Kentucky, 1990).

41. Juliet Mitchell, *Mad Men and Medusas: Reclaiming Hysteria* (New York: Basic Books, 2000).

42. In his extraordinary 1925 essay "Some Psychological Consequences of Anatomical Distinction between the Sexes," Freud explores masculine and feminine identities within patriarchy. Writing of penis-envy—a theory that can only be recuperated as "desire for power in our culture," as Freud's French reinterpreter Jacques Lacan did—Freud remarks that one of its consequences "seems to be a loosening of the girl's relation with her mother as a love-object" (1993, 19: 254). In the tragic terms that Freud lays out, the development of femininity derives in the girl from

> her narcissistic sense of humiliation which is bound up with penis-envy, the reminder that after all this is a point on which she cannot compete with boys and that it would therefore be best for her to give up the idea of doing so. Thus the little girl's recognition of the anatomical distinction between the sexes forces her away from masculinity and masculine masturbation on to new lines which lead to the development of femininity. [The thus far unseen manifestation of the Oedipus complex now occurs when] . . . the girl's libido slips into a new position along the line—there is no other way of putting it—of the equation "penis = child." She gives up her wish for a penis and puts in place of it a wish for a child: and with that purpose in view she takes her father as a love-object. Her mother becomes the object of her jealousy. The girl has turned into a little woman. (SE: 19: 256)

Reading Freud against the blindness's of his own argument, we can posit that he theorizes the *emotional and social consequences of the construction of femininity within patriarchy*, the *enforced* separation between mothers and daughters (which also must occur, with equally traumatic but differently registered resonances, between sons and mothers).

43. Judith Butler, "Desire," in *Critical Terms for Literary Study*, ed. Frank Lentricchia and Thomas McLaughlin (Chicago: University of Chicago Press, 1995), 375.

44. Irigaray quoted in Butler, "Desire," 376. Irigaray's original quote can be found in her *Speculum of the Other Woman*, trans. Gillian C. Gill (Ithaca, NY: Cornell University Press, 1985), 327.

45. Butler, "Desire," 376.

46. Swann, *Hawthorne*, 259.

47. Kochhar-Lindgren, *Narcissus Transformed: The Textual Subject in Psychoanalysis and Literature* (University Park: Pennsylvania State University Press, 1993), 128–29.

EPILOGUE

1. Jacques Lacan, "The Mirror Stage," in *Ecrits: A Selection,* trans. Alan Sheridan (New York: Norton, 1977). Lacan's theory evolved over time; he gave the first versions of this paper in 1936.

2. Eric Gould, *Mythical Intentions in Modern Literature* (Princeton, NJ: Princeton University Press, 1981), quoted in Gray Kochhar-Lindgren, *Narcissus Transformed: The Textual Subject in Psychoanalysis and Literature* (University Park: Pennsylvania State University Press, 1993), 12–13.

3. Kochhar-Lindgren, *Narcissus Transformed,* 12.

4. Ibid., 9.

5. Ibid., 6–7.

6. Judith Butler, "Desire," in *Critical Terms for Literary Study,* ed. Frank Lentricchia and Thomas McLaughlin (Chicago: University of Chicago Press, 1995), 383. My interpretation of the Lacanian theory of the formation of the subject through language is influenced by Butler's reading.

7. A proper comparative discussion of Hawthorne and Freud and their views far exceeds the scope of this epilogue, of course. A disquisition on the valences between *The Marble Faun* and Freud's enduringly provocative 1929 work *Civilization and Its Discontents* could easily be the central focus of a book-length work. My focus here is on the Hawthorne side of things, but it should be noted that Freud uses, as does Hawthorne in this novel, Rome as a metaphor for the human mind and for the individual's endlessly vexed relationship to history.

8. Terada, *Feeling in Theory: Emotion after the "Death of the Subject"* (Cambridge, MA: Harvard University Press, 2003), 31.

BIBLIOGRAPHY

Abelove, Henry. "Freud, Male Homosexuality, and the Americans." *Dissent* 33 (Winter 1986): 59–69.

Adamson, Joseph. "Guardian of the 'Inmost Me': Hawthorne and Shame." In *Scenes of Shame: Psychoanalysis, Shame, and Writing,* edited by Joseph Adamson and Hilary Clark, 53–82. Albany: State University Press of New York, 1999.

Allen, David W. *The Fear of Looking: Or, Scopophilic-Exhibitionistic Conflicts.* Charlottesville: University Press of Virginia, 1974.

Angelides, Steven. "Historicizing Affect, Psychoanalyzing History: Pedophilia and the Discourse of Child Sexuality." *Journal of Homosexuality* 46, no. 1/2 (2003): 79–109..

Arac, Jonathon. "The Politics of *The Scarlet Letter.*" In *Ideology and Classic American Literature,* edited by Sacvan Bercovitch and Myra Jehlen, 247–66. New York: Cambridge University Press, 1986.

Ayers, Mary. *Mother–Infant Attachment and Psychoanalysis: The Eyes of Shame.* New York: Brunner-Routledge, 2003.

Babiiha, Thaddeo K. *The James–Hawthorne Relation: Bibliographical Essays.* Boston: G. K. Hall, 1980.

Baker, Carlos. *Emerson Among the Eccentrics: A Group Portrait.* New York: Viking, 1996.

Barber, Stephen B. and David L. Clark. *Regarding Sedgwick: Essays on Queer Culture and Critical Theory.* New York: Routledge, 2002.

Barker-Benfield, G. J. *The Horrors of the Half-Known Life: Male Attitudes towards Women and Sexuality in Nineteenth-Century America.* New York: Routledge, 2000.

Barlowe, Jamie. *The Scarlet Mob of Scribblers: Rereading Hester Prynne.* Carbondale: Southern Illinois University Press, 2000.

Bartsch, Shadi. *The Mirror of the Self: Sexuality, Self-Knowledge, and the Gaze in the Early Roman Empire.* Chicago: University of Chicago Press, 2006.

Baym, Nina. "The Heroine of *The House of the Seven Gables;* Or, Who Killed Jaffrey Pyncheon?" *The New England Quarterly* 77 (2004): 607–18.

———. "Revisiting Hawthorne's Feminism." In Bell, *Hawthorne and the Real: Bicentennial Essays,* 107–24.

Bayer, Ronald. *Homosexuality and American Psychiatry: The Politics of Diagnosis*. Princeton, NJ: Princeton University Press, 1987.
Bell, Michael Davitt. *Culture, Genre, and Literary Vocation*. Chicago: Chicago University Press, 2001.
———. *The Problem of American Realism: Studies in the Cultural History of a Literary Idea*. Chicago: University of Chicago Press, 1993.
Bell, Millicent, ed. *Hawthorne and the Real: Bicentennial Essays*. Columbus: The Ohio State University Press, 2005.
———. Introduction to *Hawthorne's Major Tales*, edited by Millicent Bell. New York: Cambridge University Press, 1993.
———. Preface to Bell, *Hawthorne and the Real: Bicentennial Essays*.
Benjamin, Jessica. *The Bonds of Love: Psychoanalysis, Feminism, and The Problem of Domination*. New York: Pantheon, 1998.
———. "Master and Slave: The Fantasy of Erotic Domination." In *Powers of Desire: The Politics of Sexuality*, edited by Ann Snitow et al., 280–99. New York: Monthly Review, 1983.
Bensick, Carol Marie. *La Nouvelle Beatrice: Renaissance and Romance in "Rappaccini's Daughter."* New Brunswick, NJ: Rutgers University Press, 1985.
Bentley, Nancy. *The Ethnography of Manners: Hawthorne, James and Wharton*, 1st ed. New York: Cambridge University Press, 2007.
Bercovitch, Sacvan. *The Office of The Scarlet Letter*. Baltimore: Johns Hopkins University Press, 1992.
Bergland, Renée. "The Puritan Eyeball, or, Sexing the Transcendent." In *The Puritan Origins of American Sex: Religion, Sexuality, and National Identity in American Literature*, edited by Tracy Fessenden et al., 93–108. New York: Routledge, 2001.
Berlant, Lauren. *The Anatomy of National Fantasy: Hawthorne, Utopia, and Everyday Life*. Chicago: University of Chicago Press, 1991.
Bernal, Martin. *Black Athena: The Afroasiatic Roots of Classical Civilization*. Vol. 1, *The Fabrication of Ancient Greece, 1785–1985*. New Brunswick, NJ: Rutgers University Press, 1987.
Bernheimer, Charles and Claire Kahane, eds. *In Dora's Case: Freud—Hysteria—Feminism*. New York: Columbia University Press, 1985.
Bersani, Leo. *The Freudian Body*. New York: Columbia University Press, 1986.
———. "Genital Chastity." In Dean and Lane, *Homosexuality and Psychoanalysis*, 351–66.
Bersani, Leo and Ulysse Dutoit. *Caravaggio's Secrets*. Cambridge, MA: MIT Press, 1998.
Bingham, Dennis. *Acting Male: Masculinities in the Films of James Stewart, Jack Nicholson, and Clint Eastwood*. New Brunswick, NJ: Rutgers University Press, 1994.
Blair, Sara. *Henry James and the Writing of Race and Nation*. Illustrated edition. New York: Cambridge University Press, 1996.
Bloom, Harold. *The Western Canon: The Books and School of the Ages*, 1st ed. New York: Riverhead Trade, 1995.
Bridge, Horatio. *Personal Recollections of Nathaniel Hawthorne*. 1893. Honolulu: University Press of the Pacific, 2004.
Brodhead, Richard H. *Cultures of Letters: Scenes of Reading and Writing in Nineteenth-Century America*. Chicago: University of Chicago Press, 1993.
———. *The School of Hawthorne*. New York: Oxford University Press, 1986.
Brooks, Ann. *Postfeminisms: Feminism, Cultural Theory, and Cultural Forms*. New York: Routledge, 1997.
Brown, Gillian. *Domestic Individualism: Imagining Self in Nineteenth-Century America*. Berkeley: University of California Press, 1990.

Brown, Nathaniel. *Sexuality and Feminism in Shelley.* Cambridge, MA: Harvard University Press, 1979.

Bruhm, Steven. *Reflecting Narcissus: A Queer Aesthetic.* Minneapolis: Minnesota University Press, 2001.

Budick, Emily Miller. "Perplexity, Sympathy, and the Question of the Human: A Reading of *The Marble Faun.*" In Millington, *The Cambridge Companion to Nathaniel Hawthorne,* 230–50.

Buitenhuis, Peter. "Henry James on Hawthorne." *The New England Quarterly* 32 (1959): 207–25.

Bulfinch, Thomas. *Bulfinch's Mythology.* Vol. 1, *The Age of Fable.* New York: Signet, 1962.

Bumas, E. Shaskan. "Fictions of the Panopticon: Utopia and the Out-Penitent in the Works of Nathaniel Hawthorne." *American Literature* 73, no. 1 (2001): 121–45.

Burstein, Andrew. *Sentimental Democracy: The Evolution of America's Romantic Self-Image.* New York: Hill and Wang, 1999.

Butler, Judith. *Bodies That Matter: On the Discursive Limits of "Sex."* New York: Routledge, 1993.

———. "Desire." In Lentricchia and McLaughlin, *Critical Terms for Literary Study,* 369–86.

———. *Gender Trouble: Feminism and the Subversion of Identity.* New York: Routledge, 1990.

Castiglia, Christopher. *Interior States: Institutional Consciousness and the Inner Life of Democracy in the Antebellum United States.* Durham, NC: Duke University Press, 2008.

Chasseguet-Smirgel, Janine. *The Ego-Ideal: A Psychoanalytic Essay on the Malady of the Ideal.* Translated by Paul Barrows. 1975. Reprint, New York: Norton, 1985.

Cheng, Anne Anlin. *The Melancholy of Race: Psychoanalysis, Assimilation, and Hidden Grief.* New York: Oxford University Press, 2001.

Cheyfitz, Eric. "The Irresistibleness of Great Literature: Reconstructing Hawthorne's Politics." *American Literary History* 6, no. 3, Curriculum and Criticism (Autumn 1994): 539–58.

Chodorow, Nancy J. *Femininities, Masculinities, Sexualities: Freud and Beyond (The Blazer Lectures).* Lexington: University Press of Kentucky, 1990.

———. *The Power of Feelings: Personal Meaning in Psychoanalysis, Gender and Culture.* New Haven, CT: Yale University Press, 1999.

Cixous, Hélène. "Castration or Decapitation?" In *Contemporary Literary Criticism,* edited by Robert Con Davis and Robert Scheifler, 488–90. 1976. Reprint, New York: Longman, 1989.

———. *Three Steps on the Ladder of Writing.* New York: Columbia University Press, 1993.

Coen, Stanley J. *Between Author and Reader: A Psychoanalytic Approach to Writing and Reading.* New York: Columbia University Press, 1994.

Coffler, Gail. "Classical Iconography in the Aesthetics of Billy Budd, Sailor." In *Savage Eye: Melville and the Visual Arts,* edited by Christopher Sten, 257–76. Kent, OH: Kent State University Press, 1991.

Cohen, Josh. *How to Read Freud.* New York: Norton, 2005.

Colacurcio, Michael J. "Nobody's Protest Novel: Art and Politics in *The Blithedale Romance.*" *The Nathaniel Hawthorne Review* 34 (2008): 1–39.

———. *The Province of Piety: Moral History in Hawthorne's Early Tales.* Durham, NC: Duke University Press, 1995.

Cole, Sarah Rose. "Aristocrat in the Mirror." *Nineteenth-Century Literature* 61 (2006): 137–70.

Coleridge, Samuel Taylor. *Table Talk of Samuel Taylor Coleridge.* London: George Routledge and Sons, 1884.

Copjec, Joan. *Read My Desire: Lacan Against the Historicists.* Cambridge, MA: MIT Press, 1994.
Cott, Nancy F. "On Men's History and Women's History." In *Meanings for Manhood: Constructions of Masculinity in Victorian America,* edited by Mark Christopher Carnes and Clyde Griffen, 209–13. Chicago: University of Chicago Press, 1990.
Courtmanche, Jason Charles. *How Nathaniel Hawthorne's Narratives Are Shaped by Sin: His Use of Biblical Typology in His Four Major Works.* Lewiston, NY: Edwin Mellen, 2008.
Crary, Jonathon. *Techniques of the Observer: On Vision and Modernity in the Nineteenth Century.* Cambridge, MA: MIT Press, 1990.
Creed, Barbara. "Horror and the Monstrous-Feminine: An Imaginary Abjection." In *The Dread of Difference: Gender and the Horror Film,* edited by Barry Keith Grant, 35–65. Austin: University of Texas Press, 1996.
———. *The Monstrous-Feminine: Film, Feminism, Psychoanalysis.* New York: Routledge, 1993.
Crews, Frederick. *The Sins of the Fathers: Hawthorne's Psychological Themes.* 1966. Reprint, Berkeley: University of California Press, 1989.
Crimp, Douglas. *Melancholia and Moralism: Essays on AIDS and Queer Politics.* Cambridge, MA: MIT Press, 2001.
Crompton, Louis. *Byron and Greek Love: Homophobia in 19th-Century England.* Berkeley: University of California Press, 1985.
Cvetkovich, Ann. *An Archive of Feelings: Trauma, Sexuality, and Lesbian Public Cultures.* Durham, NC: Duke University Press, 2003.
Daly, Robert. "Fideism and the Allusive Mode in 'Rappaccini's Daughter.'" *Nineteenth-Century Fiction* 28, no. 1 (1973): 25–37.
Davidson, Edward Hutchins. *Hawthorne's Last Phase.* New Haven, CT: Yale University Press, 1949.
Davis, Clark. *Hawthorne's Shyness: Ethics, Politics, and the Question of Engagement.* Baltimore: Johns Hopkins University Press, 2005.
Davis, Whitney. *Queer Beauty: Sexuality and Aesthetics from Winckelmann to Freud and Beyond.* New York: Columbia University Press, 2010.
Dean, Tim. *Beyond Sexuality.* Chicago: Chicago University Press, 2000.
Dean, Tim and Christopher Lane, eds. *Homosexuality and Psychoanalysis.* Chicago: Chicago University Press, 2001.
Denning, Michael. "'The Special American Conditions': Marxism and American Studies." *American Quarterly* 38 (1986): 356–80.
Derrick, Scott. *Monumental Anxieties: Homoerotic Desire and Feminine Influence in 19th Century U. S. Literature.* New Brunswick, NJ: Rutgers University Press, 1997.
DeSalvo, Louise. "Nathaniel Hawthorne and the Feminists: *The Scarlet Letter.*" In *The Scarlet Letter,* edited by Leland S. Person, 500–512. New York: Norton, 2005.
Diffee, Christopher. "Postponing Politics in Hawthorne's 'Scarlet Letter.'" *Modern Language Notes* 111, no. 5 (1996): 835–71.
Dixon, Wheeler Winston. *It Looks at You: The Returned Gaze of Cinema.* Albany: State University of New York Press, 1995.
Dollimore, Jonathon. *Sexual Dissidence: Augustine to Wilde, Freud to Foucault.* New York: Oxford University Press, 1991.
Dowling, Linda. *Hellenism and Homosexuality in Victorian Oxford.* Ithaca, NY: Cornell University Press, 1994.
Easton, Allison. "Hawthorne and the Question of Women." In Millington, *The Cambridge Companion to Nathaniel Hawthorne,* 79–98.

Edelman, Lee. *Homographesis: Essays in Gay Literary and Cultural Theory.* New York: Routledge, 1994.
———. *No Future: Queer Theory and the Death Drive.* Durham, NC: Duke University Press, 2004.
Edmunson, Mark. *Towards Reading Freud: Self-Creation in Milton, Wordsworth, Emerson, and Sigmund Freud.* Princeton, NJ: Princeton University Press, 1990.
Elbert, Monika M. "Bourgeois Sexuality and the Gothic Plot in Wharton and Hawthorne." In *Hawthorne and Women: Engendering and Expanding the Hawthorne Tradition,* edited by John L. Idol, Jr., and Melinda M. Ponder, 258–71. Amherst: University of Massachusetts Press, 1999.
Elfenbein, Andrew. *Romantic Genius: The Prehistory of a Homosexual Role.* New York: Columbia University Press, 1999.
Eliot, T. S. "The Hawthorne Aspect." In *The Shock of Recognition.* Vol. 2, *The Development of Literature in the United States Recorded by the Men Who Made It,* edited by Edmund Wilson. New York: Grosset and Dunlap, 1955.
Ellison, Julie. "Nice Arts and Potent Enginery: The Gendered Economy of Wordsworth's Fancy." *The Centennial Review* 33, no. 4 (1989).
Emerson, Ralph Waldo. *The Heart of Emerson's Journals.* Mineola, NY: Dover Books, 1995.
Eng, David L. and David Kazanjian, eds. *Loss: The Politics of Mourning.* Berkeley and Los Angeles: University of California Press, 2003.
Erkkila, Betsy. *Mixed Bloods and Other Crosses: Rethinking American Literature from the Revolution to the Culture Wars.* Philadelphia: University of Pennsylvania Press, 2005.
Erlich, Gloria. *Family Themes and Hawthorne's Fiction: The Tenacious Web.* New Brunswick, NJ: Rutgers University Press, 1984.
Etchegoyen, R. Horacio. "'On Narcissism': Text and Context." In *Freud's "On Narcissism: An Introduction,"* edited by Joseph Sandler et al., 54–75. New Haven, CT: Yale University Press, 1991.
Evans, Dylan. *An Introductory Dictionary of Lacanian Psychoanalysis.* New York: Routledge, 1996.
Ferenczi, Sándor. *The Clinical Diary of Sándor Ferenczi.* Edited by Judith Dupont. Cambridge: Harvard University Press, 1988.
———. *Further Contributions to the Theory and Technique of Psycho-Analysis.* 1926. London: Hogarth, 1950.
Fernie, Deanna. *Hawthorne, Sculpture, and the Question of American Art.* Burlington, VT: Ashgate, 2011.
Fisher, Benjamin F. "Poe and the Gothic Tradition." In *The Cambridge Companion to Edgar Allan Poe,* edited by Kevin J. Hayes, 72–91. New York: Oxford University Press, 2002.
Folsom, James K. *Man's Accidents and God's Purposes: Multiplicity in Hawthorne's Fiction.* New Haven, CT: Yale University Press, 1963.
Foucault, Michel. *The History of Sexuality, Vol. II.* Trans. from the French by Robert Hurley. New York: Vintage Books, 1988–90, 43.
Frank, Katherine. *G-Strings and Sympathy: Strip-Club Regulars and Male Desire.* Durham, NC: Duke University Press, 2002.
Freud, Sigmund. 1993. *The Standard Edition of the Complete Psychological Works of Sigmund Freud.* Trans. James Strachey, in collaboration with Anna Freud, assisted by Alix Strachey and Alan Tyson, 24 vols. London: Hogarth and the Institute of Psychoanalysis. Originally published in London by Hogarth, 1953–74.
Friedman, Richard C. and Jennifer I. Downey. *Sexual Orientation and Psychodynamic Psy-*

chotherapy: Sexual Science and Clinical Practice. New York: Columbia University Press, 2002.
Furst, Lillian R. *Romanticism in Perspective: A Comparative Study of Aspects of the Romantic Movement in England, France, and Germany.* London: Macmillan, 1969.
Fuss, Diana. *Identification Papers.* New York, Routledge, 1996.
Garber, Marjorie. *Shakespeare's Ghost Writers: Literature as Uncanny Causality.* New York: Methuen, 1987.
Gentilcore, Roxanne. "The Landscape of Desire: The Tale of Pomona and Vertumnus in Ovid's *Metamorphoses.*" *Phoenix* 49, no. 2 (Summer 1995): 110–20.
Gilmore, Michael T. *Surface and Depth: The Quest for Legibility in American Culture.* New York: Oxford University Press, 2006.
Godbeer, Richard. *The Overflowing of Friendship: Love Between Men and the Creation of the American Republic.* Baltimore: Johns Hopkins University Press, 2009.
Gollin, Rita K. "The Animal Department of Our Nature." *The Nathaniel Hawthorne Review* 30, nos. 1 and 2 (2004): 145–66.
———. "Estranged Allegiances in Hawthorne's Unfinished Romances." In Bell, *Hawthorne and the Real: Bicentennial Essays,* 159–81.
———. *Portraits of Nathaniel Hawthorne: An Iconography.* DeKalb: Northern Illinois University Press, 1983.
———. *Prophetic Pictures: Nathaniel Hawthorne's Knowledge and Uses of the Visual Art.* Westport, CT: Greenwood, 1991.
Goodheart, Eugene. *The Reign of Ideology.* New York: Columbia University Press, 1996.
Goodrich, Samuel G. *A Book of Mythology for Youth: containing descriptions of the deities, temples sacrifices and superstitions of the ancient Greeks and Romans: adapted to the use of schools.* Boston: Richardson, Lord and Holbrook, 1832.
Graham, Sylvester. *A Lecture to Young Men on Chastity,* 1834. Reprint, New York: Arno, 1974.
Graham, Wendy. *Henry James's Thwarted Love.* Stanford, CA: Stanford University Press, 1999.
Graves, Robert. Vol. 1 of *The Greek Myths.* New York: Penguin, 1985.
Gray, Richard. *The Life of William Faulkner: A Critical Biography.* Cambridge, MA: Blackwell, 1996.
Greenberg, Kenneth S. *Honor and Slavery.* Princeton, NJ: Princeton University Press, 1996.
Greven, David. "The Bonds of Men: A Review of Richard Godbeer's *The Overflowing of Friendship* and Brian Baker's *Masculinity in Fiction and Film.*" *College Literature* 37, no. 3 (2010): 193–202.
———. "Hawthorne and the Gender of Jewishness: Anti-Semitism, Aesthetics, and Sexual Politics in *The Marble Faun.*" *The Journal of American Culture* 35, no. 2 (June 2012).
———. *Manhood in Hollywood from Bush to Bush.* Austin: University of Texas Press, 2009.
———. "Masculinist Theory and Romantic Authorship: Hawthorne, Politics, and Desire." *New Literary History* 39, no. 4 (Autumn 2008), 971–87.
———. *Men Beyond Desire: Manhood, Sex, and Violation in American Literature.* New York: Palgrave Macmillan, 2005.
———. "In a Pig's Eye: Masculinity, Mastery, and the Returned Gaze in *The Blithedale Romance.*" *Studies in American Fiction* (2006): 131–59.
———. *Representations of Femininity in American Genre Cinema: The Woman's Film, Film Noir, and Modern Horror.* New York: Palgrave Macmillan, 2011.
Grossberg, Benjamin Scott. "'The Tender Passion Was Very Rife Among Us': Coverdale's Queer Utopia and *The Blithedale Romance.*" *Studies in American Fiction* 28, no. 1 (2000): 3–25.

Grunberger, Béla. *Narcissism: Psychoanalytic Essays.* Translated by Joyce S. Diamanti. Madison, CT: International Universities Press, 1979.
Halperin, David. *How to Do the History of Homosexuality.* Chicago: University of Chicago Press, 2002.
Haralson, Eric. *Henry James and Queer Modernity.* New York: Cambridge University Press, 2003.
Harmon, MaryHelen Cleverley. *The Mirror of Narcissus: Reflections and Refractions of the Classical Myth in the Short Fiction of Nathaniel Hawthorne.* Ph.D. diss., Florida State University, 1981.
Harries, Elizabeth Wanning. *The Unfinished Manner: Essays on the Fragment in the Later Eighteenth Century.* Charlottesville: University Press of Virginia, 1994.
Haskell, Francis and Nicholas Penny. *Taste and the Antique: The Lure of Classical Sculpture, 1500–1900.* New Haven, CT: Yale University Press, 1982, 146. Hawthorne, Julian. Vol. 1 of *Nathaniel Hawthorne and His Wife: A Biography.* 1884. Boston: Houghton Mifflin, 1892.
Hawthorne, Nathaniel. *The Centenary Edition of the Works of Nathaniel Hawthorne.* Edited by William Charvat et al. 23 vols. Columbus: The Ohio State University Press, 1962–97.
Hawthorne, Nathaniel and Richard H. Millington. *The Blithedale Romance.* New York: Norton, 2010.
Herbert, T. Walter. *Dearest Beloved: The Hawthornes and the Making of the Middle Class Family.* Berkeley: University of California Press, 1993.
———. "Hawthorne and American Masculinity." In Millington, *The Cambridge Companion to Nathaniel Hawthorne*, 60–78.
———. *Sexual Violence and American Manhood.* Cambridge, MA: Harvard University Press, 2002.
Herodotus. Book 1 of *The Histories.* New York: Penguin, 1972.
Hocquenghem, Guy. *Homosexual Desire.* Durham, NC: Duke University Press, 1993.
Hofstadter, Richard. *Anti-Intellectualism in American Life.* 1963. Reprint, New York: Vintage, 1999.
Hoganson, Kristin L. *Fighting for American Manhood: How Gender Politics Provoked the Spanish-American and Phillipine-American Wars.* New Haven, CT: Yale University Press, 1998.
Holland, Norman Norwood. *The Dynamics of Literary Response.* 1968. New York: Norton, 1975.
Holmes, Jeremy. *Narcissism.* Cambridge: Icon Books, 2001.
Horowitz, Helen Lefkowitz. *Rereading Sex: Battles Over Sexual Knowledge and Suppression in Nineteenth-Century America.* New York: Knopf, 2002.
Howe, Irving. "The Politics of Isolation." In *Politics and the Novel*, 168–69. New York: Meridian, 1987.
Howells, William Dean. "James's Hawthorne." In *European and American Masters.* New York: Collier, 1963.
Ian, Marcia. *Remembering the Phallic Mother: Psychoanalysis, Modernism, and the Fetish.* Ithaca, NY: Cornell University Press, 1993.
Irigaray, Luce. *Speculum of the Other Woman.* Translated by Gillian C. Gill. Ithaca, NY: Cornell University Press, 1985.
James, Henry. *The American Scene.* Edited by John F. Sears. 1907. New York: Penguin, 1994.
———. *Hawthorne*, 1879. New York: Cornell University Press, 1997.

Jay, Gregory. "Douglass, Melville, and the Lynching of Billy Budd." In *Frederick Douglass and Herman Melville: Essays in Relation,* edited by Robert S. Levine and Samuel Otter, 369–97. Chapel Hill: University of North Carolina Press, 2008.
Jefferson, Thomas. *Notes on the State of Virginia.* Ed. David Waldstreicher. New York: Palgrave Macmillan, 2002.
Johnson, Kendall. *Henry James and the Visual.* New York: Cambridge University Press, 2007.
Jonte-Pace, Diane. *Speaking the Unspeakable: Religion, Misogyny, and the Uncanny Mother in Freud's Cultural Texts.* Berkeley: University of California Press, 2001.
Kaite, Berkeley. *Pornography and Difference.* Bloomington: Indiana University Press, 1995.
Katz, Jonathan Ned. *The Invention of Heterosexuality.* New York: Dutton, 1995.
Kilborne, Benjamin. "Shame Conflicts and Tragedy in the *The Scarlet Letter." Journal of the American Psychoanalytic Association* 53, no. 2 (2005): 465–83.
Kimmel, Michael. *Manhood in America: A Cultural History.* New York: Free Press, 1996.
King, Thomas Alan. *The Gendering of Men, 1600–1750: Queer Articulations.* Madison: University of Wisconsin Press, 2008.
Kochhar-Lindgren, Gray. *Narcissus Transformed: The Textual Subject in Psychoanalysis and Literature.* University Park: Pennsylvania State University Press, 1993.
Koestenbaum, Wayne. *Double Talk.* New York: Routledge, 1989.
Krips, Henry. *Fetish: Erotics of the Gaze.* Ithaca, NY: Cornell University Press, 1999.
Lacan, Jacques. "The Mirror-Stage as Formative of the Function of the I." *Ecrits: A Selection,* 1–7. Trans. Alan Sheridan. New York: Norton, 1977.
———. *The Four Fundamental Concepts of Psychoanalysis.* Translated by Alan Sheridan. New York: Norton, 1981.
———. *The Seminar of Jacques Lacan.* Book I, *Freud's Papers on Technique 1953–1954.* New York: Norton, 1991.
Laffrado, Laura. *Hawthorne's Literature for Children.* Athens: University of Georgia Press, 1992.
Lambert, Royston. *Beloved and God: The Story of Hadrian and Antinous.* London: Weidenfeld and Nicolson, 1984.
Lane, Christopher. *The Burdens of Intimacy: Psychoanalysis and Victorian Masculinity.* Chicago: University of Chicago Press, 1999.
Laplanche, J. and J. B. Pontsalis. *The Language of Psycho-Analysis.* London: Karnac Books, 1988.
Laplanche, Jean et al. *Seduction, Translation and the Drives.* Trans. Martin Stanton. Ed. John Fletcher and Martin Stanton. London: Institute of Contemporary Arts, 1992.
Laqueur, Thomas. *Solitary Sex.* Cambridge: Zone Books, 2003.
Lefkowitz, Mary R. and Guy MacLean, eds. *Black Athena Revisited.* Chapel Hill: North Carolina University Press, 1996.
Leitch, Vincent B. *American Literary Criticism from the 30s to the 80s.* New York: Columbia University Press, 1988.
Lentricchia, Frank. *Criticism and Social Change.* Chicago: University of Chicago Press, 1983.
Lentricchia, Frank and Thomas McLaughlin. *Critical Terms for Literary Study.* Chicago: University of Chicago Press, 1995.
Leonard, John. Introduction to *Paradise Lost,* by John Milton, vii–xliv. New York: Penguin, 2003.
Levine, Robert S. and Samuel Otter, eds. *Frederick Douglass and Herman Melville: Essays in Relation.* Chapel Hill: University of North Carolina Press, 2008.

Lewes, Kenneth. *The Psychoanalytic Theory of Male Homosexuality.* New York: Simon and Schuster, 1988.
Leys, Ruth. *Trauma: A Genealogy.* Chicago: University of Chicago Press, 2000.
Liebman, Sheldon W. "Hawthorne and Milton: The Second Fall in 'Rappaccini's Daughter.'" *The New England Quarterly* 41, no. 4 (1968): 521–35.
Lindemans, Micha F. "Endymion." *Encyclopedia Mythica.* http://www.pantheon.org/articles/e/endymion.html.
Male, Roy R. "The Ambiguity of Beatrice." In *Hawthorne's Tragic Vision,* 54–70. New York: Norton, 1957.
Mannoni, Octave. "Je sais bien . . . mais quand meme." *Clefs pour l'imaginaire de l'autre scène.* Paris: Seuil, 1969.
Martin, Robert K. *Hero, Captain, Stranger.* Chapel Hill: University of North Carolina Press, 1986.
———. "Hester Prynne, C'est Moi: Nathaniel Hawthorne and the Anxieties of Gender." In *Engendering Men: The Question of Male Feminist Criticism,* edited by Joseph A. Boone and Michael Cadden, 135–36. New York: Routledge, 1990.
Martin, Robert K. and Leland S. Person. *Roman Holidays: American Writers and Artists in Nineteenth-Century Italy.* Iowa City: University of Iowa Press, 2002.
Martin, Terence. "*Septimius Felton* and *Septimius Norton:* Matters of History and Immortality." *The Nathaniel Hawthorne Review* 12, no. 1 (1986): 1–4.
Matheson, Neill. "Intimacy and Form: James on Hawthorne's Charm." *The Henry James Review* 28, no. 2 (2007): 120–39.
Matthiessen, F. O. *The James Family: A Group Biography.* New York: Overlook, 2008.
Mazzucco-Than, Cecilia. *"A Form Foredoomed to Looseness": Henry James's Preoccupation with the Gender of Fiction.* New York: Peter Lang, 2002.
McCall, Dan. *Citizens of Somewhere Else: Nathaniel Hawthorne and Henry James.* Ithaca, NY: Cornell University Press, 1999.
McGowan, Todd. *The Real Gaze: Film Theory After Lacan.* Albany: State University of New York Press, 2007.
McKee, Patricia. *Producing American Races: Henry James, William Faulkner, Toni Morrison.* Duham, NC: Duke University Press, 1999.
Medoro, Dana. "'Looking into Their Inmost Nature': The Speculum and Sexual Selection in 'Rappaccini's Daughter.'" *The Nathaniel Hawthorne Review* 35, no. 1 (Spring 2009): 70–86.
Mellow, James R. *Nathaniel Hawthorne in His Times.* Baltimore: John Hopkins University Press, 1998.
Melville, Herman. *Billy Budd: The Genetic Text.* Edited by Harrison Hayford and Merton M. Sealts. 1978. Chicago: University of Chicago Press, 2001.
———. "Hawthorne and His Mosses, By a Virginian Spending July in Vermont." Originally published in *The Literary World,* August 17 and 24, 1850. Reprinted in *The Piazza Tales and Other Prose Pieces, 1839–1860,* 239–54.
———. *Journals.* Edited by Howard C. Horsford and Lynn Horth. Northwestern Newberry. Evanston, IL: Northwestern University Press, 1989.
———. *Moby-Dick, or, The Whale.* Edited by Harrison Hayford et al. Evanston, IL: Northwestern University Press, 2001.
———. *The Piazza Tales and Other Prose Pieces, 1839–1860.* Edited by Harrison Hayford et al. Evanston, IL: Northwestern University Press, 1987.

———. "Statues in Rome." In *The Piazza Tales and Other Prose Pieces, 1839–1860,* 398–410.
Mendelssohn, Michèle. "Homosociality and the Aesthetic in Henry James's 'Roderick Hudson.'" *Nineteenth-Century Literature* 57, no. 4 (2003): 512–41.
Merish, Lori. *Sentimental Materialism: Gender, Commodity Culture, and Nineteenth-Century American Literature.* Durham, NC: Duke University Press, 2000.
Milder, Robert. "The Connecting Link of the Centuries: Melville, Rome, and the Mediterranean, 1856–57." In Martin and Person, *Roman Holidays: American Writers and Artists in Nineteenth-Century Italy,* 206–26.
———. "The Ugly Socrates: Melville, Hawthorne, and the Varieties of Homoerotic Experience." In *Hawthorne and Melville: Writing a Relationship,* edited by Jana L. Argersinger and Leland S. Person, 71–97. Athens: University of Georgia Press, 2008.
Miller, Edwin Havilland. *Melville.* New York: George Braziller, 1975.
———. *Salem Is My Dwelling Place.* Iowa City: University of Iowa Press, 1991.
Miller, J. Hillis. *Hawthorne and History: Defacing It.* Cambridge: Basil Blackwell, 1991.
Millington, Richard H., ed. *The Cambridge Companion to Nathaniel Hawthorne.* New York: Cambridge University Press, 2004.
———. *Practicing Romance: Narrative Form and Cultural Engagement in Hawthorne's Fiction.* Princeton, NJ: Princeton University Press, 1991.
Milton, John. "Tetrachordon." In *The Riverside Milton,* edited by Roy Flannagan, 1033. Boston: Houghton Mifflin, 1998.
———. *Paradise Lost.* Edited by John Leonard. New York: Penguin, 2000.
Mitchell, Juliet. *Mad Men and Medusas: Reclaiming Hysteria.* New York: Basic Books, 2000.
Mitchell, Juliet. *Siblings: Sex and Violence.* Malden, MA: Polity, 2004.
Modleski, Tania. *The Women Who Knew Too Much: Hitchcock and Feminist Theory.* New York: Routledge, 1988.
Moglen, Helene. *The Trauma of Gender: A Feminist Theory of the English Novel.* Berkeley: University of California Press, 2001.
Mohr, Richard. *Gay Ideas: Outing and Other Controversies.* Cambridge, MA: Beacon Press, 1992.
Moi, Toril. "Representation of Patriarchy: Sexuality and Epistemology in Freud's *Dora.*" In *In Dora's Case: Freud—Hysteria—Feminism,* edited by Charles Bernheimer and Claire Kahane, 198. New York: Columbia University Press, 1985.
Mollinger, Shernaz. "On Hawthorne, Emerson and Narcissism." *Psychoanalytic Review* 70, no. 4 (1983): 571–94.
Moon, Michael. *A Small Boy and Others: Imitation and Initiation in American Culture from Henry James to Andy Warhol.* Durham, NC: Duke University Press, 1998.
Moore, Burness E. and Bernard D. Fine. *Psychoanalytic Terms and Concepts.* New Haven, CT: Yale University Press, 1990.
Morgan, Thaïs E. *Men Writing the Feminine: Literature, Theory, and the Question of Genders.* Albany: State University of New York Press, 1994.
Morrison, Andrew. *The Culture of Shame.* Lanham, MD: Jason Aronson, 1998.
———, ed. *Essential Papers on Narcissism.* New York: New York University Press, 1986.
———. *Shame: The Underside of Narcissism.* Hillsdale, NJ: Analytic, 1989.
Morrison, Andrew and Melvin R. Lansky, eds. *The Widening Scope of Shame.* Hillsdale, NJ: Analytic, 1997.
Morrison, Toni. *Playing in the Dark: Whiteness and the Literary Imagination.* New York: Vintage, 1992.

Mueller, Monika. *This Infinite Fraternity of Feeling: Gender, Genre, and Homoerotic Crisis in Hawthorne's "The Blithedale Romance" and Melville's "Pierre."* Madison, NJ: Fairleigh Dickinson University Press, 1996.

Mulvey, Laura. "Afterthoughts on 'Visual Pleasure and Narrative Cinema' Inspired by King Vidor's *Duel in the Sun.*" *Framework* 15/16/17 (1981). Reprinted in *Visual and Other Pleasures,* 29–38. Bloomington: Indiana University Press, 1989.

———. "Visual Pleasure and Narrative Cinema." *Screen* 16, no. 3 (1975): 6–18, repr. in *Visual and Other Pleasures.* Bloomington: Indiana University Press, 1989, 14–27.

Nelson, Dana. *National Manhood: Capitalist Citizenship and the Imagined Fraternity of White Men.* Durham, NC: Duke University Press, 1998.

Newfield, Christopher and Melissa Solomon. "Few of Our Seeds Ever Came Up at All: A Dialogue on Hawthorne, Delany, and the Work of Affect in Visionary Utopias." In *No More Separate Spheres!,* edited by Cathy N. Davidson and Jessamyn Hatcher, 377–408. Durham, NC: Duke University Press, 2002.

Nichols, Mary Gove. *Solitary Vice: An Address to Parents and Those Who Have the Care of Children.* Portland, OR: Printed at the Journal Office, 1839.

Nissenbaum, Stephen. *Sex, Diet, and Debility in Jacksonian America: Sylvester Graham and Health Reform.* 1980. Reprint, Chicago: Dorsey, 1988.

"Notes of a Son and Brother." In *Henry James: Autobiography,* edited by F. W. Dupee, 479–80. New York: Criterion Books, 1956.

Nussbaum, Martha. *Hiding from Humanity: Disgust, Shame, and the Law.* Princeton, NJ: Princeton University Press, 2004.

———. *Frontiers of Justice: Disability, Nationality, Species Membership (The Tanner Lectures on Human Values).* Cambridge: Belknap, 2007.

Ovid. *Metamorphoses.* Edited by A. D. Melville. New York: Oxford University Press, 1998.

Pagels, Elaine. *Adam, Eve, and the Serpent: Sex and Politics in Early Christianity.* New York: Vintage, 1989.

Painter, Nell Irvin. *The History of White People.* New York: Norton, 2010, 61.

Perry, Ralph B. *The Thought and Character of William James,* vol. 1. Boston: Little, Brown.

Person, Leland S. "A Man for the Whole Country: Marketing Masculinity in the Pierce Biography." *The Nathaniel Hawthorne Review* 35, no. 1 (2009): 1–23.

———. "Middlesex: What Men Like in Men." *American Literary History* 17, no. 4 (2005): 753–64.

———, ed. *The Scarlet Letter and Other Writings.* New York: Norton, 2005.

Pfister, Joel. *The Production of Personal Life: Class, Gender, and the Psychological in Hawthorne's Fiction.* Stanford, CA: Stanford University Press, 1991.

Potts, Alex. *Flesh and the Ideal: Winckelmann and the Origins of Art History.* New Haven, CT: Yale University Press, 1994.

———. Introduction to *History of the Art of Antiquity,* by Alex Potts and Johann Joachim Winckelmann, 1–54. Los Angeles: Getty Research Institute, 2006.

Pugh, David G. *Sons of Liberty.* Westport, CT: Greenwood, 1983.

Pulham, Patricia. "Falling into Heterosexuality: Sculpting Male Bodies in *The Marble Faun* and *Roderick Hudson.*" In Martin and Person, *Roman Holidays: American Writers and Artists in Nineteenth-Century Italy.*

Rahv, Philip. "The Dark Lady of Salem." *Partisan Review* 8 (1941): 362–81.

Rank, Otto. *The Double: A Psychoanalytic Study.* Translated by Harry Tucker, Jr. Chapel Hill: University of North Carolina Press, 1971.

Reynolds, Larry J. *Devils and Rebels: The Making of Hawthorne's Damned Politics.* Ann Arbor: University of Michigan Press, 2008.

———. "'Strangely Ajar with the Human Race': Hawthorne, Slavery, and the Question of Moral Responsibility." In Bell, *Hawthorne and the Real: Bicentennial Essays.*

Riss, Arthur. *Race, Slavery, and Liberalism in Nineteenth-Century American Literature.* 1st ed. New York: Cambridge University Press, 2009.

Robillard, Douglas. *Melville and the Visual Arts: Ionian Form, Venetian Tint.* Kent, OH: Kent State University Press, 1997.

Robinson, Jeffrey C. *Unfettering Poetry: The Fancy in British Romanticism.* New York: Palgrave Macmillan, 2006.

Rohy, Valerie. "Ahistorical." *Anachronism and Its Others: Sexuality, Race, and Temporality.* Albany: State University of New York Press, 2010.

Rotundo, Anthony. *American Manhood: Transformations in Masculinity from the Revolution to the Modern Era.* New York: Basic Books, 1993.

Rowe, John Carlos. "Nathaniel Hawthorne and Transnationality." In Bell, *Hawthorne and the Real: Bicentennial Essays,* 88–106.

———. *The Other Henry James.* Durham, NC: Duke University Press, 1998.

Rzepka, Charles J. *The Self as Mind: Vision and Identity in Wordsworth, Coleridge, and Keats.* Cambridge, MA: Harvard University Press, 1986.

Samuels, Robert. *Hitchcock's Bi-Textuality: Lacan, Feminisms, and Queer Theory.* Albany: State University of New York Press, 1998.

Santayana, George. *The Sense of Beauty: Being the Outline of Aesthetic Theory.* 1896. New York: Dover Books, 1955.

Schaub, Thomas H. *American Fiction in the Cold War.* Madison: University of Wisconsin Press, 1991.

Scott, Joan Wallach. *Gender and the Politics of History.* New York: Columbia University Press, 1999.

Sedgwick, Eve Kosofsky. *Between Men: English Literature and Male Homosocial Desire.* New York: Columbia University Press, 1985.

Sedgwick, Eve Kosofsky and Adam Frank, eds., *Shame and Its Sisters: A Silvan Tompkins Reader.* Durham, NC: Duke University Press, 1995.

Seshadri-Crooks, Kalpana. "Psychoanalysis and the Conceit of Whiteness." In *The Psychoanalysis of Race,* edited by Christopher Lane, 353–79. New York: Columbia University Press, 1998.

Shelley, Percy Bysshe. *Shelley's Poetry and Prose,* 2nd ed. Ed. Donald H. Reiman and Neil Fraistat. New York: Norton, 2002.

Siebers, Tobin. *The Mirror of Medusa.* Berkeley: University of California Press, 1983.

Silverman, Kaja. *Male Subjectivity at the Margins.* New York: Routledge, 1992.

———. *The Threshold of the Visible World.* New York: Routledge, 1996.

Sinfield, Alan. *The Wilde Century: Effeminacy, Oscar Wilde, and the Queer Moment.* New York: Columbia University Press, 1994.

Skura, Meredith Anne. *The Literary Use of the Psychoanalytic Process.* New Haven, CT: Yale University Press, 1981.

Smith, Allan Gardner Lloyd. *Eve Tempted: Writing and Sexuality in Hawthorne's Fiction.* Totowa, NJ: Barnes and Noble, 1984.

Snyder, Katherine V. *Bachelors, Manhood, and the Novel, 1850–1925.* Cambridge: Cambridge University Press, 1999.

Sosnoski, James J. "A Mindless Man-Driven Theory Machine: Intellectuality, Sexuality, and the Institution of Criticism." In *Feminisms,* edited by Robyn R. Warhol and Diane Price Herndl, 33–50. Rutgers University Press, 1997.
Spengemann, William C. *A Mirror for Americanists: Reflections on the Idea of American Literature.* Hanover, NH: University Press of New England, 1989.
Spillers, Hortense J. "Changing the Letter: The Yokes, The Jokes of Discourse, Or, Mrs. Stowe, Mr. Reed." In *Slavery and the Literary Imagination: Selected Papers from the English Institute,* edited by Deborah E. McDowell and Arnold Rampersad. 1987. Reprint, Baltimore: Johns Hopkins University Press, 1989.
———. "Mama's Baby, Papa's Maybe: An American Grammar Book." In *The Black Feminist Reader,* edited by Joy James and T. Denean Sharpley-Whiting, 57–88. New York: Wiley-Blackwell, 2000.
Stekel, Wilhelm. *Auto-Erotism: A Psychiatric Study of Onanism and Neurosis.* New York: Grove, 1950.
Stevens, Hugh. *Henry James and Sexuality.* New York: Cambridge University Press, 1998.
———. "Queer Henry *In the Cage.*" In *The Cambridge Companion to Henry James,* edited by Jonathan Freedman, 120–38. New York: Cambridge University Press, 1998.
Stewart, Randall. *Nathaniel Hawthorne.* New Haven, CT: Yale University Press, 1948.
Stewart, Suzanne R. *Sublime Surrender: Male Masochism at the Fin-de-Siècle.* Ithaca, NY: Cornell University Press, 1998.
Stokes, Mason. *The Color of Sex: Whiteness, Heterosexuality, and the Fictions of White Supremacy.* Durham, NC: Duke University Press, 2001.
Swann, Charles. *Nathaniel Hawthorne: Tradition and Revolution.* New York: Cambridge University Press, 1991.
Talty, Stephen. *Mulatto America at the Crossroads of Black and White Culture: A Social History.* New York: HarperCollins, 2003.
Tambling, Jeremy. *Henry James.* New York: Palgrave Macmillan, 2000.
Terada, Rei. *Feeling in Theory: Emotion after the "Death of the Subject."* Cambridge, MA: Harvard University Press, 2003.
Thompson, G. R. *The Art of Authorial Presence: Hawthorne's Provincial Tales.* Durham, NC: Duke University Press, 1993.
Tompkins, Jane. *Sensational Designs: The Cultural Work of American Fiction, 1790–1860.* Durham, NC: Duke University Press, 1986.
Townsend, Kim. *Manhood at Harvard: William James and Others.* New York: Norton, 1996.
Trilling, Lionel. *The Liberal Imagination.* New York: Anchor, 1953.
Ullén, Magnus. *The Half-Vanished Structure: Hawthorne's Allegorical Dialectics.* New York: Peter Lang, 2004.
———. "The Manuscript of Septimius: Revisiting the Scene of Hawthorne's 'Failure.'" *Studies in the Novel* 40, no. 3 (2008): 239–67.
Updike, John. "Late Works." *The New Yorker,* August 7 & 14, 2006, 64–72.
Waggoner, Hyatt H. *Hawthorne: A Critical Study,* rev. ed. (1955; Cambridge: Harvard University Press, 1963), 159.
Walker, Julia M. *Medusa's Mirrors: Spenser, Shakespeare, Milton, and the Metamorphosis of the Female Self.* Newark: University of Delaware Press, 1998.
Wallace, Maurice O. *Constructing the Black Masculine: Identity and Ideality in African-American Men's Literature and Culture, 1775–1995.* Durham, NC: Duke University Press, 2002.
Walters, Margaret. *The Nude Male: A New Perspective.* New York: Paddington, 1978.

Warner, Marina. *No Go the Bogeyman: Scaring, Lulling, and Making Mock.* New York: Farrar, Straus, and Giroux, 1998.
Warner, Michael. "Homo-Narcissism: Or, Heterosexuality." In *Engendering Men: The Question of Male Feminist Criticism,* edited by Joseph A. Boone and Michael Cadden, 190–206. New York: Routledge, 1990.
Warren, Joyce W. *The American Narcissus: Individualism and Women in Nineteenth-Century American Fiction.* New Brunswick, NJ: Rutgers University Press, 1984.
Warren, Kenneth W. *Black and White Strangers: Race and American Literary Realism.* Chicago: University of Chicago Press, 1995.
Weeks, Jeffrey. *Against Nature: Essays on History, Sexuality and Identity.* London: Rivers Oram Press, 1991, 16.
Weldon, Roberta. *Hawthorne, Gender, and Death: Christianity and Its Discontents.* New York: Palgrave Macmillan, 2008.
White, Susan. "*Vertigo* and Problems of Knowledge in Feminist Film Theory." In *Alfred Hitchcock: Centenary Essays,* edited by Richard Allen and S. Ichii-Gonzales, 278–98. London: BFI, 1999.
Wineapple, Brenda. *Hawthorne: A Life.* New York: Knopf, 2003.
———. "Hawthorne and Melville: Or, the Ambiguities." In *Hawthorne and Melville: Writing a Relationship,* edited by Jana L., Argersinger and Leland S. Person, 51–70. Athens: University of Georgia Press, 2008.
———. "Nathaniel Hawthorne 1804–1864: A Brief Biography." In *A Historical Guide to Nathaniel Hawthorne,* edited by Larry J. Reynolds, 13–48. New York: Oxford University Press, 2001.
Winterer, Caroline. *The Culture of Classicism: Ancient Greece and Rome in American Intellectual Life, 1780–1910.* Baltimore: Johns Hopkins University Press, 2002.
Wood, Robin. *Hitchcock's Films Revisited.* 1989. Reprint, New York: Columbia University Press, 2002.
Wurmser, Léon. *The Mask of Shame.* Baltimore: Johns Hopkins University Press, 1981.
Zafar, Rafia. "Fictions of the Harlem Renaissance." In *The Cambridge History of American Literature,* vol. 6, *Prose Writing 1910–1950,* edited by Sacvan Bercovitch, 283–352. New York: Cambridge University Press, 2002.
Zagarell, Sandra A. "Country's Portrayal of Community and the Exclusion of Difference." In *New Essays on "The Country of the Pointed Firs,"* edited by June Howard, 39–60. New York: Cambridge University Press, 1994.
Žižek, Slavoj. *How to Read Lacan.* New York: Norton, 2006.
———. "'I Hear You with My Eyes'; or, The Invisible Master." In *Gaze and Voice as Love Objects,* edited by Renata Salecl and Slavoj Žižek, 90–128. Durham, NC: Duke University Press, 1996.
———. *The Seminar of Jacques Lacan.* Book I, *Freud's Papers on Technique 1953–1954.* New York: Norton, 1991.

INDEX

Adamson, Joseph, 8, 98, 105
Allen, David W., 106
Angelides, Steven, 52, 53
Antinous, 21, 112, 180–209 *passim*
Arac, Jonathan, 12
archival research and Americanist literary criticism, 69, 249. *See also* historicism
Ayers, Mary, 67

Barker-Benfield, G. J., 218
Bartsch, Shadi, 98, 100
Baym, Nina, vii, 118, 142, 143
Bell, Millicent, vii, 63, 212
Bentley, Nancy, 204, 207, 212
Bercovitch, Sacvan, 12, 23, 153, 212, 243, 277n64
Berlant, Lauren, 23, 71, 243, 249, 262n4
Bernal, Martin, 206
Bersani, Leo, 42, 48, 52, 87, 262n1
Billy Budd, Sailor (Melville), 21, 28, 38, 117, 128, 182–97, 199, 201, 204, 209
Bingham, Dennis, 89
Blithedale Romance, The (Hawthorne), 11, 14, 15, 20, 81, 91, 92, 94, 102, 107, 109, 111, 115–40, 144, 154, 160, 163, 206, 235
Bloom, Harold, 110–11

Bridge, Horatio, 94, 96, 102, 107, 212
Brown, Gillian, 118, 154
Bruhm, Steven, 27, 28, 78, 88, 259n14
Budick, Emily Miller, 286n49
Bumas, E. Shaskan, 271n14
Burstein, Andrew, 12
Butler, Judith, 47, 78, 238, 245, 263n15

captation, 4, 163
Castiglia, Christopher, 8, 249, 256n8, 283n10
Chasseguet-Smirgel, Janine, 32
Cheng, Anne Anlin, 226
Cheyfitz, Eric, 23, 243, 257n19
Chodorow, Nancy J., 237
"Circe's Palace" (Hawthorne), 133–36
Civilization and Its Discontents (Freud), 291n7
Cixous, Hélène, 27, 179, 223, 224
Classicism. *See* Hellenism; Medusa; Narcissus; Ovid
Coen, Stanley J., 16
Coffler, Gail, 184, 196
Colacurcio, Michael J., 84, 110, 268n41 and n42, 277n64
Coleridge, Samuel Taylor, 105, 223, 263n16, 289n23
compromise formation, 265n12

Copjec, Joan, 5, 7
Crary, Jonathan, 278n6
Creed, Barbara, 136, 275n58
Crews, Frederick, 19, 28, 41, 56, 66, 70–76, 176, 178, 261n29, 263n8
Crompton, Louis, 184

Davidson, Edward Hutchins, 218
"David Swan" (Hawthorne), 2
Davis, Clark, 89
Davis, Whitney, 203
Dean, Tim, vii, 42, 48, 53, 255n3
desire, defined, 48–49
Dixon, Wheeler Winston, 129, 130, 135
Dollimore, Jonathan, 46, 226, 227
doppelgänger. See doubles
Dora (Fragment of an Analysis of a Case of Hysteria) (Freud), 236–37
doubles, 88–89, 145, 147, 148, 181, 221
Dowling, Linda, 165
Downey, Jennifer I., 41

Easton, Allison, vii, 142, 143, 177
Edelman, Lee, 7, 135
Edward II (Marlowe), 276n61
Emerson, Ralph Waldo, 14, 126, 273n37, 276n60
Erkkila, Betsy, 216
Erlich, Gloria, 71, 94
Etchegoyen, R. Horacio, 32

Fanshawe (Hawthorne), 3, 30, 97, 112, 115, 117, 119, 125, 205, 219, 221
fear of looking, 93, 98, 101, 102, 105–9, 162, 167, 200, 208
"Feathertop" (Hawthorne), 3, 88, 99–100, 109, 115, 119, 221, 225
female gaze, 99–100, 120, 161, 167, 250
Ferenczi, Sándor, 3, 280n26
Fernie, Deanna, 284n27
fetishism, 36, 117–18, 153–57
Foucault, Michel, 5, 6, 73, 83, 147, 185, 252
Fragment of an Analysis of a Case of Hysteria. See *Dora*

Freud, Sigmund: on female sexuality, 154–57, 234–37; on fetishism, 153–57; on homosexuality, 31–33, 40–57, 78; on Medusa myth, 59, 169, 173, 175, 281n29; on narcissism, 40–57, 226–30, 250–53; on Oedipus complex, 28, 41, 46, 47, 51, 55, 56, 61, 65, 75, 76, 78, 261n17, 290n42; on voyeurism, 105–6, 121–22; on shame, 105–6, 121–22. See also fetishism; homosexuality; Lacan; masochism; Medusa; narcissism; psychoanalytic criticism; shame; voyeurism; *titles of individual Freud works*
Friedman, Richard C., 41
From the History of an Infantile Neurosis (Freud), 261n27
Furst, Lillian R., 297

Garber, Marjorie, 125
gaze, the: and film theory, 5–6; and Foucault, 5–6; Hawthorne, biographical basis for treatment of, 62, 89–90, 94; Lacan's theory of, 5–6, 34–35; Mulvey's theory of, 35–37; varied and multiple, 114. *See also* fear of looking; female gaze; masochistic gaze; narcissistic gaze; pornography and pornographic gaze; returned gaze; voyeurism
Gentilcore, Roxanne, 158
"Gentle Boy, The" (Hawthorne), 19, 30, 37, 39, 40–68, 82, 91, 92, 127, 141, 205, 240
Gilmore, Michael T., vii, 268n40
Gollin, Rita K., 211, 275n56
Goodrich, Samuel G., 182, 191, 281n30
Graham, Sylvester, 10, 11, 120, 121, 148, 164, 223, 256n17
Grossberg, Benjamin Scott, 125, 126
Grunberger, Béla, 28, 29, 30

Halperin, David, 185
"Haunted Mind, The" (Hawthorne), 11, 120
Hawthorne, Elizabeth Clarke Manning (mother of Hawthorne), 61

Hawthorne, Elizabeth Manning (sister of Hawthorne), 61, 257n25
Hawthorne, Louisa (sister of Hawthorne), 61
Hawthorne, Nathaniel: and Andrew Jackson, 11–14, 17, 29, 41, 61, 92, 94, 103, 126, 257n25; 261n17; and Civil War, views of, 210, 211, 212, 215, 217, 219, 288n20; as a psychoanalytic author, 6–7, 248–49; biographical basis for treatment of the gaze, 62–63, 93–94; biographical elements in treatment of shame, 101–2; biographical basis for theme of traumatic narcissism, 30–31; Brook Farm experience, 94–95, 127; gendered writing, 223–25; in relation to Lacan, 34–35; in relation to Melville, 38–39, 180–209; in relation to Mulvey, 35–36; late works, critical evaluation of, 218–19; pacifism, 104, 266n25; passivity, 12, 13, 14, 104, 105, 106, 200, 257n19, 277n64; prefaces, significance of, 145, 150, 219, 246, 247; question of effeminacy, 12, 61, 63, 73, 94, 98, 99, 116, 126, 127, 128, 137, 140, 166; question of same-sex desire, 11, 19, 32, 65, 103, 113, 128, 184–85, 187, 224; question of race, 92, 204–6; 211–16; question of misogyny and representation of women, 141–45, 179, 234–40; religious views, 144–45; travel and notebook writing, 197–201. *See also* Antinous; fear of looking; Freud; gaze; Hellenism; history; homosexuality; intertextual poetics; Lacan; Laocoön; Medusa; murderous narcissism; narcissism; Narcissus; psychoanalytic criticism; race; shame; textual narcissism; traumatic narcissism; voyeurism; Winckelmann; young man/old man split; *titles of individual Hawthorne works*
Hawthorne, Sophia Peabody, 62, 120, 126, 127, 128, 189, 200, 270n11, 272n36, 273n38, 274n43
Hellenism, 77, 165, 189, 190, 204, 214; and race, 206–7, 214–15. *See also*
sculpture; transatlantic homoerotic aesthetic culture
Herbert, T. Walter, 12, 103, 266n23
Herodotus, 263n14
historicism, 15, 69–70, 74, 185
history, Hawthorne and the question of, 249–54
Hocquenghem, Guy, 137
Hofstadter, Richard, 13, 14, 15
Holland, Norman Norwood, 15
homosexuality, and narcissism, 7, 31–33, 43–47; question of the historical emergence of, 184–86; and transatlantic homoerotic aesthetic culture, 187–88
House of the Seven Gables, The (Hawthorne), 112, 117, 148, 149, 167, 235

Ian, Marcia, 53, 74
"Infantile Genital Organization" (Freud), 281n29
"Instincts and their Vicissitudes" (Freud), 286n50
intertextual poetics, 144, 145, 171–74
Irigaray, Luce, 238

Jackson, Andrew, 13–15, 17, 41; Hawthorne's investment in masculine presence of, 257n25
James, Henry, 62, 94, 188, 212, 221
Jefferson, Thomas, 232
Jews, representation of, and anti-Semitism, 179, 208, 213, 229, 287n9, 297
Johnson, James Weldon, 231
Johnson, Kendall, 206, 207, 212
Jolie, Angelina, 206
Jonte-Pace, Diane, 169

Kaite, Berkeley, 114
Keats, John, 186
Kilborne, Benjamin, 98
Kimmel, Michael, 12
Kochhar-Lindgren, Gray, 77, 79, 240, 244, 245
Kohut, Heinz, 256n14
Krips, Henry, 271n20

Laocoön (classical sculpture), 188, 190, 191, 192
Laocoön (Lessing, 1766), 284n27
Lacan, Jacques: on desire, 48, 53; on the gaze, 5–6, 34–35, 37; on language and the subject, 4–7, 244–46; mirror stage, 4–7, 34–35, 48, 75, 81, 88, 198, 215, 244–46; on relation of ideal ego to ego ideal, 227–28; on voyeurism, 123. *See also* gaze, the
Laplanche, Jean, 29, 52, 53
Lessing, Gotthold Ephraim, 192, 284n27
Life of Franklin Pierce, The (Hawthorne), 91, 92

Male Medusa, 125, 168; in *The Blithedale Romance,* 124–29; 272n28
Male, Roy R., 144
Mannoni, Octave, 252
Marble Faun, The (Hawthorne), 2, 3, 30, 97, 112, 138, 146, 148, 156, 174, 179, 180, 182, 189, 200, 202–9, 212–13, 216, 220, 229, 240, 243, 250–53
Martin, Robert K., vii, 127, 273n41
masochism, 47, 66, 114, 116, 122, 133, 208; masochistic narcissism, 286n50
masochistic gaze, 204–9
McGowan, Todd, 36
Medoro, Dana, 281n31
Medusa, 21, 59, 60, 124–29, 192, 193, 195, 272n27, 280n26, 281n30; antebellum descriptions of relationship between Athena and, 281n30; and correspondences with the Narcissus myth, 168–71; Ferenczi's theory of, 280n26; Freud's theory of, 59, 169, 173, 175, 281n29; and intertextuality, 171–74; and feminist protest, 174–79. *See also* Freud; Male Medusa; Narcissus
"Medusa's Head" (Freud), 21, 59, 169, 192, 272n27, 280n25, 281n29
Mellow, James R., 273n40
Melville, Herman, 21–22, 28, 37, 38, 95, 110, 124, 128, 180–209, 210, 223, 228, 239, 245; on Antinous, 186; *Billy Budd, Sailor,* 21, 28, 38, 117, 128, 182–97, 199, 201, 204, 209; "Hawthorne and His Mosses," 197, 239; *Moby-Dick,* 124, 181, 223, 255n1; "Statues in Rome," 190, 193, 194; travel journal and impressions of classical beauty, 186, 193, 194, 199, 200
Milder, Robert, 285n39
Miller, Edwin Havilland, 257n5, 276n60
Miller, J. Hillis, 108
Millington, Richard, vii, 94, 267n39
Milton, John, 29, 31, 144, 146, 149, 152, 155, 157, 158, 160, 161, 171, 172, 173, 174, 179, 191
"Minister's Black Veil, The" (Hawthorne), 101, 108, 110–11, 115, 232, 233
Mitchell, Juliet, 61, 237
Moi, Toril, 236–37
Mollinger, Shernaz, 8, 100
"Monsieur du Miroir" (Hawthorne), 1
Moon, Michael, 283n19
Morgan, Thaïs E., 99
Morrison, Andrew, 8, 98, 105, 106, 259n14
mothers, seduction (Laplanche), 52–53; shame and, 66–68
mulatto, gender and, 231
Mulvey, Laura, 9, 19, 20, 26, 35–37, 82, 83, 97, 115, 116, 117, 118, 120, 130, 142, 214, 269n3
murderous narcissism, 76–81, 173
"My Kinsman, Major Molineux" (Hawthorne), 81–89

narcissism: as psychic agency, 29; auto-eroticism as distinct from, 32; Lacan's theory of, 4–5; primary and secondary, 32; Copjec on, 5–6; Edelman on, 7; Freud's theory of, 28–33, 43–57; longstanding views of as pathological, 8–11; narcissism and the Oedipus complex, 20; shame and, 98, 105–6. *See also* fear of looking; gaze; homosexuality; mirror stage; murderous narcissism; narcissistic gaze; textual narcissism; traumatic narcissism; voyeurism

narcissistic gaze, 20, 81–89, 109, 142, 208
Narcissus (Greek myth), 1, 4, 8, 24–28, 34, 48, 53, 55, 77, 79, 81, 96, 98–99, 100, 148, 157–58, 161, 165–66, 168, 170–71, 179, 181, 183, 194, 244–48, 255n1, 280n24; and effeminacy, 99; as homoerotic icon in the Pater-Wilde tradition, 280n24
Nichols, Mary Gove, 10, 121, 148, 264. *See also* onanism and antebellum America
Nussbaum, Martha, 104

Oedipus complex, the, 28, 41, 46–47, 51, 54, 55, 56, 61, 65, 68, 75, 76, 77, 78, 80. *See* Frederick Crews; Sigmund Freud
onanism: and antebellum America, 101, 103, 114, 121, 125, 148; as distinct from autoeroticism in psychoanalytic theory, 268n42
"On Narcissism" (Freud), 19, 32, 43, 49–57, 171
Ovid, 19, 21, 24, 25, 26–28, 48, 53, 100, 101, 144, 157, 158, 159, 168, 171, 172, 176, 226, 255n1. *See also* Narcissus; Medusa; Vertumnus

Pagels, Elaine, 279n12
Painter, Nell Irvin, 214
Peabody, Elizabeth, 62, 273n37
Person, Leland S., 92, 261n17
Pfister, Joel, 124
Pierce, Franklin, 91, 92, 202, 216
Poe, Edgar Allan, 180, 223, 230, 231, 263n10, 268n42
"Pomegranate Seeds, The" (Hawthorne), 183
pornography and pornographic gaze, 114–15
Potts, Alex, 203, 204
psychoanalytic criticism, value of, 15–18, 69–71, 74–75
Pugh, David G., 12

race: and antebellum America, 204–7, 230–34; and Hellenism, 206–7. *See also* Nathaniel Hawthorne
Rank, Otto, 53, 88
"Rappaccini's Daughter" (Hawthorne), 3, 11, 80, 110, 112, 141–79, 184, 191, 213, 238, 246, 273n40
reaction-formation, 280n19
Rear Window (Hitchcock), 137–40
Reynolds, Larry J., 12, 104, 211, 212
"Roger Malvin's Burial" (Hawthorne), 20, 71, 76–81, 165, 184, 224
Riss, Arthur, 204, 212
Robillard, Douglas, 283n22
Rohy, Valerie, 74, 232, 249, 283n10
Rotundo, Anthony, 12, 128
Rowe, John Carlos, 12, 23, 212, 243

Samuels, Robert, 122
same-sex desire and antebellum America, 11, 185, 188, 189. *See also* homosexuality
Scarlet Letter, The (Hawthorne), 3, 65, 71, 98, 109, 148, 153, 156, 198, 199, 200, 212, 214, 235, 247, 266n23
scopophobia. *See* fear of looking; traumatic narcissism
sculpture, 284n27
Sedgwick, Eve Kosofsky, 88, 151, 267n29
Sedgwick, Ora Gannett, 94, 95
self-overseeing, 109–11
Seneca, 100, 266n18
Septimius Felton (Hawthorne), 2, 9, 22, 80, 81, 101, 164, 177, 202, 207, 210–42, 287n2
Seshadri-Crooks, Kalpana, 211, 287n3
shame, 8, 9, 11, 19, 20, 25, 37, 41, 47, 66–68, 91–113, 120–22, 133, 163, 173, 200; allegorical figure of in Hawthorne, 11, 120
Shelley, Mary, 223
Shelley, Percy Bysshe, 9, 10, 105, 186, 278n5, 283n19
Siebers, Tobin, 170, 171, 173
Silverman, Kaja, 35, 269n4, 274n52

Skura, Meredith Anne, 18
Socarides, Charles, 260n11
"Some Psychological Consequences of the Anatomical Distinction between the Sexes," 290n42
Stekel, Wilhelm, 10
Stewart, James, 119, 138
Stewart, Suzanne R., 116
Stokes, Mason, 226, 227
Swann, Charles, 211, 218, 233, 240, 287n5

Tanglewood Tales (Hawthorne), 133, 134, 183
Terada, Rei, 251
textual narcissism, 243–49
Thompson, G. R., 86, 264n21
Three Essays on the Theory of Sexuality (Freud), 44, 45, 46, 106, 122, 126
Todd, John, 10, 121, 148, 223
Tompkins, Jane, 101, 266n20
Tompkins, Silvan, 267n29
tourist gaze, 271n19
transatlantic homoerotic aesthetic culture, 187–88
traumatic narcissism, 7, 30–31, 107, 112, 167, 221

Ullén, Magnus, vii, 144, 211, 278n3, 287n4
Updike, John, 211, 220

Vertigo (Hitchcock), 117, 152, 269n3
Vertumnus (Roman myth), 146, 157–60. *See also* Narcissus
visual identity, 38–39, 180–209
voyeurism, 111–13, 114–40, 165–67; repressed homosexual, 200; sadism and, 114, 164

Waggoner, Hyatt H., 144, 145
"Wakefield" (Hawthorne), 3, 97, 113, 163, 235, 238
Walker, Julia M., 171, 172
Walters, Margaret, 194, 195, 284n35
Warner, Marina, 275n53
Warner, Michael, 43–44, 46, 53, 162, 259n14
Warren, Joyce W., 8, 9
Weeks, Jeffrey, 282n9
Weldon, Roberta, vii, 272n31
White, Susan, 269n3
Wilde, Oscar, 81, 101, 188, 280n24
Winckelmann, Johann Joachim (1717–68), 22, 165, 188, 189, 190, 192, 193, 195, 198, 199, 200, 203, 204, 207, 209, 214
Wineapple, Brenda, vii, 61, 62, 276n60, 287n2
Winterer, Caroline, 184
Wonder Book, A (Hawthorne), 124
Wood, Robin, vii, 72, 262n3
Wurmser, Léon, 105, 106

"Young Goodman Brown" (Hawthorne), 1, 28, 30, 80, 88, 97, 129, 235, 268n42, 273n40
young man/old man split in Hawthorne, 59, 76, 80, 81, 84, 88, 148, 224; in Poe, 263n10

Zafar, Rafia, 231
Zagarell, Sandra A., 206
Žižek, Slavoj, 88, 227–28